THIS REALM OF ENGLAND
1399 to 1688

A History of England
General Editor: LACEY BALDWIN SMITH

THE MAKING OF ENGLAND: 55 B.C. to 1399
C. Warren Hollister
University of California, Santa Barbara

THIS REALM OF ENGLAND: 1399 to 1688
Lacey Baldwin Smith
Northwestern University

THE AGE OF ARISTOCRACY: 1688 to 1830
William B. Willcox
Yale University

BRITAIN YESTERDAY AND TODAY: 1830 TO THE PRESENT
Walter L. Arnstein
University of Illinois, Urbana

Third Edition

THIS REALM

Lacey Baldwin Smith
Northwestern University

OF ENGLAND
1399 to 1688

D. C. HEATH AND COMPANY   LEXINGTON, MASSACHUSETTS/TORONTO

ORIGINAL WOODCUTS BY HUGH PRICE

MAPS BY NORMAN CLARK ADAMS

TO J. R. S.

Foreword

Carl Becker once complained that everybody knows the job of the historian is "to discover and set forth the 'facts' of history." The facts, it is often said, speak for themselves. The businessman talks about hard facts, the statistician refers to cold facts, the lawyer is eloquent about the facts of the case, and the historian, who deals with the incontrovertible facts of life and death, is called a very lucky fellow. Those who speak so confidently about the historian's craft are generally not historians themselves; they are readers of textbooks that more often than not are mere recordings of vital information and listings of dull generalizations. It is not surprising then that historians' reputations have suffered; they have become known as peddlers of facts and chroniclers who say "this is what happened." The shorter the historical survey, the more textbook writers are likely to assume godlike detachment, spurning the minor tragedies and daily comedies of humanity and immortalizing the rise and fall of civilizations, the clash of economic and social forces, and the deeds of titans. Anglo-Saxon warriors were sick with fear when Viking "swift sea-kings" swept down on England to plunder, rape, and kill, but historians dispassionately note that the Norse invasions were a good thing; they allowed the kingdom of Wessex to unite and "liberate" the island in the name of Saxon and Christian defense against heathen marauders. Nimbly the chronicler moves from the indisputable fact that Henry VIII annulled his marriage with Catherine of Aragon and wedded Anne Boleyn to the confident assertion that this helped produce the Reformation in England. The result is sublime but emasculated history. Her subjects wept when Good Queen Bess died, but historians merely comment that she had lived her allotted three score years and ten. British soldiers rotted by the thousands in the trenches of the First World War, but the terror and agony of that holocaust are lost in the dehumanized statistic that 750,000 British troops died in the four years of war.

In a brief history of even one "tight little island," the chronology of events must of necessity predominate; but if these four volumes are in any way fresh and new, it is because their authors have tried by artistry to step beyond the usual confines of a textbook and to conjure up something of the drama of politics, of the wealth of personalities, and even of the pettiness, as well as the greatness, of human motivation. The price paid will be obvious to anyone seeking total coverage. There is relatively little in these pages on literature, the fine arts, or philosophy, except as they throw light upon the uniqueness of English history. On the other hand, the complexities, the uncertainties, the endless variations, and above all the accidents that bedevil the design of human events—these are the very stuff of which history is made, and these are the "truths" that this series seeks to elucidate and preserve. Moreover, the flavor of each volume varies according to the tastes of its author. Sometimes the emphasis is political, sometimes economic or social; but always the presentation is impressionistic—shading, underscoring, or highlighting to achieve an image that will be more than a bare outline and will recapture something of the smell and temper of the past.

Even though each book was conceived and executed as an entity capable of standing by itself, the four volumes were designed as a unit. They tell the story of how a small and insignificant outpost of the Roman Empire hesitantly, and not always heroically, evolved into the nation that has probably produced and disseminated more ideas and institutions, both good and bad, than any state since Athens. The hope is that these books will appeal both, as individual volumes, to those interested in balanced portraits of particular segments of English history and, collectively, to those who seek the majestic sweep of history in the story of a people whose activities have been wonderfully rich, exciting, and varied. Erasmus once wrote: "The important thing for you is not how much you know, but the quality of what you know." In this spirit these volumes were originally written and have now been revised for a second time, not only to keep pace with new scholarship, but equally important to keep them fresh and thought-provoking in a world that is becoming both more nostalgic and more impatient of its past.

Lacey Baldwin Smith
Northwestern University

Contents

I   Medieval Twilight: 1399 to 1485

     1   *The Curse of Disputed Succession*   3
     2   *Economic Collapse and Social Dislocation*   25
     3   *The Lion and the Unicorn*   43

II   Reconstructing Society, Tudor Style: 1485 to 1547

     4   *Economic Resurgence and Social Change*   67
     5   *Old Bottles, New Wines: The Reign of Henry VII*   80
     6   *This Realm of England Is an Empire*   99
     7   *The Floodgates of Reformation*   117

III   Uneasy Equilibrium: 1547 to 1603

     8   *The Little Tudors*   137
     9   *Elizabeth of Good Memory*   157
     10   *Crisis and Recessional*   175

IV   The Demise of the Tudor State: 1603 to 1660

     11   *Straining the System: The Reign of James I*   197
     12   *Charles I and the Royal Road to War*   211
     13   *Profiteers and Pioneers*   228
     14   *The Anatomy of Rebellion*   244

V   Society Restyled: 1660 to 1688

     15   *Charles II and the Fruits of Revolution*   267
     16   *The Triumph of the Oligarchs*   287

Bibliography   307

Index   321

ILLUSTRATIONS

Henry IV   10
Henry V   16
The Dance of Death *by Hans Holbein*   32
Richard III   58
Soldiers Pillaging During the Wars of the Roses   61
Robbery and Its Consequences   96
The Amputation   98
Henry VIII by Hans Holbein   110
Thomas Cromwell   113
Frontispiece of the Tyndale Translation of the Bible   115
Henry VIII in Later Life   128
The Three Children of Henry VIII   130
Edward Seymour, Earl of Hertford and Duke of Somerset   141
Mary Tudor   149
Elizabeth I   156
Execution for Breaking the Fast   162
Robert Dudley, First Earl of Leicester   166
Sir Francis Drake   173
Execution of Mary Queen of Scots   180
The Ark Royal   183
Elizabeth and the Parliament of 1584   187
James I   199
George Villiers, First Duke of Buckingham   205
Charles I   212
London, 1616   236
The Execution of Charles I   252
Oliver Cromwell   259
Charles II   270
The Great Plague of London, 1665   279
Titus Oates   285
James II   290
The Double Coronation of William and Mary   297
Old and New St. Paul's Cathedral   300
Hampton Court, 1724   304

MAPS

English Possessions in France   20
Dynastic Inheritances of Charles V   106
Areas Under Royal Control During the Civil War   248
London, Showing the Extent of the Great Fire, 1666   280

GENEALOGICAL TABLES

The Lancastrian Claim   8
The House of Valois   15
The Houses of Lancaster and York   23
Yorkist and Neville Lines   53
The Tudor Claim to the Throne   60
Rivals to the Tudors   81
The Habsburg Dynasty   105
The Tudors, 1485–1603   139
The House of Stuart   289

CHARLES, DUC D'ORLEANS AS A PRISONER IN THE TOWER, CA. 1416. *British Museum.*

I

MEDIEVAL TWILIGHT
1399 to 1485

The Curse of
Disputed Succession

1 There is nothing quite so satisfying as a good, clean, substantial fact. It can be cherished and recorded, memorized and scrutinized, dropped casually in the middle of a conversation, or used with impressive effect to begin or destroy an argument. It is indeed a fact that Richard Plantagenet, King of England, died during the first weeks of the year 1400. On closer inspection, however, it is by no means certain that this event is one of those tidy and unadulterated facts, devoid of controversy and free from confusion and mystification. The manner of the royal passing remains in doubt; whether Richard II was strangled, starved, or "perished heart-broken" of sheer melancholy is very much in dispute. Moreover, the fact of the king's death, though a matter to be recorded, attains historical significance only in terms of what went before and after. In death Richard was infinitely more important than in life because of another not-so-simple fact: he was the last of the legitimate Plantagenet kings of England.[1]

The Fall of Richard II (1377–1399)

Richard's failure, abdication, and death have been confounded by another image. The fertile genius of William Shakespeare has conjured up the spectre of an introspective sovereign whose boastful words and eloquent appeals to God's law and the divinity of kings concealed both political

---

[1] There is no adequate political survey of the fifteenth century. The most readable account is A. R. Myers, *England in the Later Middle Ages* (Pelican Books, 1952). By far the best work on constitutional history is S. B. Chrimes, *English Constitutional Ideas in the Fifteenth Century* (1936). See also F. R. H. DuBoulay, *The Age of Ambition* (1970).

timidity and moral obtuseness. Only in recent years has Richard Plantagenet been divorced from Richard the fumbling, incompetent neurotic, whose inept urge to tyranny was translated into grand tragedy by the magic of the poet's verse. Richard, the historical reality, was the victim of the political mores of his time and of the fair words and broken promises of the man who replaced him on the throne and who engineered his "abdication." [2]

Richard's failure reflects the basic confusion and instability inherent in medieval political theory and governmental organization. The legal position of the feudal monarch was summarized in the oft-quoted words of Henry de Bracton: "the king himself ought not to be subject to any man, but he ought to be subject to God and the law." The unsolved riddle of politics was how the sovereign could be both limited and unrestrained, above man but under law. The dilemma was further complicated by the presence of a body of powerful barons who regarded themselves as the rightful watchdogs of government but whose definition of good government was sometimes synonymous with no government, and who were at pains to emphasize the dependence of the sovereign upon law as interpreted by themselves. Conversely, the aim of every great feudal monarch had been to be master in his own house, and to free himself from the factional and irresponsible interference of men, especially noblemen. As the fountain of justice, the medieval king sought to administer law and justice impartially and to root out the private law of strong and violent subjects who championed a mixture of the divine right of aristocracy and the doctrine that might makes right. That Richard had a surfeit of uncles in the shape of the dukes of Gloucester, Lancaster, and York was embarrassing but not necessarily fatal. More fundamental was the question of the king's council—was it to be an instrument of baronial rule through which the magnates could control both king and realm, or was it to be a weapon of royal authority, filled with men of the monarch's choosing, and exercising and enforcing the king's law throughout the realm?

The memory of Edward II, who had been forced to abdicate in 1327 and then had been murdered in the name of good government, together with the prolonged conflict with France in which Edward III had to rely upon his barons to fight even a losing war and a decade of minority rule under Richard II, who had come to the throne in 1377 as a boy of ten, all had swung the governmental balance heavily in favor of baronial control. In 1397, however, Richard II struck out both against his uncles and against the weight of aristocratic influence in his council and government. In a rapid coup d'etat he destroyed the authority of his baronial masters, the so-called Lords Appellant of the king's council. His uncle, the duke of Gloucester, was imprisoned and quietly smothered, the earl of Arundel was publicly

---

[2] Most of this story and the interpretation of Richard II have been taken from H. F. Hutchison, *The Hollow Crown: A Life of Richard II* (1961). For two other quite different views see A. Steel, *Richard II* (1941) and Shakespeare's *Richard II*.

tried and executed for high treason, and the earl of Warwick was exiled to the Isle of Wight. Then in order to build an aristocratic faction loyal to himself, Richard created five new dukedoms from the lands and estates of Gloucester and Warwick. Whether this was tyranny or merely the efforts of a monarch determined to be master in his own council is not a question of fact but of opinion. Richard failed and the dynasty which followed him on the throne branded his actions as tyrannical and despotic. Yet it may be well to recall the words of the proverb: "Treason never prospers, what's the reason? Why if it prospers, none dare call it treason."

Rightfully or wrongfully, Richard placed a dangerous interpretation upon the formula that the sovereign should be subject to no man. His enemies claimed that he voiced the extreme doctrine that "laws were in his own mouth and frequently in his own breast and that only he himself could change and make the laws of his realm." More dangerous yet, in February of 1399, he translated theory into practice when, on the death of his uncle, John of Gaunt, Duke of Lancaster, he confiscated the estates and dignities of the duchy of Lancaster. From one perspective Richard's actions fitted the pattern of strong medieval kingship—the extension of royal authority and the destruction of provincialism, privilege, and private law. The duchy of Lancaster was in effect a state within a state where the old duke had maintained his own council and exercised his own justice, and where royal writs held no authority. Stated differently, Richard committed an act of unmitigated tyranny. He ignored the ancient constitution which said that "to the king belongs authority over all men, but to subjects belong property," and he denied to his cousin, Henry Bolingbroke, Earl of Derby and son of Gaunt, his rightful inheritance.

When Richard seized power in 1397 from the Lords Appellant, he did not touch, but he had not forgotten, two other important noblemen: his cousin, the earl of Derby, and the duke of Norfolk, both of whom had been associated with the Lords Appellant in their rule of England. In 1399 Norfolk and Derby fell out, and the earl accused Norfolk of complicity in the murder of the king's uncle, the duke of Gloucester. The truth of the accusation has never been settled, nor was the voice of the deity allowed to decide the issue, for, though a trial by combat was ordered, Richard called off the ordeal and exiled both noblemen—Norfolk for life and Derby for ten years. The king, however, promised the exiles that their right of inheritance would be recognized. When Richard sequestered the lands of old Gaunt, he broke his bounden word, and in denying the right of Derby to inherit from his father, Richard touched the most sensitive chord in all men of property. Shakespeare may have misrepresented the mainspring of Richard's character, but he does not overstate the case when he has John of Gaunt turn to his royal nephew and exclaim: "Landlord of England art thou now, not king!" The duty that a subject owed his sovereign was placed in doubt when the monarch himself violated the rights of his peoples. So when Henry Bolingbroke, Earl of Derby, returned to England in defiance of the king's will in order to claim his inheritance to the dukedom of Lancaster, he landed not as a traitor but as a liberator who could call upon the support of all men who sought to safeguard their rights from the encroachment of arbitrary government.

Returning from exile, Henry landed at Ravenspur on the 4th of July, 1399, and immediately proclaimed to the four corners of the realm his rightful claim to the duchy of Lancaster. The response was overwhelming; dangerously so, since many of the great baronial clans—the Percys of Northumberland and the Nevilles of the northern shires—lent their support, not so much to win Bolingbroke his ducal title as to seize for themselves the control and direction of government and to secure their independence from royal interference in the conduct of their own affairs.

Suddenly Richard found himself alone at Conway castle in northern Wales, facing an army thirty thousand strong. Shakespearean legend has it that Richard meekly bowed to the inevitable and allowed himself to be led captive into the presence of his cousin of Derby. In reality, Richard's surrender involved Bolingbroke's deceit, not the king's spinelessness. Conway castle was a military stronghold with escape by sea to Ireland and France, and it was not easy to induce the king to leave the safety of his fortified port. As yet Bolingbroke had made no claim to the throne, and he sent Henry Percy, Earl of Northumberland, to offer terms and lure Richard from his sanctuary. Derby, who now styled himself duke of Lancaster, demanded recognition of his rightful inheritance and the surrender of five of the king's council to be tried before a full parliament. Growling darkly that he would "flay some people alive," Richard agreed to his rival's terms and accepted Northumberland's promise of safe conduct to London. Once enticed from Conway, the king was ambushed and taken to the Tower, where he was "guarded as strictly as a thief or a murderer."

The seizure of a king is one thing; legally to remove his crown is another. By what authority could the anointed king be dethroned and divested of powers conferred upon him by God? The question facing Henry was how to legalize a revolution. With Richard securely in the Tower of London, his first step was to reorganize the royal court and council, removing his enemies and rewarding his friends. Actually there was surprisingly little change in administrative personnel, which casts doubt upon the Lancastrian claim that the crown was usurped in the name of justice and honest government for the realm. More significant was the appointment of those two colleagues in arms, Henry Percy, Earl of Northumberland, and Ralph Neville, Earl of Westmorland, to high office—the one as lord constable, the other as lord marshal.

Control of the machinery of government still did not give title to the throne. Henry now had to come out into the open and publicly claim the crown. Three roads lay open to him—he could demand title by family descent, by parliamentary decree, or by right of conquest. The duke's hereditary rights were chimerical from the start, for if there was a legal heir to the throne it was the eight-year-old Edmund Mortimer, eighth Earl of March, who was Edward III's great-great-grandson by his third son Lionel, Duke of Clarence. Henry of Lancaster was closer to Edward III in generations but more distant in legal descent since his father was John of Gaunt, Edward's fourth son. The best that the new government could do was to accuse Richard of "perjuries, sacrileges, unnatural crimes, exactions from his subjects, reduction of his people to slavery, cowardice, and weakness of rule," and to demand that he be deposed by "the authority of the clergy and people." Dimly, hesitantly, a new and pregnant concept was being voiced—that a king could be tried and deposed by a parliament which presumably embodied the "authority of the clergy and people." There were, however, serious drawbacks to claiming the throne on the basis of a parliamentary mandate. Historically, parliament could be activated solely by authority of the crown; it could only be summoned by the king; and it could act only if it had been convened by legal writs of summons. In deposing the monarch, parliament was in effect destroying itself, and once the sovereign had been set aside it was highly questionable whether parliament retained sufficient authority to bestow the crown on anyone, let alone Henry Bolingbroke.

If the constitutional issue was obscure, the danger to Henry in claiming his throne by grace of parliament was manifest. The duke was already sufficiently beholden to the great lords for their military assistance against Richard, and he was at pains to suppress any notion that he had received his crown as a gift, given him on the basis of baronial authority in parliament. Henry insisted he was king by right of inheritance and conquest, although the former was the sheerest fabrication and the latter was darkly suspect in the eyes of constitutionalists who wondered how Bolingbroke could justify his actions against Richard on the grounds of law and yet deny to his royal cousin his legal right to be king.

England in the summer of 1399 had to have a king who could rule. Right, in the person of the reigning monarch, was powerless; but might, in the guise of the duke of Lancaster, lacked the mantle of legality. Under the circumstances the best compromise was to engineer an abdication in which Richard II would step down of his own free will; Richard's own parliament, legally summoned, would declare his throne vacant; and Henry would claim the crown by right of lawful descent. On these foundations the Lancastrian legend was concocted. Richard cheerfully (*hilari vultu*) abdicated his sovereignty and surrendered his signet seal to Henry. In fact, there is no evidence of cheerfulness, only of an angry and embittered man who had been denied fair trial and had been ordered to sign on the dotted line. Next, on the thirtieth of September, parliament was assembled to acknowledge the abdication and declare Richard as being "utterly unworthy and useless to rule and govern the realm." In fact, the parliament convened

The Lancastrian Claim

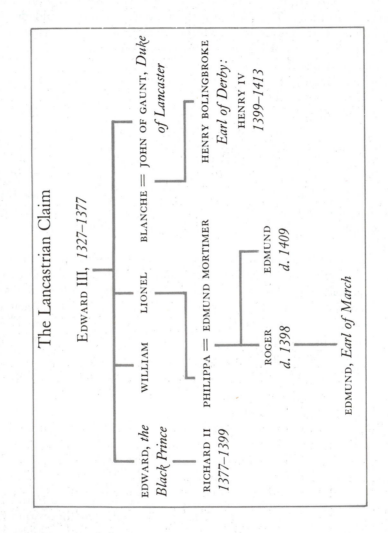

EDWARD III, *1327–1377*

EDWARD, *the Black Prince*

RICHARD II
1377–1399

WILLIAM

LIONEL

PHILIPPA = EDMUND MORTIMER

ROGER
d. 1398

EDMUND
d. 1409

EDMUND, *Earl of March*

BLANCHE = JOHN OF GAUNT, *Duke of Lancaster*

HENRY BOLINGBROKE
Earl of Derby:

HENRY IV
1399–1413

was no legal body since it lacked a legitimate king and its members were heavily outnumbered by a disorderly host of London citizens, most of whom were favorably disposed to the Lancastrian cause. At best the assemblage which met at Westminster might be called a convention or *ad hoc* parliament; at worst it was a gathering collected to lend the appearance of legality to outright revolution. Finally, Henry rose and "challenged the throne," stating that "God of His grace" had sent him with the aid of his friends and kin "to recover" the crown of England and to claim it as his due right. On October 13 Bolingbroke was crowned king and anointed with the "true" and sacred oil used at the coronation of Edward the Confessor. The fact that the oil had been conveniently rediscovered just in time for the ceremony casts doubt, if not upon the efficacy, at least upon the authenticity of the fluid. Henry was now king by God's grace, and Richard became "Sir Richard of Bordeaux, a simple knight." The only remaining impediment was the physical existence of Sir Richard, who was helped to a "natural" death within five months of his cousin's coronation.

Henry IV (1399–1413)

The right by which Henry IV ruled was uncertain. Force of arms had placed him upon the throne, and he would have to fight again and again to keep the crown upon his head. The new monarch claimed all the rights and prerogatives of his predecessor, but a precedent, nevertheless, had been established: a legitimate king had been forced to abdicate and had been replaced not by a legal heir but by an overmighty subject. Once the house of Lancaster faltered in its power, the curse of disputed succession would haunt the English throne. Henry's victory was not so much the triumph of law and justice over tyranny as it was a giant stride in the direction of royal and governmental subservience to aristocratic domination. A Neville and a Percy had been instrumental in elevating a baronial colleague to the throne; within three years Percy would endeavor to help him down again, and within two generations another Neville would bear the name of king-maker.

The man who assumed the burdens of monarchy in October of 1399 was a veteran of forty-two, skilled in war and government. The first step in Henry's newfound royalty was to free himself from his many allies who expected rich rewards for their services. The king's original council was aristocratic in composition, reflecting the influence of those "natural councillors" of the crown who claimed a seat on the royal council on the grounds of birth, breeding, and services rendered. During the first year of the reign an average of fifteen barons were invited to attend, but the number rapidly fell to seven while the proportion of professionally-trained administrators steadily rose. The new monarch drew heavily from those who had run the duchy of Lancaster, and the three most important governmental posts—the chancellor, the treasurer, and the keeper of the seal—were all filled with

HENRY IV: HENRY BOLINGBROKE, EARL OF DERBY, DUKE OF LANCASTER
"A precedent . . . had been established: a legitimate king had been forced
to abdicate and had been replaced not by a legal heir but by an overmighty
subject." *National Portrait Gallery.*

humble but loyal servants of the king. Yet no matter how hard he tried, Henry IV was never able to free himself entirely from baronial influence and interference.

The same was true of church and parliament. Immediately after his coronation, Henry called a new parliament in his own right and a new convocation of the clergy. In the latter, he tried to win ecclesiastical support for his dynasty by promising to exterminate the heresy of Lollardy; in the former he was more demanding, and insisted upon a tax on the export of wool for a period of three years. The king's relations with his parliaments throughout the reign were rarely harmonious. Even with the addition of the revenues from the duchy of Lancaster, Henry was financially more dependent upon parliament than his predecessors had been. A multitude of baronial "friends" had to be rewarded with fat annuities and grants taken from crown lands, while those who demanded too much had to be destroyed, an even more expensive procedure. Richard's income had averaged over £100,000 annually; Henry rarely equaled this figure, yet his expenses during the first eight years of the reign rose to £140,000 a year. The deficit was made up by parliamentary taxes called subsidies, imposed on land, by an export tax on wool and by import and export duties known as tunnage and poundage. The dilemma of all feudal governments was the fact that financial reality did not correspond to political theory and even a strong monarch could not finance his government from his normal or private sources of revenue. In other words, he could not live on his own. Unfortunately, this was exactly what political theory required, and parliament clung tenaciously to the unrealistic doctrine that during normal times the king should support himself by means of rents from crown lands, fees from the administration of justice, and the profits from feudal law. Parliamentary sources of money, it was argued, should be reserved for extraordinary occasions of great emergency.

Both Lords and Commons tended to view the financial plight of the crown in terms of governmental extravagance, corruption, and inefficiency, and not on the basis of economic reality. The theories and demands voiced by the Stuart parliaments in the seventeenth century had a long and distinguished heritage under the parliaments of the Lancastrian kings. Parliament's definition of good government tended to be cheap government, and in the name of efficiency and economy it began to encroach upon royal authority. Commons demanded that the king refrain from alienating crown lands and rewarding his friends with lucrative annuities; it insisted that income from parliamentary subsidies and excise taxes be audited, and that the expenses of the household be curbed and inspected by a parliamentary committee. Henry IV endeavored to resist these pressures, but his financial situation was such that he dared not antagonize this essential source of money. In 1406 he told the Commons that kings were not wont to render account to parliament, but he allowed the auditing of monies granted him two years before. There were, however, limits to how far he was willing to go; and Henry curtly dismissed the claim that members of his council should be personally responsible for any part of the grant which parliament felt had been misspent.

Henry's elevation to the throne had been made possible by the united opposition of all men of property to the violation of ancient law. Public sentiment had supported Bolingbroke's claim to the duchy of Lancaster but his seizure of the throne shocked important elements of the landed classes. Moreover, the baronial leaders soon discerned that in elevating Henry to the throne they had a tiger by the tail, and they began to question the wisdom of having replaced the unstable and emotional Richard with a veteran campaigner such as Lancaster. The first of the king's allies to fall out was Harry Hotspur, the son of Henry Percy, Earl of Northumberland. Hotspur had won fame by his defeat of the Scots in 1401, and, as a consequence of his victory, he held the earl of Douglas prisoner. The Percys were becoming increasingly restless under Lancastrian rule, and Harry refused to yield the earl of Douglas to the king, claiming the ransom money for himself on the ground that the cost of victory had been heavy and that to the victor belonged the spoils. At issue was the historic right of the crown to hold all important prisoners of war, and it was clear that Hotspur's action constituted open defiance of royal authority. Henry had no choice but to crush his erstwhile friend, and Hotspur was defeated and killed at the battle of Shrewsbury in 1403.

Equally serious was a second uprising of the earl of Northumberland in league with Owen Glendower and Sir Edmund Mortimer, uncle to the young earl of March, and himself a possible contender for the throne. Glendower was the leader of a Welsh insurrection against English rule and influence, and his daughter was Sir Edmund's wife. He had been Hotspur's ally in 1402, and four years later he entered into the infamous tripartite agreement to divide England—Glendower to take Wales and the adjacent English shires, Northumberland the northern counties, and Mortimer what was left, which wasn't much. Henry now faced not one but three potential usurpers, and it took two years of continual fighting to defend his kingdom and secure his crown. In the end Glendower was driven back into his inaccessible Welsh hills, Northumberland was caught and executed, and Mortimer was trapped in 1409 at Harlech Castle, where he chose starvation rather than surrender.

Henry spent fourteen weary years scolding his parliaments but never daring to dispense with them, plucking down the baronial caterpillars of his commonwealth but never having the strength to wipe them out, and struggling with a dread of disease and infection. The strain of constant campaigning and the weight of regal responsibility slowly destroyed the king's health, and he degenerated into a neurotic hypochondriac, plagued by eczema which contemporaries took for leprosy visited upon him by God in retribution for his usurpation of the throne. The concluding years of his life were troubled by the basic dilemma of all monarchies—the relationship between a father who is a ruling sovereign and a son and heir who is a potential king. The story that young Prince Hal tried on the crown whilst his father still lived is legend, but it does symbolize the strain that existed between the two men. As the years slipped by, it became painfully apparent that the elder stood for senility, sickness, and death; the younger for youth, energy, and life. All who looked to the future, who hoped to profit from change, turned away from the dying sovereign to his dynamic son. The end came on March 20, 1413, and Prince Hal succeeded his father upon a usurped throne, breathing new life and vigor into the Lancastrian dynasty.[3]

Henry V (1413–1422) and the War Against France

Every society creates its own particular brand of horror, and every civilization has its own methods and reasons for fighting wars. Often the ideals that lend distinctive vigor and vitality to a society breed the wars which in the end destroy those same ideals. The revival of conflict between France and England in the fifteenth century is a case in point. Feudal society, for all its Gothic spires and exquisite medieval illuminations, rested upon a military ideal—the code of the armed and mounted knight. Appeal was made to violence. Lawlessness was not entirely a matter of the lack of law enforcement; instead it was built into the creed itself. When the major pastime of the leaders of society was the mock warfare of the joust, and when feats of arms were the mark of social success, the human instinct to settle personal and international disputes by recourse to arms was not only unrestrained, it was elevated to a position of virtue. That the cannon, the musket, and the longbow were rapidly replacing the armored knight in battle mattered not at all; the medieval military code remained esteemed. Knights were by tradition, if not in reality, full-time soldiers; the language of military chivalry still held in bondage the minds of men; and the kingly ideal continued to be Richard Coeur de Lion, not Henry II or Edward I. The fact that the first Richard had drained his realm of coin and lived in England less than six months in a reign of ten years, while Henry II and Edward I had labored long and hard at the edifice of strong royal government, was of no importance. Richard I had united chivalry with piety, military prowess with the spread of God's word. His was the ideal to be followed, especially by the youthful Henry V who was anxious to prove his manhood and his kingship. Given the nature of the feudal code as embodied in the expenses of Prince Hal's education ("eight pence for harpstrings, twelve pence for a new scabbard, four pence for seven books of grammar in one volume"), it was inevitable that the young king should turn his eyes

---

[3] If due allowance is made for Shakespeare's Tudor bias and dramatic license, his historical plays remain, if not good history, at least vital and exciting history. There is no recent biography of Henry IV, but for his son read E. F. Jacob, *Henry V and the Invasion of France* (1947).

toward France, remember the glorious days of Crécy and Poitiers, and renew the ancient conflict between the two kingdoms.

The Hundred Years War was certainly an outgrowth of the structure and code of feudal society, but there is evidence to indicate that war in the fifteenth century was even more closely related to a particular aspect of medieval government—the difficulty of maintaining law and order at home. Behind the fatuous claims of the English to the throne of France lay the reality of domestic politics. A combination of lawlessness and heresy confronted the new reign in 1413 and the simplest solution to the internal turmoil was to send the troublemakers to fight in France. Heresy and sedition marched hand in hand in 1414 when Henry's old colleague in arms, Sir John Oldcastle, turned against his sovereign. Oldcastle, had he lived two hundred years later, would have been called a militant Puritan who sought to apply the standards of heaven to the affairs of man. He was aghast at the perfidy and corruption that existed in church and state, and he demanded the liquidation of what was generally regarded as the source of all ecclesiastical evil: the church's landed wealth and temporal powers. Behind him stood the restless knights of the shires, who cast covetous eyes on ecclesiastical lands, and an array of men, some desperate, some ambitious, some idealistic, who had one thing in common—the desire to change the existing order of things. The old warrior seems to have organized an ill-conceived and subterranean plot to kidnap the king and lead the city of London in a revolt against the godless leaders of society. The plan came to nothing, and though Oldcastle escaped capture until 1417, his followers were systematically hunted down and hanged as traitors or burned as heretics. In the end the old knight was caught in Wales and executed. He died a martyr to ideals that would not be realized for two centuries, and an example of the restlessness and violence of his age. Under such circumstances, it was not surprising if men argued that the prestige of a doubtful monarchy and the peace of the realm would be enhanced if such domestic strife were directed into foreign parts and if England were to gain victory abroad.

The international scene was peculiarly propitious for such a policy. France, like England, was moving into a century of overmighty subjects, irresponsible magnates, insane monarchs, minority rule, and wicked princely uncles. Unlike England, however, France had no Henry V to catch the imagination and to curb the forces of anarchy and misrule. In 1380 the death of the able Charles V and the succession of the eleven-year-old Charles VI exposed France to a combination of minority government and monarchy crippled by a sovereign who passed from adolescence into imbecility. The situation was made worse by the consequences of French dynastic policy. The kings of France had introduced a policy of endowing members of their family with the ducal titles of the various semi-independent provinces of the kingdom in the hope that bonds of blood would secure those territories more closely to the crown. King John in 1361 had presented

The House of Valois

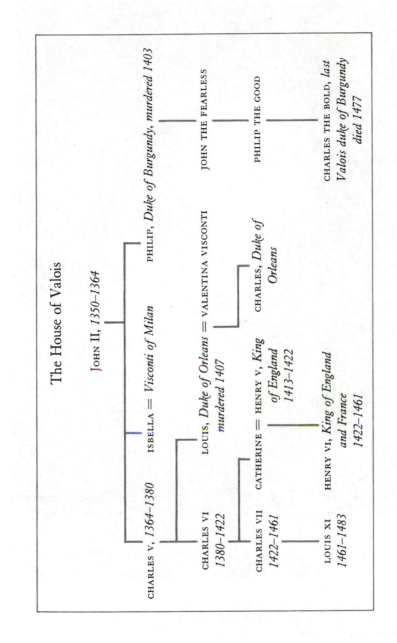

JOHN II, 1350–1364

PHILIP, *Duke of Burgundy, murdered 1403*

JOHN THE FEARLESS

PHILIP THE GOOD

CHARLES THE BOLD, *last Valois duke of Burgundy died 1477*

CHARLES V, *1364–1380*

ISBELLA = *Visconti of Milan*

LOUIS, *Duke of Orleans murdered 1407*

VALENTINA VISCONTI

CHARLES, *Duke of Orleans*

CHARLES VI *1380–1422*

CATHERINE = HENRY V, *King of England 1413–1422*

CHARLES VII *1422–1461*

HENRY VI, *King of England and France 1422–1461*

LOUIS XI *1461–1483*

HENRY V
"Hard, domineering, overambitious, bigoted, sanctimonious, priggish . . . describe a king who had most of the least attractive qualities of a warrior-saint." *National Portrait Gallery.*

the duchy of Burgundy to his son Philip, while Charles VI invested his brother Louis with the duchy of Orleans. The results were the opposite of those expected. When Charles went mad in 1392 his ducal relatives began to fight over the control of the royal government, and factional rivalry deteriorated into armed conflict in 1407 when John of Burgundy, the successor of Philip, connived at the murder of the duke of Orleans. Racked by civil discord and paralyzed by an insane monarch, France in 1414 was ripe for the picking when Henry V of England revived the Plantagenet claim to the French crown. The claim was absurd, for the house of Lancaster had only a doubtful right to its own crown, let alone the throne of France. But legality is by necessity a question of interpretation, and Henry V had no doubt as to the just and righteous nature of his title. The king's attitude was more a reflection of his character than a matter of Salic law and legal niceties.

Henry V the hero, the paragon of kingly and soldierly virtues—loyal, just, upright, honorable, able, chivalric, and pious—turns out on closer inspection to have had feet not of clay but of iron. "Hard, domineering, over-ambitious, bigoted, sanctimonious, priggish" are better words to describe a king who had most of the least attractive qualities of a warrior-saint. The wonderful image of an irresponsible prince associating in escapades of juvenile bravado with that engaging and boisterous bag of wind, Sir John Falstaff, is Shakespearean legend, not history. At sixteen Prince Hal was an adult, educated to war and the trials of campaigning in the Welsh mountains. When he mounted the throne at twenty-five, he was a veteran, the most effective kind of military man: a conquistador, adventurer, and professional soldier who combined boundless energy with the mystic appeal of leadership and an absolute conviction that God was at his elbow. Conventionally orthodox in his religious creed but almost a fanatic in the intensity with which he adhered to his faith, Henry believed implicitly that victory in war was a question not of numbers but of "the power of God." The justice of his right to the duchy of Normandy and to the crown of Valois France came close to being a religious obsession for which no price was too great to pay.

The army which crossed over to France in August of 1415 and the war that was fought there reflected most of the new forces operating in late medieval society. The ancient and always somewhat theoretical method of raising troops on the basis of military service rendered in return for land tenure had long since disappeared. Instead an indenture system was used whereby captains contracted to raise specific numbers of archers and men-at-arms. The contract or indenture set the size of the company, its rate of pay, the length of service, the place of assembly, and the composition of the unit, which generally consisted of mounted knights with their esquires and pages, mounted and foot archers, and pikemen. By the fifteenth century such armies had developed extensive headquarters—staffs of armorers, surgeons, clerks of the stable, carpenters, trumpeters, fiddlers, and the like. The more important members of the headquarters unit supplied their own archers—

the sergeant of the king's tent brought 28, the master-smith and master-carpenter had 41 and 124 respectively, and the yeomen of the king's bed chamber financed 86.

The war that such men fought was more brutal than chivalric, more businesslike than glorious. Except for moments of personal heroism and occasional pitched battles, the conflict consisted of dreary months of destructive campaigning, guerrilla operations, and the tedious battering of walled towns. In the French city of Alais the taxable property was estimated at £40,000 in 1338, at £26,000 in 1405, and at £19,000 in 1440. Paris saw wolves in the streets at night for the first time in a hundred years, and 24,000 houses stood ruined and deserted. In the provinces the devastation was worse; peasants dropped their rakes and fled to the safety of the neighboring walled towns whenever they heard the alarm bell, and even the pigs grew so conditioned to the sound that when the bell tolled they ran for safety of their own accord. The Black Death accounted for a portion of this depopulation but armed bands of marauding soldiers, many of whom were not English but mercenaries hired by both sides, completed the destruction. As France starved and bled, the hope of gain and the creed that depicted war and violence as positive virtues prevented any early termination of the conflict. Each side was fated to fight to the point of total exhaustion no matter what the ultimate price.

Henry landed with a force of 2,000 mounted men-at-arms, 6,000 archers (half of whom were also on horseback), and possibly another 1,000 in his headquarters company. The French channel port of Harfleur was the first objective and in late September it surrendered in the face of English cannons. The king was so convinced of the moral and military weakness of the French that he determined to march his tiny army overland through Normandy to winter quarters at Calais. On October 25 a wet, tired, and isolated English force found itself confronted by a French host that may have numbered as many as 50,000. At Agincourt Henry's belief that God, not man, gave victory was confirmed by the crushing defeat of the French army. English archers, the cramped nature of the battlefront which prevented the French from capitalizing on their numerical superiority, and the sodden state of the battlefield contributed to victory, but to contemporaries the hand of God was manifest in a battle that resulted in the butchery of the flower of French chivalry. The French dead included three dukes, a grand constable, eight counts, 1,500 knights, and four to five thousand men-at-arms. The English lost less than 300 men including the duke of York, the earl of Suffolk, and six or seven knights.

Agincourt was a staggering moral victory, but further conquests and the English bid for the French crown were made possible by two other factors: first, hard and unheroic fighting in which "the King's Daughter, the Messenger, the London" (all names of siege cannons used to breach the walls of French towns) were more important than armored knights; and second, the Burgundian alliance caused by another eruption of the Burgundian-Orleans feud. On August 28, 1417, the leaders of the Orleans faction, in league with Charles VI's son, the dauphin of France, arranged a meeting with John of Burgundy to discuss the plight of France and the possibility of concerted action against the English. The hope of unity was dashed by the murder of John of Burgundy, who was attacked and killed by the Orleans party. Instantly his son Philip joined the English, and together in 1420 they dictated the treaty of Troyes to a torn and prostrate France. Charles VI was allowed his crown, but Henry V was to marry the king's daughter, the Princess Catherine, and was pronounced his true and rightful heir. In return, Henry undertook to defend all of France which acknowledged the treaty and to reduce those sections which still held out for the disinherited dauphin. In May of 1420 the English parliament ratified the treaty and bound its members, "their heirs and successors to observe and fulfill its terms." The dual monarchy had been created; it now remained to be seen whether a defeated France would accept it or a victorious England could enforce it.

The first and most disastrous blow to the success of the dual kingdom came with the death of Henry V on August 31, 1422. He died of dysentery and exhaustion, victim of an obsession and martyr to a defunct ideal: a medieval Europe devoid of national consciousness and tolerant of an international ruling elite which placed chivalry, piety and nobility above Englishness or Frenchness. Had he lived two months longer he would have become king of both realms, for Charles VI of France followed him to the grave on October 11. The heir to the two kingdoms was now a nine-month-old babe —Henry, the sixth of his name.

The momentum of English victories was not stopped by the king's death; under Henry's brother, the duke of Bedford, the tide of conquest spread deep into France. By 1429 the reality of a dual kingdom seemed almost within grasp. The dauphin of France, the future Charles VII, remained uncrowned, unloved, and ineffective, and an English army stood at the gates of Orleans, the last major bastion holding out for Charles. Bedford's successes, however, were more a symptom of French moral and military paralysis than a sign of English strength or an indication of real enthusiasm for the infant Henry VI. In 1429 the tide of war began to ebb as rapidly as it had risen, and step by step the conquerors were driven back into the sea. The story of Joan of Arc and the resurgence of French arms is an oft-told tale. Joan poured new spirit into France; she even goaded the feckless dauphin into activity, and finally persuaded him into forcing his way to Rheims to be crowned. Urged on by her voices, who told her "fille de Dieu, va, va, va! Je serai à ton aide," she accomplished a miracle. Today we question that miracle, preferring to explain her success in terms of nationalism, politics, and the power of finance. But the fifteenth century thought otherwise, and it seemed to the English of the utmost importance to prove that she was a "disciple and limb of the fiend." When she was captured by the Burgundians and bought by the English for 10,000 gold

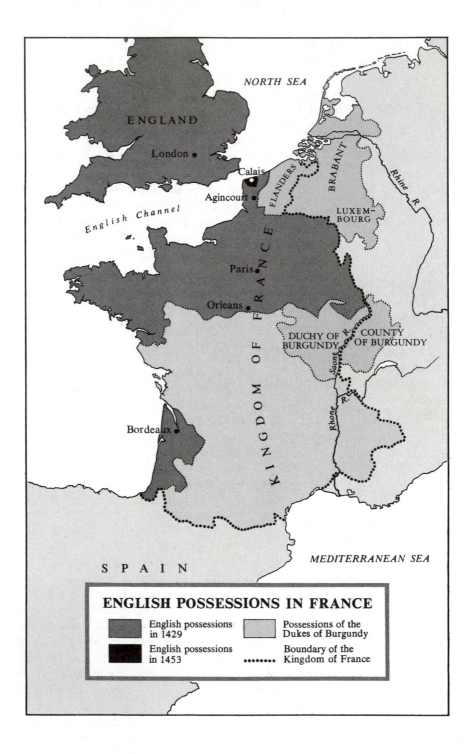

NORTH SEA

ENGLAND

London

English Channel

Calais

Agincourt

FLANDERS

BRABANT

Rhine R.

LUXEM-
BOURG

Paris

Orleans

KINGDOM OF FRANCE

DUCHY OF
BURGUNDY

COUNTY
OF BURGUNDY

Saône

Rhône R.

Bordeaux

SPAIN

MEDITERRANEAN SEA

ENGLISH POSSESSIONS IN FRANCE

English possessions
in 1429

English possessions
in 1453

Possessions of the
Dukes of Burgundy

•••••• Boundary of the
Kingdom of France

crowns, Bedford considered the prize cheap at twice the price. The moral influence of the Maid of Orleans had, at all costs, to be destroyed, and Joan was sacrificed upon the altar of a child king and the dual crown he wore. She was tried, found guilty of heresy and witchcraft, and burned at the stake at the age of nineteen on the 30th of May 1431. Though Bedford acknowledged the deed to be an act of political necessity, an English soldier at the scene cried out: "God forgive us; we have burned a saint." [4]

When Bedford died in 1435 exhausted by his impossible labors defending the regal title of his young nephew, and when in the same year Burgundy deserted its English ally, the tide of defeat turned into a flood. At home in England, a bankrupt crown, a child king, a weary and uncooperative parliament, and an increasingly irresponsible aristocracy paralyzed the English will to fight, and it became simply a matter of time before the invaders were driven into the channel.

Henry VI (1422–1461) and the Corruption of Government

Henry V's death in 1422 had left England in a desperate position. The government was committed to the defense of a dual monarchy, but the financial condition of the realm made the task well-nigh impossible. In 1433 the normal expenses of the government were estimated at £57,000 while the cost of the war in France added another £44,800. The traditional peacetime revenues of the crown, derived mostly from the duchy of Lancaster and other crown lands, amounted to £38,000 but after a multitude of fixed fees and annuities had been deducted, it fell to only £8,400. The customs on wool yielded £27,000 and parliamentary and ecclesiastical taxes supplied approximately £45,000 or a total of £80,400. Consequently, the government was operating at a deficit of over £21,000 a year and faced an accumulated indebtedness of £164,815. The constant burden of war made the English insistent that the conquered territories in France pay for their own defense and contribute to the financial support of the dual kingdom, but such a policy merely ended by alienating whatever affections Henry's French subjects may have felt, and earned for the English the nickname of "God-damns."

The budget figures reveal something more than bankruptcy in war; they help to explain further weaknesses which began to appear the moment Henry V's strong hand was removed, for England was now exposed to the uncurbed consequences of aristocratic corruption in government and the rule of a simple, if not simple-minded, sovereign. By the terms of Henry V's will, his brother Humphrey, Duke of Gloucester, was to be regent in

---

[4] There has been a great deal of nonsense written about Joan of Arc. The reader is advised to start with E. Perroy, *The Hunded Years' War* (tr. W. B. Wells, 1951). G. B. Shaw's *Saint Joan* is great literature and possibly not as bad history as it appears on the surface.

England while Bedford was made responsible for the defense of France. The great barons, working through parliament, rejected this arrangement and forced Gloucester to accept the inferior position of protector appointed by and at the pleasure of the council. As in the days of Richard II, government soon deteriorated into a family preserve in which royal uncles maneuvered to control their nephew. Bedford preferred to stand aloof, but the young king's powerful relatives, Henry Beaufort, Bishop of Winchester, and Edmund, Duke of Somerset, sought to organize conciliar opposition to Gloucester.

In the midst of this surfeit of cousins and uncles, Henry VI was, from the start, a cipher more suited to the monastery than the throne. The fiction of personal government was carefully maintained even to the point of requiring the infant sovereign to order his own educational disciplining. At the age of two, he informed his "very dear and well beloved" council that, because it was necessary for a king to learn good manners, he gave permission "to reasonably chastise us from time to time as the case shall require," and he further assured his teachers that they would "not be molested, hurt or injured for this cause in future time." The great lords of the council had nothing to fear, for the king "took all human chances, miseries and afflictions of this life in so good part as though he had justly, by some offense, deserved the same." It was said that he "gaped not after riches, and was careful only of his soul's health." The strongest word he was ever heard to say in anger was "forsooth," and his associates correctly guessed the truth when they noted that he had not "the heart or manliness to be a king." Generous to the point of lunacy, oblivious to the dirt of politics around him, and constantly begrudging the few demands on his time required by his royal office, the saintly Henry was a perfect pawn in the hands of his Lancastrian relatives, the great magnates and crown officials, all of whom enriched themselves at the expense of the royal income and made a mockery of the king's justice throughout the realm.

The deterioration of good government set in early in the reign, but it reached its culmination during the decade of the 1450s when the bickering of factions within the council became entangled with the question of the succession to the throne. The brothers of Henry V died without issue and by 1447 the only Lancastrians left, other than the young king, were members of the Beaufort family—Edmund, Duke of Somerset, Margaret Beaufort, and a grandson and great-granddaughter of John of Gaunt by his mistress Catherine Swinford. The descendants of that union had been legitimized but barred from the succession, so that the line of descent jumped to Richard, Duke of York, who was the grandson of Edmund, fifth son of Edward III and the great-great-grandson, through the female line, of Lionel, third son of Edward. When Henry VI married Margaret of Anjou in 1445 and a son was born eight years later, Richard of York's position relative to the throne was markedly changed. The original purpose of the marriage had been the hope that it might end the war in France and stop

The Houses of Lancaster and York

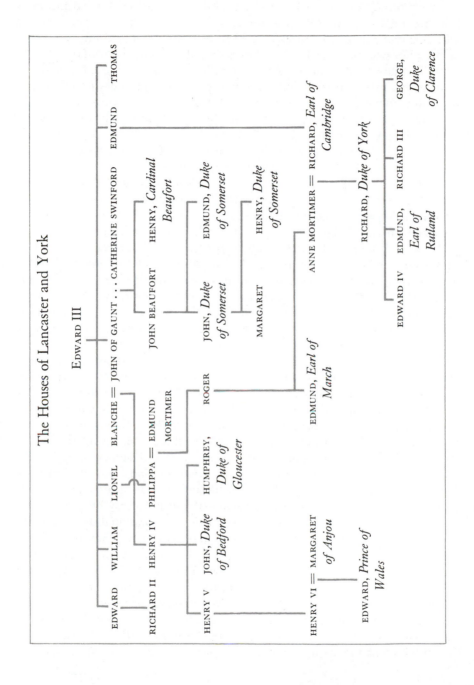

the long succession of English defeats. All it did in fact was to introduce into the English court a young, forceful, and determined French princess, who dominated her regal husband and transformed Henry from an insignificant cipher who preferred to stand outside politics into the titular head of a royal faction. United in dangerous misalliance were a baronial clique of Lancastrian sympathizers, determined to preserve the fruits of misgovernment for themselves, and a tactless and alien queen who was equally determined to secure the succession for her infant son, Edward, Prince of Wales. Opposed to both stood Richard, Duke of York, and his Yorkist followers who claimed to be indignant at Lancastrian corruption but who actually desired a share in the profits of government.

In 1449 the erosion of government both at court and throughout the realm had become so serious that parliament declined to grant money for troops to defend England's last remaining strongholds in France for fear that such soldiers might be employed by the great lords for war at home and not in France. The following year a popular insurrection, known as Jack Cade's rebellion, occurred in the counties about the city of London. The uprising was an upper-class movement of country squires and yeomen who had suffered from the consequences of corrupt government. Jack Cade called himself "John Amend-alle," and the list of his grievances was testimony to the scope and degree of Lancastrian misgovernment. Six points were singled out for reform: the king was giving away too much of the crown land and consequently could not live on his own; there was extensive corruption in the collection of royal revenues; members of the House of Commons were not elected freely and had fallen to the status of agents of the rich and mighty who controlled their elections; court parasites were using royal justice to seize for themselves the lands of their opponents and poor folk who had no influence at court; England was losing the war in France, which was a disgrace to the memory of the heroes of Agincourt; and high offices of state were given to favorites and men of mean and humble station. Cade was killed, and his brothers in arms ended on the gallows, but the criticism of the government did not die with them.

As the war with France moved toward its humiliating and costly conclusion, England slipped into anarchy and civil war. "Pray for us," said one of the soldiers still fighting in France, "that we may come soon out of this unlusty soldier's life into the life of England." In the early 1450s England saw her chickens come home to roost. Among them were hardened soldiers anxious to follow a more lucrative career at home; barons ready to use force and violence to control the profits of royal government or to unseat their adversaries on the king's council; and a Yorkist claimant to the crown who was impatient to replace the descendants of Henry IV upon the throne.

Economic Collapse
and Social Dislocation

2 The tabloid of wicked uncles and royal murders, of heroism at Agincourt and corruption at Westminster, and of dynastic dissension and baronial bullying must be framed by the prosaic details of demographic, economic, and social reality.[1] The twilight years of medieval England were darkened by the shadow of economic and spiritual depression and social irresponsibility which settled not only upon England but over all of Europe. To understand these decades of despair, it is necessary to go back and pick up the story of events some of which had their beginnings well before 1399.

Throughout Europe there was something approximating a general failure of leadership in state and church. In England the hundred years between 1360 and 1460 were punctuated with minority rule, governmental incompetence, and periodic lapses into royal senility or insanity. France was exposed to a prolonged and dreary line of inept sovereigns, and Germany disintegrated into a confusion of princely families competing for the moribund dignity of the imperial office. Even the papacy, during the Great Schism (1378–1415), was torn by competing popes, each anathematizing his rival, and each setting up separate ecclesiastical systems replete with law courts, cardinals, and taxes. Something more than bad luck must have been at work when so large a part of Europe suffered from the collapse

---

[1] The best works on the economic, social and intellectual impulses of the fifteenth century are European in orientation, not English: see E. Cheyney, *The Dawn of a New Era* (1936); and J. Huizinga, *The Waning of the Middle Ages* (1st ed., 1924). Excellent newer works are J. R. Lander, *Conflict and Stability in Fifteenth-Century England* (1969) and J. M. W. Bean, *The Decline of English Feudalism, 1215–1540* (1968).

of both royal and clerical leadership. It has been postulated that "no civilization can endure unless its members are occasionally willing to sacrifice immediate personal advantages for ultimate social gains." [2] The question, however, still remains why the balance between individual selfishness and self-sacrifice seems to vary from one generation to the next. Possibly, it can be argued that civilizations, as well as individuals, when confronted with a series of unprecedented and catastropic events, become increasingly insecure and unwilling to risk much on the future or sacrifice much for the present. Certainly the feudal standards and institutions of the past had become rigid and unwieldy by 1400. In the face of social revolution from below, prolonged economic depression, plague, and heresy, the old ways became more and more anachronistic and unrealistic, merely the fossilized relics of an outmoded past. Yet those same ideals and methods, those time-honored precedents established back in the "good old days," were blindly adhered to by men and women who had nowhere else to turn when confronted by forces which were endangering the old patterns of behavior and thought.

Changes in the Structure and Spirit of Feudalism

By the early years of the fifteenth century the cornerstones of the ancient feudal edifice were rapidly disintegrating. Three hundred and fifty years before, the overwhelming need had been for immediate and massive local defense. The armed knight, who did military service in return for land tenure, had then been a necessity and a reality; the fief and the manor had worked reasonably well as an economic and legal means of uniting land and labor into a productive union sufficient to support the knight and his retainers; and the economy of England and Europe had been so marginal as to make any other form of military or political organization unrealistic. By 1400 all this had radically changed. The king's law and the king's peace had long since secured a sufficient, if not complete, defense of the realm. The knight, though he still clung tenaciously to his warrior ideal, had lost most of his military reason for being, and the military obligations connected with his land tenure had dwindled away. Though the term "knight" lingered on either as a personal dignity or as a generic term to describe those worthy of a seat in the House of Commons, the status of knighthood was evaded by most landed proprietors who were anxious to avoid the financial and military duties associated with the position. As the fifteenth century advanced, the feudal knight tended more and more to become the sixteenth-century gentleman. Typical of the class were such boisterous and aggressive country gentlemen as Thomas Paston and John Howard, who fought a noisy duel for local preeminence in Norfolk, not with the venerable weapons of war but with lawsuits, disputed elections to parliament, rival mercantile

---

[2] J. R. Strayer and D. C. Munro, *The Middle Ages* (N.Y., 1942), p. 442.

ventures, marriage alliances, and occasional jail sentences, depending on which one had been able to exercise greater influence at court or intimidate the larger number of judges and juries in the shires.

The ideal of knighthood was the theme of Sir Thomas Malory's *Morte d' Arthur* (1472), in which the knights of the Round Table were all sworn to observe the chivalric code. They were bound "never to do outrageousity, nor murder, and always to be free from treason." They were expected "by no means to be cruel, but to give mercy unto him that deserveth mercy." Upon pain of death they were sworn "always to do ladies, damsals, and gentlewomen succour," and no knight was to "do battle in a wrongful quarrel for no law, nay for no world's goods." Yet reality was quite otherwise; the knightly order was branded as "mere disorder," and the knight who took to the field of battle was described as laden "not with steel but with wine, not with spears but with cheese, not with swords but with wine-skins, not with javelin but with spits." You would think, this critic of knighthood concluded, "they were on their way to feast and not to fight."

Sir Thomas Malory's life was the perfect expression of his class and century; he was twice imprisoned for "rape" yet could produce a wonderful allegory, deeply symbolic in meaning and style. Malory's Arthurian legend was placed in a magic kingdom where the knightly ideal became an allegory of heroic battles, courtly loves, romantic bowers, and ruined chapels. This chivalric world was a land of whites, greens, and reds in which the color white represented eternal peace, green symbolized the fruitfulness of the earth, and red reflected the violence and violation of mankind. As the joust in the fifteenth century had deteriorated into a spectacle hedged in by regulations, wooden barriers, and rigid pageantry, and had lost all relationship to the realities of war, so the chivalric ideal had become a social myth totally out of line with the actions of living men. Even Froissart, the chronicler of the Hundred Years War, had a singularly commercial view of chivalry. In one breath he claimed to be recording the "honorable and noble adventures of feats of arms" as encouragement to the "brave and hearty" of future generations. In the next breath he decried the English slaughter of their prisoners, not because it was an act of unchivalric brutality but because it was unprofitable; "one with another" the captives would have been worth "400,000 francs."

As for the fief and manor, those economic keystones of the medieval past were deteriorating with each passing generation. The fief was a political division of the land and it was held by the vassal of a lord in return for feudal services. The manor was a unit of agrarian exploitation and consisted of the union of land, labor, and legal rights. A fief often included many manors, or might include only part of a manor depending on the productivity of the soil. Private property in the modern sense did not exist; instead the lord of the manor, who was usually, but not always, a baron or a member of the knightly class, possessed only rights to the fruits of the soil.

He did not own the land itself. Only the king can be said to have owned land, and all medieval land tenure was grounded upon this concept of proprietorship whereby property rights were limited to the profits of the land, and landholding was carefully prescribed by the custom of the manor or by the terms of the tenure. In the same way that the vassal held his fief from someone above him in the feudal structure in return for rather hypothetical military services, so within the manor itself the land was held by freemen and bondsmen on the basis of various types of tenurial relationships.

The property of the manor was generally of three kinds: (1) demesne land over which the lord of the manor possessed full proprietorship and which he exploited directly through his slaves, serfs, or hired laborers, or which he leased to tenants for life or for a set number of years; (2) freehold land held of the lord for a fixed rent and passed from generation to generation unchanged in the family of the freeholder; and (3) copyhold land held on the basis of the custom of the manor, which might involve financial or personal services whereby the holder was required to give to the lord of the manor a percentage of his labor, or his produce, or both. The nature of these obligations might be recorded in the manor court, and, if so, the tenure was known as a copyhold, or the tenant's rights and services might be unwritten, resting on the historic custom of the manor. In both cases it was possible for the lord of the manor to modify and increase the nature of the services attached to the property; or, in the case of tenure protected only by custom, he could claim it as demesne land, evict the peasant and rent the fields to whomsoever he pleased at the highest price he could command. The landholding which eventually proved most resistant to the encroachment of the lord of the manor and to the vagaries of economic fluctuations was freehold property, which tended to become a fixed and permanent tenure approaching that of private property.

The labor supply of the manor was of two types—free and bond. By 1500 most laborers were free, but in 1399 perhaps a third to a half of the peasant population remained in a state of bondage—owing personal service to the lord of the manor, exposed to death and inheritance taxes and other financial extractions, and still legally bound to the land. It was quite possible for a serf or unfree laborer to hold free land and conversely it was not uncommon for freemen to farm unfree property, and for both, bond and free, to lease demesne land from the lord of the manor. The tendency by 1399 was for two things to happen. First, freemen with freeholds evolved into substantial landed proprietors, and this was the agricultural element out of which the yeoman class of the fifteenth century developed. Starting as freeholders or wealthy peasants, some of them even rose to be lords of the manor in their own right, and as a group they soon began to amalgamate with the lower fringes of the knightly class. Second, the bondsmen and copyholders tended to fall to the level of wage laborers, usually free, occasionally renting land, but generally working the soil for wages paid them by the lord or yeomen of the manor. The result of this twofold process was the weakening and eventual destruction of the bonds that had once welded land and labor into an economic unit in which both lord and peasant had legal rights and shared in the produce of the soil.

Finally the simple agrarian economy of the medieval past disappeared along with the professional knight and the fief. The merchant, the money-lender, the financial speculator, and the cloth manufacturer had become, by the fifteenth century, just as important to society as the knight and the cleric. It was true that laws regulating the just price in trade and commerce continued on the statute books; the doctrine that "riches exist for man, not man for riches" remained the official creed; and the military-chivalric ideal held captive the mind of men. But for all this, commerce and a money economy predominated. Long before 1399 the crown had become dependent upon the wool trade as a source of revenue, and the customs on wool equaled in importance land subsidies granted by parliament.

The Black Death (*1348, 1361, 1369*)

It is appropriate that Warren Hollister's *The Making of England* should conclude with a description of the demographic catastrophe that marked the spiritual, statistical, and symbolic end of English medieval society; but it is equally proper that this volume should commence with the story of the Black Death, for if any single factor contributed to the economic dislocation, emotional instability, and spiritual malaise of the fifteenth century, it was the Black Death or bubonic plague which struck England in 1348. It descended without warning like a stroke of divine retribution, striking three times in twenty years, and liquidating possibly twenty million souls. After 1370 the plague became chronic, joining cholera and smallpox as one of the three cardinal scourges of Europe. With each succeeding generation it became less and less virulent as the black rats, which carried the disease, were destroyed by their more ferocious colleagues, the brown rats, and as their breeding grounds were demolished through purely accidental acts of hygiene such as the fire of London in 1666 which cleaned out three-fourths of the metropolis.

For contemporaries the plague was incomprehensible except in terms of the wrath of God or the vicious actions of men. They were unaware of the role of the rats which spread the infection along the trade routes from Eastern Europe to Iceland, or of the fleas which attacked the rats and moved on to man, or finally of the bacillus which was the ultimate source of the pestilence. To the men of the fourteenth century the visitation of death on such a scale had to be the diabolic work of Jews poisoning the wells of Christendom, or a divine punishment for the manifold sins of humanity. As one chronicler put it: "Bands of women dressed in the gorgeous clothing of men were wont to join the sport of the joust and the tournament. There and thus they spent and lavished their possessions and wearied their bodies with fooleries and wanton buffoonery." But God brought marvelous punishment, for "that same year and the next came the general mortality throughout the world." If today we no longer blame the ladies, we are still mystified by the sudden appearance of the plague and its place of origin. It may have originated in the Far East, but China's responsibility has never been proved, and it is fashionable to attribute most things unpleasant and alien to the Orient. More probable, the plague was the result of a mutation in an already existing bacillus which made it suddenly more virulent and against which neither man nor rat had immunity.

Whatever the origins, the Black Death left behind it a path of unparalleled destruction; the long night of medieval society had commenced and not every night ends with dawn. The number of dead is beyond calculation. The figures offered by contemporaries indicate the magnitude of the affliction but are otherwise unreliable, since the medieval world was in no way a slave to statistical accuracy. It was reported that the city of Norwich lost 57,000, which seems questionable since the city at its most populous never reached 17,000. It is customary to say that between 30 and 40 percent of the population died; in round and unreliable figures this means that some twenty million were dead in Europe, and in England two million out of a total population of between four and five million.

These figures are meaningless; the mind rebels at such numbers and refuses to comprehend death on such a scale, but when statistics and percentages are translated into the realities of daily life, the picture becomes both more credible and more terrible. The Black Death wrought havoc at law; cases literally died away before they could be brought to trial. On the 28th of April, 1349, a suit involving a husband and wife over a question of the woman's dowry was introduced into court; by the day of the trial all of the wife's witnesses were dead and so was her husband. In May of the same year, five petty disputes involving sixteen men either as principals or as witnesses were taken to court. By the day of the hearing eleven of the sixteen were dead. On May 22, three suits for debt were filed; the defendant in one case, the plaintiff in the second, and both the plaintiff and defendant in the third were dead before the cases could be heard in court. The manor court records of a single manor indicate that in thirty-one cases relating to land ownership or inheritance only women or children were alive to inherit, and in nine cases there were no heirs at all.

The ecclesiastical records tell an equally dreadful story. In a single year eight hundred parishes lost their priests; eighty-three lost them twice and ten thrice over. In an Augustinian house the prior and all the monks died, while in the counties of Norfolk and Suffolk nineteen religious foundations lost their priors or abbots. In all, possibly 40 to 50 percent of the parish clergy died. The middle ages were accustomed to death, but not in such proportions that there was neither gravedigger nor priest to attend the dead and dying.

The spiritual consequences of the plague are incalculable; whether there is a causal relationship between the communal graves of the plague victims and what followed chronologically—social revolt, civil anarchy, and heresy—is impossible to say, but the Black Death set the framework in which these events took place. The life and vigor of the high middle ages had been declining long before the Black Death descended, but in a sense they too were buried with the plague victims. What remained was a dead facade: the universities withered but the Hundred Years War ground endlessly on and the supply of soldiers keen on looting and rapine was seemingly unaffected; the great medieval scholars perished but the church, soulless, continued as a vast and worldly bureaucratic machine. The spirit, the aims, and the ideals of the past corroded, leaving in their place only greed and violence. More and more, late medieval society began to assume the grotesque appearance of Dante's hell—a civilization held together by fear, fraud, and force.

Nowhere were the emotional effects so manifest as in religion. The church was held up to scorn for its inability to cure the sick, alleviate pain, or placate a wrathful God. The prayers of priests and pope were of no avail. Rich as well as poor died, and the living found it difficult to believe in a god of mercy who could inflict such suffering upon his flock. There seemed to be but two possible explanations for death on such a scale: either God was a god of wrath and vengeance to be feared, or mankind had fallen into a sinfulness which was beyond redemption and the church had lost its right to administer God's grace to man.

Religious expression turned away from reason and intellect to unreason and imagination. The intelligible God of the great medieval scholastics seemed quite incomprehensible: what good and sufficient reason could there be for a supposedly rational deity to bring upon mankind the catastrophe of the Black Death? Confronted with such unreason, the medieval world looked instead toward a God who need not be understood intellectually but who could be experienced emotionally and imaginatively. In the years following the Black Death, England and most of Europe were exposed to a wave of flagellant monks garbed in black who marched from town to town, waving flags, singing doleful chants, and bearing red crosses before them. They read letters purporting to come from Christ himself, condemning sinners to everlasting perdition, and they taught self-flagellation as the true communion since, they said, the blood of man must mingle with that of Christ in order to achieve the Blessed Land. Such groups were, of course, evangelical, but they were something more: they were symptoms of the widespread practice, both within and without the church, of deliberately exciting the imagination to achieve a more intense religious sensation. The excruciating suffering of Christ upon the cross and the agonies of sinners in hell were pictured in the mind's eye and experienced by means of imaginative realism. In art the most terrifying expression of this kind of imaginative realism was achieved in Germany by Matthias Grünewald, who was commissioned by the monastic hospital of Isenheim to paint a diseased and crucified Jesus hanging in agony on the cross. The hospital specialized in the care of incurable syphilitics who sought relief from their own suffering by witnessing that of Christ.

THE DANCE OF DEATH, BY HANS HOLBEIN THE YOUNGER
"The prayers of priests and pope were of no avail. Rich as well as poor died, and the living found it difficult to believe in a god of mercy who could inflict such suffering upon his flock." *The Granger Collection.*

The economic consequences of the plague are just as difficult to evaluate as the spiritual, but somewhat easier to record. Depopulation of the countryside followed in the wake of disease; crops were left to rot and entire villages disappeared. In Oxfordshire the parish of Steeple Barton boasted in 1300 a new church and sixty tenants. Fifty years later the water mill had ceased to turn, thirty-two of the village's sixty customary tenants were dead, and six hundred acres of farmland lay unattended. The lord of the manor had at one time received fifty-four shillings from yearly rentals; now the same land was leased for six shillings, nine pence, while the perquisites of the manor court fell from forty shillings to forty pence. By 1353 the manor house had fallen in, the dovecote was empty, and nearly twelve hundred acres of fertile land were uncultivated for want of farm hands and tenants. The silence that had settled over Steeple Barton spread throughout the kingdom. At first the lords of the manor had little difficulty in finding laborers, because the rural population in the previous century had been so abundant that not even the catastrophic crop failures and famines of the early decades of the century plus the disaster of the plague could entirely decimate their ranks. By 1400, however, the cumulative impact of the Black Death along with the Gray Death of 1361 began to take effect, and England moved into a century of contracting economy: the prevailing economic theme was one of land surplus with seriously curtailed rentals, and labor shortage with consequent high wages. Taking 100 as par, food prices during the first decade of the fifteenth century stood at 84, wages at 119. In contrast, the last ten years of the century saw food prices move up to 94 and wages drop to 105. For the large landed proprietors who were dependent on rents and farm labor, a major agricultural recession commenced in 1400 and lasted for the better part of the century.

Economic Crisis (1400–1475)

The economic crisis which reached its height during the 1440s was not caused solely by the plague; other factors were involved, both domestic and international. Certainly the Hundred Years War with its ugly stepsisters, rapine, piracy, and violence, lay heavy upon Europe, driving up the risk of commerce and reducing the buying power of some of the most prosperous areas of northern France. War can act as an economic stimulus, but prolonged guerrilla warfare, such as was being fought between France and England in the fifteenth century, may end by destroying the very basis of trade—a reasonable chance for making a profit and customers who are able and willing to buy. For centuries England's major export had been sacks of raw wool sent to Flanders and Florence for manufacture into cloth, but in the fifteenth century war began to curtail this trade. In 1448 French pirates looted the Kentish coast, burning towns located many miles inland and destroying warehouses filled with wool. In the same year England's traditional ally, the duchy of Burgundy, actively joined France in the Hundred Years War and closed her Flemish ports to English wool. The results are recorded in the trade statistics of the town of Sandwich in Kent. In 1448 one hundred and eighty-two sacks of wool were sent overseas; a year later exports had dropped to twenty-five, while imports of wine fell from 1,042 to 271 tuns.

Throughout the fifteenth century English merchants faced increased competition from abroad and at the same time were less able to defend themselves. This was particularly true in relation to the Hanseatic League, a union of German towns which exported corn, timber, pitch, and fur and controlled the sale of Flemish cloth. As the century progressed, the Hanseatic merchants were able to extend their extraterritorial rights in England, securing the virtual independence of their place of business in London. The Steelyard, as the area was called, became a state within a state and the Hansa merchants claimed immunity from English law. At the same time they were able to gain economic concessions in the form of the right to export wool at special rates which were, in some cases, more advantageous than those regulating English merchants. The crowning blow came in 1450 when Hanseatic merchants drove the English out of the Baltic and closed the lucrative Icelandic waters to English traders and fishermen.

If care is taken in the selection of the data, the economic picture of the first half of the century can be made to appear black and oppressive. Towns experienced a long decline in population: Coventry dropped from ten thousand in 1280 to under seven thousand by 1400, and York shrank from eleven to eight thousand. Wool exports from 1448 to 1450 were off 35 percent, miscellaneous trade was down 23 percent, and wine imports were cut by 50 percent. The earls of Northumberland were faced with a 25 percent cut in land revenues during the first fifty years of the century, and it has been estimated that throughout the kingdom the decline of rents may have exceeded the drop in prices by as much as 11 percent. The poverty of the realm is reflected in the reduction of the crown's income; the parliamentary subsidy for the county of Surrey was set at £587 in 1334 but by 1440 the estimate had been reduced to £506.

Like most economic matters the total design is difficult to distinguish. Economic recession and agricultural depression hurt many, but they also helped certain individuals and groups. Certainly the overall economic profile is not one of unrelenting gloom. England before the plague was approaching the point of "critical population density," which is a social science euphemism for describing starvation in a society where the population outstrips its food supply. Agriculturally the kingdom was desperately underdeveloped, and probably farm production was no better than in twentieth-century Ghana where one worker can only feed one and a half persons (in the United States in 1970 he could feed forty-two). Though the total economic pie shrank after 1349, for those who survived the Black Death there was more of almost everything to go around; uneconomic marginal land was left uncultivated and real wages may have doubled.

The decline in the export of wool, if taken alone, would indeed be an alarming index of commercial disaster, for the average number of sacks exported during the 1390s had stood at 19,357 and by 1446 it had fallen to 7,654. These figures, however, must be presented against the equally dramatic rise in the export of woolen broadcloth, for it was during the century following the plague that England moved from a wool exporting into a cloth manufacturing economy. In 1354 the export of wool broadcloth was 4,774 pieces; by 1440, the average had risen to 56,317, and by 1509 it had reached 84,789 pieces. Export figures can be translated into mercantile success, or failure, depending upon the interests involved. The Staplers, an association of 300 to 400 merchants with their headquarters (or staple) located at Calais, were on the decline during the century, but their commercial welfare was geared to the export of raw wool. Conversely, the Merchant Adventurers, a newer organization concentrating in and eventually monopolizing the export of wool broadcloth, were increasingly prosperous throughout the same period. The truth of the matter is that economic boom or depression varied from individual to individual and group to group, and had very little to do with the total picture of expansion or contraction.

The Peasantry

Of all the elements of medieval society which were being shaped by economic impulses, the peasantry remained the largest in numbers, the weakest in influence, the most important to the economy, and the dullest in wit. Medieval recorded history has been the story of a small, dominant, and literate minority who have taken the trouble to document and preserve their opinions and activities. Consequently, the historian's image of the voiceless and inarticulate majority is haphazard at best and heavily distorted by feudal upperclass prejudice against manual labor, and the medieval conviction that social groups were ordained by God to play a prescribed function within the social organism—the merchant to pay taxes, the aristocracy to lead, the clergy to pray, and the peasants to labor "with their hands from dawn to vespers." In the eyes of those who could record their sentiments, the typical toiler of the soil was "marvellously ugly and hideous. His head was big and blacker than smoked meat; the palm of your hand could easily have gone between his two eyes; he had very large cheeks and a monstrous flat nose with great nostrils; lips redder than uncooked flesh; teeth yellow and foul. . . . Upon his back was a rough cloak; and he stood leaning on a huge club."

Richard II summed up the aristocratic attitude toward the peasantry when he exclaimed, "Villains you have been and are; in bondage you shall remain," but economic reality determined otherwise. Time, if not politics, was on the side of the serf. Unpleasant to the sight and nose as the peasant may have been, his economic position was improving. The plague and the consequent shortage of labor accelerated a process that had for decades been working in favor of the serf, transforming him into something other than a bondsman, tied to the land, "owning nothing but his belly," and subject to his lord's legal and economic domination. Faced with a depleted labor supply, the lord of the manor was forced to grant far better terms to his serfs. Bondsmen became freemen either by formal agreement or by the informal lapse of ancient obligations. Occasionally the serf simply ran away to a distant manor where the local landed proprietor asked no questions and hired him for wages. The peasant's most valuable asset, his labor, was suddenly placed at a premium and he could use it to win his legal freedom. As the years passed, the lords of the manor found it easier to pay wages than to enforce personal service or labor statutes. By 1500 the serf was almost extinct. His place had been taken by three groups: the wage-earning rural proletariat which was free but landless; the free customary tenant or copyholder who paid rent but had a right to bequeath and inherit his land "according to the custom of the manor"; and the freeholder who had become in fact, if not yet in theory, the owner of land which owed no service.

The Yeomanry

Standing above the rural laborer in the social hierarchy was another group, less definable and even more elusive than the peasantry. This was the element sometimes referred to as freeholders, sometimes as yeomanry, and sometimes simply as prosperous peasants. Whatever the nomenclature, they constituted an agricultural elite which by dint of hard work and efficient farming had prospered as a consequence of the agricultural depression and labor shortage. Rents were low and leases were easily negotiated on long-term bases, and many a humble man who may have started life as a serf ended up a substantial farmer, controlling a freehold, leasing a sheep run, and employing a handful of laborers. Possibly there were five thousand such farmers, earning anywhere from five to twenty-five pounds a year. They were the lowest level within the ruling elite that represented scarcely 2 percent of the total male population. Bishop Hugh Latimer's father was one of this group, owning no land but leasing two hundred acres, raising a hundred sheep and thirty cows, hiring six laborers, and himself working from dawn till dusk to send a son to college, finance good marriages for his daughters, and pay for the hospitality which more than anything else was the mark of social status and success.

The Knights and Esquires of the Shire

The higher in the social pyramid, the more capricious the economic and financial situation became. Above the yeomanry were some 1,200 esquires with incomes ranging from twenty to forty pounds a year, and another 1,000 lesser and greater knights who controlled yearly revenues up to

£300. Though no clear division can be drawn between the knights and the barons above them and the yeomen below, the knights and esquires of the shires do seem to have been confronted with a major economic crisis during the 1440s and '50s. The decline in the demand for wool, the incessant cry for higher wages, and the collapse of rental income from land hit them hard. Plagued with curtailed means, large families, and indigent younger sons, an unknown percentage sought relief through war, lordship, and litigation.

In the long run the strain of war, and the economic dislocation which followed, worsened the financial position of the larger landed proprietors, but certain individuals perceived that the profits and wages of war might offer a solution to their economic woes. The hope of ransom money and booty was never-dying. When war in France proved more fatal than profitable, there always remained the possibility of war at home. The existence in society of a body of impecunious professional military men constantly searching for an outlet for their specialized talents constituted a menace to internal peace and security. Willing to fight in either France or England, such men sought employment in the households of the great magnates who could use their talents, and who could offer them status and position in an age which still accepted the obligations of lordship as the most important ties within society.

Lordship

Feudalism is often pictured as a political structure shaped like a pyramid, and held together by interlocking contractual relationships based on proprietorship, or *dominium* over land which had been given in return for military and feudal service. Historically speaking, however, feudalism was neither particularly systematic nor rational, and from the start it was more a state of mind than a formal political system. It is difficult for the twentieth century to sniff the feudal atmosphere which often reeked of the worst aspects of provincialism and privilege. Used in its broadest and least constitutional sense, feudalism embodied most of man's innate fears and virtues: his instinctive dislike of change, his atavistic clinging to custom, his deep suspicion of authority, his myopic loyalty to friend, kin, and village, and his preference for private settlement over public law. Belonging to the group —a guild, a town, a monastery, a college, a family or the entourage of a great nobleman—was more meaningful than membership within the realm. The individual might regard himself as being the king's man but he did so primarily because the monarch could inspire his loyalty; as yet there was only the faintest idea of service offered on the grounds of a subject's duty to the crown.

Medieval society thought in terms of lordship which was in large measure a reflection of the feudal relationship existing between a vassal and his overlord and the obligations entered upon by both parties, but it was also something more; it was the mentality that judges a man by the color of his livery and the authority of his overlord and patron. Today the nation demands a monopoly of the individual's loyalty and in return it gives him both a sense of belonging in the form of citizenship and a sense of importance and status. The man without a country has no place in the twentieth century. In medieval times the man without a lord lacked social position and influence. The hold which the concept of lordship exercised over men's minds was on the wane in the fifteenth century, but political, social, and in large measure financial success still remained geared to lordship, and the fifteenth-century gentleman was advised to "get yourself lordships for it is the law and the prophet."

The link between declining estate revenues, lordship, and the use of force in daily life can be seen in the case of Mr. Thomas Hargrave, who returned in haste from the Yorkist victory over the Lancastrians at Tewkesbury in 1471, ready and willing to capitalize upon the military success of his party. Hargrave's purpose was to evict Peter Marion from lands which Marion had held for years but which Hargrave coveted. The unfortunate Mr. Marion was suspected of Lancastrian sympathies and lacked friends or influence in high places. Hargrave seized his rival, tied him up with a dog collar around his neck, and chained him in the great hall of the manor house which had once been his. Then Hargrave sent for the recorder of Winchester, who arrived to discover the new "owner" mounted upon a raised chair with Marion cowering at his feet. Under the circumstances it is not surprising that Marion was persuaded to deed the manor to Hargrave, or that the transaction was duly recorded at law, or that Marion, the instant he achieved his freedom, repudiated his act and sought the aid of important men who could help him regain his property. It is impossible to say what percentage of the responsible elements of society were like Hargrave, but when the social element which represented the natural rulers of society, and from which sheriffs and justices of the peace were drawn, was using force, fraud, and favoritism to gain its ends, the total collapse of good government and the advent of civil war was simply a matter of time.

The Baronage

On a legal and restricted pinnacle far above the ranks of lesser men stood the baronage of England, exclusive in numbers but not always financially distinguishable from the wealthier knights of the shires. In 1436 there were only fifty-one barons, and though their number varied from decade to decade, there were rarely more than a baker's dozen who were of sufficient age, ability, and wealth to exercise real power. Their average income was in the neighborhood of £865 a year, but the lower economic echelons of the group managed with as little as £300 while the favored few rose as high as £5,000.

The lesser barons faced many of the economic problems confronting the gentry and renter classes, and they took similar steps to alleviate the situation. Like their cousins the knights of the shires, they also turned to violence, law, and lordship. The social composition of the men who joined Lord Hastings' household, for example, and looked to him for support at court and at law indicates the extent and upper-class nature of the system of lordship. Of the ninety retainers who owed Lord Hastings service and wore his livery, twenty were described as gentlemen, fifty-nine as esquires, nine as knights, and two as peers of the realm, and all were closely related to prominent county families.

The great barons were in a more favorable position, since social and economic forces were conspiring to concentrate in their hands unparalleled wealth and potential political power. The closer they stood to the crown in birth and association, the greater were their revenues. Richard, Duke of York, commanded an income of £3,231, and possibly twice this sum if his Welsh manors are included. Richard, Earl of Warwick, jogged along on £3,116 and could count on another £2,422 from his Welsh estates. The duke of Buckingham managed with £4,400, and the Percys of Northumberland trailed with £2,825.

The principle "to him who hath shall be given" prevailed. Not only the incomes but the estates of the great magnates tended to grow larger as the vagaries of marriage, mortality, and violence began to operate at an accelerated pace. As families died out, estates escheated back to their overlords or were passed through the female line into the great baronial clans whose daughters were legion. The greatest, the most prolific, the most predatory, and therefore the most successful and dangerous of these noble dynasties were the Nevilles. Younger than the Percys in noble rank, but their rivals for control of the northern shires, the Nevilles began their spectacular rise with John, third Baron Neville, who, by the judicious marriage of his many sisters and daughters, converted a distinguished northern baronial family into a dynasty equal in wealth and power to such royal clans as York and Lancaster. His eldest son Ralph (1364–1425) became first earl of Westmorland and carried on the family policy of marital aggrandizement. Ralph married twice and his second wife was Joan Beaufort, daughter of John of Gaunt by his mistress, Catherine Swinford, and thus a half-sister of Henry IV. In all, Ralph had eleven sons and twelve daughters, and hardly an important family in England escaped a Neville son or daughter-in-law. Neville daughters became duchesses of Norfolk, Buckingham, and York; Neville sons inherited through their wives such important titles as Latimer, Furnival, Fauconberg, Salisbury, and Abergavenny. Through the marriage of his daughter Cecily, Ralph was the father-in-law to the Yorkist heir to the throne and grandfather of the two Yorkist kings of England—Edward IV and Richard III. By his son Richard, he became the grandfather of the mightiest baron of them all—Richard, Earl of Warwick, better known as the kingmaker. When the kingmaker entered London in February of 1454, he marched at the head of six hundred men dressed in brilliant livery and decorated with the Neville heraldic emblem of the ragged staff. When he sat down to breakfast, six oxen were consumed by his household, and the earl was reputed to have been so lavish that all were invited to eat with him who could claim connection with his clan. He offered his guests as much roast as they "might carry upon a dagger," and it was said that six thousand friends and acquaintances came to celebrate the installation of his brother George as archbishop of York in 1467. If the number cited is correct, the entire ruling clique of England must have been gathered together at a single function. This total should not be dismissed simply as another example of picturesque but inaccurate medieval exaggeration; it is just possible that six thousand persons actually did dine with the Neville brothers for one excellent reason: the earl of Warwick had the economic means and political influence to be not only a kingmaker but also a king.

The Church

No picture of the fifteenth century would be complete without a word about the church, that international Leviathan with its heart in Rome and its ecclesiastical arteries spread the length and breadth of Christendom. Nowhere in the century was the failure of leadership so obvious or the process of fossilization so pronounced; nowhere did medieval corporate pride and exclusiveness thrive so vigorously as in the church which had, throughout the centuries, been preeminently successful in preserving its historic privileges and wealth. Originally the estates belonging to the church had been given by men anxious to show their respect for an institution which not only held the keys to the kingdom of heaven but which also practiced a higher and better way of life on earth. By the fifteenth century the ecclesia still held the keys to the kingdom of heaven but it tended to equate entrance into paradise with paying tithes and taxes. As an institution the church remained immensely wealthy,. possessing between one-fourth and one-third of all arable lands, but it had used up much of the goodwill and respect which had originally inspired these gifts. Rich, autonomous, and privileged, the ecclesia lost its early spiritual drive and became rigid and bureaucratic, eying with the deepest misgivings all new ideas, especially those which might endanger its financial and material well-being. By the fifteenth century the medieval Catholic Church had become a universal great-aunt with more of the madam about her than the martyr. It had chosen the path of safety in which church and state joined in an alliance to maintain the status quo. Pope, priest, and friar preached a single truth: payment of taxes and obedience to authority were necessary to the soul's salvation. In return the Lancastrian crown assumed the responsibility for enforcing religious orthodoxy and exterminating heresy.

Anticlericalism and the wish to purify and elevate the ecclesia were as old as the medieval world, and in the past the church had always been able to absorb and profit from the demand for reform. Fifteenth-century criticism of clerics and their comfortable and worldly way of life was different; it lay outside of a church that had grown so rigid and unyielding that it could do nothing but brand all reform as heresy and turn to the Lancastrian kings and parliamentary statutes to exterminate the ideas of John Wycliffe (1320?–1384) and his Lollard followers.

From the established church's point of view, Wycliffe expounded three darkly pernicious doctrines. First was the alarming emphasis which he placed upon the Bible and upon individual interpretations of the Scriptures as the source of spiritual inspiration and the guide for a moral life. Clerics could never sanction such a notion because it implicitly denied the authority of the ecclesia to interpret God's will and administer His grace. Even more explosive was his insistence that the man was more important than the ecclesiastical office. The wicked priest, in Wycliffe's view, vitiated the benefits accruing from the sacraments despite the authority vested in him by his sacerdotal office. Conversely, the good man, filled with a sense of divine grace, could administer the sacraments just as effectively as the ordained priest. The central issue of the church's spiritual authority was being challenged; Wycliffe was questioning the privileged status of the clergy as an ordained and separate caste within society. Finally the Oxford scholar attacked the temporal and monetary endowments of the church, insisting that Christ and his apostles had lived in poverty without benefit of gold plate and exorbitant rents. Pomp and circumstance, he said, were corrupting the spiritual health of the priestly order, and monks with their "red and fat cheeks and great bellies" were more interested in the cure of hams than of souls. In denying the right of the church to possess wealth and land, Wycliffe was only a step away from questioning its position as the custodian of the conscience of Christendom.

For a time in the fourteenth century, Wycliffe and his Lollard followers were immensely popular, and they "multiplied exceedingly like budding plants and filled the whole realm everywhere." Barons who resented ecclesiastical control of high royal offices found comfort in the Lollard belief that a good churchman "dwelleth at home and keepeth well his fold." Likewise knights of the shire in parliament must have listened with sympathy in 1410 to the Lollard suggestion that if church lands were nationalized and redistributed to deserving lords and gentlemen there would be sufficient estates to create fifteen earldoms, 1,500 knights, 6,200 esquires, a hundred almshouses, fifteen universities, and leave £20,000 for the royal treasury. Such a suggestion found wide support among landlords, both orthodox and heretic, who envied the church its wealth, power, and independence.

But it was with the lesser sort that Lollardy was most popular. A few of the converts were eccentric and impious fellows such as the man who split the statue of St. Catherine into kindling to boil his cabbage, or the singular gentleman who took a consecrated wafer used in the mass and consumed one-third of it with oysters, one-third with onions, and one-third with wine, as rather extraordinary proof that it was common bread and possessed no miraculous qualities. But by and large Lollards were devout and ordinary folk, drawn from the urban and artisan classes or from the lesser gentry. They represented a numerous, if not powerful, element of the population that was in desperate need of spiritual comfort which the established church either would not or could not give.

By the fifteenth century Lollardy was considered to be far more dangerous than it had been in the fourteenth, for the ruling classes began to suspect that novelty in religion walked hand in hand with social revolution. The Peasants' Revolt (1381) and the Lollard heresy coincided in time, and rightly or wrongly, anxious priests and frightened landlords were quick to assume that heresy in faith produced revolution in society, and that church and state must stand shoulder to shoulder if Christendom were to exterminate the heretical and seditious doctrine that "all goods should be held in common and no one ought to be allowed to have property." Persecution got under way with the triumph of a Lancastrian dynasty anxious to win ecclesiastical support for its shaky throne. Parliament passed laws in 1401 making unrepentant heresy punishable by burning, but such legislation did little but harass and irritate the Lollards. On the death of Henry IV, however, a stern and orthodox monarch, anxious to earn the favor of God, mounted the throne. By 1422 the prisons were full to overflowing with heretics awaiting trial or execution, and by 1431 Lollardy as a political or religious force was destroyed. Thereafter, the movement went underground, to become the seedbed for the spiritual and constitutional revolution which destroyed the medieval church in the sixteenth century.

The Lion and the Unicorn

3 In the last chapter Richard Neville, Earl of Warwick, was left entertaining six thousand guests. It is now time to "sit upon the ground and tell sad stories of the death of kings," for the economic and political milieu that created the kingmaker also produced the Wars of the Roses in which the houses of York and Lancaster competed noisily for the throne of England.[1] Those "gaudy, blabbing, and remorseful" days of civil war and dying medievalism have sometimes been termed the age of bastard feudalism, sometimes the century of substitute feudalism; but whatever the description, the sense remains the same. Medieval society had somehow gone wrong.

Deeply significant change is often difficult to discern except in terms of mood and atmosphere. In essence, bastard feudalism was a matter of spirit, not of institutional form; the structure of society remained the same but the aspirations of individuals and groups were no longer those of the twelfth century. By 1450 feudal society had lost its sense of direction. The barons had ceased to regard themselves as the watchdogs of good government; instead they usurped the machinery of royal government for their own narrow and irresponsible designs. The crown had become pusillanimous and bankrupt, and abdicated its traditional position of leadership to anyone who could offer political initiative. Even parliament proved itself incapable of growth or leadership and was unwilling and unprepared to operate except within the rigid confines of its feudal past.

---

[1] Shakespeare's historical plays are standard reading for the Wars of the Roses, but they should be carefully balanced by J. R. Lander, *The Wars of the Roses* (1965); R. L. Storey, *The End of the House of Lancaster* (1966); P. M. Kendall, *Warwick the Kingmaker* (1957) and *Richard III* (1955); F. Thompson's convenient survey, *A Short History of Parliament, 1295–1642* (1953); and W. H. Dunham, *Lord Hasting's Indentured Retainers, 1461–83* (1955).

The Great Magnates

Anarchy and violence remained close to the surface of medieval society, only lightly restrained by respect for royal authority, by a sense of communion in a common Christian faith, and by the realization that Englishness was a quality shared by all Englishmen. The most explosive centrifugal force in the late fourteenth and fifteenth centuries was the mounting economic independence and privileged status of a small coterie of barons who began to regard themselves as being outside the law, and who embodied the ugliest and most irresponsible aspects of bastard feudalism. Coincidence of timing made matters still more serious. Growing self-consciousness on the part of the hereditary magnates was accompanied by agrarian recession and commercial dislocation, and both took place at a time when the crown was exposed to almost fifty years of saintly but ineffective leadership. By 1450 a handful of barons, who already claimed hereditary membership in a closed corporation known as the House of Lords and who asserted the divine right of aristocracy, were ready and willing to accept the mantle of political authority the moment the monarchy renounced its position as the natural leader of society.

Political power bears direct relationship to economic wealth, and Sir John Fortescue correctly analyzed political reality when he pleaded that kings should be worth twice the gold of their greatest subjects. When a Warwick or a Percy or a duke of York could command cash revenues greater than that of their sovereign, it was clear that subjects were mightier than kings. Capitalizing upon their influence and wealth, certain barons began to construct family empires. In the northern shires and along the Welsh border the greater and lesser magnates were always able to subvert and occasionally prevent the operation of royal law. The voice of a Percy, as warden of the North, was more often heard than that of the monarch in distant London. The great nobles kept their own courts, councils, chancelleries and exchequers. They were in fact kings in all but name and, like any sovereign prince, they maintained private armies for defense and aggrandizement. Their wealth and political power attracted lesser men into their service and livery. By procuring indentured henchmen who served him in law and commerce as well as in war, a lord could surround himself with men committed "to take his full part and quarrel and be with him against all persons save the King." Hired retainers were more than private soldiers. In return for services rendered, the aristocratic purchaser offered to be "good and tender lord" to his followers. What "good and tender lord" meant is the crux of bastard feudalism, for the barons were not simply petty kings in their own feudal domains; they were also the political and social bosses of an intricate and inclusive system of patronage which permeated the entire realm.

The nobles used their position and their influence on the royal council to line their pockets with fat salaries and annuities drawn from crown lands and also to provide their friends, servants, and retainers with lucrative government offices. The king's chancery, his exchequer, even the king's law were invaded, used, and warped, thereby distorting the royal service into a vast system of jobbery. "Men," said Mr. John Paston, "do not lure hawks with empty hands," and the great magnates, if they wanted lesser men to look to them for aid and comfort, had to produce the plums of political patronage. Power in the fifteenth century was judged in terms of hospitality, for the number of those who sat down to eat in a baronial hall was in direct proportion to the extent of the nobleman's political patronage since his dinner guests tended to be either his hired henchmen or newcomers seeking office.

The structure of politics was perceived by Sir John Fortescue when he noted that the king's council was controlled by the great lords who were so occupied with the concerns of "their kin, servants and tenants that they attended but little to the king's matter." No question, he added, that was treated in the council "could be kept privy, for the lords told their servants how their causes had fared and who was against them." Success even in the shires was related to knowing the right person and wearing his livery. If a squire was faced with litigation he turned to his noble patron to insure that the judge would pass favorably on his plea and that the jury would be packed with good friends and close relations. On occasion, if legal extortion failed, outright intimidation of the judge and jury was attempted, as when Lord Fanhope sat outside the town hall of Bedford with fifty armed retainers in order to secure a proper judgment. Political power was equated with the ability to confer favors and meddle at law, and it was crucial to the baron's social and political reputation that he control the machinery of justice in the counties. Consequently Lord Hastings selected his ninety henchmen with care: twenty were sheriffs of the shires and thirty-three were justices of the peace.

The aim of all the great barons was not the destruction of law and order but the redirection of the profits of royal government into their own pockets and the control of crown and local agencies. The result, of course, was that "the law serveth naught but to do wrong," and respect for both royal proclamations and parliamentary statutes collapsed. Ultimately the magnates reached a point of lawlessness where they no longer bothered to compete with one another in the council over who should whisper self-interested advice into the king's ear. By the 1450s a more direct and violent approach to political control was being used: the barons fought openly to decide which of their party candidates would wear the crown. From the start the Wars of the Roses were not so much a dynastic struggle between royal houses as a political conflict between baronial cliques. The magnates sided with either the white rose of York or the red of Lancaster because of family hatred and personal rivalry, not because of principle. Lord Bonville was a Yorkist because the earl of Devon was a Lancastrian, and it was sufficient cause for Bonville to switch his allegiance when Devon became a

Yorkist. The lords strove to control royal government; they fought to decide who should be king on grounds of self-interest, self-aggrandizement, and self-esteem in an age which glorified warfare, condoned violence, and accepted the barons as the natural rulers of society until they had proved their incompetence a hundred times over.

The Lancastrian Crown

Aristocratic irresponsibility and independence would have been impossible had not the feudal crown as well as the feudal baronage gone wrong. "The kingdom," as one contemporary put it, "was out of all governance" for the "king was simple and led by covetous council and owed more than he was worth." The chronicler who made these observations put his finger upon the three flaws of the fifteenth-century: Henry VI was always simple and on occasion insane, royal government had fallen into the hands of men more interested in personal and family profit than good office or sound government, and the crown was hopelessly insolvent.

The financial plight of the monarchy was threefold: (1) royal inability to collect revenues in a century convulsed by lawlessness and economic dislocation; (2) the channeling of the king's resources and lands into private and baronial hands; (3) and most serious of all, the narrowing of the gap between the public revenues of the crown and the private incomes of certain overmighty subjects whose economic means were greater than those of the monarch. As the royal coffers were plundered, Commons was increasingly reluctant to grant taxes, and the knights and esquires of the shires, plagued by high wages, low rents, and contracting markets for wool and wheat, demanded economy and retrenchment in government. Import and export duties and the customs on wool declined and, at the same time, income from crown lands was depleted by the lavish generosity of Henry VI, who cared nothing for money and had little comprehension of the relationship between wealth and power. Rents from royal lands should have been supplying nearly £40,000 annually but, by the time that fixed obligations had been paid off and royal officials had dipped their fingers into the till, the amount came to only slightly over £8,000. By the 1450s the actual cash income of the king was down to £5,000, while the normal operating expenses of the royal household amounted to £24,000 and the royal debt stood at £372,000. Under the circumstances, it is not surprising that reformers should have demanded that crown property be returned to the king, that salaries and annuities to court favorites and party henchmen be cut, and that the monarch be assured a fixed and nonparliamentary personal income of at least twice that of his wealthiest subject.

When the crown became an instrument of party strife, a mere political football in the game of baronial aggrandizement, royal law and respect for royalty were almost impossible to maintain. The armor of the mighty afforded protection to the privileged few who could enforce their legal claims with the unsheathed sword, but lesser people, who looked to the king's law for defense, saw only corruption and injustice. For the first time in medieval history the anguish of common folk in the midst of lawlessness has been preserved. The voices of middling people who suffered from events over which they had no control can be heard in the letters of the Paston and Stonor families, people of local weight but never in the van of national politics.[2] Theirs was a more humble existence than that of their noble neighbors. Their wives complained about beatings "twice on a day" and their heads being "broken in two or three places." The Pastons worried about seats in parliament; they sought help in their perennial lawsuits; and they wrote about their unmindful children and the need for strong discipline. The clash of battles and the death of kings are rarely heard, but the repercussions sound in every word, and there are passages "so washed with tears that hardly ye shall read it." County families had more and more to say as they found the time and the education to record their fears and aspirations. Mr. John Paston was at pains to relate in 1450 how Lord Moleyns with a thousand men had ejected Mrs. Paston from her manor house of Gresham and then had secured a letter from Henry VI instructing the sheriff of Norfolk to "make such a jury as to acquit the Lord Moleyns." When the Lancastrian monarch was openly sanctioning the ugliest aspects of bastard feudalism, he could no longer expect all his subjects to regard him as king of England. In the eyes of John Paston he had become a party chief, the titular head of one of two competing dynasties.

The Failure of Parliament

The story of political collapse in the fifteenth century is incomplete without reference to parliament. The body that met in 1399 to acknowledge Henry IV as king of England, and to which the first Lancastrian monarch promised "not to be guided by his own will nor his own desire or individual opinion but by common advice, counsel and assent," had long since outgrown its early medieval origins. By 1400 the organization of parliament had evolved into something resembling its present-day structure. What yet remained to develop was the modern legislative mind and the privileges, traditions, and responsibilities of a national body representing all interests and estates within the realm. That process was not completed until the end of the seventeenth century.

The fifteenth century saw the evolution of a body of lords and a group of commoners who were becoming increasingly aware of their own separate and corporate existence. By 1450 the Lords had successfully transformed what had originally been a group of the king's advisers, appointed by the

---

2 The Stonor and Paston letters are available in a number of editions. The standard ones are *Paston Letters*, ed. by J. Gairdner, 6 vols. (1904), and *Stonor Letters*, ed. by C. L. Kingsford, Camden Soc., 2 vols. (1919).

monarch and composed of those individuals whom the king wished to call to his court, into a closed instrument of oligarchical and aristocratic rule. Royal judges and non-noble elements had been removed by aristocratic pressure, and the barons had been successful in claiming a seat in the House of Lords based solely on inheritance and noble title and not upon royal favor. Magna Carta and later royal charters had formulated the baronial right to advise the sovereign; by 1400 that right of advice had become tantamount to control of the royal government, and the king was allowed to rule only upon the sufferance of his nobles.

The temporal lords were fairly constant in their attendance in parliament; possibly half their number sat during any given session. In Henry IV's first parliament, ninety-seven peers were summoned and sixty-three sat. Thereafter the number of those who could claim noble dignity either by royal writ or by inheritance fell to around fifty and once dropped as low as twenty-three. As for the spiritual lords, the two archbishops and nineteen bishops of the realm were fairly regular, but their brothers, the abbots of the monasteries, were erratic in the extreme; of the twenty-seven who had an historic right to sit, only a handful ever attended. Until the Reformation in the third decade of the sixteenth century, the spiritual lords outnumbered the temporal but power resided with the lay barons who were the natural leaders of the realm, the possessors of economic and social strength outside of parliament, and the advisers and controllers of royal government. At one time five Neville brothers sat in the House of Lords—four barons and one bishop—and it was family association such as these, more than rank or numbers, that guaranteed political authority.

The Commons was far behind the Lords in corporate self-identity. The term itself simply meant that which was general or public, and only slowly did it acquire institutional significance. Over three hundred individuals sat in the House of Commons in 1422: two knights from each of the thirty-seven shires, one hundred and eighty-eight representatives from the chartered towns or boroughs, and possibly thirty to forty others appointed by the crown, such as the king's justices and councillors. By 1450 competition for a seat in Commons was sufficient to produce rowdy campaigning and disputed elections. The lower house had become so much an upper-class preserve for landlords, merchants, and lawyers that in 1430 legislation was passed to prevent men "of small substance and no worth" from voting, and the right to vote in the shires was restricted to men of property who held sixty acres of free land producing an annual income of forty shillings. At the same time borough elections tended to become limited to a small oligarchy of municipal officers and substantial citizens. If the House of Lords was becoming the closed corporation of the magnates, the House of Commons was developing into a preserve of men of lesser, but still great, wealth. There was nothing common about the incomes or social positions of Commons.

Originally the role of Commons had been that of the humble petitioner: the old formula for law enactment in the fourteenth century stated that statutes were made "with the assent of the earls, prelates and barons at the request of the knights of the shires and commons in Parliament." By the middle of the fifteenth century a significant change in phraseology had evolved; one which embodied a revolution in legislative function. Now the formula read: "Be it enacted by the King's Majesty with the advice and consent of the Lords spiritual and temporal and the Commons in the present parliament assembled and by the authority of the same." Commons had achieved partnership with the Lords, and was no longer simply a petitioner but now a co-creator of law.

Equally important was the new dignity embodied in the phrase "by the authority of the same." The impecuniousness of the Lancastrian crown and its financial dependence upon parliamentary sources of income added weight to Commons' voice. Moreover, the new dynasty's doubtful legitimacy and its abdication of political leadership under Henry VI transformed parliament from a high court of justice into a legislative organ of government capable not only of translating the king's will into law but of enacting its own opinions as well. The authority of that indivisible trinity—King, Lords, and Commons—was "so high and so mighty in its nature that it could make law and unmake that which was law."

On the statute books and in the annals of constitutional history parliament looks impressive. Six times between 1341 and 1407 it successfully claimed the right to audit royal accounts. It chose the king's councillors in 1404 and selected the council of regency during Henry VI's minority. In 1367 it impeached a royal minister for dishonesty, and in the fifteenth century it demanded the privileges of freedom of speech and immunity from arrest, and the right to hold annual sessions. Such pretensions, however, were more illusory than real. Behind the glitter of parliamentary activity stood serious constitutional and psychological limitations which in the end assured that the Lancastrian parliaments would be as ephemeral as the Lancastrian dynasty. As early as 1399 it was being said of members that "some stammered and mumbled and did not know what they meant to say. Some were afraid to take any step without their master's orders. Some were so pompous and dull witted that they were hopelessly involved before they reached the end of their speeches, and no one could make out what they wanted to say.... Some went with the majority whichever way they went, while some would not commit themselves; and some were so afraid of great men that they forsook righteousness." Embedded in these words are the reasons for parliament's failure to slough off its feudal origins and develop into a modern representative institution. Constitutionally, parliament was as yet incapable of exercising powers that would insure legislative independence, because psychologically it was unable to picture itself in the alien role of a sovereign authority rivaling the king. The basic paradox of the medieval constitution remained: only a strong monarch could enforce parliamentary law and win respect for it throughout the land.

Parliament was the creature of the king, and it continued to be a matter of debate, albeit somewhat theoretical and pedantic, whether parliament could legally exist without the physical presence of the imbecilic Henry VI. The king still issued the writs that summoned parliament into being. He prorogued and dismissed it, he controlled its agenda and he maintained his right of veto and amendment. In fact it was not absolutely clear whether royal ordinance might not be equal to parliamentary statute, and no one took seriously the suggestion that parliament should meet annually irrespective of need or emergency.

A more serious failing was that parliament never developed any idea of itself as the watchdog of government or as being responsible for good government; the former duty belonged to the barons on the council, the latter to the crown. At best parliament's image of its proper role was simply that of a rectifier of bad administration. So long as there was no financial emergency, corruption of law, or royal mismanagement, it did not expect or desire to be summoned. Lords and Commons may have had most of the forms and structures of their modern counterparts, but they still thought of themselves as feudal institutions, meeting occasionally to exercise their extraordinary powers of taxation and legislation. The king was limited by historic law, not by parliamentary statute; the crown was still expected to live on its ordinary and nonparliamentary sources of income; and if affairs of state were running according to form and custom, parliament was not expected to interfere. The political and economic crisis of the fifteenth century produced the extraordinary and largely misunderstood situation in which parliament had to be in constant emergency session. Royal bankruptcy and ineptitude insured parliamentary existence, but Lords and Commons regarded both as being undesirable, and they approved of strong, solvent, and competent monarchs who had no need to summon them. As late as 1560 Sir Thomas Smith was still voicing this traditional if unrealistic view when he wrote: "What can a Commonwealth desire more than peace, liberty, quietness, little taking of their money, few parliaments?" The great nineteenth-century constitutional historians to the contrary, the Lancastrian parliaments had little sense of their manifest destiny and less appreciation of the forces that were making their existence necessary and assuring their future history.

Though parliament was legislatively active, its failure was most obvious in the realm of law enforcement. As one contemporary put it: "Many acts of parliament/Few kept with true intent." The power to legislate is worthless without the means to compel obedience, and parliament was dependent upon a strong national monarch to enforce its will, and to assure its prestige and position as a body representing the voice of the entire land. With monarchy moribund and the machinery of justice and law enforcement in the hands of the great magnates, parliament was dominated by ruthless noblemen who possessed the economic and military means to implement or to ignore statutory law as they saw fit. Law regardless of whether it was royal or parliamentary, fell victim to the greed and brutality which recognized no authority other than the drawn sword. The evils of livery (the hiring of private armies) and maintenance (the corruption and intimidation of juries and law courts) were legislated against with vigor, but they continued to flourish despite endless laws to the contrary. In 1404 the earls of Northumberland and Westmorland waged private war; the loser was ultimately brought to trial, accused not of high treason but merely of trespassing! Again in 1411 parliament thundered against lawlessness and rioting but such pious, if statutory, platitudes became ludicrous when in the following year Sir Robert Tirwhit, Justice of the Courts of Common Pleas, ambushed Lord Roos with five hundred armed men, and pleaded ignorance of the law as his defense.

Even the traditional signs of parliamentary strength and independence were little more than further evidence of baronial predominance and royal pusillanimity. The case of Mr. Thomas Yonge is often cited as a milestone in the development of parliamentary freedom of speech and immunity from arrest. In 1451 in the House of Commons Yonge proposed that the duke of York be named as heir apparent to the throne. The Lancastrian barons surrounding the king were anything but pleased by the idea and promptly clapped Mr. Yonge into the Tower of London for his presumptuous suggestion. After a twelve-month sojourn in jail, he was released and four years later Mr. Yonge successfully brought suit against the government for damages. On the surface his success represented a victory for the principle that members of parliament "ought to have their freedom to speak without any manner of challenge, charge, or punition." In reality, his freedom was made possible by an uneasy reconciliation between the two parties in April of 1451, and the damages he was able to collect were the result of the duke of York's appointment as protector of the realm in 1455. Mr. Thomas Yonge won his liberty and his parliamentary privilege more because he was the duke of York's man than because he was a member of Commons.

Good government as well as healthy parliaments were based upon a proper and harmonious balance between crown, parliament, and barons. In the fifteenth century the elements of this trinity consisted of an inept king, an effectual legislative body, and an irresponsible baronage. Under the circumstances, it was only a matter of time and personality before the kingdom was rent in twain and any semblance of good governance lapsed into civil war.

The Wars of the Roses

The Wars of the Roses, symbolically represented by the white rose of York and the red of Lancaster, were the result of an amalgamation of baronial blood feuds, dynastic disputes, and local aristocratic land rivalry. These three spilled over into civil war when it became more profitable to replace a Lancastrian king, who had become the instrument of factional favoritism, than to try to breathe self-interested direction into his pious but leaderless administration. The crisis commenced in the crowded year of 1453. In July England experienced her final military humiliation with the loss of Gascony; in August the king finally moved from simple-mindedness into eighteen months of insanity; and in October his queen bore him a son.

Richard, Duke of York, was named temporary protector of the realm, but Yorkist control lasted only as long as the king's madness. When Henry VI regained his senses, his queen and her Lancastrian associates recovered their influence over royal administration. Confronted with a Lancastrian heir to the throne and with the queen and the Beaufort family firmly in control of the king's person, York turned to force of arms to rid the realm of "evil councillors" and to restore his henchmen to a place in the political sunshine about the king. This was the situation when the duke of York and his first cousin, the earl of Warwick, presented Henry VI with an ultimatum which struck at the heart of the feudal monarchy and made a mockery of the divine right of kings. "Please it, your Majesty Royal, to deliver up such as we will accuse [of our enemies]. This done you to be worshiped as a most rightful King." The Battle of St. Albans which followed in July of 1455 sowed the dragon seeds of hatred and family revenge: one baron fell with his "brains dashed out, another with a broken arm, a third with a cut throat, and a fourth with a pierced chest, and the whole street was full of dead corpses." The battle was a dress rehearsal and preview of coming attractions. It won the Yorkists preeminence within the royal council and rid them of their rival, the Beaufort duke of Somerset, killed upon the field of war. It did not change, however, the fact that Queen Margaret of Anjou was scheming to turn the tables; that a young Lancastrian prince of Wales lived to carry on his royal line; and, most important of all, that blood once shed could not be stanched and that Somerset's son was waiting to revenge his father.

Four years passed in which all semblance of government collapsed and both parties secretly prepared for further war. Then in 1460 the inevitable happened: Richard, Duke of York, gave up trying to rule through a puppet king and claimed the throne as his legal birthright (see genealogy, page 53). This was the signal for civil war in earnest. At Wakefield in December of 1460 a small Yorkist force, which was out foraging during a Christmas truce in the hostilities, was ambushed and annihilated. The duke was killed, his battered head capped with a paper crown and mocked as a "king without a kingdom." His second son, Edmund, Earl of Rutland, was captured and died at the hands of young Lord Clifford, whose father had been killed at St. Albans. When Rutland begged for his life, Clifford coldly answered: "By God's blood, thy father slew mine, and so will I do thee and all thy kin!" On both sides vengeance was the order of the day, and three months later York's eldest son, Edward, Earl of March and now the Yorkist claimant to the throne, had his revenge. Together with his cousin, Richard Neville, Earl of Warwick, Edward inflicted a crushing and

Yorkist and Neville Lines

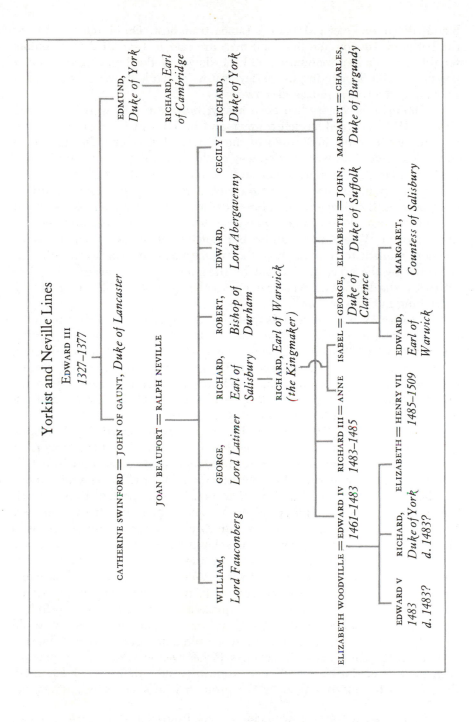

bloody defeat on Queen Margaret's Lancastrian host. On March 29, 1461, at the battle of Towton, ten thousand men are said to have died in a conflict fought in a blinding snowstorm, and the flower of the Lancastrian nobility perished while floundering in the icy waters of Cork stream, a tiny brook swollen by the winter rains and snow.

The price of victory had been heavy, but the results were ephemeral. Edward IV had earned himself a crown and his Lancastrian rival, Henry VI, now resided in quiet abdication in the Tower of London. The new king soon discovered, however, that crowns could be readily won upon the field of battle but that keeping them and exercising royal authority involved endless hours in the counting house, not heroics in the jousting court or conquests on the dance floor. Moreover, Margaret of Anjou had escaped capture and had fled to France where she spent her time teaching her son, the prince of Wales, "nothing else but cutting off heads or making war." Of more immediate consideration, the young monarch soon learned that he ruled not by the grace of God but by the power of his cousin, the earl of Warwick, the kingmaker who seemed, in the eyes of one observer, "to be everything in this kingdom."

Edward IV was nineteen, handsome, dissolute, and ruthless, and in the end both king and kingmaker realized that "it is a matter of being either master or varlet." The crisis came to a head in 1464 when Warwick decided on a French alliance. Peace with England's ancient enemy would destroy the hopes of the Lancastrian exiles and secure conditions necessary to the growth of trade; but amity with France was unpopular, unhistoric, and unheroic, and it was not to the liking of King Edward.

The treaty with France was to be secured by the marriage of the king to a Gallic princess, but the earl's designs were blasted and the kingmaker publicly humiliated when Edward calmly announced to his council that he was already secretly married to Lady Elizabeth Woodville. The new queen and her family were social and political nonentities who had little to their credit except incomparable good looks and equal ambitions. Mistress Woodville had been married to Sir John Grey, a staunch Lancastrian who had died of his wounds following the second battle of St. Albans, and she had had by him two sons. Edward IV married not only a complete family but a veritable dynasty, replete with five Woodville brothers and as many sisters. The new queen's sisters were quickly matched with the most elevated blood of the realm while the thrice-married duchess of Norfolk, a rather dressy dowager of almost eighty, was wed to the twenty-year-old John Woodville, the queen's brother. As an ultimate insult to ancient lineage and baronial exclusiveness, Elizabeth's father was elevated to the peerage with the title of Earl Rivers. Warwick and the old nobility were disgusted, their feudal feelings outraged by the promotion of such "new and strange men."

The kingmaker's foreign policy received its final blow when Edward concluded an alliance with France's traditional enemy, the duchy of Burgundy, and married off his sister Margaret to Duke Charles. Insulted and slighted, Warwick turned to Louis of France to help him destroy his ungrateful monarch. A diplomatic revolution followed in which Louis XI, that master of Renaissance ruthlessness and intrigue, engineered and financed the ultimate moral bankruptcy of the English nobility. In 1469 Yorkist Warwick and Lancastrian Margaret of Anjou patched up their historic feud. It was a bitter pill for the queen to accept as an ally the man most responsible for the defeat of her dynasty. When Louis XI suggested that her son, Edward, marry Warwick's younger daughter, she cried out "What! Will he indeed give his daughter to my son, whom he has so often branded as the offspring of adultery?" Politics, however, triumphed over moral outrage, and the two children, one aged thirteen, the other ten, were duly pronounced man and wife. The queen and the earl were joined in political misalliance by George, Duke of Clarence, the mercurial and covetous brother of Edward IV. He married Warwick's elder daughter, and in the fall of 1470 the kingmaker, the disgruntled duke, and the militant queen declared the doddering Henry VI to be rightful king of England. In September they invaded the realm; Edward fled to Burgundy; and Warwick triumphantly entered London, reinstating Henry on his rickety throne. The restored monarch, however, was too confused to realize what had happened and sat "amazed and utterly dulled with troubles and adversities."

Warwick had achieved a staggering victory, but it proved more fleeting than any he had ever won before. The Lancastrian lords refused their support even though the earl was now backing a Lancastrian monarch; the populace demanded peace and the restoration of royal authority, not a continuation of baronial misrule; and Edward, who had escaped to Burgundy, was planning his revenge. By March of 1471 he was back in England at the head of a tiny army. Instantly Warwick's grand design collapsed and old enemies as well as erstwhile friends rallied to Edward's banner. At the Battle of Barnet, fought in the midst of a dense fog, friend could not be distinguished from foe and the dying "looked up for heaven and only saw the mist." Richard, Earl of Warwick, aged forty-three, fell trying to escape, and Edward IV, having triumphed over the real strength of the Lancastrian forces, defeated the queen a month later at the Battle of Tewkesbury. Margaret was captured and her son killed in, or possibly murdered after, the battle. With the Lancastrian prince of Wales dead, Edward IV now had no reason to keep the father alive, and on May the 23rd, 1471, in the fiftieth year of his life and the forty-ninth of his reign, Henry VI died in the Tower of London "of pure displeasure and melancholy."

Edward IV (1471–1483)

It is customary to end the Wars of the Roses with Edward's victory at Tewkesbury in 1471, for henceforth he was the undisputed master of the realm. Under Edward IV, England experienced the blessings of that essential element of good government—a strong sovereign. Dissolute, lazy, and greedy, Edward of York nevertheless had three qualities that served well the revival of monarchy: he was charming, ruthless, and knew the worth of his servants, and under the first Yorkist monarch England prospered as she had not done for over fifty years.

Inheritance and confiscation went a long way to rectify the deficit in the king's finances. As his father's heir, Edward could call upon the immense resources of the Yorkist lands, and the bloodbaths of Towton, Barnet, and Tewkesbury had at least one beneficial result: the king was able to repossess the confiscated estates of the fallen Lancastrian nobility, which helped to free him from parliamentary grants and interference. Edward was in fact the only English sovereign since Henry II to die solvent. In government the king turned away from the aristocracy and sought the support of men of middling social position—knights, lawyers, clerks, and merchants. Instead of favoring the ancient organs of state—the Exchequer, the Treasury, and the Chancery—he relied on the more intimate instruments of government—the royal council and household—where his influence was more readily felt. In the northern shires royal authority was enforced for the first time in decades when his brother, Richard, Duke of Gloucester, was given the title of the king's lieutenant in the North.

New life was infused into the law in 1462 when Edward sat in person upon the Court of King's Bench and later accompanied his judges in their perambulations about the kingdom. In 1478 his younger brother, George, Duke of Clarence, tried his hand at treason for a second time and was destroyed—a lesson to all that the king's law recognized no exceptions. But, when on April 9, 1483, Edward died at the age of forty of overweight and overindulgence, twelve years of strong Yorkist rule proved insufficient to secure Edward's line from the machinations of yet another wicked uncle.

Edward V (April 9–July 6, 1483)

Edward's successor was his twelve-year-old son, Edward V, the product of that hated Woodville marriage. A hundred years of anarchy and violence had left their scars. Richard II came to the throne at ten but lived to manhood; Henry VI exposed the realm to seventeen years of minority government and another thirty-two of royal incompetence, but it was only after five decades of pious ineptitude that he was finally put away. Edward V, however, lasted barely three months. It is often said that popular fear of further misrule and civil war under yet another minority made possible Richard of Gloucester's seizure of his nephew's throne. In actual fact the brevity of Edward's reign is merely further evidence of the disrespect into which monarchy had fallen and the extent to which the ancient bonds of loyalty had corroded during a century of palace revolutions and royal assassinations.

The duke of Gloucester was Edward IV's younger brother, who has come down in history as Richard Crookback—malevolent and crooked both in body and soul. The Shakespearean portrait, however, is a stranger to the

historical man. Gloucester had been the faithful servant of his brother and
the successful bastion of royal authority in the turbulent northern shires,
where he watched Nevilles and Percys as closely as the Scots. Richard was
the natural choice as protector for his brother's son. The queen's family, the
Woodvilles, were new and suspect upstarts, and Gloucester had little trouble
wresting power from them and seizing control of the government in the
name of his royal nephew. In the fifteenth century death was the price of
political failure. The Woodvilles and their allies would have destroyed
Gloucester had they been able to manage it. When they failed, they were
destroyed; in June the young king's Woodville uncle, Earl Rivers, and his
half-brother Richard Grey were executed. Then Richard of Gloucester fulfilled the legendary role of the wicked uncle: on June 22 Edward V was
declared a bastard; on July 6 the duke mounted the throne as rightful heir
to his brother; and a year later the young prince, along with his ten-year-
old brother, conveniently vanished, some say murdered in the Tower of
London.

Richard III (1483–1485)

Murder has magic and can transmute the most sordid politics and
vicious designs into grand tragedy. Recently the disappearance of the little
princes has been the subject of endless detective research, journalistic speculation, and partisan efforts to whitewash Richard III.[3] The primary suspect
for murderer, however, remains Richard III, who continues to be the
legendary villain and who certainly had motive, means, and opportunity.
No matter where the ultimate responsibility lies, the timely disappearance
of the two princes proved once again the inadequacies of a political system
in which murder was the only answer to an ineffectual monarch, be he an
irresponsible Richard II, a saintly Henry VI, or a child Edward V.

Murder failed to make Richard's throne secure, and the forces of
violence and hatred that had dethroned Henry VI continued unabated under
the Yorkist dynasty, especially now that Richard III had deposed his royal
nephew. No matter how hard the new king tried to restore the luster of
the crown by carrying out his brother's policies with vigor, the fact remained
that an important percentage of his kingdom regarded him as a usurper.
Where forced loans extracted from wealthy subjects had been termed "be-
nevolences" under Edward IV, under his brother they were branded
"malevolences." Even fate seemed to be against Richard, for in April of 1484
his only son died. Throughout 1485 exiled Lancastrians were strengthened

---

[3] The mystery of the little princes has become the subject of modern detective fiction:
J. Tey, *The Daughter of Time* (1953). See also P. M. Kendall, *Richard III* (1955);
A. R. Myers, "The Character of Richard III," *History Today*, IV (1954); Shakespeare's
Richard III; and J. Gairdner, *The Life and Reign of Richard III* (1898).

RICHARD III
"The legendary villain." *National Portrait Gallery.*

by banished Woodvilles and disgruntled magnates who had failed to gain from Richard all that they felt should be their due. By the spring of 1485 intrigue and avarice had done their work, and the throne of England was once again staked upon the throw of the military dice.

The Battle of Bosworth Field

With the death of Henry VI and his son in 1471 the Lancastrian line had run dry, but the Lancastrian faction remained, and it became necessary to discover a true and rightful claimant to the throne. The desperate plight of the Lancastrian position was revealed by the fact that the mantle of party authority fell to Henry Tudor, Earl of Richmond, whose birthrights and claim to the crown were twice damned. Henry's Plantagenet blood came from the wrong side of the blanket; his mother had been a Beaufort, the great-granddaughter of John of Gaunt by his mistress, Catherine Swinford, whose children had been legitimized but barred from the succession by act of parliament. His father may also have been born out of wedlock; Edmund, Earl of Richmond, was the product of the union of Catherine, widowed queen of Henry V, and a clerk of her wardrobe named Owen Tudor, and the precise legal status of their relationship has never been established. Helped by Louis XI of France, Henry Tudor made one of the most reckless gambles of history: on August 2, 1485, he landed at Milford Haven in Wales with nothing to his credit but a handful of men and a doubtful claim to the throne. Of Welsh stock, he drew support from his native Wales, but even so the army that met Richard III on the 22nd upon the high ground two miles from the market town of Bosworth was smaller and far more desperate than its opponents. Tudor historians to the contrary, neither God nor righteousness prevailed. Richard III was left dead upon the field of battle and his white rose trampled underfoot by the forces of Lancaster because key magnates deserted their king at the crucial moment, and because Lord Thomas Stanley and his brother William maintained the doubtful tradition of kingmaking by standing aside so as to equalize the military balance between the armies.

Bosworth Field augured nothing but continued civil strife. If the past was any mirror for the future, the future looked bleak indeed for Henry Tudor, who now styled himself King Henry VII. England had experienced eight monarchs in eighty-six years and simple mathematics indicated that the new sovereign might reign for a decade at most. In fact, the first ten years seemed proof of the prophecy that Bosworth was simply another swing of the pendulum in the vicious game of baronial feuding, for Henry fought yet another pitched battle to save his crown and had to execute two pretenders to his throne. That a second decade was allowed him and that it was a period of relative security and prosperity was something that few people in 1485 would have cared to predict.

Thirteen battles were fought during the Wars of the Roses, between

The Tudor Claim to the Throne

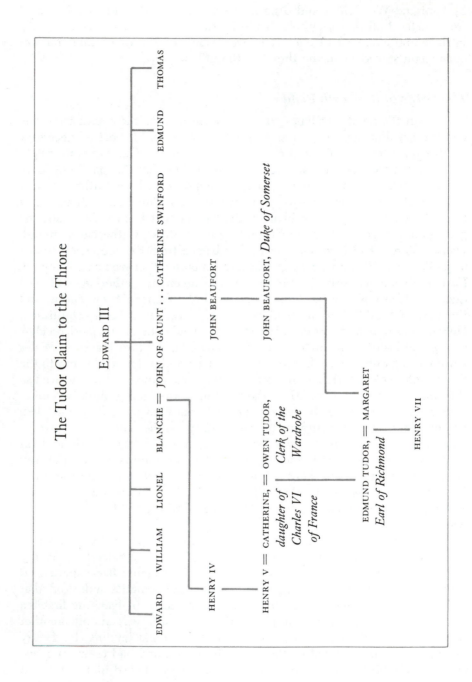

SOLDIERS PILLAGING DURING THE WARS OF THE ROSES
"Men went wet-shod in wine, and then robbed the town and bore away bedding, clothes, and other stuff and defouled many women."
British Museum.

1455 and 1471, and if the dates are pushed forward to include the year 1487 at least two more engagements must be added to the list. It is usual to dismiss the wars as the unsavory but exclusive pastime of the great nobles who, like college football teams, fought ferocious and not very effectual battles with their paid, liveried retainers. Philippe Comines, chronicler and statesman of fifteenth-century France, noted with considerable envy that in England "no buildings [were] destroyed or demolished by war and there the mischief of it falls on those who make the war." But the horror that the memory of those years could engender in the minds of later generations makes it difficult to believe that the Wars of the Roses were simply a matter of a Lancastrian unicorn and a Yorkist lion noisily prancing up and down the land. At Ludlow in 1459 a Lancastrian army sacked the town so that "men went wet-shod in wine, and then robbed the town and bore away bedding, clothes, and other stuff and defouled many women." The Wars of the Roses were associated in the popular mind with violence, anarchy, and corruption. Whether the civil wars caused lawlessness and peculation in government or whether bastard feudalism produced both is unimportant. To sixteenth-century eyes, aristocratic irresponsibility and civil discord were intimately linked, and that association in the public mind was the greatest single political asset bestowed upon the new Tudor dynasty.

In 1485 the standards of the age were still medieval. Henry V, *sans peur et sans reproche,* remained the heroic model and pattern for all that society believed to be best in life and death. Henry VI was the last king-saint in English history, and the fact that he was incompetent was less important to contemporaries than that he was pious. The economic and intellectual background, however, was changing. The successful king would soon replace the devout sovereign in popular esteem; the solvent monarch would be more honored than the heroic. Henry VII was no messianic statesman, no gifted governmental architect guided by the image of a future monarchical absolutism. He was no better and no worse than the fourth Henry; both were hardworking, careful, and unobtrusive sovereigns who sired sons more glamorous but not necessarily more successful than themselves. But while the first Lancastrian struggled and ultimately failed to rebuild royal authority or to control the forces of dying medievalism, the first Tudor succeeded because time and tide were on his side.

HENRY VIII AND FRANCIS I AT THE FIELD OF THE CLOTH OF GOLD, 1520.
The Lord Chamberlain's Office.

II

RECONSTRUCTING
SOCIETY, TUDOR STYLE

1485 to 1547

Economic Resurgence
and Social Change

4 The fifteenth-century historian is confronted with a paradox: if the generation of the Lancastrian kings was archaic and medieval, it was also forward-looking and modern. The pious peasant, the indolent cleric, and the disorderly baron were part of a receding feudal profile; the clothier and the financier, the explorer and the religious reformer, the humanist and the landed country gentleman belonged to the image of the future. The era, however, was not the product of a polarity between the old and the new, not a matter of "either or," but instead a balance between "more or less." Hope and depression, chivalric nonsense and Machiavellian calculation, peace and war, laity and clergy, baronial relic and capitalistic gentry existed side by side. Often one aspect of the dichotomy was happily unaware of its opposite; sometimes the tension between the two was unbearable; but always the fifteenth-century man was more or less a composite of all elements.[1]

Prosperity

As barons tore themselves to pieces and priests and prelates turned deaf ears to the voice of reform, new impulses and new ideas were stirring. The day was dawning when a Venetian ambassador would admire the

---

[1] In addition to the works cited in Chapter 2 see M. Gilmore, *The World of Humanism* (1952); F. Caspari, *Humanism and the Social Order in Tudor England* (1954); G. N. Clark, *The Wealth of England* (1946); L. A. Clarkson, *The Pre-Industrial Economy of England, 1500–1750* (1971); J. Clapham, *A Concise Economic History of Britain* (1949); J. Thirsk, *Tudor Enclosures* (Historical Assoc. Pamphlet No. G. 41); and S. Thrupp, *The Merchant Class of Medieval London 1300–1500* (1948).

wealth and power of the first Tudor monarch, and another foreigner would remark that in England yeomen ate as well as gentlemen, and nobles rivaled European kings in the lavishness of their tables. The duke of Buckingham fed two hundred guests in his great hall on Christmas day; Sir Edward Montague, a mere social upstart, dispensed food to 1,200 who begged at his door; and the duchess of Norfolk customarily sat down to a table set for twenty and served as her first course two boiled capons, a breast of mutton, a piece of beef, seven chevons, a swan, a pig, a quantity of veal, two roast capons, and a custard. The bounty of the rich man's kitchen was an economic necessity, for everybody from the household staff to the beggars in the street ate the crumbs from his table. The pastures were rich and the fields were "fat, fruitful and full of profitable things," and though the methods of distribution were unjust by modern standards, there was enough food for all.

The land lay green and pleasant, and as the country slowly recovered from agricultural depression and bubonic plague, the horse, costly to feed but efficient to work, replaced the cumbersome ox. Though sheep runs and wheat fields pushed deep into virgin timber, England remained in the year 1500 a realm rich in the most essential of all medieval resources—woodlands. The squirrel could no longer "jump from tree to tree from Blacon Point to Hillbree," but the ancient forests of Epping, Sherwood, and Arden still stood untouched, affording a plentiful supply of ribs, planks, and masts for a growing navy and an expanding merchant marine, the lumber to construct the jerry-built houses of an exploding city of London, and the charcoal for the furnaces of the ironsmiths. Shrinking timber stands might at some future date confront the kingdom with an acute shortage but, for the moment, they meant prosperous farmlands and successful commercial enterprises.

Another sign of prosperity was an expanding population. Before the Black Death in 1348–50 the population may have exceeded four million; after the plague it probably dropped as low as two and a half million. By 1400 the kingdom had started on the long path of demographic recovery: the population may have reached three million by 1500, over four million by 1600, and just short of six million by 1700. Population figures in an age blissfully free from statistical exactitude are understandably vague, but the results were everywhere evident. More mouths to feed, more backs to clothe, more vanity to satisfy, and more homes to construct meant busy artisans, eager merchants, and an insatiable commercial appetite. Wool chapmen skipping from shop to shop "as if they were at leapfrog," tradesmen as active as "dancing galliards," and scavengers and apprentices, weavers and dyers, all "as busy as county attorneys" pleading cases in the shire courts—this was the dominant picture throughout most of the sixteenth century, for England in 1500 stood upon the threshold of three generations of un-precedented economic prosperity.

Of all the new impulses within late medieval society, the strongest was the growing export of woolen cloth. Traditionally England was Europe's most important source of raw material—tin and grain, lead and leather, and above all, raw wool and unfinished cloth. The lord chancellor sat on a wool sack, the crown lived off of the tax on the export of wool, merchants grew fat from its sales, landlords rented sheep runs or raised their own flocks, and one thankful beneficiary of the "golden fleece" wrote:

> I thank God and ever shall,
> It is the sheep has paid for all.

By the middle of the fifteenth century the emphasis had shifted from the export of raw wool to the manufacture and export of broadcloth or unfinished woolen fabric. The change simply enhanced the profits and importance of the trade, for the demand for English woolens continued to expand as the European market recovered from the ravages of war and anarchy.

Slowly, painfully, but irresistibly economic prosperity wrought political, social, and moral revolution. The harbingers of change were the gentlemen sheep raisers, the urban cloth manufacturers, and the Merchant Adventurers who supplied the continent with English woolens. Demand stimulated supply, but large-scale production was only possible after fundamental organizational changes. The manufacture of wool cloth could not be fitted into the rigid and fragmented guild system of the medieval past. Sheep raising on the farm, carding and spinning in the cottage, weaving and dyeing in the town, and storing and exporting to foreign markets were steps that required careful synchronization of time and material. Eventually there evolved the coordinator or clothier who bought raw wool in large quantities, delivered it to the spinners, transported the yarn to the weavers and carried the finished product to the drapers and merchants to be sold. The fifteenth-century clothier soon became the prototype of the modern industrial entrepreneur, supplying raw material and transportation, paying wages on the basis of piecework or by the hour, utilizing the farmer's wife and child as a source of labor, and avoiding the older towns with their hampering guilds and trade restrictions. Occasionally such industrial organizers took the final step and brought the weavers together under a single roof, converting their own homes into nascent factories where the weavers became their hired servants. Sometimes they rented looms to craftsmen who lost their independent status as artisans and became industrial sharecroppers. Whatever the organizational method, the economic rewards were spectacular. Mr. Thomas Paycocke of Coggeshall could afford to found a magnificent chantry for the sake of his commercial soul and the souls of his parents, his wife, and his father-in-law; John Winchcomb, better known as Jack Newberry, refused a knighthood, preferring to "rest in russet coat, a poor clothier to his dying day," but he could afford to entertain Edward IV at his urban home. It was appropriate that merchant John Fortey on his funeral brass should have represented himself as standing with one foot upon a sheep, the other upon a sack of wool.

Paycocke and Winchcomb were clothiers and incipient industrialists;

their mercantile counterparts were the merchant princes of the city of London. "Some men of noble stock were made, some glory in the murder blade; Some praise a Science or an Art, but I like honourable Trade!" Commerce if organized on a large enough scale was not only honorable, it was also immensely profitable. The cloth merchants of London aimed at the formation of a commercial cartel. They organized themselves into a corporate fellowship known as the Merchant Adventurers and successfully maintained that membership in their society was necessary for anyone trading with Antwerp. Provincial merchants were driven into joining or into bankruptcy, and in the end the Adventurers made good their legal claim to a monopoly of the cloth trade between England and the Netherlands. They received official recognition in 1486, and with each passing year their influence was more keenly felt. Largely on their recommendation, Henry VII negotiated in 1496 the trade treaty known as the Intercursus Magnus, easing the commercial restrictions which had limited the lucrative London-Antwerp mercantile axis. Finally in 1497 the Merchant Adventurers were granted the coveted right to impose a fee upon all newcomers who hoped to poach upon their trade monopoly with Antwerp.

Inflation

As clothier and merchant enlarged their remunerative web of trade, all England was caught up in the larger pattern of European and world commerce. Inflation, that unseen economic monster with an insatiable appetite, devoured fixed incomes and savings, wiped out ancient debts, and injected new life into the economic sinews of society. Between 1500 and 1540 prices doubled, and doubled again during the next twenty years. Wheat in 1450 still cost what it had in 1300; a hundred years later the price had risen threefold. By 1600 the general price level had increased by a factor of five. The late medieval man was confronted with a crisis as baffling, as mystifying, and as misunderstood as the Black Death. The feudal world had assumed that war, plague, and famine stemmed from God as retribution for the sins of man, and so it had blamed economic distortion and rising prices upon human avarice and sin. The sixteenth century was still sufficiently close to its medieval and Christian heritage to seek an explanation for economic evil in man, not in social systems. The corruption of Eve and the fall of Adam, not the malfunction of God's perfect society, were the sources of economic evil and the high cost of food. Social critics such as Sir Thomas More spoke against the greedy hoarders of grain who held out for famine prices, and against the grasping landlords who pushed up rents or converted wheat fields into sheep runs, thus producing food shortage and high prices. The lust for lucre, the vanity of courtiers, and the greed of parvenus were the culprits of economic life. Fashion demanded that "whole estates" be worn upon a courtier's back, and when Sir Nicholas Vaux was willing to pay £1,000 for a suit, it is understandable that social critics jumped to the conclusion that vanity was forcing up the cost of living.

Vanity confused the issue, for scarcity—especially a growing shortage of food and land in the face of an expanding population—was a cardinal factor in producing inflation. It was not, however, until 1574 that Europe awoke to the fact that high prices had nothing directly to do with human greed. Jean Bodin, the French political philosopher, was one of the first to realize that a new and impersonal factor was at work: gold and silver were suddenly abundant. In the fifteenth century Europe's scarcity of precious metals began to abate. New silver mines were found in Central Europe; new sources of gold were discovered in West Africa. The supply became a flood when in 1545 the Spanish stumbled upon the silver mines of Bolivia. By 1572 the world's output of silver was six times what it had been at the turn of the century. As the wealth of the Americas poured into the European market, it drove down the value of money, reduced the purchasing power of traditional coinage, and forced up the relative cost of services and supplies.

Inflation and the wool trade together created an economic whirlwind that swept away ancient landmarks and time-honored habits. Despite the false simplicity of economic determinism, the fact remains that a growing population, inflated prices, and an insatiable demand for wool reversed the social and economic cycle prevailing before 1460. They transformed the early fifteenth-century pattern of land plenty, labor shortage, and high wages into land hunger, labor surplus, and rising rents. Behind changing economic design loomed the millions of sheep which outnumbered humans by three to one. To the social critics of the age sheep were devouring the realm, eating up fields that had once grown wheat, pushing back the forests, depopulating the countryside, and creating hunger and unemployment. With wool in incessant demand, the lord of the manor discovered that lands for which he had once been unable to find renters or laborers could now be converted into sheep runs. A single shepherd and his dog were all the labor required; the sheep did the rest. Once the landlord was liberated from a scarcity of labor and assured of a market for wool, the value of his land soared. In the midst of land hunger, landlords cast covetous eyes upon the common lands of the manor and sought ways of modifying the ancient land tenure. Two paths were open to them: breaking the medieval system of community rights to the fruits of the manor and enclosing the commons, or evicting peasants who could not prove their historic title to the land.

Enclosures

The ease with which the lord could enclose land or raise rents so as to keep them abreast of the inflation depended upon local conditions and the nature of the prevailing tenure. Demesne land, which to all intent and purpose had become a form of private property owned by the lord of the manor, and freehold land controlled by the freeholders of the manor presented no problems. Short-term leases could be renegotiated as the inflation took its course, and demesne and freehold fields which were often scattered indiscriminately throughout the manor could be brought together into a consolidated unit by buying up adjacent strips and by constructing hedges and digging ditches. Once enclosed, such property could be turned into sheep runs or utilized for more efficient farming methods without regard to the communal customs of the manor. This kind of enclosure caused relatively little social disturbance, and though the lord of the manor had the most to gain, freeholders, wealthy peasants, and even enterprising copyholders were anxious to convert their arable strips into consolidated and workable farming units.

What produced a howl of social indignation was the lord's efforts to enclose all or a portion of the common land and to evict peasants who held their property either by copyhold tenure or by the custom of the manor. The division and enclosure of the common pasture spelled economic ruin for many villages and for peasants who held little arable land but who survived by pasturing their few cattle, sheep, and swine upon the communal lands. Even more serious than the destruction of the commons was the inability of many peasants to withstand the lord's legal and economic encroachment upon their rights and tenures within the manor. By one of the most ironic twists of history, the peasant's hatred "copy," preserved in the manor court and recording the conditions of servitude by which the land was held, suddenly became in the sixteenth century his best defense against eviction or increased rents. The "copy" stated the fixed fees and financial obligations owing to the lord, but in an era of inflation such obligations tended to become more and more nominal, and consequently the lord was anxious to claim copyhold property as demesne land so that he could raise rents at will. If the peasant could produce no proof or "copy" of his tenure, he found it difficult to defend himself at law.[2] Where a copy existed and rents were fixed, the lord had other means of coercion. He could arbitrarily raise the heriot or death tax. If the copyholder's descendants were unable to pay the tax, the land reverted back to the lord of the manor. Where the peasant held his tenure simply upon the unwritten custom of the manor, he was even more at the mercy of the lord, and though in theory both historic, unwritten tenure and copyhold tenure were protected in the king's courts, neither of them successfully withstood the pressure of landlords who were determined to enclose land and raise rents. Whatever the ethics involved, inflation, eviction, enclosure, and a booming trade in wool introduced a revolution in rents. Land in Yorkshire that had leased for four pence an acre in the fifteenth century rose to nine pence by 1548, and finally two shillings, four pence by 1621 and, for the record, was up to twenty-two shillings, seven pence by 1930.

The extent of enclosure and peasant evictions is difficult to estimate.

---

[2] One of the reasons why many tenants in the sixteenth century could claim no "copy" was because their ancestors had broken into the manor court and destroyed such records during the Peasants' Revolt of 1381.

Accurate statistics were scarce, popular indignation profuse. Possibly not more than 3 percent of the land was actually enclosed during the sixteenth century, but to contemporaries the legion of evicted and dispossessed peasants seemed dangerously large. The presence of able-bodied paupers in Tudor society caused great consternation. Charity was meant for the infirm, the malformed, and the helpless, not for the economically unemployable, and the existence of an army of lusty beggars in a century that lacked adequate poor relief or police control was deeply frightening to government magistrates and property owners. The records indicate that between 1455 and 1607 in thirty-four counties only 516,573 acres of land were enclosed, or 2.76 percent of the total, and that some 50,000 persons were evicted from their property. The most disturbing aspect of the land revolution was not acreage statistics, nor even the existence of a vagrant and unemployable labor supply, but the introduction of what men feared most—change. New names, new methods, new blood broke the static timelessness of village life. Suddenly the oldest peasant families found themselves dispossessed and landless. The ancient equality of the medieval manor, in which the economic status of the lord had not been far removed from the cottager and copyholder, was collapsing. Exactly how far the process could go was dramatized at the manor of Apsley Guise where in 1275 each peasant had held equal holdings of approximately fifteen acres. By 1542 four lucky and hardworking farmers held sixty acres or more; only three tenants continued to possess their original fifteen acres; and all the rest had been forced to give up substantial portions of their holdings. It seemed grossly unjust and against all proper proportion in the divine plan that the rich should be getting richer and the poor poorer. As one poet put it:

> The poor at enclosing do grutch
> Because of abuses that fall.
> Lest some man should have but too much
> And some again nothing at all.

The Age of the Gentry

The new relationship between land and labor, the steady rise of prices and the relative fall of wages, the growing tension between landlord and peasant, and the mounting wealth of city merchants and Essex clothiers produced more than extremes of riches and poverty, beggary and opulence; they changed the social and political face of England. The age of the gentry was beginning; the future belonged to the landed country gentleman and his blood cousins in oligarchy, the merchant, the lawyer, and the parish rector. Not until 1689 would the landed country gentleman come of age, but already in 1500 the indispensable conditions for both his moral and political ascendancy were taking shape. The fifteenth-century squire and knight of the shire were changing from desperate, irresponsible, and litigious proprie-

tors, ready to fish in the muddy waters of barional feuding, into the backbone of Tudor respectability. The secret of change was wealth. Enclosure
and eviction, rising prices in the wool market, and increased profits to be
had from land gave the country gentleman the means to finance his new
class consciousness, while his newfound prosperity created the need for a
political security and tranquility in which he could enjoy the fat of the earth.

Money and political influence, not blood and social origins, were the
motifs of the sixteenth century. The landed country gentleman and the
city merchant lived by the commercial rule that "conscience is a pretty
thing to carry to church" but he who "pursueth it in a fair market or shop
may die a beggar." Knavery could be forgotten: rich estates could earn
social respectability for even the basest family. The merchant adventurer,
the clothier, and the landlord had the means, the desire, and the opportunity
to manufacture the tokens and emblems of class consciousness. The sixteenth
century became, *par excellence,* an age of heraldry, and pedigrees were
carefully recorded in the College of Arms. For the historian, the visitations
of the Garter King of Arms, by which the authorities checked into the
economic and historic claims to gentility, are invaluable sources of social
history, but they read like genealogical fairy tales in which imagination and
artistry are more evident than truth. Money and influence could conjure
up and legalize the most pretentious heraldic claim. Russels and Guildfords,
Cecils and Cavendishes, Pagets and Cromwells sought to obtain by wealth
and marriage the symbol of class status—the right to bear heraldic arms.
The College of Arms was of late feudal origin but the Tudors reorganized
and systematized it, and the privilege of bearing arms was limited to those
"of good name and fame and good reknown" and to those who could show
a yearly rental of ten pounds. In actual fact, political influence was more
weighty than gentle origins in persuading the College to sanction what it
must have suspected to be the sheerest fabrications.

The economic and blood ally of the landed country gentleman was the
city merchant, united by a two-way traffic in trade and land, and in sons and
daughters. Land was the acme of respectability; trade and law, though
tolerated if practiced on a grand enough scale, stood as poor relations.
Merchants and lawyers were quick to buy estates not only because land was
profitable but also because it brought social recognition. Conversely, the
sons of landed families went into trade and married the daughters of rich
merchants who could sweeten the odor of their tawdry social origins with
a fat dowry. Landed squires, urban lawyers, and merchant princes were
upper middling people, but they were distinctly not, if they could help it,
of what is described today as the middle class. The standards and aspirations of the age were landed and aristocratic. Second sons of country
gentlemen might move to town and even turn to trade, but their spiritual
and social souls belonged upon their fathers' estates, and, as quickly as they
could manage it, either through sharp practices or sharp marriages, they
returned to their natural habitat. So also did the merchant. The draper, Mr.
Thomas Cony of Bassingthorpe, commenced his career with a commercial

income of £200. At his death sixty years later he was worth £450 from land and had cut his ties with the wool business. By means of changing the source of his income Mr. Cony expected to change his social status.

The day would come when a peer might marry an alderman's daughter (1597) but, for most of the sixteenth century, the nobility left the commercial matrimonial field to the country squires. This did not mean that the peerage was untouched by the commercial spirit or left trade entirely to middling gentlemen and upstart merchants. The successful man—be he a member of the noble elite or of the gentry—went in for raising rents, enclosing lands, and dabbling in trade. Howards and Herberts, Staffords and Latimers owned ships and iron mines and speculated in commerce. Peers may have declined to enter the counting house or the parlor of the commercial sort, but they were perfectly willing to take their 10 percent and to profit from the new impulses of the century.

The Education of the Gentry

The gentry in their newfound social consciousness and economic prosperity began to send their sons to college. Whether the quest for learning was a symptom of deliberate class exclusiveness or a sign of the new intellectual forces of the century is anybody's guess, but in education and in the "New Learning" the landed gentleman, the merchant, and the lawyer found a badge and an intellectual rationale for their class which was even more important than carefully designed pedigrees. Heraldic devices were part of lesser men's efforts to ape their feudal predecessors and social superiors; education set the gentleman off from the old feudal nobility, and Oxford and Cambridge were transformed from feudal seminaries for clerics into Renaissance schools for gentlemen.

Learning in the medieval past had been the preserve of ecclesiastics, and the feudal knight had regarded formal education with scorn, preferring to "hunt and blow a horn, leap over lakes and dikes, setting nothing by politics." The feudal squire learned a way of life but he rarely received academic training. He was taught to sing and dance and compose on harp and virginal, to speak well, and to move with grace and ease. He learned to ride and hunt, to hawk and fight. His education prepared him for a military existence in which the highest ideals were those of chivalry and his greatest obligations were to his lord. All this he learned in the entourage of kings and barons, not within the cloistered confines of Oxford and Cambridge.

The new students of the sixteenth century sought a formal academic education of the mind rather than training in the physical and social graces of society. By accident or by that curious tendency of men to discover what they need in order to survive, gentry class-consciousness found in humanism an educational creed to its own tastes. The Renaissance spirit, which came to be called in northern Europe the "New Learning," moved slowly northward from Italy breathing the warm air of intellectual criticism and curiosity into the chilly climes of sterile scholasticism. Secular in mood, slavishly classical in form, and essentially skeptical in spirit, the "New Learning" laughed at the old ways as the "grossest kind of sophistry" and claimed that rhetoric, history, and the classics were the new gods of the educational world. The man who did most to liberate Cambridge University from its bondage to the gloomy ignorance of the medieval schoolmen was Desiderius Erasmus who, though he could not stomach English beer and weather for more than two years, prepared the text of his *New Testament* while in residence at Cambridge. Returning to the original Greek, Erasmus held the Scriptures up to the same critical standards that Lorenzo Valla (1406–1457) had applied to the *Donation of Constantine and* William Grocyn (1446–1519) to Dionysius' *Ecclesiastical Hierarchy*.

In Italy, humanistic education was geared to the training of man so that he could attain his fullest potentiality, and *uomo universale* was viewed as the highest achievement of individualism. In England aristocratic education had a more social and practical end. The study of human affairs as they were revealed in the "Poets, Orators and Historians" of the ancient world was the essence of sixteenth-century education. It was Sir Thomas Elyot's *The Governour* (1531) and Roger Ascham's *The School Master* (1570) that set the educational aspirations and methods of Tudor England. Training of the mind was to be undertaken not so much for the sake of man as for the benefit of the state. In the university the young gentleman was expected to learn "to be a most loyal servitor of his prince," and to serve the body politic "in parliament, in council, in commission and other offices of the commonwealth." The rights of blood and gentility to a high position in society were never denied, but the medieval notion of a divine right of aristocracy which demanded a share in government gave way to the idea of a moral obligation on the part of an educated gentry, anxious to dedicate their talents to the kingdom. The changing state of affairs was even recorded in statute when parliament noted that "the wanton bringing up and ignorance of the nobility" had forced "the prince to advance new men" who could serve him. A successful and parvenu Tudor crown needed the support and the brains of equally successful and upstart clothiers, lawyers, and landlords. The fact that Henry VIII took as his second wife a young lady whose great-grandfather had been a merchant and lord mayor of London, and whose father was a country gentleman, may indicate that the Tudor dynasty had grown so secure by 1533 that it could afford to go slumming, but it also signifies the speed with which commercial elements were achieving respectability and the economic and social importance of the gentry class.

The Nation-State

Education was to be dedicated to the service of the state, not to God, and it is in this transfer of purpose that there resides one of the most momentous of all intellectual and political revolutions. Service to the state is predicated upon the idea of statehood and the existence of a social body that has outgrown its feudal, corporate, and fragmented nature and has evolved into a nation. The forging of political unity and the transformation of a medieval realm into a modern nation were largely the result of the strong-arm tactics of the great Tudor monarchs, but spiritual nationalism— a sense of oneness and Englishness—was far advanced before the first Tudor seized the crown at Bosworth Field.

It is said even today that every Englishman's class is branded upon his tongue; in the fifteenth century, it might be added that his geographic as well as his social origins were indelibly imprinted upon his speech. The indispensable condition of nationhood—linguistic unity—had developed far enough by 1400 so that the babble of innumerable tongues had given way to a single dominant speech: that of English as spoken in the neighborhood of the city of London. The conquered tongue of the Anglo-Saxon, much modified and corrupted, had triumphed over Norman French, and possibly nothing better signifies the growing exclusiveness, national consciousness, and sense of separation from the European and continental community than the victory of native English over alien French. By the fourteenth century Chaucer was writing in English, and French had ceased to be the sole speech of polite society, although the upper classes tended to remain bilingual. Cases in the sheriff's court in London were pleaded in English in 1356, and six years later parliament decreed that all law suits presented to the royal courts should be conducted in the native tongue. That peculiar English pride in speaking no language save one's own was already manifest in 1404, when a knight and a doctor of law were sent as ambassadors to France and both admitted: "We are as ignorant of French as of Hebrew." By the reign of Henry V, the kings of England considered English to be their mother tongue, and "learned, unlearned, old and young, all understood the English tongue."

The King's English, richly intermingling Saxon and French, might never have become the common tongue of the realm had it not been for Mr. William Caxton and his printing press established in 1477 "at the sign of the Red Pale" in the royal borough of Westminster. Caxton was a wool merchant turned savant who joined the service of Edward IV's sister, Margaret, Duchess of Burgundy. Inspired by the Renaissance atmosphere of the city of Bruges, "the Florence of Flanders," and encouraged by the duchess, Caxton put aside his wool ledgers in order to translate into English the *Recueil des Histoires de Troye.* He did not, however, take kindly to the fate of the medieval copyist whose eyes were dimmed from "over much looking on the white paper," and like any astute businessman he sought some faster and easier means of disseminating his translation. On a business trip to Cologne in 1471 Caxton encountered an extraordinary device for "putting in enprinte," and he immediately set about mastering the new art of printing with movable type. Six years later he moved his press from Flanders to Westminster and published the first book ever to be printed in England—*The Dictes and Sayengs of the Philosophres,* translated by no less a person than the king's brother-in-law, Earl Rivers. Perhaps a hundred works came off of Caxton's press: not limited editions designed for monks and princes but relatively cheap prints for all who loved Chaucer's *Canterbury Tales*, Boethius' *Consolations of Philosophy*, Lydgate's *Temple of Glass*, or Malory's *Morte d' Arthur*. It was certainly a difficult job, as the printer confessed, "to please every man because of diversity and change of language"; but Caxton's English, his choice of "old and homely" words, became familiar to every literate Englishman.

English in the fifteenth century dominated but it did not monopolize. Cornishmen still spoke a variant of their ancient Breton tongue; Yorkshiremen, though they claimed their guttural sounds were English, were incomprehensible to natives of Kent; and so tenaciously did the Welsh cling to their Celtic speech that Queen Elizabeth felt it necessary to learn that language. But the growth of a single medium of expression, the increasing reference to English as the mother tongue, and the dying use of French and Latin were signs of evolving national cohesiveness. The day was not far off when an archbishop of Canterbury, who was no longer appointed by a foreign and Italian-speaking pontiff, would remind his countrymen that strength lay in national unity. "It is an easy thing," Thomas Cranmer warned, "to break a whole faggot when every stick is loosed from another." Bishop Edmund Bonner asserted that "in matters of state individuals were not to be so much regarded as the whole body of the citizens." Once Englishmen became conscious of a sense of Englishness, once they transferred their loyalty from locality and estate to realm and state and began talking about England as that "blessed isle," a sentiment had been set loose which would destroy the last shreds of lingering medieval internationalism. English became the means by which Cornishmen and Yorkshiremen alike could express their loyalty to the land, and once the new Tudor monarchs were able to associate themselves with the Englishman's love of England, then they had become, as one contemporary noted, not only kings "to be obeyed" but idols "to be worshipped."

The Heart of the Realm

The center of the Tudor melting pot, the grotesque and growing heart of the realm which conservative social critics complained was devouring the rest of the body politic, was the city of London. In 1335 the city had possessed three times the wealth of any other community in the kingdom; by 1520 the ratio was fifteen to one and still increasing. Though the size and influence of the metropolis upset the political sensibilities of Tudor theorists, it was nevertheless a source of immense pride to the loyal Englishman who exclaimed: "What can there be in any place under the heavens that is not in this noble City either to be bought or borrowed?" London was indeed the "store house and mart" of all the world. The metropolis and its suburbs were the residence both of the royal court and of the courts of law, and by the second decade of the sixteenth century the offspring of the gentry were crowding into the Inns of Court or law colleges for a year of what might be described as postgraduate work. Knowledge both of the law and of the ways of the city was an indispensable attribute to a landowning class which regarded litigation almost as a pastime. There, in the borough of Westminster, resided His Majesty's High Court of Parliament, and as the century progressed the agitation on the part of country gentlemen to participate in the legislative destinies of the nation and to share in the responsibilities of government became a demand that Tudor kings found it expedient to heed and Stuart monarchs ignored at their peril. From the full-bosomed prostitutes practicing their trade at the Cardinal's Hat and the Swan to the magnificent royal mansion at Whitehall in Westminster, London encompassed every variety of Tudor subject. Gentleman and varlet walked side by side and the ancient barriers of class and feudal privilege gave way before the violence and opulence of urban life.

To many Englishmen London was cancerous, evil, and seditious, and its denizens so fickle that "one moment they will adore a prince and the next moment they would kill or crucify him." But for all this, the city was the key to England and to Tudor authority. An overgrown provincial town of possibly 50,000 in 1500, a century later London had grown into a metropolis of close to 200,000, a rate of growth ten times that of the population of the rest of the realm, which only rose from 2.6 to 3.7 million. Early in the sixteenth century it became the political counterbalance to the feudal northern shires, and with each passing decade the political and economic scales dipped more heavily in favor of the city and the south of England. The Tudors were secure upon the throne as long as they held captive the hearts of Londoners. Catholic prelates, feudal snobbery, and even the sensibilities of all Christendom could be shocked and violated as long as the city remained loyal. It was here in London that the crucial audience for Tudor pageantry resided, and it was in London that the drama of Tudor history would unfold.

Old Bottles, New Wines:
The Reign of Henry VII

5 Fashions in history are as unpredictable as tastes in clothing. Why flat chests and high skirts should be sexually appealing to one generation and accentuated breasts and long skirts to another is no whit more comprehensible than why Henry VII should be the perfect "new monarch" to Victorian historians and a medieval relic to modern scholars. Along with such terms as "Lancastrian constitutionalism" and "Tudor despotism," the "new monarchy" is out of fashion. Sometimes newness is denied to Henry VII on the grounds that he was nothing but an efficient emulator of his Yorkist predecessors, Edward IV and Richard III. Sometimes scholars push newness forward into the reign of his son Henry VIII and leave the first Tudor behind as a medieval man. Historians, however, are like Humpty Dumpty: a word means just what they choose it to mean—"neither more nor less." This being the case, the term "new monarch" as applied to Henry VII is not without justification.[1]

The "New Monarchy"

Since 1399 Plantagenet heirs had been feuding over the royal patrimony of the murdered Richard II. In 1485 a usurper and a foreigner snatched the coveted crown from them. Henry Tudor's stolid Welsh blood and distaff

---

[1] Henry VII's new look can best be read in G. R. Elton, *The Revolution in Tudor Government* (1953) and W. C. Richardson, *Tudor Chamber Government* (1952), both of which are fairly heavy going; J. P. Cooper, "Henry VII's Last Years Reconsidered," *Historical Journal*, II (1959); G. R. Elton, "Henry VII: Rapacity and Remorse," *Ibid.*, I (1958) and his "Henry VII: A Restatement," *Ibid.*, IV (1958) and his "Henry VII: IV (1961). See also a fine new biography: S. B. Chrimes, *Henry VII* (1972).

Rivals to The Tudors

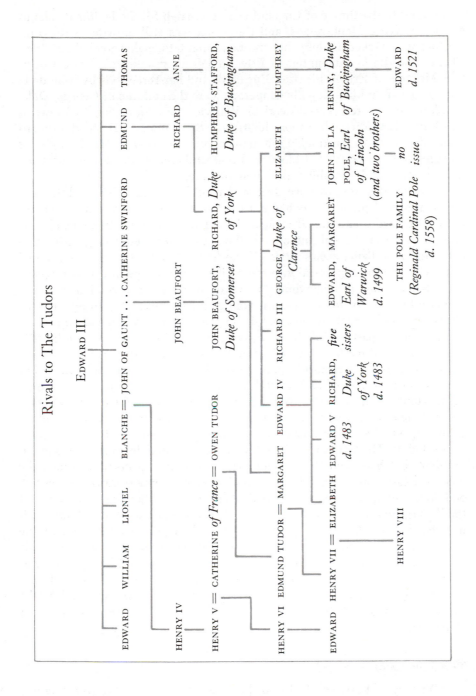

pretensions to the throne of England were no match for the legitimate claims of the surviving Plantagenets, and the arena was still crowded with competitors who lacked nothing but military might to make good their titles. There were the five daughters of Edward IV, his grandson Edward Courtney, Marquis of Exeter, his sister Elizabeth and her three sons by John de la Pole, Duke of Suffolk. Equally dangerous were the children of George, Duke of Clarence: the ten-year-old earl of Warwick and Margaret, Countess of Salisbury. Less direct but more legitimate than Henry VII stood Edward Stafford, Duke of Buckingham, a descendant of Edward III through his youngest son. If novelty of blood and doubtfulness of title confer newness, then the first Tudor qualifies as a "new monarch."

Medieval historians never tire of noting that Henry VII did little that his great feudal predecessors had not done or had not aspired to do. Henry II and Edward I had aimed at financial solvency, the enforcement of law, and the exercise of royal authority without the interference of greedy magnates and moralizing ecclesiastics. If the first Tudor had a conscious model from which to draw political inspiration, it was the image of a strong feudal king. Some rather peculiar things, however, occur when sovereigns begin to emulate history. If, for instance, a young girl discovers her grandmother's clothes in an old trunk in the attic, if she proceeds to dress herself up in the fashions of the past, and if she goes about announcing to all and sundry that she is her grandmother, then it is time to call in the psychiatrist. This hypothetical and highly neurotic damsel may think she is her grandmother, but her slavish imitation of archaic styles can resurrect the past no more than could Henry VII. The first Tudor may well have thought of himself as a feudal king and may have seen himself as conforming to the "true" medieval tradition, but this did not make him a medieval monarch. His very success prevented it. He introduced into the ancient feudal formula the one ingredient that had been lacking—efficiency. In doing so he transformed the medieval forms into something new and modern. Opportunistic, mercurial, cunning, brutal, and always practical, these are the adjectives that suit best the Tudor dynasty. The enforcement of law was more important than legality; the king's will was of greater concern than political theory; and the duties, not the rights, of subjects were proclaimed in every royal edict. The institutional bottles remained centuries old, but a new and heady wine was being poured into them, a vintage nourished upon the bright sun of economic expansion and social dynamism. Success was in the air; and as the cautious clothier and the hard-headed landlord were successful so also was Henry VII.

The Succession Secured

Victory at Bosworth Field on the 22nd of August, 1485, won a crown for Henry Tudor, Earl of Richmond, but the new king was soon to learn the truth of the Machiavellian axiom: "There is nothing more difficult to plan, more doubtful of success, more dangerous to manage than the creation of a new system ... for ... the nature of people is fickle and it is easy to persuade them of something but difficult to keep them in that persuasion." The first step in keeping irresponsible barons and doubtful friends in line was the securing of the succession.

Henry VII outraged the theory of legitimacy and insulted the memory of Edward III by claiming the throne by lawful descent, but he also emphasized the fact that the crown had been won by force of arms which, though not exactly legal, was obviously a sign of God's will and favor. The "disposition of God" could only be "known by manifest, certain and authentic revelation" of which victory in battle was presumably the surest indication. As proof of divine sanction Henry announced that his reign had commenced on the day before Bosworth Field, which was a convenient way out of the legal dilemma facing the new reign: how to attaint for high treason loyal Yorkists who had fought for Richard, their liege lord and lawful king. In official parlance Richard III was styled "King in deed but not of right." A new parliament was summoned for November 7, 1485, which dutifully acknowledged God's will and Henry's position as king and obediently referred to the victor as "our new sovereign lord, King Henry." Parliament did not, however, confer regal authority upon the conqueror; this, Henry maintained, had already been achieved by military triumph at Bosworth Field.

God's will and Henry's title to the throne still had to be defended against a multitude of real and mythical claimants. One of the foremost contenders, Elizabeth of York, Edward IV's eldest daughter, was removed from the list by marriage to Henry himself. The murder of Edward's sons, presumably by their uncle Richard III, was a blessing to the new sovereign, since it left no direct male Plantagenet heir except the ten-year-old earl of Warwick, who was promptly ensconced in the Tower. The descendants of Edward's sisters and daughters remained a plague, but only the de la Pole family were serious contenders and they were hunted down and exterminated. More difficult by far were two legends against which Henry had no defense: the persistent story that the two little princeling sons of Edward IV had not been murdered but had miraculously escaped; and the equally strong belief that the child earl of Warwick was still at large, claiming his rightful title as the legitimate Edward VI. Despite the parading of the real and incarcerated earl of Warwick and the assurance that a wicked uncle had in fact dispatched both Edward V and his little brother Richard, the myths persisted and became the center for Yorkist conspiracies and artful impersonations. Less than two years after the victory at Bosworth, Yorkist and baronial discontent rallied to the banner of a young boy by the name of Lambert Simnel who proclaimed himself to be the authentic and liberated earl of Warwick. Ireland and Burgundy became the haven for exiled Yorkists and the springboard for the hopes of restoring the true dynasty. Led by John de la Pole, Earl of Lincoln, and manned with Burgundian and Irish mercenaries, the white rose of York made a desperate bid to capture the throne. At the battle of Stoke on June 16, 1487, Henry Tudor was again victorious; the earl of Lincoln was killed; and Simnel was captured, pardoned, and demoted from a potential king to a scullery boy in the royal kitchen where, by dint of hard labor, he earned the rank of king's falconer.

Impersonating monarchs was not over. Four years later in 1491 Richard, Duke of York, the brother of the murdered Edward V, suddenly reappeared in the person of a young and handsome Flemish lad of seventeen who was blessed with a regal appearance and a facile mind. Perkin Warbeck is historic evidence not only of the imaginative mentality of the age but also of the fact that legendary tales of royal pretenders are grounded on a single element of truth: that people believe what they want to believe. Warbeck or the rightful Richard IV, depending on the color of one's rose, was recognized in the courts of Vienna and Burgundy, where the Emperor Maximilian proclaimed him lawful king of England and the duchess of Burgundy accepted him as her nephew. Fortunately for Henry Tudor this elegant mountebank was a better impersonator of royalty than leader of men. For six years Warbeck maintained his act and involved braver men in treason. In the end he was captured in an abortive invasion of England in 1497. Again the king showed surprising mercy and allowed the imposter to live, but two years later Warbeck sealed his own fate and that of the real earl of Warwick. Twice he endeavored to escape, and in his second attempt he involved the earl. In 1499 both men were executed in their twenty-fifth year. The earl, as befitting his Plantagenet blood, died by the axe; Warbeck was hanged by the neck.

By the very nature of kingship, the elimination of rival contenders to the throne through exile, battle, or execution became the foundation of government policy, for in sixteenth-century monarchy there was no place for legal opposition. The individual who attracted political support to himself, whether through blood like the earl of Warwick or through wealth and power like the kingmaker, had to be destroyed. This policy of extermination did not die with the first Tudor. Anyone unfortunate enough to be tainted with royal blood learned to step warily and lived constantly beneath the shadow of the sword. The duke of Buckingham lasted only until 1521; the sister of the young earl of Warwick, Margaret, Countess of Salisbury, was executed in 1541 and her descendants were systematically harried out of the land and destroyed. By 1525 the curse of Edward III's fecundity had worn itself out, the Plantagenet line was all but extinct, and the Tudors had become the primary possessors of royal blood. Dynastically, Henry VII did his job well. Not only did he destroy his rivals, but his queen also gave birth to eight children, of whom four lived to adolescence and three passed on the united blood of York and Lancaster to their descendants. Arthur, the elder son, died of consumption in 1502; Henry, the second son, ascended the throne in 1509; Margaret married James IV of Scotland and became the link through which the Stuart dynasty succeeded the Tudors in 1603; and Mary, the youngest child, eloped with her brother's close friend, Charles Brandon, Duke of Suffolk.

The secret of political power and the security of the throne involved more than seizing the crown, eliminating rivals, and propagating the regal race. If Henry VII's subjects were to stay in the proper "persuasion," the new king had to offer them more than royal bratlings; he had to achieve governmental solvency and enforce the laws of the realm. The power of money and the effectiveness of the king's courts were the pillars upon which Tudor security rested.

Financial Solvency and Fiscal Feudalism

The fifteenth century had revealed something which might be described as the anatomy of usurpation. The successful contender to the throne had to be lavish with his promises, assuring reformation to reformers and offering the hope of gain to all who were greedy of land, title, and position. If the royal aspirant were fortunate enough to survive the field of battle and become a king, the fair and easy pledges which he had so generously bestowed to win allies suddenly had to be made good. "Friends" had to be rewarded, potential rivals bought off, enemies defeated, and in the end the spoils of victory were consumed and the new crowned monarch found himself dependent upon the bounty of those mightier than he. This had been the fate of the Lancastrians, and this might have happened to the Yorkists had not Edward IV brought with him the immense private resources of his clan. With Edward's elevation to the throne in 1461, the richest magnate of the realm became king. When the kingmaker was finally destroyed in 1471, the crown fell heir to many of the Neville properties. Long before Henry VII "inherited" his kingdom, the financial recovery of the monarchy had commenced. Edward IV had brought not only new estates to the crown but also more efficient administration of the royal domain; at the same time his customs receipts had profited from the revival of the wool trade with Europe.

The new Tudor monarch simply outdid his Yorkist predecessors. Henry's first move was to use parliament as the legal instrument to assure to the crown all its ancient possessions, and to attaint the estates of Yorkist adherents and add them to the crown lands. Legislation was also passed restoring to the king all properties alienated as far back as the days of Edward III. If power is related to finances, Henry VII started his reign as secure as Edward IV had ended his. Income from crown lands in 1485 totaled £29,000; which was probably more than Edward had been able to extract. By the end of the reign in 1509, land revenues had risen to £42,000 and the profits of the duchy of Lancaster had increased from £650 to £6,500. The customs, reflecting the growing prosperity of the century, rose from just over £30,000 a year to an average of £40,000 by the time Henry died.

If Henry VII thought in medieval terms, he at least did so in an effective fashion. He viewed the historic income of his crown as no more than his just desert, assets from which he should neither have to beg nor bargain. Feudal kings had traditionally lived off rents from royal estates, revenues from the customs, fees from the administration of justice, and monies extracted on the basis of a vassal's duty to his overlord. The last two sources had been sorely depleted as weak and vacillating kings had allowed royal law courts to fall into disrespect and had let slip their feudal rights. The Tudors aimed not so much at the destruction of medieval feudalism as at its adaptation to the financial needs of the new dynasty. Henry demanded his feudal rights, particularly those involving money payments, and it was this insistence that earned for him the reputation of a miser and extortionist. Despite the unpopularity of his fiscal policies, Henry at least succeeded in fulfilling the medieval dictum that kings should live on their own.

The price that society paid for such financial solvency was the exercise of a variety of fiscal feudalism whereby the sovereign extracted from his subjects the last measure of his historic rights. In 1504 he demanded two feudal aids, the first when his eldest daughter married James of Scotland and the second for the knighting of his son Arthur. The artificiality of the demand was apparent from the start; Arthur had been knighted fifteen years before and had been dead two years. Moreover, parliament voiced the sentiments of most landowners when it offered Henry £40,000 on condition that he refrain from searching into the records in order to discover the exact obligations of ancient land tenures. Resistance to the revival of feudalism, however, was difficult since military land tenure carried with it endless responsibilities which the crown could transform into a lucrative source of income. As late as the middle of the sixteenth century Sir Thomas Smith could still write that "no man holdeth land simply free in England but he or she that holdeth the crown of England; all others hold their land in fee." The king's feudal tenants-in-chief owed a form of inheritance tax known as relief; if they were minors, they became wards of the crown and their lands passed into the temporary possession of the government; and if a tenant died without heirs his land reverted back to the king. These had all been ancient obligations based upon the military nature of feudalism, and they operated at every level of the feudal structure. Wardship, for instance, was an understandable condition since the overlord had originally given the land in return for military service. If his vassal were a minor and unable to fulfill his military duties, it was only natural that the fief should be returned to the lord until the vassal came of military age and competence. Relief, aids, wardship, and the like were terms governing the relationship existing between any lord and his vassal; but the king, as the greatest lord of them all, derived the most profit.

All these feudal liabilities were legal, but most of them had been ignored or disobeyed for a century or more. In reviving them, Henry VII demanded nothing more than his own, and he systematically went about inquiring into the conditions of landholding throughout his kingdom. If he could prove that a man held his land as a knight's fee originally presented to him by the king, then Henry exacted his feudal due. A year after he became king, Henry established a commission to inquire into land tenure, and the crown began to scrutinize the *inquisitiones post mortem* of its subjects in order to determine the extent and nature of their estates. As a further safeguard to the crown's feudal incomes, Henry's son insisted in 1536 upon legislation known as the Statute of Uses to prevent landowners from escaping relief or wardship by legal trickery. The protest on the part of landowners in parliament, however, was so great that the crown decided to compromise, and by the Statute of Wills in 1540 it allowed those who held their property by knight's service to bequeath two-thirds of their land without obligation and subjected only one-third to the burdens of wardship.

Justice and piety were the two attributes of medieval kingship most highly esteemed. Piety was gratuitous, but justice had the added attraction of being profitable. Use of the king's courts was a privilege, not a right, and in order to start the machinery of justice a sizable fee had to be paid. More profitable, but less certain, were the fines levied as punishment by the king's courts. With his eye upon the exchequer, Henry VII tended to chastise his wayward subjects with the economic whip more than with the executioner's blade. Barons who indulged in treason or broke the many laws against livery, powerful men who tried to subvert justice by bribing or intimidating judges and juries, and merchants who evaded governmental regulations and customs duties, all paid for their transgressions with their monies, not their lives. The story that Henry extracted £10,000 while on a social visit to the earl of Oxford for a technical breach of the law against the keeping of liveried retainers is probably apocryphal, but the king's words are symptomatic of the spirit of his reign. As he was leaving, Henry turned to his baronial host and said: "My lord, I thank you for my good cheer, but I may not endure to have my laws broken in my sight; my attorney must speak with you."

A final source of income which reflected the growing strength of the government was the collection of benevolent loans extracted from those most able to pay—wealthy individuals and corporations. The royal tax collectors confronted both rich and poor with the dilemma known as Morton's Fork. The victim was persuaded to pay if he were wealthy and lived lavishly, because high living was obviously proof of the ability to contribute generously to the king. He was equally persuaded to part with his money if he lived in poverty, for this presumably was evidence of frugality and the existence of savings, a portion of which should be donated to the support of the kingdom.

Even in diplomacy, concern for the welfare of his exchequer was paramount in Henry's calculations. Early in the reign he revived the Yorkist policy of friendship with the Habsburg interests in Europe because he valued the goodwill of whoever controlled the markets of the Lowlands and could threaten the crown's revenues from the export duty on woolen broadcloth. Similar fiscal considerations stood behind the marriage of Henry's eldest son, Prince Arthur, to Catherine, the daughter of Ferdinand and Isabella of

Spain. The match was first proposed in 1488, but the children were young, Spain wanted to see whether the Tudor line would survive, and both Henry VII and Ferdinand required time to settle the most important element of all—Catherine's dowry. By 1496 the terms of marriage had been hammered out and the dowry was set at 200,000 crowns; five years later the wedding took place, and within five months Arthur was dead and Catherine a widow in a foreign land. Though Henry grieved for the loss of his son, he had no intention of losing his daughter-in-law's dowry as well; and after two more years of bargaining it was decided in 1503 that Catherine should be betrothed to young Prince Henry, six years her junior. For diplomatic reasons the Spanish princess had to wait still another six years before the fateful marriage finally took place.

In war as well as diplomacy Henry was able to realize a profit. England joined Spain in 1489 in a war to prevent France from absorbing the duchy of Brittany, and the king was quick to use the expenses of sending an army to France as an excuse for extracting £100,000 from parliament. Henry made noisy military gestures to satisfy his ally and to allay parliamentary suspicions about the purpose for which its grant was being spent, but in December of 1492 he was delighted to sign the unheroic yet extremely lucrative treaty of Etaples by which he agreed to put aside his claim to the French throne in return for a handsome monetary tribute.

When the first Tudor died he had accomplished a revolution in finances. The royal income in 1485 has been computed at £52,000; twenty-four years later it may have reached £142,000, but £113,000 may be more accurate. The Venetian ambassador correctly analyzed the transformation when he wrote home in 1500 that England was "perfectly stable by reason, first of the King's wisdom whereof everyone stands in awe; and secondly on account of the King's wealth." Henry VII had rectified one essential set of statistics: economically speaking there were no more overmighty subjects; instead noblemen were "nothing more than rich gentlemen in possession of great quantities of land." The king was immeasurably the wealthiest individual in the realm, and Sir John Fortescue's formula that monarchs should be twice as wealthy as their greatest subjects had been put into effect many times over. Henry Tudor as a landlord was worth £42,000 annually; his nearest rival could scarcely muster £4,000.

The Resurgence of Royal Authority and the Rule of Law

The wisdom of the king amounted to more than a deep regard for pounds, shillings, and pence. Money could buy power and enforce a grudging respect; but the traditional role of kingship and the source of its esteem was the position of the monarch as supreme judge and administrator of the realm. The crown was regarded as the fountainhead of justice and the wellspring from which flowed "a flood of all that is good or evil." Evil lay in inactivity; if Henry were to fulfill the proper role of kingship, he had to enforce his laws upon both great and small, and see that the machinery of government operated without respect to rank or person. No Tudor was deliberately a revolutionist, and neither Henry VII nor his son desired the destruction of the old governmental or social system. Instead they endeavored to harness it and to utilize the existing structure. Their purpose was to convert feudal barons into domesticated peers who regarded themselves as servants of the state—not independent leaders of society—and to transform the structure of government from a preserve of aristocratic privilege into an effective instrument of royal authority. The task involved neither the annihilation of the nobility nor the creation of new organs of government; the secret lay in making the inherited system operate.

Henry VII summarized the problem that confronted him at the commencement of his reign when he summoned the peers of the realm and required them to swear not to shelter felons, not to impede or ignore royal writs, not to corrupt or intimidate juries, not to maintain private armies of indentured retainers, and not to sanction riots and foster violence. The fundamental job was to impress upon a hierarchically structured society the fact that "it was not fit that private men should carve out their redress which way they list" and that "obedience is the best in each degree." In this task the king was immeasurably helped by the extinction of the old nobility during the Wars of the Roses, which had so reduced their ranks that only eighteen barons were called to Henry's first parliament. The nobleman, be he Yorkist or Lancastrian, who gave faithful service to the monarchy, irrespective of the man who wore the crown, was rewarded; the magnate who continued to play the risky game of kingmaking was destroyed. It was no accident that Thomas Howard, Earl of Surrey, who had fought for Richard III at Bosworth Field, was freed from the Tower in 1491 and his lands restored, while Sir William Stanley, whose timely betrayal had won Henry the battle, was executed for treason four years later. The former had accepted and was willing to live by the axiom: "what pleaseth the prince hath the force of law"; the latter harkened back to an older generation of nobility that had no place in the Tudor world.

The first Tudor had the financial wherewithal to purchase a standing army in the style of European sovereigns. He chose not to; yet rebels had to be chastised, the realm defended, and wars fought. The two hundred yeomen of the guard established early in the reign as a personal bodyguard for the king were mere window-dressing to royalty, not an effective weapon of coercion. Henry VII had no use for expensive mercenary troops; he preferred the historic system of recruitment whereby the great magnates armed their own tenants and placed them at the service of the crown. The problem was to limit the system of recruitment to the king's command. This was done by the use of Commissions of Array, appointed by the king for each county and composed of notable personages of the shires who were ordered to arm a prescribed number of men at their own expense. Private liveried armies were anathematized, but noblemen who failed to raise their quota were brought before the king's Star Chamber to explain their delinquency. For example, Lord William Howard, though he complained bitterly about the cost, was commanded to raise one hundred men-at-arms and thirty archers for the king's use. So long as such troops were at the king's command and not under oath to some noble lord or wearing his livery, they constituted an effective fighting force with which to secure the crown and defend the realm.

At law the most glaring needs were neither new statutes nor new courts but the "just execution of laws, reformation of faults, giving out of commandments" and impartial justice. For the past hundred years justice had been forfeited to influence, and the aristocracy had successfully exercised a form of judicial patronage in which local concerns prevailed over royal interests, money over legality, force of arms over the evidence, and baronial privilege over the crown's right. Humble folk either did not bother to take their grievances to law or, if they did, they took them to the man who could control the outcome of the case. Common law could no longer furnish protection. It had become rigid and archaic, ponderously slow and intricately technical, and the bastion of wealth and influence. Only the rich could afford it, and the common law, depending as it did on juries, was constantly exposed to bribery and intimidation.

Common law was not the only kind of justice available to Englishmen. The king, who was the wellspring "of all that was good or evil," could hear complaints and administer justice directly or through his council. His decisions were not hampered by juries, precedents, or legal technicalities. Royal justice tended to be commonsense justice, and lesser people found swift, impartial, and equitable decisions whenever they brought their pleas to the king or his council. Such law, sometimes called equity law, was inherent in kingship, and the king's council could administer justice in its master's name. The Court of Chancery enforced equity law, and by 1485 it was already a venerable division of government; but Chancery had the disadvantage of being restricted to civil cases. Though the court increased in stature and in business under the Tudors, there still remained a pressing need for some competent organization to hear criminal cases. Men were being urged to bring their grievances directly to the sovereign, and the lords of the council began to reserve certain hours of the day and a particular location in the king's palace at Westminster to hear criminal disputes. They met in the Star Chamber and, as the years passed, a number of the king's servants came to specialize in such criminal cases, and their meetings assumed the name of the Court of the Star Chamber. Under Henry VII the court never became visibly separate from the rest of the council; but after 1509 it took on "great augmentation and authority," joining the Court of Chancery as an instrument by which "obedience" was taught to the baronial few as well as the common multitude.

Obedience, as Henry knew, was the daughter of respect for royal authority. A proper and humble regard for the king's will could be cultivated by maintaining a deep financial distinction between the sovereign and his subjects, and it could be fostered by making the king's courts havens of justice, but the most effective method was by brutally insisting upon the supremacy of law in every corner of the realm. The legacy of the medieval past has been a kingdom divided into semiautonomous franchises, such as the episcopal palatinate of Durham, the duchy of Lancaster, and the Welsh Marches, where border lords paid scant heed to the king's writs and clung tenaciously to their cherished liberties. Under the first Lancastrian king, the duchy of Lancaster had been absorbed into the royal domain; but even as late as 1534, twenty-five years after Henry VII's death, it was still being said that "the King's rights are attacked by all manner of liberties, his felons and outlaws are clothed and maintained by stewards and bailiffs of these liberties, so that his process has no place and his laws are not dread." The first Tudor did his best to curb the independence of these ancient franchises by creating the King's Council for Wales and the Marches, but he left it to his son, Henry VIII, to bring the king's law into the mountains of Wales. In 1534 parliament finally passed legislation abolishing the right of the semi-independent Welsh principalities to give sanctuary to felons who had escaped the long arm of royal law. Two years later statutes were enacted "making the laws of Wales the same as those of England" and reorganizing the 136 lordships of the Welsh Marches into five new shires under royal law and administration. By April of 1536 the independence of almost all of the self-governing franchises throughout the kingdom had given way to the sole jurisdiction of the crown. The only peace that could now be broken was the king's peace, the only justices were royal judges, and the only right to pardon a crime was the king's right.

The destruction of provincialism was easier than the curbing of baronial privilege; the lesson of equality before the law had to be drilled into a peerage which had been for four centuries happily operating in the tradition of feudal independence and irresponsibility. The old nobility had to learn that the king's servant, no matter what his degree, had "a sufficient warrant to arrest the greatest peer of this realm." With calculated cruelty the Tudors insisted that the great should be struck down while the weak, protected by the mantle of royal authority, should inherit the earth.

Long after Henry VII's death his son was still carrying on his father's policies. In 1541 Henry VIII struck straight at the heart of feudal exclusiveness when two members of the baronial elite were hanged by the neck as common criminals. The case involved one of the most cherished of all feudal prerogatives—hunting rights. Those who harked back to the carefree days of the previous century when great men were laws unto themselves were reluctant to give up hunting at their pleasure in the countryside. As the enclosure of land grew more frequent, the exercise of this right became increasingly difficult. The crisis was brought to a head when young Thomas Lord Dacre of the South and his brother-in-law, John Mantell, together with fourteen of their friends were accused of murder. The young gentlemen, in the language of their indictment, had illegally conspired "how they might best hunt the park" of Mr. Nicholas Pelham "with dogs and nets and other engines." They had "bound themselves to slay any of the King's lieges who might resist them in their illegal purpose." When Mr. Pelham's men tried to stop them, one of his servants was fatally wounded, and the culprits, ranging from a lord to a Sussex yeoman, were arrested, indicted, and sentenced to be hanged.

The trial of Lord Dacre, since he was a baron of the realm, could not take place in a court of common law and had to be handled directly by the king's council. Dacre insisted that the killing had been accidental and demanded a judgment by his peers. The young man was wealthy and had influential friends at court, and one member of the council, Lord Cobham, was "very stiff and vehement" in refusing to view the affair as anything more than a high-spirited escapade on the part of a band of well-connected delinquents. The council persuaded Lord Dacre to give up his demand for a trial, and "upon hope of grace" confess his guilt and throw himself upon the king's mercy. Henry VIII was adamant, and the terrible sentence was executed. The court and feudal society were appalled at the spectacle of a rich and socially respectable young blade being treated as if he were a common cutpurse and murderer. In shocked words the Spanish ambassador reported that Lord Dacre had been hanged from "the most ignominious gibbet, and for greater shame dragged through the streets to the place of execution, to the great pity of many people, and even of his judges, who wept when they sentenced him, and in a body asked his pardon of the King." The aspect of the tragedy which provoked the most astonishment was that only Dacre and Mantell with two of their closest friends were executed while the others were granted the king's pardon. The moral was perfectly clear; if Englishmen lived under a single law, it was then a denial both of God and monarchy to assume that the estate of nobility could claim exemption or operate as a law unto itself.

The Art of Government

The tortoise of institutional change pays slight heed to the random, if brilliant, antics of the dynastic hare. Under Henry VII a new attitude of mind was at work, a new approach to government which had little to do with victory on the battlefield or the death of kings. In the medieval past, government had been viewed primarily as a necessary evil; by the sixteenth century men were beginning to whisper the extraordinary proposition that it might be a positive good. Statecraft had a long way to go before it evolved into the science of the modern bureaucratic state, but by 1509 in England, and earlier in Italy, government had come to be regarded as an art in which men made a conscious effort to calculate policy and to act accordingly. The ends of diplomacy were to be measured in terms of material benefit, not of spiritual or chivalric purposes. The amoeba-like quality of the feudal past in which there was little or no distinction between the legislative, executive, and judicial aspects of government was slowly giving way to a more precise notion of governmental function.

The most celebrated expression of the new spirit that was pervading the courts of kings as well as the mansions of merchants was the publication in 1516 of Sir Thomas More's *Utopia,* a treatise that has won for its author the questionable distinction of being one of the founders of political science. In part a medieval dream reflecting the perfect harmony of monastic life, in part a fantasy inspired by the discovery of the New World, and in part a learned joke in which Sir Thomas could indulge in the fiction of chamber-pots made of gold and children playing marbles with precious gems, the *Utopia* was above all else the first English example of the application of reasoned thought to the problems of good government. For the first time it was assumed that man by the exercise of his own rational mind could construct a reasonably perfect society. More's *Utopia* was here on earth and was the work of human beings; now mankind no longer had to wait for heaven and the operation of divine grace to achieve peace and happiness.

The accomplishments of Henry VII were a far cry from the reasoned society outlined in More's *Utopia,* but it can at least be said of Henry that he "was not afraid of an able man" and that he "was served by the ablest men that were to be found without which his affairs would not have prospered as they did." The secret of effective government lay not so much in the existence of strong kings as in the presence of able councillors: men dedicated to the single ideal of serving their master. New and strange men in government were not unique to the Tudor dynasty. The same complaint had been directed against Henry I, Richard II, and Edward IV. What set the first Tudor apart from his predecessors was the mentality of those who surrounded him. Chastened magnates sat on the royal council by invitation, not by divine right. Literate and educated ecclesiastics had traditionally been the prop and stay of governments which tended to flounder in the hands of warrior kings and illiterate peers, but the single-hearted service that Bishop Fox offered Henry VII was different both in kind and degree. It was said of him that "to serve the King's turn, [he] would agree to his own father's death." Fox was first the king's servant and only second an official of the church, owing obedience to God and to a foreign pope. Bushy, Green, and Scrope were the creatures of Richard II as Empson and Dudley were the servants of Henry VII, but there was a fundamental difference between Plantagenet favorites and Tudor workhorses. Richard's humble councillors were hardworking, loyal knights of the shire. Henry VII was surrounded by men who embodied in their careers the three new influences beginning to predominate in most sixteenth-century states: attention to administrative and fiscal detail, a conscious desire to increase efficiency, and a growing appreciation that government, though it operated in the king's name, had a life and spirit of its own.

The art of government, the Renaissance mind as applied to the problems of administration, belonged to no single innovator or individual genius. Henry VII was well served, and much which was branded as rapacious during his reign was in fact only the efforts of his officials to introduce order and logic into the chaos of medieval government. Sir John Lovell and Sir John Heron, the king's treasurers, laboriously worked out a relatively rational system of fiscal collection, appropriation, auditing, and disbursing. Sir Richard Empson and Sir Edmund Dudley, those hated legal advisers to the monarch, earned their evil reputations not so much because they were unscrupulous as because they were highly efficient. In the sixteenth century, however, the king's government was only as good as the monarch himself, and it was Henry's own vigilance, energy, and constant labor that gave life and direction to his reign.

The traditional image of the king is of a man, slight of build, sallow of face, and sparse of hair, who was more at home in the counting house than in medieval armor. But it should also be remembered that Henry won his crown in a fair fight upon the battlefield and that one chronicler acknowledged that "his mind was brave and resolute and never, even at moments of the greatest danger, deserted him." Tudor England had great difficulty with Henry's personality, and it may not be a coincidence that Shakespeare never wrote a play about him. A sovereign who acquired a reputation for avarice, who meticulously initialed each page of his financial ledgers, who actually covered four folios of one of his treasurer's account books with his own figures, and who rejoiced in converting Utrecht guilders, Flemish pounds, and Venetian ducats into "good sterling" was hardly a subject of great interest to a dramatist. Only later, in the seventeenth century, was the king praised as a sovereign of unusual ability and character who gave himself unstintingly to the affairs of state.

Whatever the monarch's manifold failings in the eyes of traditionalists who viewed kingship in terms of Henry V and Agincourt, Henry Tudor possessed two qualities that insured success in an age of "new monarchs" who practiced Machiavellian diplomacy and financial extortion: Henry VII paid close attention to administrative detail and was immensely hardworking "so that no one dared to get the better of him through deceit and guile." When he died in 1509, in the fifty-third year of his life and the twenty-fourth year of his reign, he bequeathed to his son something unique in English history: a safe throne, a full treasury, and a prosperous realm.

The Smell and Flavor of the Kingdom

The writing of history, like the painting of a picture, seeks to trick the eye into seeing something that is not there: an intelligible shape and an aura of sensibility. The art of government with its emphasis upon reason and calculation was little more than a flitting smile upon the face of Tudor

England, which remained far more medieval than modern in its conception of the universe and in the structure of its thought. The pomp and circumstance of the sixteenth century and the actions of a handful of titans obscure the realities of the existence of the unwashed multitude whose only history is the faceless, mindless record of demographic statistics dealing with births, marriages, and deaths.

Tudor society was cruel, vicious, and dangerously lacking in social inhibitions. Men were as quick to anger as to love, and no one, not even the clergy, walked unarmed at night. Unlit streets and the king's highways were the haunts of criminals—disabled soldiers, debtors, starving peasants, professional assassins, and an army of outcasts for whom society felt no particular responsibility. In London there was little that a rudimentary police force of 240 constables could do except to make frightful examples of those luckless enough to be caught or to answer the shouts of the victims with the words: "God restore your loss [we] have other business at this time." The degree of violence is difficult to judge. In terms of recorded felonies, the sixteenth century may have been as safe as the twentieth. Under Elizabeth the average yearly crime rate was 20 per 10,000 people in the turbulent shire of Essex, while in 1965 the rate for all England was 95.4 per 10,000; but modern means of crime detection and thoroughness of recording make these comparisons meaningless. Certainly contemporaries thought there was "no country in the world where there are more robbers and thieves than in England," and though the actual number of homicides may have been low, the incidence of rioting, feuding, brawling, and thieving seems to have been extremely high. Moreover, the number of apprehended criminals who slipped through the law's net and escaped punishment entirely was inordinately great. More serious, crimes of bodily violence—such as rape, murder, and manslaughter—were, at least in Essex, highest among the gentry, that element of society which was not only the most lethally armed but also in theory the most responsible.

In contrast to law enforcement, law enactment was detailed, ferocious, and ritualistic. With a fine appreciation that the punishment should fit the crime, the law prescribed that traitors be drawn to the gallows on a sled, hanged and cut down alive, castrated, disemboweled, decapitated, and quartered. Poisoners were boiled alive, witches and heretics burned at the stake, and murderers hanged 'til dead in chains. A Tudor execution was a carefully staged public spectacle in which the condemned man, as the traitor Friar Stone discovered in 1540, was the principal actor upon whom the government was ready to spend a great deal of money.

The most common engine of justice was the gibbet, and any theft over one shilling could be punished by hanging. Lesser offenses warranted lesser but almost as unpleasant consequences. Fraudulent merchants and slanderers were chastised on the pillory—there the culprits were forced to stand, neck and wrists pinioned, and, on occasion, their ears nailed to the

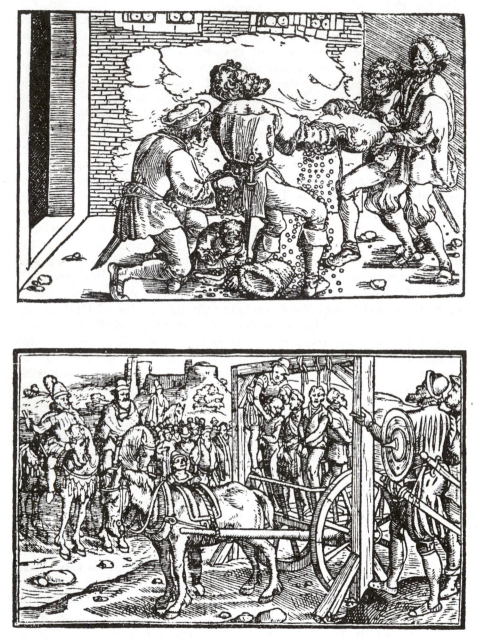

ROBBERY AND ITS CONSEQUENCES
"Unlit streets and the king's highways were the haunts of criminals—
disabled soldiers, debtors, starving peasants, professional assassins and an
army of outcasts for whom society felt no particular responsibility."

for half a ton of timber to make a pair of gallows for to hang Friar Stone	2s. 6d.[2]
to carpenter to build them	16d.
to laborer to dig holes	3d.
to men who helped set gallows up	7d.
for drink to them	1d.
carriage of timber to the Dungeon	4d.
for a hurdle	6d.
for load of wood and horse to draw him to Dungeon	2s. 3d.
to 2 men who set the kettle & parboiled him	12d.
to 3 men who carried his quarters to the city gates and set them up	13d.
halter to hang him	1d.
2 halfpenny halters	1d.
sandwich cord	9d.
for a woman to mind the kettle	2d.
executioner's fee	4s. 8d.

board behind their heads. The stocks were reserved for drunkards, rioters, namecallers, bawds, and scolds. False jurors were forced to ride "with their faces to the horses' tails" and paper caps on their heads; the village ducking stool was kept for gossips and scandal mongers; and public whipping was the customary method of discouraging idleness and prostitution. The law was without pity, but so also was life. "At any season," lamented Bishop Fisher, there were "beggars or poor folks that be pained and grieved with hunger and cold lying in the streets." Though Fisher preached compassion it was not easy to feel much inward pity when every city had its share of those who lacked "their arms, feet, hands, and other features of their bodies." Everyone's life was an agony of itches, toothaches, gout, bladder stones, ulcers, and sores, and all men walked in dread of the plague and smallpox. The torment of the traitor's death had to be set against the agony of the soldier whose bravery had brought him to the operating table to face the surgeon's saw without benefit of anesthesia, or that of the lover whose delights were more than repaid by the horrors of uncontrollable syphilis.

Death in one grisly guise or another was everywhere, yet life was made endurable and explicable by the knowledge that nothing existed—suffering, love, disaster, good fortune—which did not somehow fit into the pattern of God's ultimate design. The Tudor cosmos was tidy, sensible, and psychologically satisfactory, for every part fitted together to create a universe in which man was the most important actor, earth the center of

---

[2] S stands for shillings, d for pence. Thus the total came to 13 shillings, 3 pence in an era which accounted 50 shillings a year to be a living wage. The quote is in Terence Murphy, "The Maintenance of Order in Early Tudor Kent: 1509–1558" (unpubl. Ph.D. diss., Northwestern University, 1974) from Canterbury Cathedral Library MSS, F/A/13/ff. 69d–70.

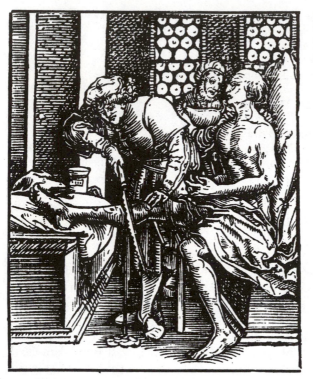

THE AMPUTATION
Facing "the surgeon's saw without benefit of anesthesia."

the stage, and God the producer, playwright, and director.[3] The universe possessed both spiritual and physical meaning: it was the stage on which man enacted the drama of his salvation, choosing either good or evil, heaven or hell; and every event—from the birth of Siamese twins to hurricanes that destroyed the harvest—betokened God's purpose and signified some celestial clash between the soldiers of God and Satan, who were eternally waging war for the souls of men. The macrocosm and the microcosm of existence were meshed in a divine web that extended from the butterfly to God, from man's society to the outer reaches of the firmaments, for all things in heaven and earth were linked in an endless "chain of being."

> God hath set an order by grace between Himself and angel and between angel and angel; and by reason between the angel and man and between man and man, man and beast; and by nature only between beast and beast; which order from the highest point to the lowest God willest us firmly to keep.

It was in this essentially medieval world, which believed that life was a moral issue, that the dramatic events of Henry VIII's reign and the Reformation took place.

---

[3] For a description of medieval Tudor cosmology see page 299.

This Realm of England
Is an Empire

When Henry VII died on April 21st, 1509, two men fell heir to his authority: his eighteen-year-old son, Bluff King Hal, and Thomas Wolsey, the child of an Ipswich butcher. While the young monarch cut royal capers, spent his father's treasures—which were not as large as legend pictures them—and enjoyed the role of a lavish and athletic prince graced with inexhaustible charm and a magnificent physique, the business of government was quietly assumed by the late king's almoner.[1]

King and Cardinal

At thirty-four Thomas Wolsey was a man of insatiable ambition, and Henry VIII was more than willing to gratify his servant's pretensions in return for relief from the burdens of kingship. The offices of church and state were thrown open to Wolsey's cupidity: archbishop of York in 1514, lord chancellor and cardinal legate of all England in 1515, and papal legate for life in 1524. For a time it seemed as if the realm possessed two kings—one in blood and name; the other in ability and fact. The cardinal exercised

---

[1] The works, both good and bad, on the reign of Henry VIII are legion. The following is a small sampling of the controversy surrounding Henry VIII as a human being. A. F. Pollard, *Henry VIII* (1902) is a classic and the starting point for any study of the king's character. F. Hackett, *Henry VIII* (Bantam Classics, 1963) is a controversial and rather dangerous popular biography. H. F. M. Prescott, *The Man on a Donkey* (1952) is a brilliant historical novel in which Henry is cast as the villain. The most recent treatments are J. J. Scarisbrick, *Henry VIII* (1968); and L. B. Smith, *Henry VIII, The Mask of Royalty* (1973).

an authority which no medieval monarch had wielded: as lord chancellor and cardinal legate he united in his ample person the spiritual and temporal powers of the realm. His residences at Hampton Court and York Palace housed an entourage of 400 courtiers who waited upon his pleasure, and though the ancient nobility hated him for his pride and humble birth, they also danced to his lordship's fancy. The cardinal's legatine authority brought papal power directly into England; both the archbishop of Canterbury in his palace and the simple monk in his monastery were subject to his scrutiny. As lord chancellor, Wolsey made the Court of Chancery and the Star Chamber the core of his temporal authority, shaking the great barons "by the ear" and teaching them respect for the king's law. Long before the real king assumed plenary power over his subjects' souls as well as their bodies, the Great Cardinal had marked the way.[2]

Wolsey's major interests were directed more toward diplomacy than toward reform within the church, and in his young master he found a student eager to step out upon the continental stage and make England's weight felt in the diplomatic balance of power. Young Henry with his golden beard and angel's face was the hope of philosophers, the friend of scholars, the image of physical perfection, and the pride of England. The whole world rejoiced "in the possession of so great a Prince" and all things were suddenly "full of milk, of honey and of nectar." In the words of the Venetian ambassador, the king united "such corporal and mental beauty as not merely to surprise but to astonish all men." Though he wasted his patrimony and turned the chilly court of the first Tudor into a glittering palace of dance and music, the prince carried out at least one of his father's deathbed wishes: in 1509 he married the twenty-four-year-old Catherine of Aragon. The new queen had been a friendless and penniless exile in England ever since the death of her first husband, Prince Arthur, in 1502. Whether a frail boy of fourteen and a Spanish lass of fifteen were ever active in the connubial bed will never be known. Years later, when the question was of vital importance, Catherine swore the marriage had never been consummated and that Henry was free from sin in marrying his brother's widow. Certainly the young Henry was fond of his Spanish wife, if not especially faithful. Catherine did her best; she produced three stillborn children, two infants who died within the month, and the Princess Mary. The birth of the princess in 1516 gave new hope to the royal couple. "They were both young," Henry said, and "if it was a daughter this time, by the grace of God the sons will follow." That God's grace might not be forthcoming was a possibility that the king would not consider; he was far too concerned with feats of war to worry about such an improbability.

---

[2] For the controversy over Wolsey's character, see the first half of Scarisbrick's *Henry VIII*, A. F. Pollard, *Wolsey* (1929), and C. W. Ferguson, *Naked to Mine Enemies* (1958).

The Lessons of Diplomacy

War and diplomacy in the sixteenth century were the last aspects of society to divest themselves of the language and mentality of the medieval past. The old confusion between war and peace prevailed; the goals of diplomacy were rarely commercial or economic; and war was still viewed as a glorious end in itself and not as an instrument of foreign policy. The moment that an eighteen-year-old sovereign replaced an elderly and parsimonious parent upon the throne of England, it was to be expected that he would cast his eyes toward Europe and join the noisy and complex game of continental diplomacy in which the dramatic, the magnificent, and the romantic were of more concern than the practical, the calculated, or the profitable. Young King Henry entered the European arena because he was "not unmindful that it was his duty to seek fame by military skill," and because he wanted to "create such a fine opinion about his valour among all men that they would clearly understand that his ambition was not merely to equal but indeed to excel the glorious deeds of his ancestors." Chivalry may have been dying in the dark attic of the exchequer, but it was very much alive in the glitter of the courts of kings.

The admiration of all men was devoutly to be wished, but the opinions that counted most in diplomatic circles were those of two rival princes— Francis I, the Most Christian King of France, and Charles V, His Most Catholic Majesty of Spain and Emperor of the Holy Roman Empire. Both sovereigns were young and came to power within six years of Henry's succession to the crown. Among the three a boisterous and chivalric rivalry existed, and it was indicative of the intimate nature of international relations that, when Francis ascended his throne, Harry of England should have immediately inquired of the French ambassador whether the new king had a well-turned leg. When the ambassador admitted that his sovereign's legs were "sparse," Henry proudly indicated his own thigh and boasted, "Look, here! And I have also a good calf to my leg."

Despite a shapely limb and a full treasury, Henry was at a disadvantage when it came to European war and diplomacy. Compared to France and Spain, England was weak in wealth and population and, geographically, she was located on the periphery of the diplomatic arena. She could not strike at France without risking Scottish invasion through her back door; she could not antagonize Charles of Spain since he was also archduke of Burgundy and lord of the Low Countries, where English wool found its way into the European market. Italy, Milan, Venice, Naples, and the Papal States were the central attractions in the chivalric antics of diplomacy and war which were carried on furiously, if inconsequentially, between Valois France and Habsburg Spain. Italy was the courtesan of the European community of nations, and the younger powers fought in a noisy and ostentatious fashion for her doubtful virtues and manifest charms. The young princes of Europe had learned to tax their subjects, and they hastened to send their armies into Italy to plunder or purchase the art and luxury of the Renaissance. Francis I offered to choke Benvenuto Cellini with gold if he would condescend to practice his goldsmith's trade in Paris. Henry VIII had the money to buy his way into the diplomatic game but he could enter the Italian scene only by proxy.

One final personality must be added to this already crowded international scene: the great Cardinal Wolsey, who advised his young sovereign, catered to his youthful pride, and used diplomacy to further both his own ambitions and the peace of Europe. As a diplomatist Wolsey served three masters—the dynastic desires of his king, the interests of the papacy which had conferred upon him the unprecedented title and authority of legate *a latere,* and finally his own aspirations to be the honest broker in the Habsburg-Valois controversy. Though the cardinal strove manfully, he ultimately proved the impossibility of serving three masters well, especially in diplomacy where calculation and reason were constantly thrust aside by chivalric whim and the chances of war.

Henry VIII's first taste of foreign politics was disagreeable but salutary. In 1511 he entered the Holy League of doubtful name in order to help the Roman pontiff hold the balance of power between Spain and France. England, Venice, Spain, and the papacy confronted the aggressive actions of the French in Italy. English troops were sent into southern France where they promptly got sick on green wine, mutinied, and returned home without orders—hardly the heroic picture the young king had in mind. The following year Henry went in person to earn military renown in France, and in August of 1513 at the Battle of the Spurs he succeeded in defeating a French army. More enduring and possibly even more glorious, despite the king's absence, was the victory over the Scots that his soldiers won in September of 1513 at Flodden Field. Ten thousand of the king's enemies are said to have fallen there, including James IV of Scotland, while the English, led by the earl of Surrey, lost less than three hundred men. It is little wonder that contemporaries felt divine intervention to be manifest in such a feat, and Queen Catherine promptly wrote her husband in France to be sure he offered thanks to God. Henry may have been irritated at a deity who sanctioned such a marvelous victory in his absence, but he did the gentlemanly thing and rewarded Surrey with the dukedom of Norfolk.

The war with France was punctuated by the usual broken promises, diplomatic turncoats, and bad feelings among the erstwhile allies. In the end Henry and Wolsey found it to their advantage to make peace with France and to marry off the king's youngest sister, Mary Tudor, to Louis XII. The marriage was a mere diplomatic escapade, for Louis was sixty, his English wife eighteen, and the French king only survived three months of wedded bliss. In 1514 dynastic rivalry was intensified by the accession of Francis I, who commenced his reign with a major bid for French hegemony in Italy. At Marignano in 1515 Francis crushed the armies of the duke of Milan, and all of northern Italy lay prostrate before him. The battle of

Marignano badly upset the diplomatic balance, and Cardinal Wolsey began to worry lest the Roman pontiff become a French chaplain and the church be brought captive a second time to Avignon. The diplomatic scene was again changed in 1516 by the appearance of the third of the princelings of Europe; Charles, Duke of Burgundy, "void of all excess, either of virtue or vice," became king of Aragon and Castile. Wolsey quickly allied England to the new master of Spain, at the same time joining the pope and the Emperor Maximilian of Germany in an effort to curb French pretensions in Italy. When Maximilian died in 1519, however, any idea of countering the French menace was put aside, and the three royal gentlemen of Europe competed loudly for the imperial election and title. Charles, as the late emperor's grandson, was the inevitable winner, and suddenly the immense power of Spain, the Holy Roman Empire, and the Lowlands, together with the Spanish gold and silver of the New World, were united in a single person.

Despite the dangerous preponderance of power in the emperor's hands, Wolsey and his king continued to favor an imperial alliance. In part the decision reflected economic necessity since Charles could terminate at will English trade with the Lowlands; in part it was habitual since no one could remember a time when England had not been at war with its inveterate enemy France; in part it was dynastic since the new emperor was the nephew of Henry VIII's wife, Catherine of Aragon; and in part it was personal since Charles dangled the bait of a papal election before the covetous eyes of Cardinal Wolsey and his ambitious master. Consequently, in 1522 England again found herself at war with France; but the hollowness of English diplomacy was revealed three years later when it became apparent that a victory for the emperor was tantamount to a defeat for England. In 1525 at Pavia, Charles destroyed a French army and took captive the Most Christian King of France. Italy and for a moment all Europe fell before the emperor. England, from being the fulcrum of the European balance of power, sank to the level of a second-rate principality that was suffered but not seriously considered by the Imperial Leviathan. The realities of power were obvious in 1527 when Spanish troops, sent to remind His Holiness that he was no longer a French flunkey but a Spanish chaplain, mutinied and sacked the holy city. The situation for Wolsey was serious in the extreme; just when his spiritual master had become the helpless prisoner of Spanish troops, his royal master demanded something that only the emperor or an independent pope could grant: a divorce from his fat, sterile, forty-two-year-old wife, Catherine of Aragon.

The King's Great Matter

It is not necessary to enter into the debate over whether Henry was infatuated by a young lady of the court named Anne Boleyn who indignantly refused to become his mistress and held out for marriage and a crown, or whether he actually felt the need for a male heir to secure the succession.

Nor is it particularly profitable to speculate whether the king was sincerely pricked in his conscience after eighteen years of married life with Catherine of Aragon because she had been his brother's wife, or whether, in the words of Shakespeare, "his conscience has crept too near another lady" of the court. Only three facts are beyond dispute. First and most obvious, Henry wanted to marry Anne Boleyn, and to do so he needed an annulment, which only the pope could grant. Second, the succession was endangered by the existence of a legitimate female heir, the Princess Mary, and an illegitimate male heir, the duke of Richmond. Finally, there were the inescapable diplomatic facts that his wife's nephew was the most powerful sovereign in Europe and the pope dared not antagonize the man who controlled the silver mines of Peru, the markets of the Netherlands, the military might of Spain, and the destinies of Italy.

Henry in 1527 was in no hurry, and was content that Wolsey should accomplish the divorce [3] through the usual diplomatic and military means. The pope had to be rescued and freed so that he could grant a legal divorce. The only way to achieve this was through alliance with France and war with Spain—but such a policy lasted only so long as there was reasonable expectation that the emperor could be defeated in battle. By the summer of 1529 any such hope had become a figment of the cardinal's desparate imagination, and the evidence was mounting that Henry would never get his divorce through the normal channels. Caught between a rebellious king of England and an adamant emperor, the pope procrastinated. He refused to grant Wolsey authority to decide the divorce case in England, but he did send Cardinal Campeggio to open hearings. By late spring, however, Clement VII had decided to "live and die an Imperialist," and he dispatched secret orders to Campeggio to "decide nothing, for the Emperor is victorious and we cannot afford to provoke him." In July he commended Henry's case to Rome, and the court's ultimate decision was a foregone conclusion when, in August, France and Spain signed the Treaty of Cambrai, leaving Italy to Charles, and Wolsey to face his outraged master. Henry's reactions were ruthless and immediate. Cambrai was signed on August 3, 1529; the cardinal was jettisoned on October 9; and by November Henry had taken the first hesitant steps toward sundering the ancient and constitutional ties with Rome and establishing an independent Church of England.

Wolsey had served his master sufficiently well but in the end the authority that he prized the most—his legatine powers stemming from the spiritual core of Christendom—destroyed him, for suddenly it was remembered that his office of papal legate was a blatant violation of the ancient Statute of Praemunire, which outlawed the acceptance of direct papal jurisdiction. For all those who hated him, this was enough. The king was no sentimentalist either. Once the cardinal lost his usefulness, he was without

---

[3] Divorce is the term invariably used, but in fact the king did not ask for a divorce, since he argued that he had never been legally married in the first place.

The Habsburg Dynasty

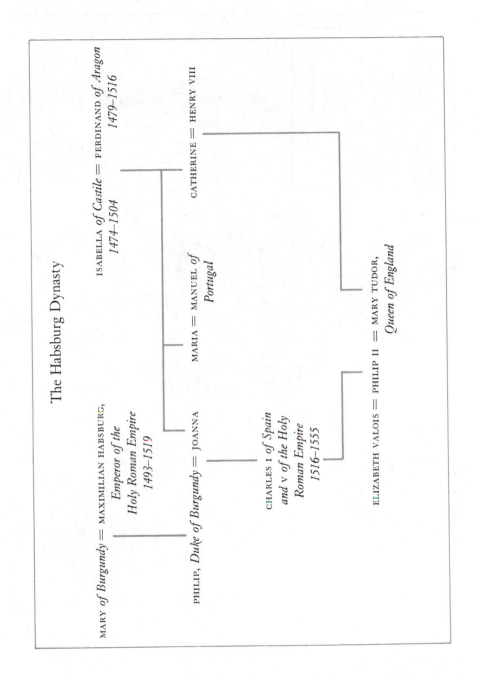

MARY of Burgundy = MAXIMILIAN HABSBURG,
Emperor of the
Holy Roman Empire
1493–1519

ISABELLA of Castile = FERDINAND of Aragon
1474–1504   1479–1516

PHILIP, Duke of Burgundy = JOANNA

MARIA = MANUEL of
Portugal

CATHERINE = HENRY VIII

CHARLES I of Spain
and V of the Holy
Roman Empire
1516–1555

ELIZABETH VALOIS = PHILIP II = MARY TUDOR,
Queen of England

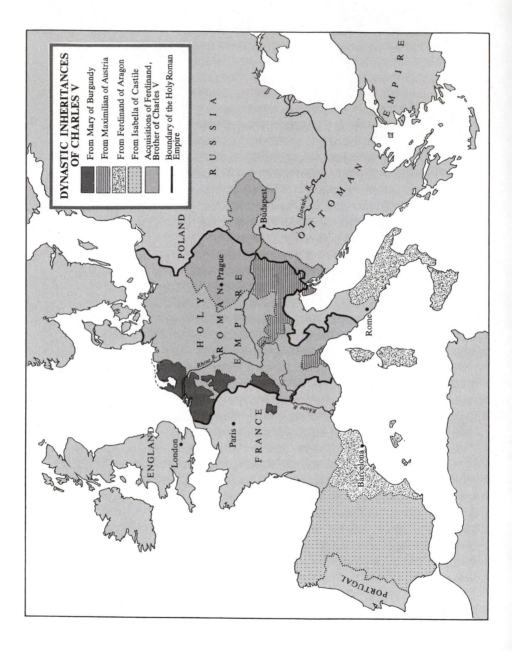

DYNASTIC INHERITANCES OF CHARLES V

- From Mary of Burgundy
- From Maximilian of Austria
- From Ferdinand of Aragon
- From Isabella of Castile
- Acquisitions of Ferdinand, Brother of Charles V
- Boundary of the Holy Roman Empire

RUSSIA

POLAND

OTTOMAN EMPIRE

Budapest

Danube R.

H O L Y

R O M A N • Prague

E M P I R E

Rhine R.

Rhône R.

Rome

ENGLAND

London •

Paris •

FRANCE

Barcelona •

PORTUGAL

defense, and Henry allowed the law to operate even though he himself had broken it by sanctioning Wolsey's legatine authority. There had once been a time when the Great Cardinal had believed himself the equal of his sovereign, but the loss of the things he prized most—wealth, authority, and respect—was evidence that ultimate power rested with the king. Had not death intervened, Wolsey might have faced the charge of high treason.

The king was justifiably perturbed by the course of events. Anne Boleyn continued to refuse him the full enjoyment of her charms, the pope showed every sign of denying his divorce, Charles V remained the obstinate defender of his aunt's marital rights, and Henry still needed a legitimate male heir. This last was the rub that made it impossible for him to listen to the various compromises presented by a pontiff frantic to please both king and emperor. Clement offered to grant a dispensation sanctioning the union of legitimacy and illegitimacy through the marriage of the Princess Mary to the king's bastard, Henry Fitzroy, Duke of Richmond; he urged Henry to take Anne as his mistress and promised to legitimize the children born out of wedlock; he tactfully suggested that Catherine retire into a nunnery, thus allowing him to permit Henry to remarry; he even toyed with the notion of sanctioning bigamy. But all of these fertile, if questionable, schemes fell afoul of the king's conscience and his determination that his offspring be unimpeachably legitimate. To achieve this end he needed a legal divorce and a legal wife, and these Clement was unable to give.

With Wolsey and his legatine powers gone, Henry sought some new authority to carry through his divorce, and in November of 1529 the Reformation Parliament was summoned. The body that met was unprecedented: it lasted seven years, enacted 137 statutes, of which 32 were of vital national significance, and exercised an influence in the affairs of God and church that no feudal parliament had ever dreamed of claiming. The divine and absolute authority of king in parliament was called forth, and the law as willed by Henry and proclaimed by parliament became "a never erring judge"—the instrument of revolution by which the medieval church was swept away.

In November of 1529 there was no real thought of risking a permanent break with Rome, but parliament, restless in its anticlericalism, was viewed as a useful cudgel with which to belabor the pope and possibly frighten that unhappy ecclesiastic into a more amiable frame of mind. In 1530 parliament passed a series of statutes aimed at the more obvious clerical abuses. A Mortuaries Act and a Probate Act were passed, limiting a lucrative source of ecclesiastical income from the probate of wills and the arranging of funerals. The following year the king turned on convocation and threatened to lay the entire church under ban of outlawry for having violated the Statute of Praemunire in recognizing Wolsey's legatine powers. The threat was sufficient to persuade the church to part with £119,000 and, more important, it was the lever by which Henry forced convocation to acknowledge him as the church's "singular protector, only and supreme lord, and as far as the law of Christ allows even supreme head." In angry silence bishops and priests submitted, and Archbishop Warham in presenting the new title wisely decided to accept silence as the equivalent of assent.

With the church thoroughly intimidated and the potential authority of the king as spiritual as well as temporal leader of the realm acknowledged by convocation, the government struck at the nerve center of the papacy—its sources of revenue. In the first Statute of Annates of 1532, parliament gave the king authority to abolish the traditional payment to the pope of the first year's income of all newly installed bishops. Unfortunately His Holiness remained more frightened of an emperor in his backyard than of a king in distant England, and it became painfully evident that if Henry were to have his divorce, it would have to be procured in defiance of the pontiff. Moreover, patience and time were running short, for Anne Boleyn had finally been bribed into compliance. In September of 1532 she was created marchioness of Pembroke with an annual income of £1,000; three months later she was pregnant; and on the 25th of January she was secretly married to the king. If Henry were to be saved from bigamy and his heir born on the right side of the blanket, less than eight months remained in which to divorce Catherine of Aragon.

Chance played into the king's hands, for in August of 1532 Archbishop Warham died. Unexpectedly Henry appointed in his stead an obscure forty-three-year-old Cambridge don who had first come to the monarch's attention for his strenuous, if scholarly, defense of the King's Great Matter, as the divorce was termed in academic and diplomatic circles. Both as a man and as one of the heroes of the English Reformation, Thomas Cranmer is difficult to judge, if only because he was the most timid, backsliding, and reluctant martyr ever to face the stake.[4] Cranmer united a rare literary talent, which could capture in prose the emotional intensity of religion, with a political naïveté that once led Henry to shout out in exasperation: "Oh Lord God! What simplicity have you" to permit every knave and enemy to take advantage of you? Yet the new archbishop's simplicity was his greatest asset, for he alone of the king's servants earned his master's love, and though in theology he shortly passed his sovereign by, the two were agreed on one vital tenet: Henry, not the pope, spoke for God.

The relationship between Henry and his deity was elementary: in return for a punctilious fulfillment of his religious obligations, God rewarded him with material success and eternal salvation. Should such blessings be withdrawn, then Henry assumed that he had inadvertently sinned, had somehow failed to carry out the exact religious formula, and therefore had earned God's wrath. When Catherine of Aragon failed to secure the suc-

---

[4] One's picture of Thomas Cranmer, who died a martyr's death in the reign of Catholic Mary, is still largely a matter of which book one reads. A. F. Pollard, *Thomas Cranmer and the English Reformation* (1904) and J. Ridley, *Thomas Cranmer* (1962) are by far the best.

cession with a male heir, the king searched his conscience for the source of such obvious divine malediction, and discovered in Leviticus the terrible warning that "if a man shall take his brother's wife, it is an unclean thing . . . ; they shall be childless" (20:21). God had long ago passed sentence upon that marriage, and it was up to Henry to right the wrong and propitiate his deity so that he might once again merit all the good things that heaven could bestow. Others might suffer from a sense of their own inadequacies and endure a feeling of sin and undeservingness, but Henry remained serene in the citadel of his faith—as a man, as a Christian, and as a king he knew God to be his ally. He treated his heavenly partner as he did his earthly colleagues; he expected God to live up to His duty and fulfill His side of the bargain by presenting the king with what he most desired: Anne Boleyn and a legitimate heir.

The moment that a frightened and demoralized pope sanctioned the appointment of Thomas Cranmer as archbishop, clerical reformation moved swiftly into ecclesiastical revolution. Before any divorce granted by the archbishop's court could be permanent, the queen's right of appeal to Rome had to be denied; this could only be achieved by cutting the constitutional links between England and the papacy. Therefore in April of 1533, one month after Cranmer's installation, parliament somewhat hesitantly obliged the king by enacting a statute of simple name but of momentous implication —the Act in Restraint of Appeals. By a stroke of the legislative pen it was decreed that all spiritual cases "shall be from henceforth . . . definitely adjudged and determined within the King's jurisdiction and authority" and "not elsewhere." A month later Henry appeared before a tribunal, whose authority now stemmed from the crown, to hear sentence delivered by a bishop of his own selection. To no one's surprise the king's marriage to Catherine was declared null and void, and Henry was able to present Anne Boleyn to the world as his lawful wedded wife. When on June 1, 1533, Anne was crowned queen, the final step in a carefully calculated plan was completed. Henry and his ministers had done their best to assure a legitimate male heir; the rest was up to God and Anne Boleyn, both of whom signally failed in their duty. To "the great shame and confusion of physicians, astrologers, witches, and wizards, all of whom affirmed that it would be a boy," the child that was born at three in the afternoon on September 7, 1533, turned out to be Elizabeth Tudor.

The Royal Supremacy

Henry was outraged that he should have been made ridiculous in the eyes of Catholic Europe. He had risked his crown and endangered his soul, and all he got for his efforts was yet another useless daughter to complicate the succession. A certain amount of consolation, however, could be taken in the knowledge that the child was healthy and the mother fertile. God would not forever withhold His favor; and in the meantime Elizabeth's

· ANNO · ÆTATIS ·   · SVÆ · XLIX ·

HENRY VIII, BY HANS HOLBEIN THE YOUNGER
"God and Caesar were joined." *Alinari.*

rightful claim to the throne had to be protected, the break with Rome completed, and Englishmen re-educated on the subject of religious truth. By the Act of Succession passed in March of 1534 subjects were warned to acknowledge in their hearts as well as their actions the fact that Henry's marriage to Anne was "undoubted, true, sincere, and perfect." During the spring the king was given authority to make all clerical appointments; a second Statute of Annates severed the financial ties with Rome; papal revenues were redirected to the king's treasury; the pope's name was stricken from the church's service; and in November of 1534 the constitutional revolution was solemnized by the Act of Supremacy, which acknowledged that Henry Tudor was "Supreme Head of the Church of England." The saving phrase, "as far as the law of Christ allows," which had been insisted upon by convocation four years earlier, was quietly omitted. God and Caesar were joined, and the medieval tenet that divine law stood higher than either man or society vanished when Henry VIII monopolized all secular and spiritual jurisdiction.

The doctrine of royal supremacy signaled the ultimate destruction of the monasteries. International monastic foundations were an anomaly within a national church, and they were soon viewed by the crown as seminaries of "factious persons" who recognized at heart, if not at law, an authority higher than that of the state. They constituted a sort of sixteenth-century fifth column and were a potential danger to the new ecclesiastical regime. Bishops and archdeacons, almoners and even simple priests had for centuries been in fact, if not in theory, servants of the crown, and the secular church had been the competent and complacent scullery maid of kings; but the monasteries and nunneries were different. They lived by their own rules, they were often exempt from episcopal discipline, and they traditionally advocated papal authority as a convenient balance to prying bishops and interfering monarchs. Though they bowed to the royal supremacy, they did not accept it in their hearts for, as one inmate confessed, he acknowledged the king "as supreme head for fear" but "could not find in his conscience" to believe it. Henry knew full well that a little conscience could be a dangerous thing, and it was deemed necessary and godly that monks and monasteries, nuns and nunneries should go.

The destruction was financially lucrative as well as politically expedient. Between 1536 and 1539 those "putrified oaks," as one contemporary called the monastic foundations, gave way, and land worth nearly two million pounds was nationalized. In destroying the monasteries, the state violated the law of God and man, for by confiscating almost one-tenth of the property of England, it accomplished, as Bishop Bonner complained, the shameless "breaking of the dead men's testaments, and their most godly intents and ordinances." Godliness, however, was forced to retreat before financial and political need. The treasures of the first Tudor had been squandered upon the wars and diplomacy of the second; the royal coffer was empty; and parliament, though willing to bless ecclesiastical revolution, was, as usual, reluctant to grant taxes. With the destruction of the monasteries Henry's income almost doubled, making him one of the richest sovereigns in European history; if he and his children had been able to retain the monastic loot, the English crown might have been assured a sufficient revenue, free of parliamentary purse strings. In that case parliament might never have found the instrument with which to transform the monarch into the servant of the landed classes. For better or for worse, Henry, his son, and his daughters had to sell the profits of the Reformation, and the monastic lands passed out of the hands of the crown. Country gentlemen who served well the Tudor dynasty profited the most, but merchants, lawyers, corporations, and well-to-do yeomen were all quick to purchase monastic estates from a government that faced bankruptcy.

The legend of a "golden shower" of lordships thrust upon a glutted market at bargain prices has been dissipated by modern economic research, which indicates that the estates and manors of the monasteries were sold by a government determined and usually able to get a good price. The picture of the king dispensing largesse with total financial abandon must be modified. Some property was doubtless given away to deserving Tudor workhorses and key officials of the shires, but the bulk was sold in order to pay for the king's wars and foreign policy. The effect, either intentional or accidental, was to commit the governing elements of the realm to the idea of a national church. Though the transfer of the monastic wealth to these groups ultimately destroyed the Tudor monarchy by depriving it of an independent landed income, it assured the permanent triumph of the Reformation, for the most important classes of the realm now had a vested interest in protecting property which a return to papal Catholicism might jeopardize.

The man who engineered the break with Rome, and who understood far better than the king the parliamentary means by which the old ecclesiastical constitution was being replaced, was Thomas Cromwell, whose father had been a brewer and blacksmith known for his drunkenness, disorderliness, and illegal commercial practices. In a short but feverish career, Cromwell encompassed soldiering in Europe, banking in Italy, marketing in the Netherlands, and practicing law in London. After Thomas Wolsey's fall from grace in 1529, Cromwell soon replaced the cardinal as Henry's chief minister, becoming principal secretary in 1534, vicar general in 1535, lord privy seal in 1536, and the architect of the new sovereign and theocratic state. Cromwell brought to government the same attitude of mind that an Italian banker brought to money—detachment, calculation, and practicality. Coldly factual and analytical, he belonged to that variety of councillor who saw government in terms of efficiency and effectiveness. He endeavored to construct a rational structure of government from the chaos of feudal privilege and overlapping medieval jurisdictions. His fiscal system was indicative of his tidy and categorical mind. For each kind of royal revenue a separate office was established, six courts or departments in all—the Exchequer to collect parliamentary grants and income from the customs, the Court of General Surveyors to administer all crown lands except the duchy of Lancaster (which had its own collecting agency), the Court of Augmentation to administer and milk monastic property, the Court of Wards to oversee the crown's feudal income, and finally the Court of First Fruits and Tenths to administer church revenues.

Whether it was the king or his minister who inspired the Reformation in England remains one of the most baffling questions of the reign. The

THOMAS CROMWELL
"Cromwell brought to government the same attitude of mind that an Italian banker brought to money —detachment, calculation, and practicality." *National Portrait Gallery.*

two men, one looking as much like a professional athlete as a king and the other more like a publican than a vicar general in matters spiritual, were different sides of the same coin. Henry "beknaved" his chief councillor twice a week, but Cromwell kept "as merry a countenance as though he might rule all the roost." And rule the roost he did, for Thomas Cromwell was the indispensable technician of the English Reformation, the man who phrased the key statutes that tore apart Christendom, who hammered out the details of the break with Rome, and who organized the destruction of the monasteries. The king's first great minister, Cardinal Wolsey, had been a priest and a papist, Cromwell was a lawyer and an M.P., whose encyclopedic mind and mastery of parliamentary techniques made possible the king's supremacy. The vicar general, however, was never more than the brains behind the king; he was no *alter rex*, and Henry himself supplied the willfulness and drive that sustained the revolution. It was truly said: the king was determined to "show his absolute power and independence of anyone."[5]

---

[5] The relationship between Cromwell and Henry VIII is discussed by G. R. Elton, "King or Minister?: The Man Behind the Reformation," *History* 39 (1954). The classic biography of Cromwell is R. B. Merriman, *The Life and Letters of Thomas Cromwell*, 2 vols. (1902). The best modern account is Elton, *Reform and Renewal: Thomas Cromwell and the Common Weal* (1972).

The new church that rose upon the ashes of the old remained Catholic and orthodox in every particular save one—it was English and Henrician, not Roman and papal. The man who assumed the mantle of ecclesiastical authority was no heretic; in his own estimation, Henry warranted the title of Defender of the Faith as much in 1534 as in 1522 when a grateful pontiff had presented that dignity in acknowledgment of the king's diplomatic support and his vigorous attack on Martin Luther. The church was in need of liberation, not reform, and Henry's ordained task was to free it from the devilish and foreign ministrations of a petty Italian potentate. The king's loyal subjects remained "obedient, devout, catholic and humble children of God." Canon law was still valid in English courts, the rights and authority of the ecclesia to excommunicate were maintained, and the church continued as an ordained and privileged institution with power to censor opinion, shape the minds of men, dictate morals, and, if necessary, to withhold the keys of paradise to those judged unworthy of God's salvation.

Henry had "destroyed the Pope but not popery," and ardent reformers, who demanded that the Supreme Head "get rid of the poison with the author," suspected with some justification that "the rich treasures, the rich income of the church, these are the gospel according to Harry." Though "zely people" found the king a sore trial, Henry himself was supremely confident that his religious *via media* was pleasing to God. The structure of his church, which reflected more the spirit of a generation which thought in hierarchical terms than the will of a consummately egotistical sovereign, was depicted in a woodcut showing Henry sitting in his majesty with the hand of God bestowing upon him the Book of Truth. At his feet in humble supplication kneel the archbishops, bishops, and ministers of the church, respectfully listening to Henry's interpretation of God's Word. At the bottom of the picture are the laity, obediently accepting their faith from on high, believing what those in authority tell them, and loyally reciting: "vivat rex." The "wine of obedience" and the "fatness and substance of religion" were carefully equated in a church that remained authoritarian to its core.

If the church remained largely Catholic and unreformed, the state did not. The Reformation in England called forth the modern Leviathan, the sovereign national state. What Henry II had tried, the eighth Henry achieved: the subjugation of an international priestly order which adhered to a spiritual and legal jurisdiction outside of and above the crown. The Act of Supremacy not only gave the monarch the authority of the pope, it also expressed a political creed that smashed once and for all the essential international duality of medieval Christendom. The fact that Caesar had won over the bishop of Rome in the struggle to monopolize God's representation on earth was nothing new. Caesaropapism had been customary for centuries in the eastern half of the Roman Empire. What was unique was the organ through which Caesar voiced his will. As the pope spoke through and for the international medieval church, so now the king spoke through and for the state. As the church could not err, so now the state claimed infallibility.

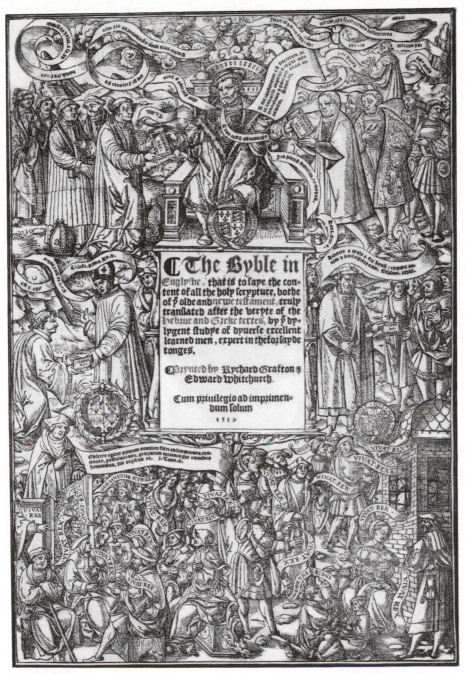

"VIVAT REX"

The frontispiece of the Tyndale translation, the *Byble in Englishe* of 1539.
British Museum.

Englishmen were confronted with the "new found article of faith" that a statute made by the authority of the entire realm could not be thought to "recite a thing against the truth." The nation-state, above which no power stood higher and which could make or unmake truth on the grounds of *raison d'état*, was heralded in the preamble to the Act of Restraint of Appeals, which read: "this realm of England is an empire . . . governed by one supreme head and king," and that the monarch is imbued with "plenary, whole and entire power, pre-eminence, authority, prerogative and jurisdiction to render and yield justice and final determination to all manner of folk."

Such was the story of the king's Great Matter and the break with Rome. Two questions, however, remain: how was Henry able to get away with a revolution that involved the nationalization of a fourth of all arable property, shocked the sentiments of possibly two-thirds of the population, and defied the sensibilities of all Christendom? And how did he exercise his new authority of "Pope, King and Emperor" in England?

The Floodgates of Reformation

7 If there is a lesson to be gleaned from history, perhaps it is the recognition of the perversity of causal relationships. It is astonishing in the extreme that the rage of spiritual battle known as the Reformation should have had its English inception in diplomacy, not psychology, in the accident of marriage, not the design of heaven, and in the court of kings, not the house of God. Across the channel in Europe the anguish of souls in mortal fear lest they fall into eternal damnation led such men as Martin Luther to regenerate and revolutionize the ancient church. When the medieval ecclesia would not or could not give them the spiritual aid and comfort for which they clamored, they turned their backs on Rome, defied its anathemas and set about constructing for themselves a new and deeply personal spiritual edifice in which they could find contentment. In England the constitutional cart came well before the spiritual horse. Only after the church had been established by an act of state were the floodgates opened and a spiritual reformation begun that continued unabated until 1660.[1]

The fact that the English Reformation commenced as a revolution of legal forms and not of religious content goes a long way toward explaining why Henry VIII succeeded in bringing the old church to heel. The king instinctively perceived a profound truth about his subjects: the inadvisabil-

---

[1] Even today it is difficult to find works dealing with the Reformation that are free from bias. The best description of the church before 1530 is H. M. Smith, *Pre-Reformation England* (1938). Three quite different but excellent surveys of the Reformation period are F. M. Powicke, *The Reformation in England* (1941); P. Hughes, *The Reformation in England,* 3 vols. (1954); and A. G. Dickens, *The English Reformation* (1964). For a new interpretation see G. R. Elton, *Policy and Police, the Enforcement of the Reformation in the Age of Thomas Cromwell* (1972). For the Scottish experience see G. Donaldson, *The Scottish Reformation* (1960).

ity of upsetting their traditional religious beliefs. The break with Rome involved few fundamental doctrinal or ceremonial changes. Except for omitting the name of the pope in their prayers, Englishmen continued to pray and kneel, to worship and to think in the old familiar ways. In fact, it is quite possible that in the more distant shires humble folk were unaware that any Reformation had taken place at all. For the moment, at least, Henry had achieved the impossible, for he was like "to one that would throw down a man headlong from the top of a high tower and bid him stay when he was half way down." Catholicism without the pope was the king's religious solution, a sort of *via media,* and the chronic problem of the last twelve years of Henry's reign was how to prevent the ecclesia of his own creation from falling further into Protestant heresy or sliding back to Rome.

The Failure of the Old Church

Though Henry enforced God's Word with Draconian measures, the secret of his success in maintaining the *via media* involved two other factors: the dearth of Englishmen willing to risk their lives in defense of the old ecclesiastical institutions, and the existence of a small but highly vocal minority, who viewed the rooting out of papal authority as the prelude to the creation of the kingdom of heaven on earth. In nationalizing the church, Henry did little more than give statutory recognition to the fact that time and history had passed the old ecclesia by. As a vast, ponderous, and conservative body, heavy with vested and corporate interests, the church of the early sixteenth century was the institutional incarnation of dying medieval cosmopolitanism. Kings and representative bodies had begun to forge special geographic preserves for their own laws and jurisdiction, transforming feudal kingdoms into nation-states and shattering the emotional and cultural unity of Christendom. The international church was out of touch with a generation that had turned away from the seamless cloak of Christ. God was French or English or German; and His vicar in Rome was finding it increasingly difficult to speak so many languages.

From the fourteenth century on, there had been growing resentment in England of the papacy and of the international character of the church. Englishmen darkly suspected that their interests and their taxes were being sacrificed to the aspirations of a foreign potentate residing in Rome. In 1417 the Pontiff, Martin V, bestowed a cardinal's hat upon Bishop Beaufort of Winchester, the richest subject of the English crown and the half uncle of Henry V. The pope failed to inform the English king of his decision, and Henry V angrily told his uncle that if he accepted the cardinal's hat he would have no bishopric to go with it since he would be deprived of his see. Not until 1427 did Beaufort attain the coveted title, and his promotion was bitterly resented by laymen and nobles who feared that he might support the interests of Rome in preference to those of England. Anti-foreign feelings were running so high by 1526 that the stolid English duke of Norfolk informed Cardinal Wolsey, on the occasion of his appointment as papal legate, that he gave not "a straw" for the cardinal's legatine and foreign powers but that he honored him because he was archbishop of York and cardinal within the English church, "whose estate of honour surmounteth any duke now being within the realm." A subject was to be known by his rank within the English hierarchy and not by some intruding authority from abroad.

The church, as the special vehicle by which God bestowed His grace upon man, maintained that it must be free to judge human transgressions without interference from temporal interests. The medieval ecclesia had been a state within a state, and over the course of centuries it evolved an intricate legal machinery to administer its own laws. Priests and clerics lived under the jurisdiction of the church, claiming benefit of clergy or immunity from the operation of royal law. Conversely, the crown's subjects found themselves under the church's jurisdiction in cases of divorce, disputed marriages, probate of wills, and other matters where moral and religious judgments were involved. The core of the problem revolved around the dichotomy of divergent loyalties. The Christian division of man into body and soul was paralleled in the medieval world by the duality of state and church, in which the spiritual and temporal authorities shared responsibility in the eyes of God for man's welfare, and divided between them the profits of his labors. In practice, however, this harmonious balance collapsed into a struggle over ultimate authority in which the church, by the sixteenth century, was the outstanding loser.

By the early years of Henry VIII's reign all the signs were pointing to a major crisis between church and state, and by 1514 public opinion was so inflamed against clerical pretensions that Richard Fitzjames, Bishop of London, had to ask the king to protect the bishop's chancellor from trial for murder. The case involved one of the most tragic mysteries of Lollard persecution. On the morning of December 4, 1514, Mr. Richard Hunne, merchant-tailor and suspected heretic, was found hanging by the neck from a beam in his prison cell. Ecclesiastical officials dismissed his death as suicide committed by a dangerous and deranged heretic, and a court of three bishops and twenty-five lesser clerics decreed that his body be burned. Public reaction was immediate and portentous. It was said that Hunne's arrest for Lollard heresy was nothing but a punishment inflicted upon a man who had refused to give up his dead child's winding-sheet as a burial fee to the local priest. A coroner's jury, far from accepting the story of suicide, returned a verdict of willful murder against Hunne's jailor and the bishop's chancellor, Dr. William Horsey. By English custom, Horsey would have stood trial before the king's court, but his benefit of clergy would have protected him from any sentence handed down by a secular tribunal. In order to protect his chancellor from an irate London jury, Bishop Fitzjames called on the king to prevent the trial, and he appointed Richard Kidderminster, Abbot of Winchcombe, to preach in convocation a reminder that trying a cleric in a royal court was contrary to the law of God, to the liberties of the church, and to a recent papal decree claiming that benefit of clergy exempted all priests in holy orders from any contact with secular authority. Kidderminster's sermon produced an uproar, and parliament petitioned Henry to allow a public hearing on the principle of benefit of clergy. The king himself presided, and, though the regal theologian remained a loyal and dutiful son of the church, there could be only one decision in such a clash between royal and papal claims. "Kings of England," Henry pronounced, "have never had any superior but God alone." When the young king became Supreme Head of the Church in 1534, he simply gave title to what he and his whole generation had known for twenty years.

The insistence by an international ecclesia upon a double standard—one for clerics and another for laymen—might have been accepted had not the church exposed itself to the charge of corruption. Corruption is an explosive word meaning different things to different people. Is the unchaste priest as corrupt as the judge who accepts a bribe? Is the student who cheats to be compared with the merchant who knowingly sells impure drugs? Was the church of pre-Reformation England as corrupt as passionate and righteous reformers claimed; was it, in fact, a bedlam of fornicating clerics, proud prelates, and unclean ritualists? The heart of the question is not so much a matter of comparing degrees of depravity as of establishing some standard of judgment. The medieval church had aimed high; it had claimed to be the possessor of a better way of life; and men tended to judge it in terms of those ideals.

Corruption in the church more than any other issue highlighted the contrast between the ideals of medieval life as taught by the ecclesia and the realities of daily existence as practiced by laymen and clerics alike. On all sides the ideals of society stood in stark and sorry contrast to the actual world. The church preached that the surest path to paradise was the way of the monastery; yet all of Christendom knew that monasteries and nunneries had become boarding houses for wealthy pensioners such as Lady Audley, who insisted on being accompanied at church by her twelve vocal dogs. Ideally bishops and prelates were good shepherds, healers of the soul, and guardians of the conscience. In fact, absenteeism and pluralism were destroying the spiritual health of the church; by 1520, in Oxfordship alone, 58 of the country's 197 parish priests were absentees. Everywhere it seemed as if the church had fallen to the temptations of the world, engaging in business, administration, and finance, and judging the good official to be more pleasing to God than the good cleric. By almost any ecclesiastical standard the church stood condemned; by the high ideals that it set for itself, the clergy was indeed "a source of pollution to the whole earth."

Had Henry faced an ecclesia with nothing to lose but its spiritual existence and a church backed by the respect of the laity, he never would have risked the break with Rome. Possibly he never would have thought of it and would have executed Cromwell as a dangerous and perverted radical. Concern for religion was not lacking, but respect for the old forms was obviously on the wane when Erasmus could write to an English bishop in support of the argument that "the expenses laid out on a monastery had better been bestowed on the poor."

As it was, the image of the ecclesia presented to both king and subject was the picture of Cardinal Wolsey loitering in his lordships and embodying in his person the most invidious clerical abuses. At the apogee of his power in 1527, besides being cardinal and papal legate, he was bishop of Winchester, archbishop of York, and abbot of St. Albans, the richest monastery in England. His ecclesiastical revenues approached £10,000, while the profits of justice and the gratuities and pensions presented by foreign princes and humble supplicants in his Court of Chancery raised the total to the princely sum of £50,000 per annum. Here indeed was a magnate of the church who would ultimately have to answer for the sin of avarice. Busy with the burdens of state, the cardinal never visited any of the dioceses of which he was bishop, and only at the end of his life did he travel northward for the first time to his archdiocese of York. His legatine authority from Rome gave him the means to sweep clean the ecclesiastical stables, but the man who was in the pay of both France and Spain could hardly be expected to take seriously the abuse of simony. The priest who sired a son and a daughter did not feel obliged to enforce the church's laws of celibacy; the prelate who built sumptuous mansions fit for kings (both York Palace and Hampton Court were taken over by Henry VIII) scarcely had time to relight the dying embers of spiritual zeal within the church; and the man who left the cure of souls to vicars and suffragans was in no position to criticize his ecclesiastical colleagues for absenteeism and pluralism. Worse, Wolsey used his legatine powers not to reform the church but to extend his personal control, building a vast structure of jobbery, the profits of which flowed into his silken pockets. The cardinal was the living symbol of the proud, unpreaching prelate. For many men and women the old church, the Roman Church, was the memory of the Great Cardinal, and the bishop of Rome was nothing more than a Wolsey writ large without the redeeming quality of being English. If the heart of the ecclesia had turned to gold and its soul had been consumed with greed, it is little wonder that few men could be found to defend it. England remained deeply religious but vocally anticlerical. A supreme head in Westminster Palace could be no worse than a cardinal legate in York House or a pope in Rome. Moreover, the royal prince was not to be judged by the same standards as the spiritual father. The Supreme Head could not be accused of pluralism, simony, absenteeism, and immorality. Henry made no pretense of a higher way of life. Papal bastards remained the scandal of Christendom, but royal escapades into infidelity neither shocked Christian sensibilities nor weakened respect for the crown. Henry was a man of the world, not of God, and he made no hypocritical claims to a more moral existence.

When a church can no longer engender respect, when it can no longer present a living example of a better and higher way of life, then it may endure as a fossil but it cannot expect men to sacrifice their lives for its protection. The largely bloodless nature of the English Reformation, more than any other symptom, revealed the apathy in the hearts of men.[2] The blood of the martyrs was not only the seed of the early church, it was the very soul of the ecclesia; and when the spirit of martyrdom died, so did the medieval church. Statistically, the break with Rome, the divorce of Catherine of Aragon, the enactment of the Royal Supremacy, and possibly even the destruction of the monasteries would have been voted down in a democratic election. But Tudor England fervently believed that the "better part" of society was more capable of leadership than the "more part," and neither part cared enough to defend to the death the institutions of the past. Archbishop Warham was no Thomas á Becket, and the "better part" of the realm was more concerned with preserving its skin than its soul, more interested in the citadel of man than in the City of God. Englishmen, one and all, knew well the adage "power is present, holiness hereafter."

Signs that the church was faltering in its leadership and losing its hold over the laity were everywhere manifest. In 1510 Dean John Colet elected to place the management of St. Paul's School under the guardianship of London businessmen and not in the hands of the clergy. There was, he said, "nothing certain in human affairs, yet he found the least corruption" in men who lived without hypocrisy by the standards of this world. The same doubts were evident in the economic decline of the monasteries. In Norfolk, Yorkshire, and Buckinghamshire the capital wealth of the religious foundations between 1480 and 1540, a period of considerable inflation, increased by only 1.13 percent, which was not enough to offset the normal depreciation caused by fire, decay, and inefficiency. In Norfolk only £136 or 2.6 percent of the monastic revenues went into the distribution of alms, and in Yorkshire the figure had fallen to less than 0.14 percent. When one of the essential spiritual justifications for monastic establishments was limited to such trifling sums, many laymen began to look elsewhere for more healthy means of fulfilling their charitable aspirations.

As the century wore on, Tudor England increasingly bred men like Sir Richard Riche, a devoted government workhorse who perjured himself at the trial of Sir Thomas More, attended to the torturing of Protestant Anne Askew, became a hot gospeler under Edward VI, and returned to the religion of his youth with Catholic Mary, founding a boys' school so that future generations could be brought up in the true faith. He finally resumed his Protestant creed under Elizabeth and personally destroyed the popish ornaments with which he had endowed the chapel of his school. Sir Richard

---

[2] Sir Thomas More, Bishop Fisher, and a handful of Carthusian monks were the only ones to lay down their lives in 1535 in defiance of the Act of Supremacy.

and his generation were content to bend with the variable wind of government policy and political expediency. They agreed with the old gentleman who argued that it was "safest to be of the religion of the king or queen . . . for he knew that he came raw into the world," and accounted it folly "to be broiled out of it."

Apathy and expediency were dignified by the political philosophy of Erastianism. The sovereign who had assumed the papal tiara as well as the royal crown could anathematize those who defied his doctrine even more effectively than could the Roman pontiffs, and the Tudors elevated political obedience into a creed sanctioned by God, legalized by statute, and enforced by the engine of the state. The question whether the king was beyond law and was protected by the divinity that "doth hedge a king" was a political and theological issue left in studied vagueness. Only one consideration prevailed: obedience to the king. He "who has not obeyed his Prince, let him die the death," for a man "owed all things save his soul" to his sovereign. Even his soul was closely scrutinized for the cancer of sedition, and it was promised a warm welcome in hell should it prove disloyal to God's lieutenant on earth. Bishop Richard Sampson stated the Erastian gospel of obedience in its most succinct form when he wrote, "the Word of God is to obey the King and not the Bishop of Rome."

The Reformation Spirit

Apathy and the creed of obedience explain much, but they do not account for the presence of a handful of men, righteous in their spiritual strength and adamant in their stand against evil, who saw the Reformation as something more than the removal of the pope's name from the liturgy and the lead from the roofs of monasteries. Throughout Europe and England men of faith were searching for a sense of spiritual security in the midst of worldly uncertainty. As the zeal of the old church declined and its leadership lagged, the medieval ecclesia could no longer offer the spiritual solace for which men of tender conscience so ardently sought. The prescribed formula, a balance between faith in divine grace and good works whereby the faithful strove to attain salvation, no longer offered certain men relief from sin and the hope of paradise. In Germany Martin Luther hurled inkpots at the devil in his despair and practiced his monastic calling until he was warned that his health could be endangered by such ceaseless prayers, vigils, and mortification of the flesh. "If ever a monk got to heaven by monkery," Luther confessed, "it was I." In England too a Cambridge scholar sought to find spiritual comfort to merit salvation by following the rules of prayer to the very letter. Little Thomas Bilney, because "our Lord doth bid us when we will pray to enter into our chamber and shut the door," thought it "a sin to say his service abroad and always would be sure to have his chamber door shut" when saying his matins. But Thomas Bilney could no more shut the door on his doubt and sense of guilt than Martin Luther could close his mind to the same dread, the terrifying fear that he did not deserve God's mercy.

The similarity between the religious anxiety of a Cambridge student and an Augustinian monk indicates the general failure of the old forms and rituals, which waxed all the more luxuriant as inward worship and conviction waned; the resemblance between their solutions is equally symptomatic of the universal appeal of the reformed faith. Luther in his monastery and Bilney in his college turned to the Bible. Quite independently they stumbled upon a profound truth: in hopelessness lay the seed of new promise, in despair was found new consolation. Luther read: "the just shall live by faith" (Romans i, 17); Bilney read: "It is a true saying, and worthy of all men to be embraced, that Christ Jesus came into the world to save sinners" (I Timothy i). Suddenly both men discovered that it was not necessary to warrant salvation. God's grace stood above justice; no amount of striving, no amount of good works, could earn a man a place in heaven, for God's mercy saved even the undeserving. Faith and faith alone could move mountains and save sinners, and the reformers of the sixteenth century were above all else men of uncompromising faith.

Doctrinally the reformed faith stemmed from Luther, but historically the memory of John Wycliffe and his army of simple Lollard followers helped to set the emotional stage in England, for though the fifteenth-century church had largely succeeded in purging the kingdom of overt heresy, it had not been able to fill the void in men's souls. During the 1520s the Lutheran heresy found a receptive audience, especially among Cambridge undergraduates gathered at the White Horse Tavern where new ideas were discussed and debated. It will never be known whether Lutheran tracts made converts, or whether dissatisfied but deeply religious and questioning minds like Bilney's discovered for themselves the same wonderful experience that had thrown "open the doors into paradise" for Martin Luther. Certainly for Englishmen as well as for Germans, Paul's words of encouragement to sinners became "a gate to heaven" and the source of their spiritual strength. For those who found "marvelous comfort and quietness" of soul in Scripture, the Bible and a profound sense of God's infinite mercy were sufficient to sustain them. They needed neither church nor cathedral, image nor ceremony to fortify them in their conviction. For fervent reformers there was no need of a mediator other than Christ between God and man, for it was faith alone that redeemed man in the eyes of God and inspired him to the Herculean task of living the righteous life. "No man," said John Hooper, "can possess the joys promised in the gospel, but such as study with all diligence to live after the gospel." This was the inner spirit that three centuries earlier had led men into the monasteries and had persuaded them to give their blood in defense of the church; in the sixteenth century this was the source of the dynamism which urged them to reform the world.

Though the king neither approved of the Protestant creed nor liked such "zely people," he well knew their value as militant storm troopers in defense of the royal supremacy. If the king's supreme headship was not to "lie post alone, hidden in the acts of parliament and not in the hearts of his subjects," he had to turn to those who regarded the political gains of a break with Rome as only a first step toward the spiritual triumph of hurling the pope and all his doctrines out of the realm. The religious radicals quickly became the dangerous but essential allies of the monarchy, and they trumpeted throughout the land the evils of the pernicious doctrines of the bishop of Rome. By 1536 the Church of England and especially the episcopal bench were heavily populated with zealous exponents of royal supremacy, who urged that constitutional revolution by act of parliament should pave the way for spiritual revolution by act of faith.

Acts Written in Blood

Henry could not depend solely upon the earnest exponents of religious change who felt close upon them the joys of salvation and the fires of damnation. He knew the truth of the political dictum: "Horror waits on Princes," for "out of subjects' fear groweth Princes' safety." The king was fearful for his own safety as well as that of his church, and he agreed with Bishop Gardiner that "it is better for edicts to be written in blood than in water." The instruments of terror which were forged to strike fear into the hearts of subjects and to hold the timid to a proper respect for the new church were twofold: the Act of Succession passed in March of 1534 and the Act of Treason enacted in December of the same year. The first was essentially a loyalty test, for the Act of Succession not only acknowledged Anne Boleyn to be the king's lawful wife but required that all subjects of legal age take an oath that "they shall truly, firmly and constantly" defend the statute "and all other acts and statutes made since the beginning of this present parliament." In other words, the oath was retroactive, and Englishmen had to swear not simply to accept the political and matrimonial results of the break with Rome but also the principles on which they stood. It was on this issue that the greatest of all of Henry's subjects, Sir Thomas More, forfeited his life.

On Wolsey's fall from grace in 1529, More followed him as lord chancellor. The appointment was heralded as the dawn of a new era in which the philosopher-statesman would guide the realm toward a utopian existence, for Sir Thomas More was England's most distinguished scholar and humanist. As the king moved closer to revolution, his lord chancellor grew increasingly alarmed and finally resigned his office in May of 1532 on the pretext of ill health. The principle at stake as far as More was concerned was not the divorce, nor even the defiance of Rome, but his unwillingness to acknowledge the state as the be-all and end-all of human existence. For More the realm, the crown, parliament, and even the law were subject to the common conscience of all Christendom. In divorcing himself from Catherine and his church from Rome, Henry was violating the unity of Christendom, the common heritage of Western Europe. "I can not perceive," Sir Thomas wrote in 1534, "how any member thereof may without the common assent of the body, depart from the common head." More's view was medieval and humanistic, and it ignored the new impulses of nationalistic prejudice and the realities of Machiavellian politics. Many men must have felt as More did, but few died for such an intellectual concept. Most Englishmen agreed with the worthy Dame Alice More, who scolded her husband when she visited him in the Tower: "I marvel," she said, "that you, that have always hitherto [been] taken for so wise a man, will now so play the fool as to lie here in this close and filthy prison and be content to be shut up among mice and rats, when you might be abroad at your liberty." [3]

Sir Thomas More, Bishop John Fisher, and a handful of monastics were the sole martyrs of the old church. They were destroyed by the Act of Treason which extended the meaning of sedition to include all those who did "maliciously wish, will or desire, by words or writings, or by craft imagine" the king's death or slander his marriage. More and Fisher died in 1535 but, for most people, the words of the Treason Act were sufficient to achieve conformity to the will of the king. Fear, as Bishop Bonner later confessed, was the underlying element of the Reformation for, he said, "fear compelled us to bear with the times, or otherwise there had been no way but one." That one way was the path of martyrdom. Bonner and his colleagues learned their lesson well when in 1540 they were presented with the proof that Henry's *via media* would be written in blood. In that year three Catholics were butchered as traitors for questioning the royal authority in matters spiritual, and three Protestants were consumed in the fire as heretics for questioning the tenets of the Catholic Church of England. The French ambassador was aghast at such terrifying justice and wrote: "It was wonderful to see adherents to the two opposing parties dying at the same time, and it gave offense to both."

In maintaining Catholicism without the pope and in demanding that the man cast down from the high tower stop halfway, Henry was confronted with a serious dilemma: was not the pope's doctrine the pope? Was not all that had been sanctioned and exploited by the papacy corrupted and desecrated by that association? If the pope had been proved false and satanic, how could Englishmen be sure that such an anti-Christ had not also been leading men into damnation by preaching a false doctrine about such matters as purgatory, the sacrificial mass, and the veneration of saints and images? "The Pope's doctrine is the Pope," said William Turner to Bishop

---

[3] The bibliography on More, the humanist, the martyr, the statesman, and the social scientist is mountainous. A start can be made with R. W. Chambers, *Thomas More* (1948); T. Maynard, *Humanist As Hero* (1947); J. H. Hexter, *More's Utopia: The Biography of an Idea* (1952); and R. Ames, *Citizen Thomas More and His Utopia* (1949).

Gardiner, "and ye hold still the Pope's doctrine, ergo ye hold still the Pope." Henry VIII had no intention of accepting the doubtful logic of such a syllogism or of permitting impudent inquiry as to whether "the state of our religion" after 1500 years "be established in mere idolatry." The *via media* of Catholicism without the pope was endangered from both the right and the left, and the government after 1536 was absorbed in closing the floodgates of change and in enforcing the royal supremacy upon a people deeply troubled by growing religious dissension and bitterness.

The Pilgrimage of Grace

The first shock came from the right. In the late summer of 1536 Lincolnshire and Yorkshire rose against a Tudor national despotism that was encroaching upon the ancient privileges and provincialism of the feudal north and against a Tudor church which had callously and blatantly rent asunder the corporate unity of Christendom. In Yorkshire the rebels called themselves the Pilgrims of Grace and placed badges upon their arms depicting the five wounds of Christ. For a moment it appeared that the life expectancy of the newborn national state would be short, for the rebels showed signs of actually reaching London. Fortunately for the Tudor government, the two uprisings were badly coordinated. Moreover, the rebels knew what they did not want better than what they hoped to achieve. The Pilgrimage was essentially the culmination of widespread antagonism to every aspect of the Tudor regime. The badge of religion produced the appearance of unity, for all malcontents could unite in defense of the monasteries and the old church. Beneath the surface, however, divergent class interests weakened the Pilgrimage and gave the government time to arm. The old feudal nobility, men who lived in the tradition of the Nevilles and the Percys, were aggrieved that their family prerogatives and ancient privileges were being infringed upon by a professional bureaucracy in London which had established a district office in the northern shires—the King's Council for the Northern Parts. They complained that their traditional right to be represented on the king's council was being usurped by commoners and parvenus, and that a blacksmith's son held sway where once nobles of ancient lineage had guided the realm and advised the king. Lesser folk were agitated by high taxes, and the peasants felt themselves to be threatened by the steady encroachment of enclosures, which the government would not or could not prevent.

The immediate cause of the Pilgrimage of Grace was the publication in July of 1536 of the Ten Articles, which of all the Henrician religious formulas reflected most strongly the growing influence of reformers frantic to purge the church of both pope and popery. Specifically, the traditional seven sacraments were cut to three, and Protestant ideas about the inefficacy of prayers for souls in purgatory were accepted. One of the most persistent demands of the rebels was the return of the missing four sacraments. Henry was brutal in his handling of the Pilgrimage; his vanity was outraged by "rude commons of one shire" and the "most brute and beastly of the whole realm," who had dared to defy God's viceroy on earth and had failed to learn the truth of the dictum that "the King's wrath is death."

The monarch, however, was not blind to the dangerous discontent behind the rebellion. The moment it was crushed he turned to the question of religious uniformity, for now that he had assumed the authority of the bishop of Rome he was responsible for the faith of his flock. Three turbulent years passed, in which Henry's "simple loving subjects" spent their time "arrogantly and superstitiously" debating theological niceties and religious novelties in taverns and alehouses with ever increasing vehemence. When one impassioned but impractical reformer could advocate the reading of Scriptures in a brothel, while an equally dogmatic defender of the old faith wanted to see the heads of all the reformers impaled upon a stake, it was obviously time for the Supreme Head of the Church of England to speak *ex cathedra* so that his obedient subjects might know the truth and live in concord and quiet. The difficulty was that diplomatic and marital problems continued to bemuse and befuddle the purity of religious policy.

HENRY VIII IN LATER LIFE "The King's wrath is death." *British Museum.*

Religion, Matrimony, and Diplomacy

England's only allies were the Lutheran princes of Germany, but so long as the stubborn and historic rivalry between Valois France and Habsburg Spain continued, Henry felt his crown and his supremacy to be relatively secure. Unfortunately the diplomatic kaleidoscope continued to shift with senseless regularity, and at home the threat of disputed succession continued to hang over the kingdom. Anne Boleyn had produced a future queen, but the Princess Elizabeth in many sensitive minds remained the child of sin and bastardy. Worse, Anne was unable to fulfill her obvious wifely and royal duty by presenting the king with further live children. Whether Henry's eye was again attracted by a lady of the court or whether, having risked so much for a male heir, he was determined to try again is not clear, but once the king had set his mind upon a new wife, Anne's destruction followed with terrifying speed. On January 8, 1536, Catherine of Aragon finally died, and Henry, dressed in brilliant yellow, celebrated the occasion with a festive ball; but the old queen's death signaled the destruction of the new queen. With both wives dead, Henry could remarry and no one could claim the union illegal or the results born in sin. Within three weeks fate struck Anne the final blow—she was delivered of a dead baby on January 29. By May she had been accused of high treason and adultery, and on the 19th she was executed.

For Anne, Henry had performed miracles, taming the ancient and arrogant church and thereby transforming a medieval dragon into a modern pet; but marriage to the lady had proved to be neither fruitful in the bedchamber nor tranquil in the parlour. Anne Boleyn was a better mistress than queen, and she allowed the breath of adultery to touch her married life. The charges of adultery and incest with her own brother were patently false, but the queen had on occasion acted with indiscretion, and she soon learned that in royalty a double standard existed; kings could cut extramarital capers with impunity; queens could not be touched by even a hint of infidelity, lest the legitimacy of their children be placed in doubt. Eleven days after Anne's execution, on May 30, 1536, Henry married once again. This time he chose Jane Seymour, who left no mark upon her husband but who nevertheless fulfilled her nuptial vows to be "bonair and buxom in bed and at board." Though she died from the consequences, she gave birth on October 12, 1537, to the future Edward VI.

With Anne Boleyn dead and the succession secured, it seemed that the king might be able to settle the religious issue to his liking—in a highly orthodox fashion. In May of 1539 parliament was called upon to fulfill the ultimate logic of the English Reformation, when, for the first time in history, the faith of Englishmen was legislated upon by the authority of the sovereign national state in the guise of statutory law. The Act of Abolishing Diversity of Opinion reavowed transubstantiation, communion in one kind, celibacy of the clergy, private masses, and auricular confession. All five

MARY

EDWARD

points had been issues of growing controversy. Each was decided in a strongly Catholic manner and accepted by a realm which was still overwhelmingly conservative and viewed the bill as the "wholesomest act ever passed."

Conservative and orthodox as these measures were, they did not stand alone nor could they be divorced from diplomatic considerations. The Act for Abolishing Diversity of Opinion remained largely unenforced during the period when it was wise for England to appear less Catholic and more Lutheran. Throughout 1539 Henry was alarmed by the thought of diplomatic isolation and by the possibility that France and the emperor might patch up their ancient feuds and turn upon the schismatic enemy, England. For the moment the danger was so great that conservatism in religion was put aside, and the king allowed himself to be stampeded into an alliance with the Lutheran princes of Germany and marriage with Anne of Cleves in January of 1540. The instant, however, that Francis and Charles proved that they disliked one another more than they disliked their cousin Henry, the king returned to the conservative position. In July Thomas Cromwell

"The time to worry had arrived, for a new generation was about to take control." *National Portrait Gallery and the Lord Chamberlain's Office.*

ELIZABETH

paid with his head for having dragooned the king into the German marriage alliance with Anne of Cleves. His mistake was not simply a diplomatic one, for if any man symbolized the forces of change and Reformation it was the king's vicar general in matters spiritual. Consequently, when Henry determined on orthodoxy in religion, his minister was sacrificed to satisfy the conservative party. Within days of Cromwell's death, Anne of Cleves was divorced and became instead Henry's "loving sister." On July 28, 1540, the king married Catherine Howard, the protégé of the conservative faction at court. Mistress Catherine lasted eighteen months and left at her execution nothing but a broken, white-haired sovereign of fifty-two, who had grown suddenly old from the knowledge that his vivacious teen-age wife, the apple of his elderly eye, was not after all a "rose without a thorn." Catherine proved to be no virgin before her marriage and dangerously silly, if not overtly adulterous, afterward. She paid for her carefree delinquencies with her life in March of 1542, and a law was passed making it illegal henceforth for a maiden who was not a virgin to wed the monarch, a limitation which, the French ambassador noted, excluded most of the ladies of the court.[4]

The concluding years of Henry's reign were taken up in warring with France and Scotland, prescribing the truth for his subjects, marrying a respectable widow who could double as nursemaid for an unpredictable and increasingly difficult old man, and preparing for the day when the king must die. In Catherine Parr, Henry found his most dutiful, if least romantic, spouse; and in war he sought distraction from the afflictions of old age— gout, obesity, an ulcerated leg, and general weariness. Again the king's armies were victorious, and at the battle of Solway Moss in November of 1542 the army of yet another Scottish sovereign was routed by English troops. James V died, it was said, of shame at the behavior of his soldiers, and he left behind him a six-day-old heiress, Mary Queen of Scots, Henry VIII's grandniece and the lady whose manifest charms, questionable intrigues, and legal claim to the Tudor throne bedeviled both Scottish and English history. In France between 1543 and 1546 Henry was also victorious, but his military efforts ultimately had but one lasting consequence: the expenses of war forced him to part with a substantial portion of his monastic riches, which were quickly acquired by those harbingers of a future political system, the landed country gentlemen.

In religion, as well as war, the aging monarch exercised his will, but the results were equally ephemeral. In the *King's Book*, published in 1543

---

[4] A great deal of history can be gleaned from various novels and biographies dealing with Henry's many wives, who can be neatly recalled to mind by reciting the following:

Divorced, beheaded, died;
Divorced, beheaded, survived.

The following is a short list of some of the works on the king's spouses: G. Mattingly, *Catherine of Aragon* (1941); H. W. Chapman, *Anne Boleyn* (1974); L. B. Smith, *A Tudor Tragedy: The Life and Times of Catherine Howard* (1961); and A. Martienssen, *Queen Katherine Parr* (1974).

and carefully scrutinized by the royal eye, the Supreme Head of the Church of England presented his final opinion on religious matters. The new document was largely Catholic in creed and antipapal in sentiment, and it placed heavy emphasis on obedience. The proper role of Christians living in this world, as far as Henry was concerned, was that they should live "soberly, justly and devoutly," for the king reminded his people that God "hath ordered some sort of men to teach others, and some to be taught," and that the surest road to heaven lay along the path of obedience to "such order as is by us and our laws prescribed."

Religious sobriety lasted only as long as the king, and the *via media* of a Catholic Church without the pope came to an end almost the moment that the huge and bloated sovereign died on January 28, 1547. Henry left behind him subjects of many minds, who, oddly enough, had one thing in common—they had loved this bulging bully of a king, whose single redeeming quality of great personal magnetism had held both Catholics and Protestants loyal to his person. Neither that godly imp Edward VI nor his neurotic half-sister, Bloody Mary, was ever able to command the same devotion. Henry's church, the anomaly of a Catholic ecclesia to which had been grafted the royal supremacy, ultimately rested upon the king's massive personality. Now in the new year of 1547 a child-king sat upon the throne. During the king's lifetime men of conservative inclination, like Bishop Gardiner, had feared "not these fond malicious follies" of the Protestant reformers, but "when those that now be young shall . . . win a contempt of religion"; then was the time to worry "what is like to ensue thereof." In 1547 the time to worry had arrived, for a new generation was about to take control.

LORD BURLEIGH AND THE COURT OF WARDS AND LIVERIES, CA. 1590.
The Goodwood Picture Collection.

III

UNEASY EQUILIBRIUM
1547 to 1603

The Little Tudors

That serene and invincible prince, Henry VIII, was dead, and England stood upon the threshold of two reigns which would prove conclusively that the secret of effective government in the sixteenth century resided in the resplendent personality of the sovereign rather than in Cromwellian calculation, Wolseyan justice, or ministerial efficiency. An *alter ego* is no *alter rex*, and though Wolsey, Cromwell, and later Elizabeth's chief ministers (the two Cecils) spoke for the sovereign, they always exalted, never depreciated, regal authority which belonged solely to the king. In 1547, however, a new and dangerous situation was at hand, and the truth of the adage, "Woe to the land where the King is a child," was about to be realized. The new sovereign, Edward VI, reigned but did not rule, and an *alter rex* stood at the head of state even if he did not sit upon the throne.[1]

The Lord Protector

The succession of that godly imp, the nine-year-old son of Jane Seymour, had been established by parliamentary statute in 1543 and by his father's last will and testament. Henry bequeathed the crown imperial first to Edward, then to his daughters Mary and Elizabeth, and finally to the offspring of the marriage of his sister Mary and his old friend Charles Brandon, Duke of Suffolk. Significantly, the children of his elder sister Margaret, who had married James IV of Scotland, were not included in the

---

[1] W. K. Jordan, *Edward VI* (2 vols., 1969–70) is the best study of the king and his reign. Mary, Somerset, Northumberland, Paget, Edward VI *et al.* are beginning to attract considerable scholarly attention. See H. F. M. Prescott, *Mary Tudor* (1953), E. H. Harbison, *Rival Ambassadors at the Court of Queen Mary* (1940), B. L. Beer, *Northumberland* (1974), and S. R. Gammon, *Statesman and Schemer: William, First Lord Paget, Tudor Minister* (1974).

succession. Henry's testament was more than a bequest; it was a constitution. The ferocious personality of the old sovereign was replaced by a council of sixteen "entirely beloved councillors" who were empowered to govern the realm during the young king's minority, and Edward was strictly enjoined by his father never "to change, molest, trouble nor disquiet" his legally appointed advisers. More remarkable still, the autocratic old monarch named no single man to rule the kingdom but instead imposed a strict majority rule upon a council of regency which was composed of absolute equals. Henry's purpose is in doubt, but he had good cause to fear that once the dark shadow of his own authority had vanished, the regal sapling would be destroyed by factional intrigue and religious strife. The Tudors had come to the throne in the wake of the murder of the two Yorkist princes by an uncle of legendary wickedness. It remained to be seen whether sixty-two years of Tudor rule had sufficiently revitalized the crown so that it could withstand another Edward and another minority. History did not repeat itself, for the young king's uncle, Edward Seymour, Earl of Hertford, coveted not his nephew's throne; he was content with the dignity of lord protector.

The dead lion was to be feared less than the live rabbit. Within four days of Henry's death, his will was violated, his most dire pronouncements ignored, and Edward Seymour elevated by the council to the office of lord protector and governor of the king's person. Government by a council of regency had been the fashion in the fifteenth century, but it was regarded as dangerously anachronistic in an age that was authoritarian to its core. Most men agreed that a protectorate was "both the surest kind of government and most fit" for the commonwealth, and that no man had a better right to the office of lord protector than the new king's uncle. It was by no means certain, however, whether even a protectorate could replace the prestige of royalty and give direction to a country suddenly liberated from the will of a despotic monarch and beset with a host of economic, religious, diplomatic, and political problems.

The keystone of Tudor governmental structure was the existence of a directive authority which could determine policy and fill the bureaucracy with vitality. Devoid of leadership, the Tudor regime tended to rot; the feudal tradition that office was more a private sinecure than a public trust and that royal finances were more a personal source of profit than a governmental responsibility still thrived in such places as the Exchequer, the Chancery, and the Court of Augmentations. Personal loyalty to the monarch, heavily fortified by the fear of the king's wrath, had instilled into Henry's government a reasonable degree of honesty. Respect for the old king had been grounded upon an almost atavistic fear that Henry, as God's lieutenant on earth, could scrutinize and root out the secret treason hidden in the reaches of a subject's heart, and upon the conviction that the wages of disobedience were the soul's damnation. In puny contrast, Seymour was simply the king's maternal uncle; merely a man of "fit age and ability" to rule in Edward's stead. No Tudor blood coursed through his veins, no di-

The Tudors: 1485–1603

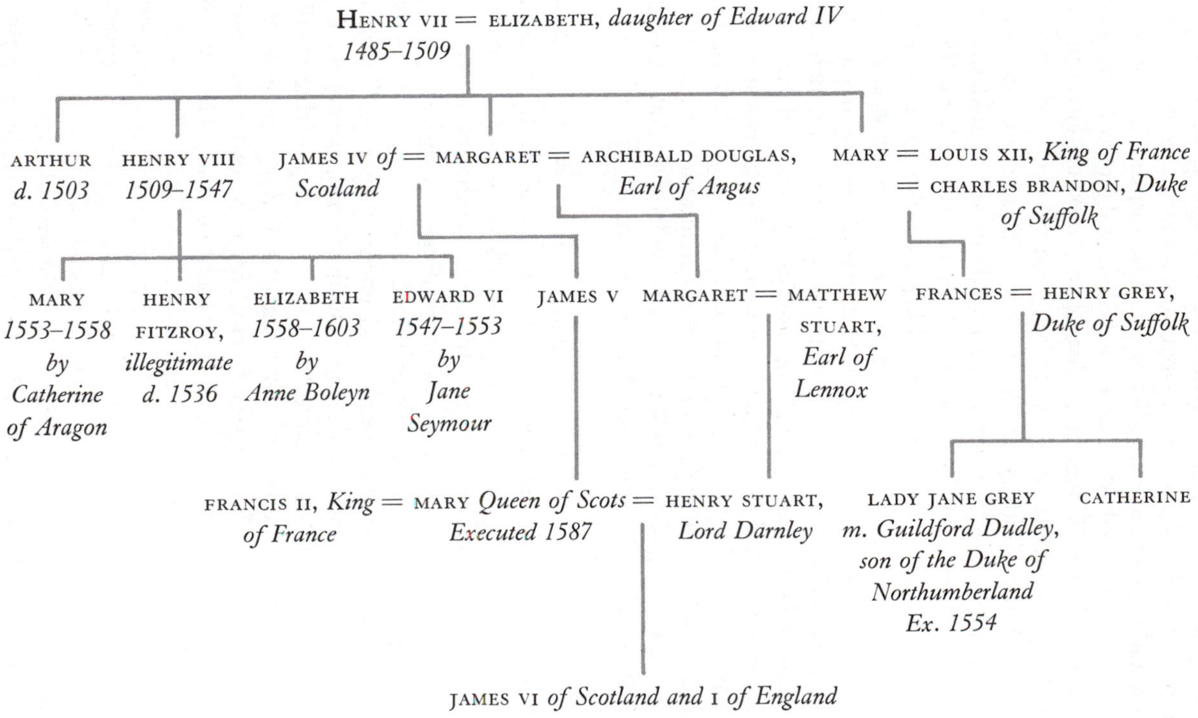

HENRY VII = ELIZABETH, daughter of Edward IV
1485–1509

ARTHUR
d. 1503

HENRY VIII
1509–1547

JAMES IV of = MARGARET = ARCHIBALD DOUGLAS,
Scotland   Earl of Angus

MARY = LOUIS XII, King of France
     = CHARLES BRANDON, Duke
       of Suffolk

MARY
1553–1558
by
Catherine
of Aragon

HENRY
FITZROY,
illegitimate
d. 1536

EDWARD VI
1547–1553
by
Jane
Seymour

ELIZABETH
1558–1603
by
Anne Boleyn

JAMES V   MARGARET = MATTHEW
                     STUART,
                     Earl of
                     Lennox

FRANCES = HENRY GREY,
          Duke of Suffolk

FRANCIS II, King = MARY Queen of Scots = HENRY STUART,
of France   Executed 1587   Lord Darnley

LADY JANE GREY
m. Guildford Dudley,
son of the Duke of
Northumberland
Ex. 1554

CATHERINE

JAMES VI of Scotland and I of England

vinity hedged his person, and respect for his office was solely contingent upon his personal ability to win esteem and exercise leadership.

In theory the authority of the Tudors stemmed from God, but in reality their power rested upon the cooperation of subjects who were constantly bullied and cajoled but who always could be inspired by the presence of the king. Henry once called himself "a father and nurse to his subjects," and in a way all the Tudors regarded themselves as governmental nannies appointed by a higher authority to rule, but ultimately dependent upon the devotion of the children of the nursery. Henry, on occasion, could be almost oriental in his aversion to his rebellious and thankless subjects whom he threatened to make "so poor that they could not have the boldness nor the power to oppose him." Yet for all his grumbling, the old king had relied upon their goodwill. No Tudor possessed a standing army or the usual instruments of coercion; consequently it was all the more important to maintain respect and obedience, if only because there were such meager means of curbing rebellion and punishing sedition. In the end Henry, as Erasmus sagely remarked, had power and sovereignty "by the consent of the people." He may have scolded and even shocked his people, but he rarely forced them to do what was not already in their hearts; and Elizabeth proved she was her father's daughter when she acknowledged that "God hath raised me high, yet this I account the glory of my crown, that I have reigned with your loves."

With Henry gone, Edward Seymour stood in *loco parentis*. Unfortunately for the endurance of his rule, the new lord protector proved himself to be a man of mercy but not of tact, of ideas but not of practicality. The protectorate was totally divorced from the symbol of regality, and it was never able to command the loyalty and allegiance owing to the prince who sat upon the throne. Unwilling to rule by the heavy hand of tyranny, and innocent in his belief that reason and goodwill were sufficient instruments of government, Seymour sanctioned disobedience, permitted corruption in government, and failed to stifle the stringent voice of factionalism.

If Edward VI's reign indicates that the Tudor regime floundered when deprived of a popular, vigorous, and divinely ordained leadership, the period also reveals another facet of sixteenth-century life: that discord was anything but dead, and that kingmakers had not disappeared with the fifteenth century. Though the structure of Tudor government may have been sufficiently resilient to withstand the passing of an autocratic and divine prince and his replacement by a protectorate of human contrivance, it was not strong enough to resist the encroachment of class and religious factionalism. The ghost of feudal feuding had never been permanently laid to rest, and it tended to reappear in different guise. The overmighty magnate of the previous century was no more dangerous to the well-ordered kingdom than the country gentleman of the sixteenth century bent on the enclosure of land, or the London clothier greedy for further profits in the booming wool trade. The proud prelate who had once claimed the special sanction

EDWARD SEYMOUR, EARL OF HERTFORD
AND DUKE OF SOMERSET
"A man of mercy but not of tact,
of ideas but not of practicality . . .
Seymour sanctioned disobedience,
permitted corruption in government,
and failed to stifle the stringent
voice of factionalism." *Wallace
Collection, London.*

of God was no more difficult to handle than the earnest reformer who was
willing to sacrifice state and church, concord and obedience in order to
achieve the kingdom of heaven on earth. The spirit of feudal anarchy would
not be permanently buried until a single political-religious faction had won
complete control of government and society. Two generations of Stuart
ineptitude, four years of civil war, two decades of interregnum, and a
Glorious Revolution would have to pass before a single element—the landed
country gentlemen in league with the city lawyer, the town merchant and
the country parson—was able to establish firm oligarchical rule.

France and Scotland

The new protector was faced with problems which stemmed from a
combination of his own personality, the uncertain nature of his office, and
the economic and religious burdens bequeathed him by the old king. The
most immediate problems of the new reign were matters of foreign and
military policy. The last years of Henry's rule had seen wars with France
and Scotland which had not been permanently concluded on the king's
death. The lord protector, who assumed the rank of duke of Somerset,
quickly proved his worth by smashing the Scottish forces at the Battle of
Pinkie in September of 1547. The victory, however, was never followed up,
and Somerset's handling of diplomacy revealed a basic flaw in his character:
he could conceive but never execute; he could start but never finish. The
protector lacked the essential characteristic of any ruler who must be his
own prime minister—attention to detail, careful planning, and endless hours

of crushing labor. Instead, he was a genial and naive dilettante who was thrust into high office by the accident of blood. He ruled over a government composed of office-seeking suitors, unscrupulous and land-hungry colleagues, and puritanical and militant religious reformers, and he lacked both the ruthlessness and the ability to control such a wolf pack. The fruits of victory at war were allowed to wither away, and nothing was done to prevent the young princess of Scotland, Mary Queen of Scots, from being sent to wed the dauphin of France, thus joining in marriage England's most dangerous enemies. In his handling of France the same fatal weakness prevailed. Somerset did little to prevent the outbreak of hostilities in 1549; he did nothing to strengthen the defenses of English holdings along the French coast; and his religious policy at home antagonized the emperor, who was the only man in Europe who could have helped in a war against France. What the lord protector never realized was that Protestantism in religion necessitated peace with France at any price; and conversely, friendship with the emperor required caution and orthodoxy in religion.

Religious Policy

The duke of Somerset's religious inclinations are difficult to gauge because conviction, either in religion or in politics, was not a strongly developed quality in any of the Edwardian ministers of state. Whatever his personal faith, the lord protector associated himself with the reforming party, and he opened up the court and the king's schoolroom to the Protestant creed. The young king had been brought up by tutors, already tainted with reforming ideas, who had not dared influence their royal protégé during his father's life, but once Henry was dead, they transformed Edward into a thoroughgoing, unremitting reformer. The moment the new government in November of 1547 repealed the Henrician treason and heresy laws, England became a haven for continental heretics, and the clamor for religious reform rose to deafening proportions. The heart of the theological controversy involved the ancient ceremony of the Eucharist, and every alehouse and tavern, pulpit and street corner became the stage for a debate in which all was either "as black as pitch, vice, abomination, heresy and folly," or "fair roses and sweet virtue."

Somerset's reaction to the mounting discord was to re-establish spiritual conformity slightly to the left of the old Henrician *via media* and to concoct a religious formula that would be sufficiently broad to satisfy all but the militant extremes in both the Catholic and Protestant camps. The crucial question was the nature of the mass: was it a miraculous ritual in which the bread and the wine were actually transformed into the body and blood of Christ whose sacrifice was re-enacted each time the ceremony was performed, or was it a commemorative service in which no change occurred except in the hearts of the communicants and which only brought to mind Jesus' sacrifice for mankind? The new Prayer Book of 1549 offered a simplified version of the ancient liturgy and a verbal revision of the Eucharist in which the exact nature of the mass was deliberately left in doubt. For a moment it seemed as if the Prayer Book, which was predominately the work of Archbishop Thomas Cranmer, might become the basis for a new religious settlement, and even the conservative and outspoken Stephen Gardiner, Bishop of Winchester, announced his compliance, and pointed out that the book was capable of a Catholic interpretation. This, however, was exactly the trouble; and the radical reformers were disgusted by a settlement that so openly threw "ambiguous expressions before posterity." In the end the Prayer Book, though a literary masterpiece, turned out to be a religious catastrophe, and the humane Act of Uniformity, which was enacted to enforce it, proved totally ineffectual. Protestants continued to clamor for further reformation, and peasants in the southwest of England rose up in revolt, calling for a return to the good old days of Henry VIII.

Economic Change and Social Reaction

Had religion stood alone without the coincidence of economic crisis, the lord protector might have been able to ride out the storm of contention and rebellion. Two interlocking economic forces reached their apex during Edward VI's reign—inflation and prosperity. The flood of specie pouring in from the New World during the decade of the 1540s was only beginning to affect the price level, but the cost of war during Henry's final years, plus the debasement of the currency, created an inflationary cycle that strained the Tudor economy beyond endurance. During the last years of Henry's reign the government was able to extract approximately £650,000 from direct taxation, another £799,310 was realized by the sale of monastic lands, and some £363,000 had been created by reissuing the coinage. But even these unheard-of sums were insufficient for Henry's military needs, and he left his son a deficit of £75,000. The pressure of debasement and the cost of war produced an inflation in which prices doubled between 1547 and 1549. Pensioners and schoolmasters, landlords and clerics trapped by fixed and customary rents, and government officials dependent upon the historic fees of their office faced economic annihilation. As a way out, landlords turned to the enclosure of lands, government minions to corruption, pensioners to patronage, and schoolmasters and clergymen to vocal but ineffectual complaint.[2]

Debasement of the coinage produced the added hysteria of economic boom, since English woolens could be purchased in Europe with uncorrupted specie at bargain prices. The woolen industry grew monstrously.

---

[2] By August of 1551 there was so much debased coinage in circulation that the council was forced to establish the value of a silver shilling at six pence, half its original value but approximately its true silver worth. Individuals who found their coins suddenly devalued by one half were badly hurt, for the government made no effort to exchange worthless currency for sound coins; it could not have afforded to do so.

Possibly the livelihood of one-third of the population was dependent in some fashion upon the manufacture and export of woolen cloth; and the entire economic health of the realm was at the mercy of a foreign market exposed to the vagaries of world commerce, dynastic wars, and the caprice of princes. By 1549 the howl of protest against peasants being evicted by merchant landlords and gentlemen farmers, who were anxious to profit from the unprecedented expansion, began to meet a receptive response among a small and idealistic group of men at court known as the Commonwealth party. Joining economic conservatism and religious radicalism, the Commonwealth men were impassioned and doctrinaire exponents of an organic, balanced, and self-sufficient body politic in which famine prices, capitalistic greed, enclosures, and a swollen wool trade dependent upon a foreign market had no place. Economic and religious reformers agreed that greed, avarice, and idolatry must be banished from the realm. Bishop Hugh Latimer spoke most loudly for outraged economic justice and religious righteousness, and he inveighed against proud and unpreaching prelates in their cathedral palaces, rent-raising landlords in their lordships, and profit-taking merchants in their countinghouses. "You landlords, you rent-raisers, I say you step-lords, you unnatural lords, you have for your possessions yearly too much."

If Latimer was the propagandist who struck at the moral decay of the kingdom, John Hales in the House of Commons was the political theorist who hit directly at wool merchants and enclosing landlords. He challenged the authority and endangered the economic well-being of the group who monopolized the Commons and who filled the offices of justices of the peace throughout the shires. Whether the lord protector was himself a Commonwealth man is not certain, but he gave his blessings to Hales' Subsidy Act of 1548 and Enclosure Commission of the same year. The first was a tax on sheep aimed at shifting the tax burden to those most capable of paying, and at rectifying the growing imbalance of an economy in which farmlands were giving way to sheep runs. The second was a moral crusade to enforce already existing but largely ignored legislation against the enclosure of land, and to insure that enclosing landlords pulled down their hedges and returned their stolen acres to the village commons. The results were disastrous to Somerset and the Commonwealth party, for Hales' actions not only antagonized the landed and mercantile classes but they also inspired the "poor commons" to revolution. When Latimer preached that landlords and rent-raisers had "yearly too much," he inadvertently sanctioned the demands of peasants who bitterly resented the actions of the rich in raising rents and enclosing the commons. At the same time the appearance of the Enclosure Commission during the summers of 1548 and 1549 gave the peasantry the idea that the "Good Duke" was their guardian angel and would approve their taking the law into their own hands.

In the summer of 1549 the results of Somerset's theological and economic policies were Catholic religious revolt in Cornwall and Devon and Protestant economic sedition in Norfolk. The Devon uprising was in the best tradition of unthinking reaction and provincialism, but Ket's Revolt, as the Norfolk rebellion was called, smattered of religious communism, something which struck fear into the ruling classes. "It is not agreeable with the Gospel," stated one champion of the underprivileged, "that a few persons shall live in so great abundance of wealth and suffer so many their Christian brothers to live in extreme poverty." A scared but determined gentry struck hard at such advocates of a social system which was in direct opposition to the Tudor doctrine of political, social, and economic inequality and hierarchy. Both revolts were promptly put down.

The Wicked Earl

In the eyes of landlords and merchants, the duke of Somerset was responsible for governmental ineptitude, mismanagement, and policies that seemed to have led directly to social and religious rebellion. In a palace revolution in October of 1549 he was arrested and deprived of office, and two-and-a-half years later he was executed on a trumped-up charge of treason. His real guilt, however, was his popularity with the great unwashed of Tudor society and his mishandling of the affairs of state.

The man who engineered the protector's destruction was his onetime colleague-in-arms, John Dudley, Earl of Warwick. It is usual to present the reign of Edward VI in terms of stereotypes—Catholic versus Protestant, idealist versus realist, the "Good Duke" versus the wicked earl. Somerset has had his impassioned apologists, but almost no one has ever had a kind word to say for Warwick. In actual fact, however, Dudley's precipitate career was not so much a fearful example of ruthlessness in politics and greed for power as of the general level of ineptitude in government. Warwick assumed power not by talent but by default. He brought to high office both the strength and weakness of the military mind; he preferred action to inaction, he was always willing to gamble on luck if he could not think of a ready solution, and he constantly took the shortest route to a given objective no matter what the ultimate consequences.

Uniting a highly developed instinct for political survival with an absolute determination to establish himself and his family as one of the great landlords of the realm, Dudley headed a governmental faction consisting of earnest Protestant reformers and unscrupulous court elements who coveted the wealth of the church. These strange political bedfellows had but a single creed in common—that clerical wealth and lordships were harmful to God's church. The earl never took the office of lord protector. Instead he assumed the title of duke of Northumberland and ruled through his influence over the twelve-year-old Edward, who was declared by law to be of age and allowed to go through the pretense of ruling, sitting in the

council, and being consulted in weighty matters of state. Actually the way
to the king's heart was financial—he was given control over his privy purse,
something which his uncle had never seen fit to do. In his own eyes Edward
had come of age, and Northumberland assiduously fostered this notion;
Somerset, to his cost, had continued to regard his nephew as a small boy
scarcely out of the nursery.

Purifying the Church

The attack on church property had commenced under the lord protector with the destruction of the chantry lands, but this was a policy left over
from the previous reign, and followed logically from Reformation theology.
The case against the chantries was clear: chantry priests, who prayed for
souls who had not managed to make it into heaven but had achieved that
level between hell and paradise known as purgatory, had lost their spiritual
reason for being; and the estates which financed such superstitious practices
deserved to be confiscated and put to more secular and political uses. Full-
scale plunder of the ecclesia got under way with the rise of Northumberland. As early as 1547 the Spanish ambassador noted, when a royal commission was sent out to inspect all English bishoprics, that the commissioners
had orders to "examine the clergymen and inquire into their knowledge,
manner of life and income," and he concluded that it "may well turn out
that the question of income is the principal one." The truth of his prophecy
was soon revealed. The Henrician bishops had for the most part been
allowed to retain their offices under Somerset, but after the lord protector's
fall in October of 1549, the surge of religious revolution quickly swept them
off the episcopal bench and into the Tower as disobedient subjects of the
crown. In their stead were selected men who advocated high thinking and
simple living for the episcopate. At a vastly reduced income, Nicholas
Ridley followed Edmund Bonner in the see of London; John Poynet succeeded Stephen Gardiner in the richest bishopric in England and accepted
a government salary of £1,300 in lieu of his predecessor's episcopal income
of £3,000; and Coverdale of Exeter managed with £500, which was one-
third the usual revenues of the see. The plunder of the bishoprics reached
its height in 1551 when Tunstal, Bishop of Durham, was deprived of his
office. No one was appointed in his place and the revenues of his diocese
were swallowed up by Northumberland.

Religious radicals were glad to return the church to its primitive
poverty, but they were shocked that reform should be the cloak behind
which avarice and economic greed could operate. On the other hand, the
Northumberland gang were fully aware that doctrinal purification was a
necessary prelude to territorial looting, and they supported the extreme
Protestant position that the mass was a commemorative service, that priests
were biblical and moral teachers, and that the church should be returned

to its original ceremonial purity. By the new Ordinal of 1550, the divinely ordained priest became a parson appointed by government patronage, and in 1552 a revised version of the 1549 Prayer Book ended any pretense at compromise with Catholicism. The clergy were required to wear plain surplices at mass instead of ornate Catholic robes, stone altars were pulled down to make way for movable wooden communion tables, and the consecrated wafer was replaced by household bread. In the same year a second Act of Uniformity was passed which, unlike its predecessor of 1549, threatened the most dire punishments for nonconformity and non-churchgoing. It would seem that the government was determined that moral turpitude should be chastised in humble folk even if corruption were condoned in high office.

Kingmaking

From the start Northumberland tried to conceal the partisan and factional nature of his government by the pretense that young Edward had come of age. The king had grown from a small and impish lad who always did his best and thanked his tutors for telling him his faults into a precocious and rather terrifying young man obsessed with a royal sense of duty and a straight-laced Puritan conscience which would never allow him to "set light God's will" merely for the sake of expediency. Edward's governors had done their work well, and the Tudor clay had been shaped into the image of an Old Testament prophet—upright and just but devoid of humanity. At sixteen Edward died in the odor of Biblical sanctity; "O Lord God," he cried, "save Thy chosen people of England. O my Lord God, defend this realm from papistry, and maintain Thy true religion."

Northumberland had no intention of leaving the defense of God's chosen people to the deity. He had tied his political star to a frail and consumptive boy, and when in January of 1553 Edward's doctors told him that the king had "a tough, strong, straining cough" and was pining away, he realized that he could only save the "true religion," not to mention his own neck, by barring the succession of Catholic Mary and launching forth upon the risky game of kingmaking. By law, by blood, and by rightful inheritance Mary Tudor was next in line to the throne, but she was a Catholic and a woman, and Northumberland persuaded the dying king to devise a new order of succession whereby both Mary and Elizabeth were declared illegitimate and the crown was willed to Lady Jane Grey, Henry VIII's grandniece, a fervent Protestant and, most important of all, Northumberland's daughter-in-law. With a certain amount of judicious rephrasing of Edward's "Device for the Succession" and a great many threats, the duke bullied the judges into accepting the change and cajoled the council into acknowledging Lady Jane as Edward's lawful heir. All this was done in the nick of time, for on July 6, 1553, Edward died, his sputum "livid, black and fetid," his feet swollen and his body smelling "beyond measure." [3]

Northumberland's triumph was short-lived. At the crucial moment the duke was overcome with a strange and fatal lassitude. Probably he was ill, possibly he sensed the futility of his desperate plan, for he failed to take the one step that might have assured the success of his scheme: he allowed the Princess Mary to slip through his fingers and to proclaim herself the rightful queen of England. Northumberland had also reckoned without one vital factor—loyalty to the Tudor line as well as to the crown. The days of kingmaking were over; it was enough for most Englishmen that Mary was a Tudor. Her faith, the confusion surrounding her legitimacy, even her sex, were of no consequence compared to the fact that she was her father's daughter and had been bequeathed the crown imperial by parliamentary statute and the old king's will. Almost without dissent, the kingdom rallied to her; Northumberland's army melted away, the council acknowledged her as queen, the duke humbly apologized for having defied the divinity of Tudor monarchs, and in nine days the reign of Lady Jane Grey was over.

Mary Tudor (1553–1558)

The new queen had endured disgrace, humiliation, submission, head-aches, fits of melancholia, and palpitations of the heart. She had suffered a surfeit of stepmothers, some callous, some silly, some abusive. But what Mary could not forget was the knowledge that she had betrayed her mother's memory and the church which had upheld the legitimacy of her birth. Unlike Bishop Fisher and Sir Thomas More, she had hesitated and at her father's command had taken the Oath of Supremacy. Now that she was queen she was determined to do penance for that moment of weakness and to turn the clock back to those golden days when her mother had been un-disputed queen of England, her father a dutiful and loyal son of Rome, and Mary herself had danced at court, freshfaced and free of troubles.

For all her many redeeming qualities, which led contemporaries to judge her to be "a Prince of heart and courage, more than commonly is in womankind," and modern historians to describe her as "the most merciful of all the Tudors," the Queen at thirty-seven was an anachronism. Time had passed her by. She passionately sought to return her errant and unhappy land to the bosom of a church that bore little resemblance to the ecclesia of her youth. The corrupt and comfortable papacy of Clement VII had died in the fury of religious wars, and by 1553 both Catholics and Protestants denied absolutely any idea that "men who live according to equity and justice shall be saved," no matter what their religious creed. The light

---

[3] Recently another interpretation has appeared. W. K. Jordan, in *Edward VI*, argues that Edward, not the wicked duke, was the driving force behind the Device for the Succession and the decision to exclude Catholic Mary.

laughter of Erasmus' humanism and the tolerance of More's *Utopia* had no place in the stern world of Cardinal Caraffa, who had founded the militant order of the Theatines and now wore the papal tiara as Paul IV. The ranks of Catholicism had closed: either one was counted among the true believers or one belonged to the devil's camp. Religious strife, persecution, and atrocities on both sides had polarized the two faiths, engulfing any middle ground where men of moderation might seek understanding and accord. The hopelessness of Mary's vision of a world sans heresy, sans doubt, sans discord, was evidenced by the sterility of her means: her fruitless marriage to Philip of Spain, the use of fire to purge her church of error, and her dependence upon ecclesiastics who were even more out of touch with reality than she was herself.

The fervent welcome accorded Henry VIII's Catholic daughter convinced her that the past could be resurrected and the Roman church restored. At first the queen's policy followed the cautious lines laid down by Stephen Gardiner, the wily Bishop of Winchester, who had exchanged the cold stone of a prison bench for the lord chancellor's soft woolsack. Four years of imprisonment under Edward VI had left their mark; but in 1553 Gardiner still remained more a politician than an ecclesiastic, more a gover-

MARY TUDOR BY
HANS EWORTH, 1554
"The Queen at thirty-seven was an anachronism. Time had passed her by."
Society of Antiquaries.

nor of men than a healer of souls. Both he and the Emperor Charles V cautioned Mary to go slowly; the Reformation would have to be unmade as it had originally been made, legally by act of parliament. For the first years of Mary's reign, tolerance and rehabilitation were practiced on all sides. Only Northumberland and two of his closest colleagues lost their lives for playing at kingmaking; the queen's council was enlarged to unworkable proportions so as to include all important men of moderate faith and politics; and distinguished Protestants were allowed, and on occasion even encouraged, to flee the realm (the duchess of Suffolk took five weeks to make her way from London to Gravesend). The church was purged of its married clergy, but, if Protestant parsons quietly put away their wives, they were allowed to serve as priests in parishes where their lapses into sin were unsuspected. Finally, in October of 1553 an obliging House of Commons reversed the divorce of Catherine of Aragon, absolved Mary of bastardy and repealed the Edwardian Reformation. Catholicism without the pope was reinstated, but further than this parliament would not go, and Mary had to live with her satanic title of Supreme Head of the Church of England. She even found it necessary to exercise its hated authority to cleanse the church and reintroduce the old ritual.

Two barriers blocked the path to reunion with Rome: opposition to Mary's marriage with Philip of Spain and the fear that spiritual absolution might entail the return of the monastic lands. On the first point the queen remained adamant, and she proved herself to have both her mother's Spanish pride and her father's savage willfulness. Against her councillors' advice, her parliament's bitter opposition, and her country's hatred of "proud Spaniards or strangers," she set her elderly heart upon Archduke Philip, heir to the Habsburg domains and the son of her mother's champion, the Emperor Charles V. "She would," as she informed her irate Commons, "choose as God inspired her," and on July 25, 1554, Philip became king of England by grace of his marriage to Mary Tudor.

On the subject of the church lands, Mary was less firm and reluctantly accepted the argument of expediency: guaranteeing the riches of the church to their secular owners was a small price to pay for the spiritual salvation of her realm. Only after the landed classes in both the Lords and Commons had been assured on this point did parliament in November and December of 1554 repeal the Act of Supremacy, petition for reunion with Rome, reinstate the old heresy laws authorizing the crown to enforce orthodoxy with fire and sword, and lift the ban of treason against Cardinal Reginald Pole, who brought back with him to England the pope's absolution for twenty years of schism and heresy. Even more than his cousin the queen, Cardinal Pole represented a lost cause; for over a generation he had suffered exile and privation as a consequence of both his faith and his blood, for Reginald Pole was not only the leading English Catholic prelate but he was also the grandnephew of Edward IV and one of the last remaining Yorkist claimants to the English throne. Spiritually as well as dynastically he belonged to an England that had long since ceased to exist.

Sedition and Heresy

Pole arrived in England, as he said "not to destroy, but to build; to reconcile, not to condemn," but both queen and cardinal "with bitterness of heart" soon discovered that heretical opinions were everywhere rampant, and that a policy of love and moderation only encouraged the devil to greater acts of sacrilege. By the end of 1554 it was becoming painfully apparent that papal absolution had brought not blessed relief from sin but further sedition.

Even before Pole arrived, the government had been presented with a clear lesson in the dangers of trying to turn back time. In her determination to marry Philip of Spain, Mary had blinded herself to the fact that the diplomatic and economic considerations which had once produced the Anglo-Spanish alliance under Henry VII had disappeared. The collapse of the wool trade with Antwerp in 1551–52, though it caused poverty and depression, had liberated England diplomatically from dependence upon the foreign power that controlled the Low Countries. Spain with her disciplined legions of tough Castilian peasants, and her golden treasures plundered from Mexico and Peru, was becoming the Leviathan of Europe and the champion of resurgent Catholicism; English merchants who encountered Iberian maritime and commercial power in the Mediterranean and Caribbean began to wonder whether Spain, not France, might be the real enemy.

Englishmen were notoriously uncivil to foreigners, and when Philip's emissaries, sent to settle the treaty of marriage, made it clear that they regarded England as a pestilent land of heretics and barbarians, anti-Spanish feeling erupted into rebellion. In January of 1554, three thousand Kentish men rose against the threat of a Spanish king and a popish mass, and marched on London. Their leader, Sir Thomas Wyatt, was a gentleman of parts, and his presence was a dangerous indication that the rebellion was no aimless agrarian revolt or senseless explosion of class hatred and revenge. The natural leaders of Tudor England as well as the many-headed multitude concealed treason in their hearts, and had London been less loyal, Wyatt more swift, or the queen less resolute, Mary might have lost her throne. As it was, the magic surrounding the Tudor dynasty held firm. The queen was magnificent; she stayed on in London, and with the usual Tudor flare for words rallied the city to her defense. "What I am," she cried, "ye might well know. I am your Queen, to whom at my coronation . . . you promised your allegiance." Therefore, "good subjects, pluck up your hearts, and like true men, stand fast against these rebels." When Wyatt swept up to Ludgate he found it closed, held by men loyal to the Tudor line. Without the city, the rebellion withered and died. Wyatt knew full well the penalty for unsuccessful treason and paid the price. But two others also paid with their lives for his ill-starred venture: less than a week after Sir Thomas entered the Tower, Lady Jane Grey and her husband, Guildford Dudley, walked out to their execution. The Princess Elizabeth was more fortunate.

She also was a threat to her sister's crown and church, but Mary's compassion and King Philip's caution saved her, though Bishop Gardiner begged to be given authority to gather evidence of her treason and complicity in the Wyatt rebellion.

When Mary had exhorted her brave Londoners to stand fast, she had also told them that should she "leave some fruit of my body behind me to be your governor," she trusted that such a blessed event would be of great comfort to the realm. In this expectation Mary reckoned without a virulent and vocal minority of Protestants who had the audacity to nail to the palace gate the defiance: "Will you be such fools, oh! noble Englishmen, as to believe that our Queen is pregnant; and of what should she be, but of a monkey or a dog."

The Smithfield Fires

The futility of turning back the hands of time was revealed in the misguided conviction that the old church could best be served by fire and brimstone. Patience and forbearing and loving understanding had proved their uselessness when confronted by obstinate heresy and sedition. Safe in Geneva, the haven of exiled Protestants from every kingdom in Europe, John Knox, that Moses of Scotland, thundered dreadful anathemas against women in regal office, declaring that Mary was "a wicked woman, yea a traitoress and bastard" and encouraging Englishmen to cast out such a Jezebel. At home the godly translated his advice into action: a priest had his nose cut off, and a church in Suffolk was set on fire while mass was being celebrated. Wyatt's rebellion and the actions of Protestant extremists seemed proof that heresy and treason marched hand in hand and that heretics waited impatiently to overthrow those two bastions of all good government: law and religion.

Had Mary burned fewer heretics and hanged more traitors she would never have earned the censure of later generations. The judgment of history has been based on a somewhat doubtful distinction: bloody is the sovereign who sets fire to men's bodies to cleanse their souls; politic is the monarch who hangs and mutilates to preserve the state. Mary, however, thought otherwise: she deemed it worthier and better for her future reputation that it be known and recorded that Archbishop Cranmer died for his heresy to God rather than for his treason to her throne. Toward rebels the queen showed herself unusually merciful; toward subjects disobedient to God she could administer only justice, which clearly stated that such obstinacy deserved death at the stake. Except for the handful of Protestant leaders who died early in 1555, it is difficult to fix the responsibility for burning some three hundred men, women, and children. Currently it is fashionable to depreciate the horror by presenting the sorry statistics of persecution elsewhere in Europe—6,000 heretics burned in the Low Countries by Charles V, almost as many executed in France by order of Francis I and his son

Henry II, 800 witches burned in Savoy, 199 sorcerers punished in Venice, and under Elizabeth of England 125 persons tried for witchcraft and 47 executed. The ugly figures merely indicate that heretics and sorcerers were accepted by the sixteenth century as murderers of the soul, who deserved death just as surely as criminals who destroyed the body. Some authorities place the blame on Bishop Bonner of London, others prefer Cardinal Pole or the queen, and still others speak of the spirit of an age which accepted it as a "work of cruelty" against both God and man to nourish heretics within the commonwealth.[4]

Wherever the ultimate responsibility may lie, the immediate decision in 1555 rested with Stephen Gardiner, who argued the belly wisdom of his old master, Henry VIII: that laws enacted in blood were more enduring than those written in water. The lord chancellor was always more interested in outward political obedience than inward spiritual conformity, and he reasoned that the agonizing spectacle of men dying by slow fire would destroy the religious ardor of even the most courageous and render them obedient. The first martyrs were a select half dozen who were sacrificed to politics, not God. Cranmer, Ridley, Hooper, Latimer and two others were ordered to face the fire in the expectation that they would fail to play the man, or that the sight of their suffering would discourage men of weaker spirit. In adopting such a policy Gardiner proved to be as unrealistic as his queen. He totally underestimated the spiritual strength that led men to endure with a smile on their faces the torments of the stake, in preference to risking their immortal souls in the agony of everlasting damnation. "Wily Winchester" could never comprehend the words of Dr. Rowland Taylor, who rushed to the fire exclaiming "now I know I am almost at home . . . and I am even at my Father's house!" Far from frightening lesser men, the sight of such conviction encouraged those of weaker hearts to be martyrs.

Within the year Gardiner sickened of the Smithfield fires, and died realizing the folly of enforcing heresy laws at the stake. But once the flame had been lit, it was difficult to put out. During Wyatt's rebellion a number of religious prisoners in the Marshalsea had been offered a chance to escape; but they had refused their freedom, stating that "as we came in for our consciences, and [were] sent hither by the Council, we think it good here still to remain till it please God to work our deliverance . . . ; whether it be life or death we are content." In the face of Protestant obstinacy, a kind of administrative exasperation set in. Spiritual conviction was beyond argument or reasoning. The law required that such folk be destroyed, and in lieu of any other solution, there was nothing to do but proceed with the grisly policy of purging the kingdom with fire. If, as is often said, "sterility

---

4 The question of ultimate responsibility remains open. See W. Schenk, *Reginald Pole* (1950); P. Hughes, *The Reformation in England*, vol. 11 (1954); and B. White, *Mary Tudor* (1935). Whatever one's religious preference or historical favorite, John Foxe's *Book of Martyrs* (*Acts and Monuments*, 1563) remains the classic and impassioned account of those terrible years.

was the conclusive note of Mary's reign," it lay primarily in the dreadful fact that nobody was able to think of anything but the stake as a way of handling heresy.

Mary's marriage was as sterile as her religious policy. The marriage had been the result of the queen's determination to recapture the past, and of Charles V's willingness to sacrifice his only legitimate son to a middle-aged spinster for the sake of Habsburg diplomatic policy. In the century-old Habsburg-Valois rivalry, the entrance of England into the Spanish-Imperial fold completed the encirclement of France and insured the vital sea link between the emperor's most valued possessions—Spain and the Netherlands. From Charles' dynastic view the marriage was crucial; from Philip's more intimate perspective the union was something less than a success, and Spaniards blatantly wondered what their king could "do with such an old bitch," who was ten years his senior. Though Philip did his father's bidding, he felt that "it would take God himself to drink of this cup," and despite the queen's prayers he remained in England for only a year and a month. He returned to Mary only once again, in March of 1557, to claim his reward: England's participation in the most recent flare-up of hostilities between Spain and France. In June, against the advice of her council and the threats of the pope, who had allied himself with France and excommunicated her husband, Mary dragooned her reluctant kingdom into a war for which it felt no liking and for which it was financially and spiritually unprepared. The ultimate fruit of her marriage was not the child for which the queen had shed so many tears and offered so many prayers, but the loss of Calais, the last English possession on the continent.

The final verdict upon a woman who was deeply compassionate but who died branded with the epithet of "Bloody" was passed by the English chronicler, Ralph Holinshed, when he said that the queen had not "the favor of God, nor the hearts of her subjects, nor yet the love of her husband," and therefore God had sent her a short reign. She died on the morning of the 17th of November, 1558, just twelve hours before Cardinal Pole. Mary had grown old, sick, and disillusioned in the struggle to make a vision come true. The dream had turned into a nightmare, and her stout subjects greeted the news of her death with jubilant ringing of bells and blazing bonfires. The prayer book that had been her constant companion was found to be tear-stained at the two places where her failure had been most complete—the prayers for the unity of her church and for women bearing children.

If the fifteenth century had been plagued by Plantagenet fertility, the sixteenth suffered from Tudor sterility. The offspring of lusty King Hal seemed to be lacking in the crucial qualities of survival: good health and fecundity. Henry's sons—Edward VI and Henry Fitzroy—both died of consumption in their teens; now Mary had perished childless and unmourned at forty-two; it only remained to be seen whether the last of his children, the Princess Elizabeth, would fare any better.

Elizabeth of Good Memory

9 The role of womankind was perfectly clear; in sermon, book, and Bible it was stated that women were frail, foolish, and inferior. Their ordained function was to bear children "till they die of it; that is what they are for." Without doubt God had created man to rule, and it was a wife's duty "if she saw her husband merry, then she was merry; if he were sad, she was sad." During the years 1558–1560 this dulce order of things was sadly upset by a plethora of ladies who failed to fit the conventional female pattern. In France, England, and Scotland the realms were afflicted with what John Knox called that enormity of nature—"The monstrous regiment of women." It was against all human and divine law that "a woman should reign and have empire above men." Yet Mary of Guise was regent of Scotland; Catherine de Medici was soon to become regent and queen mother of France; Mary Stuart was queen of Scotland; and Elizabeth Tudor succeeded her sister on the throne of England. No one questioned that the consequences of such an unnatural and undesirable situation would be discord, inconstancy, and civil strife. The regent of Scotland died in the midst of civil war; Catherine de Medici bequeathed to her heirs a kingdom convulsed by religious conflict and human atrocities; and Mary Stuart perished on the execution block. Only Elizabeth was an exception to the rule, and Englishmen were quite certain that the cause lay with the special interference of God and the divine genius of their sovereign lady.[1]

---

[1] The two best biographies of Elizabeth are J. E. Neale, *Queen Elizabeth* (1934), and E. Jenkins, *Elizabeth the Great* (1958). Both are very partial to the queen. Excellent but more general are A. L. Rowse, *The England of Elizabeth* (1951), J. Hurstfield, *Elizabeth I and the Unity of England* (1960), and W. T. MacCaffrey, *The Shaping of the Elizabethan Regime* (1968).

Elizabeth I (1558–1603)

"Vain but acute" was the judgment passed by one observer of the new queen. Her vanity was forgiven as one of the natural weaknesses of her sex; her acuteness was regarded as a gift from heaven usually reserved for men. Whatever the role of the deity in the making of a queen, Elizabeth at twenty-five was an experienced student of political survival in an age that had seen her mother executed for adultery, her uncle for incest, and her cousin Lady Jane Grey for treason. Under Edward VI she had romped with the lord protector's brother, Thomas Seymour, only to discover that his favors were given with calculation and his motives touched with treason. Under Mary she had bent with the papal wind but found that her mere existence was such a threat to her sister's throne and faith that she could not blame Mary if, out of state necessity, she had demanded the death of her Protestant sister. If Elizabeth had not served such an exacting apprenticeship and been fortunate beyond expectation, she as well as Lady Jane

ELIZABETH I. ANONYMOUS PORTRAIT, 1575
"Vain but acute." *National Portrait Gallery.*

Grey might have written on a prison wall: "to mortals' common fate my mind resign; my lot today, tomorrow may be thine."

Hard work, an infallible political instinct, and innate Tudor tact and sleight-of-hand saved Elizabeth from the common fate reserved for female rulers. The planning and labor which went into her coronation showed that from the start she appreciated that the love of her people was the surest bastion of her throne, and she carefully cultivated it by every kind of artistry and pageantry. On January 14, 1559, the eve of her coronation, the queen officially entered the city of London at the head of an immense procession. For once Elizabeth spared no cost—silks for livery and banners, timber for the seats in Westminster Abbey, delicacies for feasting important guests, food to be distributed among the poor, and even the fee to be paid the astrologer royal for setting the most propitious day for the crowning—all were financed with a single purpose in mind: to disperse the gloom that had settled upon a country humiliated in war and floundering in spiritual and financial bankruptcy for almost a decade. The cost was well over £16,000 but worth every penny of it.

Englishmen desired above all else strong, vigorous, and secular leadership devoid of fanaticism and passion. They saw in Gloriana, as her people came to call her, a monarch who could curb factions and quiet discord; a symbol of unity to which they could sacrifice their lives and give their hearts. The old king had achieved unity by elevating the crown, through his personal magnetism and the ferocious laws of parliament, to a point above party and politics. Elizabeth was her father's daughter: athletic, red-haired, autocratic, and vain, but she added a new element to royal leadership—a genius for courtship and coquetry. She wooed and won her people, transforming subjects into lovers who sought "Sweet Bessy's" hand. "Elizabeth of Good Memory" built no empires, nor sought to bring heaven to earth, but in a halting, vacillating, and often infuriating fashion she solved the three most pressing problems of the early years of her reign: she put out the spreading fires of religious hysteria; she secured the realm in a world filled with women rulers and religious frenzy; and she redeemed England's confidence in itself and in Tudor government.

The Elizabethan Religious Settlement

Like her sister, Elizabeth was the victim and the product of the past; unlike Mary, she felt no need to prove her mother right or vindicate the faith of her childhood. As the daughter of Anne Boleyn, Elizabeth had no choice—she was the hope and inspiration of English Protestantism. There is, however, little doubt that the queen had been brought up a good Henrician, and if she had had her way in 1559 she would have cut the legal cords with Rome, reestablished the Supremacy, and adapted her father's muddled *via media* to the needs of her own reign. Elizabeth was a *politique*, a firm believer that religion should be an instrument of state and a compartment of life, not the end of government or the whole of human existence. Internationally and domestically she had to walk a difficult religious tight-rope, trying to convince Philip of Spain and the Catholic world of her religious orthodoxy, endeavoring to lure the moderate members of her sister's episcopate to follow her into a second break with Rome, and striving to conciliate the extreme Protestants whose support she needed if her religious settlement were to be acceptable to the House of Commons.

In the end Elizabeth made many more concessions than she had anticipated. In February of 1559 the Supremacy Bill was introduced into parliament, where it met with the unanimous opposition of the spiritual lords in the upper house and the Protestants in the lower house. The religious radicals in parliament were well organized and supported by the Marian exiles, fresh from Calvin's Geneva, where they had been taught the militant doctrine of that "perfect school of Christ" and learned how to band together in defense of the true faith. Such men were not satisfied with a bare Supremacy and a restoration of Catholicism without the pope. They desired a purified church stripped of all its papal trappings.

By March it was evident that the Marian bishops would also have nothing to do with the Supremacy Act, no matter how Catholic Gloriana's church remained in creed and structure. Moreover the international situation had changed, for the war with France had been concluded and England no longer required the support of Catholic Spain. During the Easter recess the queen turned to the religious reformers both in and out of parliament for support. She sought to reintroduce Cranmer's Prayer Book of 1549, but she had to settle for the more Protestant 1552 version. Once she had given way on doctrine, the Supremacy Bill passed both houses in April of 1559. It named the queen Supreme Governor, a somewhat less provocative title than Supreme Head. Elizabeth's defeat, however, was far from complete. The Prayer Book of 1552 was amended to soften its Protestant severity, and ambiguous wording was introduced which once again allowed the communion service to become a mass for those who preferred a Catholic view of the Eucharist. A new Act of Uniformity was enacted to give teeth to the Prayer Book and to enforce right thinking throughout the land; and four years later, in 1563, convocation passed the Thirty-nine Articles, a religious creed that reflected the queen's determination to unite her people "into an uniform order of Religion, to the Honour and Glory of God," and to preserve the tranquillity of her realm.

Extremists in both camps complained; the Marian bishops resigned their dioceses and the religious radicals thundered against a compromise that so obviously smelled of political expediency rather than of God's Holy Word. Elizabeth's settlement, however, did in part dampen the fire of religious bigotry, and it has endured in only slightly modified form to the present day. It did so because the queen and her advisers took to heart the warning that England had bowed to four changes in faith in as many decades, and that if it "bent again it would break." Elizabeth was determined that her settlement, once established, should be final, authoritative, and founded upon her own divine and royal prerogative. She alone spoke for God, and the religious history of her reign consisted of a prolonged duel, waged against the Protestant radicals, to keep her church as she created it—comfortable, moderate, and popular.

Elizabeth's religious solution was grounded on the sound psychological principle that in England Catholics were better losers than Protestants. The old church, Mary's resurrected ecclesia, lacked the spirit of martyrdom and came to heel without a fight. Quietly and without a fuss, the Marian bishops resigned their sees and were replaced by middle-of-the-road Protestants. Few priests stood firm—only 189 out of 9,000 refused to take the new Oath of Supremacy—and fewer still of the Catholic laity placed devotion to the pope above patriotism and duty to the crown. In contrast to Mary's handling of Protestants, Elizabeth chose to treat ardent and unrepentant Catholics not as religious martyrs determined to supply the seed for a new and militant church, but as traitors who acknowledged an allegiance to a foreign potentate.

Religion and Diplomacy (1558–1572)

The Word of God had again been established by human contrivance; it still remained to defend the faith and protect the realm from foreign menace. Mary Tudor had died just in time to leave her sister the thankless task of concluding a losing war, acknowledging the loss of Calais, and facing a Henry II of France who, it was said, bestrode England, "having one foot in Calais and the other in Scotland" where a French regent ruled in the name of his daughter-in-law, Mary Queen of Scots. The treaty of Cateau-Cambrésis in April of 1559 brought peace to Europe by ending the century-old hostilities between France, England, and Spain, but it left Henry II of France and Philip II of Spain free to turn their energies to the extermination of heresy in Europe. Henceforth the soul's salvation, not dynastic ambitions in Italy, became their avowed diplomatic aim.

The death of Mary Tudor had proved a blessed liberation for Philip, since he was again free to settle his diplomatic affairs by marriage. He might have been a more serious suitor for Elizabeth's hand had not peace with France involved his marriage to Elizabeth Valois, the daughter of Henry II. His marriage by proxy in July of 1559 had a fateful and unexpected consequence. During a joust in honor of his daughter's wedding, Henry II was mortally wounded. Within ten days the king was dead and France fell prey to a three-way struggle between the ducal and militantly Catholic family of Guise, the Dowager Queen, Catherine de Medici, and the Protestant house of Bourbon. A leaderless France nominally ruled by the ailing fifteen-year-old Francis II produced a diplomatic revolution. Spain, overnight and almost by default, was transformed into the Catholic colossus of Europe, and France herself was exposed to a generation of men who regarded the voice of religious conscience as an adequate guide to domestic and international affairs.

Everywhere in Europe religious passions and hysteria were on the increase. In Rome, the Vatican breathed the extravagant air of the Counter Reformation. The new spirit was symbolized in the terrifying if apocryphal words of Pope Paul IV: "If our own father were a heretic, we would carry the faggots to burn him." Paul would have had no difficulty in detecting error even in his own father, for in 1563 the Council of Trent concluded its lengthy labors and presented the Catholic world with an authoritative pronouncement upon what the faithful were to believe. The supremacy, but not the infallibility, of the pope was proclaimed, and the papacy found in the new order of the Society of Jesus a champion of its authority and an instrument with which to revitalize the ancient faith. The Jesuits were the shock troops of Rome, militant and singleminded believers in a variety of Catholicism which left no room for doubt or uncertainty, no place for discord or disobedience. The new soldiers of the church, led by their spiritual general, Ignatius Loyola, viewed the world as torn between the forces of Satan and the disciples of God, and they called upon men and monarchs to work for "the greater glory of God." Militant, crusading, and convinced Catholicism was on the march, undoing the work of heretics, rewinning lost souls, saving whole kingdoms from damnation, throwing back the Turkish infidel, and yearning to win England again for the Catholic faith.

The Jesuits were the elite of the Counter Reformation, giving it leadership and inspiration; but Spain regarded herself as the chosen instrument of the deity and custodian of the priceless treasure of spiritual liberation. From 1545 on, the prodigious riches of the silver deposits of Peru and the loot of the Incas financed the men and arms dedicated to destroying the godless. In 1559 the trumpet to bring down the Protestant walls of Jericho was tuned and ready, but Philip was by nature cautious, preferring peace to war, marriage to battle. He waited to see whether Elizabeth could be lured into an alliance with Catholic Spain, or whether she would prove her birthright and relapse into religious error. Even after the publication of the Prayer Book and the Act of Supremacy, Philip manfully restrained any impulse to chastise his sister-in-law; Protestant Bess seemed preferable to the leading Catholic claimant to the Tudor throne, Mary of Scotland, who, though of the proper faith, was married to the dauphin of France. Only when the Spanish king became convinced that the reconquest of his own heretical subjects in the Lowlands was impossible as long as they were receiving encouragement from Protestant England did he sound the blast for her destruction.

The first victim of fanaticism was France, where the monarchy had slipped into incompetence, and the kingdom was torn by Catholic bigotry, unbending Protestant self-righteousness, family feuding, provincialism, privilege, and aristocratic ambitions. Following each other in quick and dissolute succession, the last three Valois kings personified the unhappy condition of France. The sick and insipid Francis II died within the first year of his reign; Charles IX proved to be a profligate young prince who ran the gamut of vices both natural and unnatural but managed to survive until 1574; and the last and most intelligent of the Valois, Henry III, chose to play the vicious fop, ruling over a "court of silk and blood" and a realm that despised his cynicism and perversity. Nine civil wars in forty-two years engulfed the land. The wars were fought in the absence of any effective form of central government and in the presence of abundant moral and political corruption. Frenchman butchered Frenchman as an act of Christian piety, and in 1572 on St. Bartholomew's Day, some two to three thousand Huguenots were massacred in Paris. The Protestant world was horrified, and England shuddered at the thought that there but for the grace of Elizabeth lay slaughtered English Protestants.

With civil war in France, England reaped a diplomatic harvest. On the debit side was the upset of the balance of power, leaving Spain the unrivaled giant of Europe and the leader of the Catholic crusade. No longer was it possible to insure England's safety through the time-honored policy of playing off Valois France against Habsburg Spain. On the credit side was a prostrate France torn by domestic strife and unable to join Spain in a religious war against England. For a time Elizabeth and her council toyed with the possibility of open intervention in France in the hope of recovering Calais; and in 1562, by the Treaty of Hampton Court, the queen promised the French Protestants 100,000 crowns and an army of 6,000 men in return for the port of Le Havre. The city proved to be an easy gift to receive but difficult to keep. Within the year, French Protestants and Catholics were again at peace, and Catherine de Medici was encamped in front of Le Havre with an army 40,000 strong. The English defense was neither long nor glorious, and Elizabeth learned that it was dangerous and expensive to concern herself in the domestic affairs of a foreign power. Moreover, the Spanish menace was becoming so acute that England could no longer indulge in the luxury of war with France. The new situation was reflected in the Treaty of Blois of 1572, whereby England and France pledged themselves to mutual defensive assistance. Though Anglo-French relations remained fretful throughout the century and Elizabeth sent troops to help French Protestant rebels, three centuries of rivalry had ended. Elizabeth herself never forgot nor forgave the loss of Calais, but England learned to live without her continental port, and the approaching battle with Spain for spiritual and national survival more and more consumed her energies.

John Knox and Mary Queen of Scots

English meddling in the affairs of other lands proved to be more successful in Scotland than in France. Across the border, Scottish Protestants and Catholics were at each other's throats. The northern kingdom had long been a thorn in England's side, but ever since the death of James V in 1542 the danger had increased, for Scotland had become a province of France, strategically located at England's back door. The regent was James' widow,

A WOMAN *with her sucking* INFANT, *tied together in a Bag and thrown into* a River *in* SCOTLAND; *and* FOUR MEN HANGED *at the same time for* eating Goose *on* a Fast Day.

"Scottish Protestants and Catholics were at each others' throats." *The Granger Collection.*

Mary of Guise, sister to the most powerful nobleman in France. The child queen of Scots had been sent to Paris to be educated in French ways and to marry the dauphin, and French culture and interest prevailed at Edinburgh.

James V, despite the advice offered by Henry VIII that defiance of the Vatican would open up the monastic lands to the Scottish crown, had remained loyal to Rome. The church of Scotland was in even greater need of reform than the English ecclesia, but James had been unmoved since Scottish clerics tended to be useful and worldly prelates, and since he could bestow ecclesiastical estates and offices as rewards for political loyalty rather than for service to God. After James' death in 1542 the situation began to change. With the growth of French influence at court, God-fearing Protestant preachers were able to pose as true Scottish nationalists working to liberate the church from the hands of a godless foreign power.

After a prolonged and tumultuous sojourn, first in Frankfurt and Geneva and then in England, John Knox, that irascible member of God's elect, returned home from exile in 1559. He brought with him a species of Protestantism peculiarly congenial to the restless and rebellious hearts of highland lairds who coveted the lands of the church, hated the regent for exercising royal authority, and hoped to rid the kingdom of French domination. What particularly appealed to their clannish souls was Knox's militant assurance that it was the duty of "Nobles and Estates to be as bridles to repress the insolvency of your kings." Even before Knox arrived, Scottish nobles, wise in the ways of feudal anarchy, had joined together in defense of God's Word and their own treasured independence by forming the Congregation of the Lord, part an army and part a covenant of the faithful. By the summer of 1559 the Protestant clans were in full revolt against the regent, and in February of 1560 Elizabeth reluctantly allowed herself to become involved in the expensive and risky policy of fostering revolution across the border. She had no other choice: the Lords of the Congregation were consistently defeated in battle; Mary Stuart, who in 1559–60 was already queen of Scotland and queen consort of France, was advertising her claims to be queen of England as well; and French troops were pouring into Scotland in support of the regent. For Elizabeth, intervention in Scotland was not so much a matter of defending the Protestant faith as of preserving her own throne. Helped by English soldiers and sterling and by the death of Mary of Guise, the Protestant faction finally triumphed. By the Treaty of Edinburgh, signed in June of 1560, French troops were withdrawn, and England and Scotland joined hands for the first time in 300 years; not even the arrival of Mary Stuart the following year to claim her Scottish inheritance could undo the links which the Protestant faith was forging.

With the death of Francis II in December of 1560, seventeen-year-old Mary Stuart faced the doleful prospect of leaving the center of Renaissance culture for the bleak hills of Calvinistic Scotland. Like Elizabeth she was a monarch without a spouse, but, unlike the English queen, Mary made matrimony the center of her life, not the instrument of her rule. She sought and found romance in a fashion that elevated the sordid career of one of history's silliest females into something approaching classical tragedy. Deeply religious but devoid of moral sense, Mary Stuart combined the granite stubbornness of her Scottish blood with the coquetry of her French upbringing. She was the most fatally charming and dangerously idiotic of her ill-starred Stuart dynasty.[2] She sought to win back her heretical and rebellious kingdom by tact and feminine charm, and for a time she listened to the warning administered by Preacher Knox when she asked him whether he thought "that subjects having power may resist Princes?" "If the Princes exceed their bounds" was his dour answer. It was not her Catholicism, however, but her dynastic ambition that was the queen's undoing, for Mary refused to ratify the Treaty of Edinburgh which required her to renounce her rights to the Tudor throne. Indeed, to strengthen that claim, she married on July 29, 1565, her cousin, Henry Stuart, Lord Darnley, a grandson by a second marriage of Mary's own grandmother, Margaret Tudor. Darnley was a vicious and effeminate young man, and ultimately the match resulted in double murder and the loss of her throne; but the child of Mary Stuart and Lord Darnley lived to rule Scotland for thirty-six years and England for another twenty-two.

Mary's marriage lasted scarcely nineteen months. It was destroyed by her husband's hatred for his wife's Italian and very private secretary, David Riccio, who was killed by Darnley in a jealous rage. In revenge Mary connived at and possibly arranged the murder of her husband on February 9, 1567. She then ran off with his murderer, James Hepburn, Earl of Bothwell. Catholics and Protestants alike were aghast at adultery and murder in a queen, no matter how young and charming, and the streets of Edinburgh resounded with the cry "Burn the Whore." In June she was seized and shortly forced to abdicate in favor of her thirteen-month-old son; a year later she managed an utterly romantic escape, but within the week she was defeated in a final effort to win back her kingdom. To escape renewed imprisonment or worse, she fled to England where she became Elizabeth's difficult and unwanted guest for the next nineteen years.

Throughout Mary Stuart's hectic reign, Elizabeth had made it clear that as long as she could secure her northern frontier she preferred her legitimate, though Catholic, cousin to any Protestant rebel. Even after Mary's imprisonment and abdication in 1567, Elizabeth sought her restoration; and during the years that the Stuart queen was her guest in England, Gloriana treated her as the rightful sovereign of Scotland. Only after Mary had entangled herself in the designs of Philip of Spain and persisted in dangerous intrigues to unseat her Tudor cousin, did Elizabeth finally settle

---

[2] The romance of Mary Queen of Scots and the controversy surrounding her involvement in the murder of her husband have produced a veritable library of works. Possibly the three best are T. F. Henderson, *Mary Queen of Scots* (1905), Andrew Lang, *The Mystery of Mary Stuart* (1901), and Antonia Fraser, *Mary Queen of Scots* (1969). Since they present different views, they should be read together.

her diplomatic relations with Scotland. By the Treaty of Berwick in 1586 she entered into a defensive alliance with her northern neighbor, recognized James as lawful king, granted him a handsome pension, and, though she never expressly said as much, let it be known that Mary Stuart's son was the heir to her crown.

Mary of Scotland's career epitomized the wisdom of Gloriana's decision to remain single. Virginity was Elizabeth's surest diplomatic weapon and her greatest domestic anxiety. Abroad she used the prospect of marriage to bait her diplomatic hook, and she allowed herself to be courted by almost every eligible crown prince of Europe. At home, however, a virgin queen was regarded by almost everyone as unnatural and dangerous to the realm. A husband and an heir were supremely important, but no one, least of all Elizabeth, could decide upon an appropriate spouse. The Scottish ambassador struck at the core of the problem as far as Gloriana was concerned when he tactlessly but astutely told her that "ye think that if ye were married, ye would be queen of England, and now ye are king and queen both. Ye may not suffer a commander." Elizabeth's "stately stomach" regarded marriage as incompatible with sovereignty, and she chose the risky path of virginity. In doing so, however, she exposed England to civil and religious war; as long as Elizabeth remained single, Catholic Mary Stuart was her legal heir. In 1562 the queen was brought to the threshold of death by smallpox and, when she recovered, she was boldly informed by her people that "the want of your marriage and issue is like to prove ... a plague" upon the land. Elizabeth remained unmoved, and when parliament begged her to name a husband, she tartly replied: "I will not in so deep a matter wade with so shallow a wit." Clearly the queen considered parliament presumptuous and unworthy to discuss the question of a monarch's marriage and nuptial bed; and her own wit told her that it was politically safer and diplomatically wiser to remain single. Dangerous as a maiden and childless queen might be, a royal lady who lost her independence and created a rival political power through marriage—as Mary Stuart had done—would be even more disturbing. Elizabeth preferred to keep the world and her subjects guessing and to play the delightful game of coquetry. She flirted with—and possibly she loved—Robert Dudley, Earl of Leicester, but she never forgot that the people of her kingdom were the principal audience of her courtship. "Do not upbraid me with miserable lack of children," she implored her parliament, "for every one of you, and as many as are Englishmen, are children and kinsmen to me."

The Elizabethan Body Politic

In the clash between the queen and her loyal parliament over the question of marriage, Elizabeth articulated a political creed that became the basis of her domestic policy: she would set her own house in order without the advice or interference of overmighty magnates or presumptuous

ROBERT DUDLEY, FIRST
EARL OF LEICESTER
"She flirted with—and
possibly she loved—Robert
Dudley, Earl of Leicester."
*The Collection of Mr. and
Mrs. Paul Mellon.*

commoners, and she would be master in that house.[3] The first step in revitalizing the body politic was the selection of councillors congenial to a sovereign who was secular in spirit and politic in thought, and who demanded that she alone monopolize the stage of royalty and receive the accolades of her loving people. The queen chose moderate, hardworking men who were content to remain behind the scenes, arranging the pomp and circumstance of monarchy and managing the drudgery of government. In politics Gloriana turned to William Cecil who, like Elizabeth, had been a Henrician under Henry VIII, a Protestant under Edward VI, and a nominal Catholic under Mary. He was first the queen's principal secretary and finally in 1572 her lord treasurer, and upon him Elizabeth conferred one of the few new peerages of her reign.[4] He became Lord Burghley; "a

---

[3] Absolutely essential to a proper understanding of Elizabethan England are E. M. Tillyard, *The Elizabethan World Picture* (1934); C. Morris, *Political Thought in England, Tyndale to Hooker* (1953); F. Van Baumer, *The Early Tudor Theory of Kingship* (1940); and L. Stone, *The Crisis of the Aristocracy, 1558–1641* (abridged edition, 1967).

[4] Anyone interested in the queen's great minister should read C. Read's two studies: *Mr. Secretary Cecil and Queen Elizabeth* (1955) and *Lord Burghley and Queen Elizabeth* (1960).

great heretic, and such a clownish Englishman," it was said, that he believed "that all the Christian princes joined together are not able to injure the sovereign of his country."

In religion Gloriana placed her new church in the cautious care of Matthew Parker, Archbishop of Canterbury, whose wife offended the queen's sense of clerical propriety but whose conservatism and loyalty more than compensated for his being married. In finance she turned to William Paulet, Marquis of Winchester, her lord treasurer until his death in 1572, and to Sir Thomas Gresham, an expert in international finance. With unerring political sense Elizabeth perceived that only a solvent monarchy could be a popular monarchy, and she began the long, painstaking task of rebuilding the nation's credit. The job was not easy. Her sister had bequeathed an empty treasury, a debt of £227,000, an unstable currency, and a costly and futile war. Elizabeth's own adventures into France and Scotland were not cheap, and involved the sale of £90,000 of crown lands and the borrowing of £247,000 of foreign money. Yet the queen managed somehow to perform a fiscal miracle. The debased coinage was withdrawn, and a new currency issued which improved the foreign rate of exchange and netted the government a profit of £45,000. The debt was paid off, and Elizabeth's credit rose to the point where she could borrow in the Netherlands at 8 percent interest, while Philip of Spain had to give 16 percent. By 1562 the crown was, for the first time since the days of Henry VII, living on its own historic sources of income—about £250,000 in all—with only minimal help from parliament.

In setting her house in order the queen unconsciously followed the political mentality of her age, which was soundly authoritarian in its social, religious, and political prejudices. Society was an organic and hierarchical whole in which obedience to legal authority became "the glue and solder of the public weal, the ligament which tieth and connecteth the limbs of this body politic each to the other." The favorite Elizabethan political metaphor was the human body, and Thomas Wilson assured his readers that "the true ordering of the state of a well-fashioned commonwealth" was for every part to "obey one head, one governor, one law, as all parts of the body obey the head, [and] agree among themselves." Monarchy gave the kingdom its unity and leadership, and Elizabeth told her parliament that "it is monstrous that the feet should direct the head" and "no king fit for his state will ever suffer such absurdities." The crown, however, existed only in confederation with a myriad of local and regional interests, classes, and corporations. Guilds, towns, and shires recognized their subordinate position within the state, yet each was conscious of its own identity and stubbornly retained a high degree of independence of action. In such a scheme of things the parts as well as the totality were divine. Elizabeth by necessity was a divine-right monarch, "the life, the head, and the authority of all things that be done in the realm of England." But she could claim no monopoly of divinity, for all authority in the sixteenth century was divine, all rights and duties sacrosanct. In a sense, a religiously articulated constitutionalism had developed, in which every element of the body politic was expected to cooperate but could also claim a hearing. Consequently the highest institution within the realm was that organ which could speak for all interests in the commonwealth—king in parliament.[5] When Elizabeth sat is the midst of her Lords and Commons, and legislation was enacted by the whole parliament, then the kingdom spoke *ex cathedra*. Parliament was the "highest and most absolute power of the realm" because it was said "every Englishman is intended to be there present . . . from the prince to the lowest person in England."

Not only was king in parliament the highest authority of the kingdom, but in that body the crown also found its greatest bulwark against rebellion. The Spanish ambassador spoke the truth when he said of Henry VIII that he "always fortified himself by the consent of parliament." Royal caprice was translated into statute; should rebellion arise it would not be against the king alone but against the will of King, Lords, and Commons as embodied in law. The Tudors required no standing army. They had no need to rule in "the French fashion," for the will of God and the monarch were enshrined in acts of parliament. On one point, however, Elizabeth was adamant: the controlling mind within that mystical union of crown and parliament belonged to the queen.

All the Tudors were at pains to retain the initiative in the lawmaking process, and Elizabeth scrutinized with cautious care each aspect of the legislative machinery. From the molding of public opinion so as to insure the election of "godly and Christian men," to the writing of bills and their passage through parliament, the crown supervised every step of the process and endeavored to influence the mind of its faithful Commons. No dynasty was ever more solicitous of the good opinion of its subjects or more conscious of the necessity of a proper frame of mind within the realm. Governmental paternalism by public connivance and acclaim was the Tudor goal. The art of propaganda and the deliberate manipulation of public opinion had their birth in the sixteenth century. Pamphlets and official versions of almost every historic event of Gloriana's reign were distributed for home and foreign consumption. Elizabeth's public relations man and keeper of the public conscience was her principal secretary and lord treasurer, William Cecil, whose spies sounded out popular sentiment and whose instruments shaped it. Even the works of Shakespeare were read and censored by the master of the revels, and his deletions and emendations can be read to this day.

If loyal subjects failed to send right-minded representatives to parliament, the government could exercise pressure, though it rarely tampered openly with elections. As part of their political patronage the great lords all

---

[5] Possibly the phrase should be "queen in parliament"; but the sixteenth century tended to think of royalty in masculine terms, irrespective of the sex of the sovereign.

had "pocket boroughs" which looked to them for favor at court, and the voters often left one of the two names on their election forms empty to be filled in by their patron. In controlling the peers and bishops of the realm, Elizabeth in effect held reign over a sizable proportion of the personnel of the lower house.

Once in London and at Westminster Palace, landed gentlemen, county merchants, and city lawyers, though they quickly grew wise in parliamentary precedent and procedure, needed guidance and even, on occasion, severe discipline, if a turbulent assembly of rowdy provincials was to be transformed into a legislative body. As late as 1581 it was necessary to teach the House polite manners, so that at the end of the day Commons would "depart and go forth in a comely and civil sort" and not "so unseemly and rudely to thrust and throng out as of late time hath been disorderly used." The Speaker of the House and the privy councillors were the queen's instruments of discipline. The Speaker was a royal appointee who controlled the timing of bills, curtailed debate, and passed judgment upon a close vote between the ayes and the nays. He was held strictly accountable for a properly cooperative House, and one Speaker was told by an Elizabethan privy councillor: "You, Mr. Speaker, should perform the charge Her Majesty gave you at the beginning of this parliament, not to receive bills of a nature which is not pleasing to Her Majesty."

The ultimate source of parliamentary leadership was the queen's Privy Council, most of which sat in the House of Commons. So long as members of the council were experts in procedure and precedent, drafted and piloted legislation, coordinated the labors of Lords and Commons, and determined the subject, length, and direction of debate, the House of Commons filled the role assigned to it in the divine order of things: the docile, silent, and obedient junior member in the partnership of king in parliament.

The Privy Council was more than the crown's voice in Commons; it was the mainspring of Tudor government and the channel through which direction and inspiration were infused into the body politic. Though it spoke solely in the queen's name and in theory acted only upon matters brought to it by the sovereign, the council in fact was the administrative ruler of the realm and helped the monarch determine national policy. A Tudor sovereign was only as good as his council, and was dependent upon it for accurate information and efficient execution of the royal will. The queen's council handled foreign affairs, either writing or drafting official communiqués to foreign powers; it issued proclamations dealing with every facet of Elizabethan life; it appointed local officials in the queen's name; and it was in constant touch with the most detailed aspects of provincial affairs. The price of wheat, the level of wages, the drainage of rivers, the apprehension of criminals, the construction of bridges—nothing was too slight nor too important for the council's consideration and action. Together the queen and her Privy Council were the head and heart of a commonweal in which some men were born to lead, others to follow, and all men to obey divinely constituted authority.

Beneath the council was a salaried bureaucracy of scarcely five hundred persons. The secretariat numbered no more than fifteen; the treasury, which included customs officials and exchequer clerks, amounted to possibly 265; the judiciary managed with a staff of fifty; and the various regional agencies—the duchy of Lancaster, the earldom of Chester, the Councils of Wales and of the North—completed the list with a staff of 145. This happy scarcity of bureaucrats in Tudor society did not mean that Englishmen were blessed with less government than elsewhere in Europe. Quite the contrary. Elizabethan paternalism and control over the common folk were brought directly into the shires by a regiment of unpaid amateur officials and by the political philosophy of the age, which taught that the ownership of land carried with it a responsibility for leadership and a duty to serve the crown. Whether or not the 5,000 natural leaders of society actually held title as justices of the peace, lord lieutenants of the county, sheriffs, chief constables, or commissioners of the sewers, they were expected to preserve order throughout the realm. At the apex of the ruling classes stood the sixty or so peers of the realm, who were worth anywhere from £20,000 to £100,000 in land and capital assets; at the bottom of the governing pyramid were the provincial merchants, lesser country gentlemen, government clerks, and city lawyers, most of whom possessed at least fifty pounds a year in an era that accepted two pounds, ten shillings as a minimal but adequate annual income. The group was financially and socially privileged, and enjoyed the choicest plums of office and patronage in return for single-hearted service to the throne.

Of all the unpaid officials of government the 1,500 or so justices of the peace, who represented possibly three-fifths of the whole ruling class, were the most important and effective. The JPs were chosen from men of birth and breeding by the Privy Council; they were often members of the House of Commons, and combined knowledge of law with understanding of local conditions. From forty to seventy justices were appointed in each county, and they united the judicial and administrative functions of government. Except for major crimes, they handled local justice, often hearing complaints and handing down punishment in their front parlors. Administratively, they were the eyes, ears, and hands of the Privy Council, informing the government of such local crises as floods and famines, fixing wages and watching over the needy of the parish, supervising weights and measures, and auditing the accounts of the overseers of the poor. They were ultimately responsible for the collection of parliamentary taxes and, along with the lord lieutenants, supervised the defenses of the shire and raised troops in time of emergency. Underpaid, overworked, and conditioned to ruling, the JP was the indispensable unit of Tudor government, and both queen and council were at pains to insure his loyalty and efficiency.

In no other kingdom of Europe was royal authority so effective; in Valois France the monarch spoke but no one listened; in Spain Philip's word was law, but corruption and inefficiency blunted his authority; only in Elizabeth's England was the crown able to rule with the confidence and cooperation of the landed and governing classes. The system worked reasonably well because Gloriana and her council sensed the threefold secret of political success: (1) the importance of maintaining respect for government and of encouraging the habit of obedience among leaders of society as well as the multitude; (2) the guiding through parliament of legislation agreeable to the ears of MPs who often turned into JPs when they went back to their shires; and (3) the binding of the financial and social aspirations of the ruling elite to the throne by the judicious distribution of court, county, church, and military patronage. More than her religious settlement, more than her diplomatic victory in Scotland, more even than her triumph over Spain in the years to come, Elizabeth's greatest accomplishment was her success in infusing her government and her realm with the confidence, pride, and energy that sent Drake around the globe, led Raleigh to plant nations in the wilderness of the New World, and inspired Shakespeare to speak of

> This royal throne of kings, this scepter'd isle,
> This earth of majesty, this seat of Mars,
> This other Eden, demi-paradise,
> This fortress built by Nature for herself
> Against infection and the hand of war,
> This happy breed of men, this little world,
> This precious stone set in the silver sea,
> Which serves it in the office of a wall
> Or as a moat defensive to a house,
> This blessed plot, this earth, this realm, this England.
>
> *Richard II, Act ii, sc. i*

Cultural Setting

To describe Elizabethan society with a single reference to Shakespeare (1564–1616) and none to Christopher Marlowe (1564–1593), Ben Jonson (1573?–1637), Edmund Spenser (1552–1599), Francis Bacon (1561–1626), and a host of lesser literary and philosophical giants is to describe a flower without mentioning its scent, color, and shape. No one has yet come forth with an adequate explanation of Renaissance England, where the magnetism and daring of men seemed unlimited; where the brevity and suffering of life engendered not despondency but the determination to excel in all manner of things—in literature, in feats of navigation and endurance, in philosophy, and even in saintliness and fiendishness. No one has explained what trick of sociological legerdemain produced the magic of Will Shakespeare's plays, the intellectual daring of Bacon, or the insatiable dream that led Sir Walter Raleigh (1552?–1618) at the age of forty-two to seek the legendary land of El Dorado. What created the dynamic self-confidence that induced Drake, Gilbert, and Grenville to risk their lives for God and queen? Sir Humphrey Gilbert (1539?–1583) was last seen returning home from his ill-starred effort to colonize Newfoundland. He was seated in the stern of a tiny cocklecraft in the midst of a North Atlantic storm, serenely soliloquizing: "We are as near to heaven by sea as by land." Sir Richard Grenville (1541–1591) in the *Revenge* took on the entire Spanish Atlantic fleet and had to be forceably restrained from ordering the powder magazine of his ship blown up to prevent the ignominy of the loss of one of her majesty's warships. He could not be stopped, however, from toasting the Spanish captain and then, according to legend, committing suicide by eating the goblet as his horrified captors looked on. Sir Francis Drake (1540?–1596) was an incredibly vain man, but for once vanity and achievement marched hand in hand in a naval hero who regarded it as his divine mission personally to punish Philip II for his perfidy to God, to England, and to Sir Francis Drake! His name alone—the Spanish called him El Draque, the dragon—was said to have been worth the mightiest galleon in the queen's navy. All three of these intrepid seadogs had their answer to Raleigh's proud challenge: "What shall we be, travelers or tinkers, conquerors or novices?"

Other lands and other centuries have had their demigods, but Elizabethan England was unique in that the heroes of the mind and pen paralleled the deeds of conquerors; in fact, on occasion they were one and the same person. The poet John Donne (1573–1631) went avoyaging in 1596 with Lord Admiral Howard, Raleigh, and the young Earl of Essex on their triumphant attack upon Cadiz. Sir Walter Raleigh, in the midst of military, commercial, and governmental enterprises, found time to compose some of the finest verses of the century; other professional soldiers also produced quite passable poetry; and Elizabeth herself wrote speeches that might have done credit to Shakespeare. The playwright Kit Marlowe, murdered in a barroom brawl, was probably a government informer, and Sir Francis Bacon, the most revolutionary and brilliant mind of his generation, was a politician who—even by Tudor-Stuart standards—was found guilty of misappropriating government funds. Economic prosperity, an intense sense of Protestant mission, incredible good luck, and the presence of a Virgin Queen whose personality and showmanship somehow managed to ignite the fire of boundless loyalty in most of her subjects, all contributed to the flowering of a generation which was deeply aware that style makes the man. "It is with life as it is with a play; it matters not how long the action is spun out, but how good the acting is." In one way or another the heroes of the sixteenth century regarded themselves as on display—either before God (the Puritan) or before history—and Elizabeth spoke both a political and metaphysical truth when she exclaimed "We princes are set on stages in the sight and view of all the world duly observed."

There had once been a time when men set their eyes only upon God

SIR FRANCIS DRAKE
"A naval hero who regarded it as his divine mission personally to punish
Philip II for his perfidy to God, to England, and to Sir Francis Drake.
British Museum.

and asked to be accorded immortality in heaven; but now, even for lesser men, it was also necessary that the deeds and reputations of mortals live on in the minds of future generations. As Humphry Lluyd, one of the more obscure Elizabethan mapmakers, lay dying in 1568, he set his heart not on paradise but on finishing his map of Wales; and when he had completed the task, he wrote the great Dutch cartographer, Abraham Ortelius: "Dearly beloved Ortelius, neither the daily shaking of the continual fever . . . neither the looking for present death, neither the vehement headache without inter-mission could put the remembrance of my Ortelius out of my troubled brain. Wherefore I send you my Wales not beautifully set forth in all points, yet truly depointed. . . . Take therefore this last remembrance of thy Humphry and for ever adieu." Humphry Lluyd's map of Wales was his claim to immortality.

Life was a "wide and universal theatre," but Shakespeare, Bacon, and Marlowe offered something more than a purely sixteenth-century script; they voiced ideas that have proved enduring for all men and all times. The great Shakespearean history plays which open where this text begins, with the deposition of Richard II, are both a lesson in the judgment of God upon a kingdom that had violated the divine order of things and a deeply human study in the relationship of means to ends: when men are corrupt they debase the most inspired ends; when the ends are ignoble they destroy the most noble men. Bacon's *Advancement of Learning* and *Novum Organum* are not only sustained sixteenth-century attacks on medieval scholastic thought; they also go to the root of living—Sir Francis advises his fellow Elizabethans that knowledge is power and that if man would learn to gen-eralize and experiment on the basis of empirically proven evidence he could be as the gods and possess sovereignty over the universe. Power—political, technological, and scientific—fascinated the late Elizabethans, and they were fully aware that the world was their oyster if only man himself were not a pigmy, forever in need of divine guidance. It was presumptuous but understandable that Marlowe's Doctor Faustus should seek to make a pact with the devil to gain a dominion that "stretcheth as far as doth the mind of man." But Faustus was justifiably consigned to hell when he hark-ened to the diabolical proposal: "Here Faustus, try thy brains to gain a deity." Men who seek to become gods in fact become devils; and sometimes it is not easy to be sure whether individuals like Raleigh were heroes or, as many of his contemporaries called him "the greatest Lucifer that hath ever lived in our age."

Crisis and Recessional

10 Sound management and God's special favor saw Elizabeth through the first ten years of her reign; her religious settlement was adopted with surprisingly little opposition, and her kingdom committed to a Protestant foreign policy which was as peaceful and economical as the queen could make it. Commencing in 1568 the situation began to change. The deity showed a depressing tendency to forget his special charge—"God's Englishman"—and Elizabeth and her council had to work that much harder to guide the realm through rebellion at home and crisis abroad.[1] The same centrifugal forces that were tearing France to pieces began to appear in England, and on the international front a decade of living in the same world with a touchy and pugnacious Catholic Spain began to strain even Gloriana's diplomatic finesse.

Cold War—Sixteenth-Century Style

Elizabeth had begun her reign as an ally of her Spanish brother-in-law in the conflict against France, and it had been Philip who successfully countered French influence at Rome and guarded Elizabeth against excommunication. The Most Catholic King of Spain preferred upon the English throne an independent though Protestant Elizabeth Tudor to a Catholic but French Mary Stuart. By 1568, however, Philip was beginning to wonder whether he had miscalculated; ten years later he was convinced a terrible mistake had been made and that someday Elizabeth would have to be destroyed. When Elizabeth ascended the throne, France had been strong and

---

[1] The following are a number of books which give a somewhat different flavor to the personalities and events of the reign: R. H. Tawney, *The Agrarian Problem in the Sixteenth Century* (1912); P. M. Handover, *The Second Cecil* (1959); R. Lacey, *Robert Devereux: The Earl of Essex* (1971); J. A. Williamson, *The Age of Drake* (1938); J. Hurstfield, *The Queen's Wards* (1958); and L. B. Smith, *The Elizabethan World* (1967).

united, Mary Stuart's Guise relatives had been militantly anti-Spanish, and England had been weak and struggling under her Virgin Queen. Twenty years later the situation was very different: France had ceased to be a great power, the Guise family had moved into the Spanish orbit, and England had become the champion of heresy on the continent.

Slowly but surely the diplomatic friendship between England and Spain cooled into toleration, cold war, and open conflict. From the start Anglo-Spanish relations were strained by English trading incursions into the Caribbean, which Spain regarded as her sacred preserve. In 1562 John Hawkins, his ships' holds filled with slaves from West Africa, sailed for Haiti. There he sold his contraband cargo and with handsome gifts persuaded Spanish officials to ignore their own imperial edicts outlawing all trade with foreign powers. Two years later he was back again; this time Cecil, Leicester, and even the queen herself invested in an enterprise that netted the shareholders a 60 percent profit. Hawkins' third voyage in 1567 fared less well; his squadron of ten ships was set upon by a Spanish fleet, and he was fortunate to escape with two of his vessels.

Just when Spain was ordering her colonial officials and admirals to treat Hawkins as a pirate, England decided to give unofficial but vital aid to Philip's rebellious and heretical subjects in the Netherlands. The Dutch crisis was all-important. Philip's seventeen Dutch and Flemish provinces, which were part of his Habsburg inheritance, were becoming increasingly restless under their Catholic and Spanish overlords. Open rebellion erupted in 1566 when Philip, anxious to exterminate the hateful Calvinistic faith, introduced the Spanish Inquisition. The more he tried to suppress heresy and rebellion, the more desperate grew the revolt. England became involved when Dutch heretics in the northern maritime provinces took to the ocean as "Sea Beggars," set on striking a blow for God by destroying Spanish shipping in the channel. Philip called them pirates, but Elizabeth offered them sanctuary in English ports and allowed them to take on provisions and sell their plunder to London merchants. Relations between Elizabeth and Philip came close to open war in December of 1568 when a Genoese ship, laden with gold loaned to Spain to pay for the disciplining of the Netherlands, put into an English port to escape the Sea Beggars. Gloriana promptly seized the bullion and renegotiated the loan with the Genoese bankers. Philip was outraged and regarded the action as blatant robbery. In retaliation he stopped English commerce to the Lowlands, and Elizabeth countered by freezing all Spanish assets in England.

The Northern Rebellion

Just as the diplomatic cold war was warming up, Elizabeth was confronted with her first major domestic crises: the arrival of the fugitive Mary Stuart on May 16, 1567, and the rebellion of the northern earls in the autumn of 1569. The Revolt of the North was a lesson in inept timing and evidence of the strength of the Tudor regime. Three divergent grievances were at work to produce insurrection: feudal sensibilities in the northern shires, dislike for Mr. Secretary Cecil at court, and the queen's opposition to Mary Stuart's proposed marriage to Thomas Howard, fourth Duke of Norfolk. Howard was England's sole remaining duke and the ranking peer of the realm, a cousin to Elizabeth, and an irresolute nobleman whose aristocratic sensibilities were inordinately touchy and who fancied himself as husband to a queen. He and a number of other peers were determined to destroy William Cecil, whom they felt to be the source of Elizabeth's anti-Spanish, pro-Protestant foreign policy, and responsible for her interfering and bureaucratic ways in government. Behind Norfolk stood the earls of Northumberland and Westmorland, who harked back to the irresponsible days of their Percy and Neville forefathers when feudal loyalty to kin and clan spoke louder than allegiance to the crown. The crisis came to a head in June of 1569 when Elizabeth threw her support behind Cecil, forbade Norfolk's marriage to Mary Stuart and ordered him to return to court. The duke elected discretion over valor and submitted, but the northern earls took alarm; they revolted in the name of the true faith and the good old life, which was being endangered by economic and social change. By Christmas of 1569 the last feudal uprising had collapsed, and 800 peasants died on the gallows for their loyalty to a code that no longer had a place in Tudor England.

The long deferred bull of excommunication against Elizabeth was finally issued in February of 1570, but papal thunder fell on deaf ears; in England the voice of rebellion was silenced, and abroad both Philip and Elizabeth were still reluctant to commit their kingdoms to the ordeal of war. The king of Spain was far too concerned with heresy in the Netherlands and Turkish penetration into the Mediterranean to lend teeth to an otherwise harmless spiritual threat; and Elizabeth, despite the passionate appeals of the war party in her council, had no intention of involving England in a costly war. Relatively inexpensive cold war was more to her taste.

For all their caution, however, Elizabeth and Philip were heading for armed conflict. Gloriana, despite her barefaced disclaimers, continued to give aid and comfort to Philip's Dutch rebels and to sanction English piracy against his treasure fleets. Philip in his turn encouraged Catholic sedition in England, gave support to Mary of Scotland, and slowly became convinced that he was God's instrument, chosen to rid the world of that arch heretic, Elizabeth of England.

Philip II of Spain and His Great Enterprise

On paper Philip appeared stronger by far than Elizabeth. He was not only king of Spain but after 1580 monarch of Portugal as well, thus uniting the Iberian peninsula and the empires of the New World. In Italy, the duchy of Milan and the kingdom of Naples were Spanish. The western

Mediterranean was a Spanish lake from which the Turks were driven after their defeat at the naval battle of Lepanto in 1571. The seventeen provinces of the Netherlands and the county of Burgundy were Philip's birthrights, and the profits from the commerce of Antwerp, the silver of Peru, and the trade of the entire world poured into his capital. The center of this family empire, acquired helter-skelter by the vagaries of death and marriage, was Philip's residence outside of Madrid—the Escorial. Part tomb, part palace, the Escorial reflected the king's literal turn of mind; built in honor of St. Lawrence, who had been grilled over burning coals, it was shaped in the form of a vast gridiron. There, with the eight coffins of his nearest and dearest, Philip resided, laboring into the long hours of the night over the most intimate details of his empire and allowing no decision, however trifling, to pass uninspected through his cautious hands.[2] Philip and Spain possessed the will to lead the forces of the Lord in a triumphant Counter Reformation, but they lacked the resources and the resourcefulness. The wealth of the Indies flowed into the realm but stayed only long enough to disrupt the Spanish economy, which was still agricultural and medieval, causing inflation and the illusion but not the substance of prosperity. The real benefactors were the seventeen provinces of the Lowlands which supplied Spanish armies and navies with the ingredients of war, Iberian aristocrats with luxuries imported from all parts of the world, and Catholic monks with salt herring for their fast days.

The time had been when Spanish seamen had known the North Atlantic and the English Channel as well as Hollanders and Cornishmen did. By the mid-century, though Spain ruled the oceans of the world, she was neither spiritually nor materially a great naval power. Genoese and Italians, Flemish and Portuguese captained the giant galleons which transported soldiers to fight for Christ and priests to save heathen souls in Mexico and Central America. When the Armada against England finally set sail, its best pilots were Dutchmen; and the Spanish commanding officer was Alonso Perez de Guzmán el Bueno, Duke of Medina Sidonia, a nobleman of blameless and devout life whose health was uncertain and who confessed that he had rarely ever been to sea, easily caught cold, and was always seasick. Spanish military power excelled on land. Her soldiers regarded the navy as an inferior branch of the service, and warships were used as floating platforms for musketeers and pikemen and not as mobile batteries. Her naval tradition and architecture were Mediterranean, and her ship designers built oared galleasses and clumsy, top-heavy galleons suitable to quiet waters but not to the winds and waves of the Atlantic. "To speak the truth," wrote one English naval captain, "till the King of Spain had war with us, he never knew what war by sea meant, unless it were in galleys against the Turks."

---

[2] The character of Philip II remains baffling. See R. B. Merriman, *The Rise of the Spanish Empire*, vol. IV (1934); R. Trevor Davies, *The Golden Century of Spain* (1954); and J. H. Elliott, *Imperial Spain, 1469–1716* (1963).

The approaching struggle with England was intimately associated with Philip's troubles with his rebellious Dutch subjects. In 1576 he decided on a concerted effort to destroy heresy and subdue his provinces. By a policy of force and diplomacy, the king's governor-general of the Netherlands, the duke of Parma, succeeded in splitting the provinces and rallying the southern states to the side of Spain and Catholicism, leaving only the ten northern principalities in revolt. By 1581 the northern states declared their independence, and four years later in desperation they called for English military assistance. As Parma's troops moved steadily northward, Dutch appeals became more urgent, and finally Elizabeth was induced to send an army of 6,000 soldiers under the earl of Leicester to fight in Holland. No matter how reluctant Philip was to risk war with England, by 1585 it was apparent that peace and victory in the Netherlands could only be achieved after the English heretics had been destroyed and the realm re-Catholicized. Moreover, Spain had suffered long and patiently the indignity of English piracy upon the high seas, and the violation of her imperial and commercial monopoly in the Americas.

The most blatant act of piracy had been Sir Francis Drake's global voyage of pillage and plunder in 1577. Of the five ships that left Portsmouth, only the *Golden Hind* returned thirty-four months later, having completed the second circumnavigation of the earth, but the profit was worth the cost. Elizabeth for once was lavish in her praise, England was gleeful, and Philip infuriated; for English investors, of whom Elizabeth was among the largest, had realized a 4,700 percent profit entirely at Spain's expense. More was soon to follow; in April of 1587 Drake struck again, this time with twenty-three ships carrying royal troops for the official purpose of "distressing" the king of Spain. The English fleet attacked the Spanish homeland, burned thirty ships in the harbor of Cádiz, destroyed naval installations, and blockaded Lisbon for four weeks. Sir Francis completed Philip's humiliation by sailing on to the Azores, where he seized a Spanish merchantman laden with treasure valued at £114,000, of which Elizabeth claimed £40,000 as her share.

Mary of Scotland and English Catholicism

Open war in the Netherlands and on the high seas was complicated by a series of plots and counterplots in England which led to the execution of Mary Queen of Scots on February 8, 1587. For nineteen years Mary Stuart lived in England as an unwanted and embarrassing prisoner; but this did not prevent her from meddling in high treason. Surrounded by English spies, she went from one harebrained plot to the next, any one of which would have ended on the scaffold if Elizabeth could have brought herself to execute a cousin who was an anointed queen. Mary never learned; messages continued to flow from her prison in the accustomed manner of cloak and dagger drama. Elizabeth's government, if not the queen herself, became convinced that sooner or later by the law of averages one of these plots must succeed. Parliament and council implored their queen to exterminate such a "monstrous and huge dragon," and even men of the cloth argued that mercy need not be shown to one who "hath heaped up together all the sins of the licentious sons of David—adulteries, murders, conspiracies, treasons, and blasphemies against God." After months of agonizing indecision, Elizabeth signed the warrant that sent her cousin to the block. In the end she had no other choice, for England was at open war with the man who acknowledged Mary Stuart to be the rightful ruler of the realm and who even talked about making her his wife.

As Spain readied herself for a religious crusade, English Catholics suffered from guilt by association. "No papist," so the equation read, "can be a good subject." During the first years of the reign Catholics were tolerated, but the Northern Rebellion, the papal excommunication of the queen, the threat of invasion, and the intrigues surrounding Mary Queen of Scots forced Elizabeth into a more severe policy. A new spirit of martyrdom was appearing in English Catholicism. More and more the "Cause" received

EXECUTION OF MARY QUEEN OF SCOTS (FEBRUARY 8, 1587)
"After months of agonizing indecision, Elizabeth signed the warrant that sent her cousin to the block." *Bibliothèque Nationale.*

fresh ideas and blood from the continent where Jesuits, fanatics, and exiles dreamed of a united Christendom in which England would be purged of its Protestant heresy. By 1572 Catholicism was clearly tainted with treason when Mary Stuart and the duke of Norfolk, those two veteran intriguers, were caught up in a plot manufactured out of the sanguine and fertile imagination of Robert Ridolfi, an Italian merchant and papal spy, who convinced many people that 10,000 Spanish soldiers were waiting to sail for England and that an equal number of English Catholics were ready to rise up against the queen of heretics. The plot came to nothing and Norfolk was executed, but the specter of militant and seditious Catholicism was not dispelled. Fear of Catholic treason was heightened by the arrival of seminary priests, trained at the English college at Douai in the Netherlands. They came during the 1570s by the dozens to revive the hope and courage of the faithful. Catholic resurgence received further impetus from the Jesuits under Edmund Campion and Robert Parsons who were smuggled into England to "confute errors" and to assure Elizabeth's subjects that their primary duty was to the pope and the law of God.

In the face of such provocation Elizabeth's policy of moderation and toleration collapsed, and the queen found it impossible to resist the demands of nationalists and Protestants determined upon the extermination of the Catholic menace. The penalty against saying mass was increased to 200 marks and a year in jail; Catholic priests were imprisoned; and in theory every Catholic layman faced bankruptcy if he persisted in the errors of his faith. Campion was caught, tortured, and hanged in 1581; and possibly some 200 other seminary priests and Jesuits were executed during Elizabeth's reign. Those who died were hanged and disemboweled as traitors, not heretics; the queen persecuted, but she did so in the name of the sovereign national state. Significantly, she never saw fit to call upon God as her ally; nor did she seek to justify her actions as spiritually necessary to her own salvation or that of her victims.

The Armada

The diplomatic and religious crisis came when the Armada,[3] on which Catholic prayers and Spanish gold had been lavished, finally sailed in July of 1588. One hundred and thirty ships weighing 58,000 tons, carrying over 31,000 men and 2,431 cannons, set forth to administer the vengeance of heaven and the censure of the church. The special mission of this vast effort was the destruction of a middle-aged female who was branded by the Catholic world as having been "born in adultery, an offspring of incest, a declared bastard," and a sovereign "incapable of lawful succeeding." Officers and men, sailors and soldiers had confessed and heard mass before

---

[3] By far the best modern study of the Armada is G. Mattingly, *The Armada* (paperback ed., 1962).

setting sail. Gambling and swearing were forbidden, and no unclean person was allowed to accompany the *Armada Catholica*. Twenty great galleons, floating fortresses each bearing as many as fifty-two guns, and some forty armed merchantmen, slow, seaworthy, and hard to sink, were the fighting core of the Spanish fleet. Then there were thirty-four fast sloops, the eyes and ears of the navy, and two dozen transports to carry the men and arms dedicated to God's Great Enterprise. Philip's strategy was to avoid battle if possible and to send his Armada up the channel to rendezvous with the Spanish forces under the duke of Parma stationed in the Netherlands. Reinforced with Parma's troops, the fleet would then turn and carry the army up the Thames estuary, and land south of London.

What happened every schoolboy knows—the guns of a larger, better armed, and more mobile English fleet, 200 strong and commanded by Drake, Hawkins, and Lord Howard, led the heavy Spanish galleons a merry chase. What saved England and destroyed the Armada was not so much English heroism—of which there was plenty—but Spanish inexperience at sea, the inability of Philip's fleet to make contact with Parma's land forces, and the winds and waves of the North Atlantic, which swept down upon a demoralized Armada and blew it to destruction upon the rocks of Scotland, the Orkney Islands, and Northern Ireland. Of the 130 ships that had left Corunna, perhaps four score crawled home in defeat. Of the rest: 10 had been taken, sunk, burnt, or driven aground by the English; 23 more were vanquished, in the words of one Spanish author, "by the elements, against which valour and human daring are impotent because it is God who rules the seas"; and possibly 12 others were "lost, fate unknown."

Whether accomplished by God or man, the victory was spectacular, and England proved conclusively that "twelve of Her Majesty's ships were a match for all the galleys in the King of Spain's dominions." The Counter Reformation was slowed down, Protestantism and the independence of the northern provinces of the Netherlands were assured, and Englishmen henceforth felt confident that the future and the riches of the New World were theirs. In this, however, the fates reserved a bitter disappointment. Spain learned to defend her empire and to build more seaworthy vessels. War, so brilliantly begun, deteriorated into a costly, endless struggle in Holland, France, and Ireland; and at home the kingdom grew restless under paternal restraint, and waited none too patiently for the old queen to die.

Recessional

In 1588–89 the moment of glory was over, and so in effect was Gloriana's reign. She lived on, recalling memories and watching old friends and enemies die: "her Robin," Robert Dudley, Earl of Leicester, in 1588; Henry III of France and Catherine de Medici in 1589; Marlowe in 1593; Hawkins in 1595; Drake in 1596; Philip in 1598; and her good and faithful servant, William Cecil, in the same year. More and more the world passed her by,

THE ARK ROYAL
Lord Howard's flagship during the defeat of the Armada was "a match
for all the galleys in the King of Spain's dominions." *British Museum.*

and an England emerged that Old Bess neither desired nor understood.
Once the crisis of survival had passed, new and discordant factors developed,
forces that ran counter to the central theme of the Elizabethan political
creed: the organic unity of the realm. Rid of the foreign menace, England
could afford the luxury of domestic squabbling, and factionalism appeared
once again as Puritans thundered at impiety and idolatry in the church,
politicians and parliamentarians grew critical of government restraint, and
merchants complained of economic regulations and state monopolies.

Essex and the Irish Wars

Across the Irish Sea, religion, racialism, and tribalism plus 10,000
Spanish troops and a hundred ships united to produce civil war and rebellion in 1595–96, which took eight years to quell. English rule had existed
in Ireland since the days of the Norman kings, but early English conquerors
had tended to become more Irish than English, and with the Reformation
the government in London could no longer depend even upon the loyalty
of the English Pale around Dublin. In 1596 Anglo-Irish and tribal Irish
joined in a revolt led by Hugh O'Neill, Earl of Tyrone. It cost the queen
£120,000 from the sale of crown lands, two million more from parliamentary

funds, and a debt of £473,000 before Tyrone was captured and English rule of Ireland secured.

A tragic by-product of the Irish quagmire was the destruction of Robert Devereux, Earl of Essex, the last of the queen's favorites and the greatest rebel to her crown. Essex had been the darling of the court ever since his arrival in 1586 at the age of eighteen. He was the embodiment of the Renaissance man, coveting honor and renown above all else. The earl had been granted military responsibility in France and in the naval war against Spain, where he proved himself better at personal heroics than leadership. But Essex yearned most of all for absolute command, and in 1599 he demanded that Elizabeth allow him to lead an army into Ireland to redeem English honor and crush the Tyrone rebellion. He discovered, like many before him, that the Emerald Isle was a military graveyard for English reputations. Instead of finding glory, Essex revealed his incompetence and latent treason. He came to terms with Tyrone, and in defiance of the queen's express orders returned to London to justify his actions and excuse his lack of military success. Elizabeth was patient beyond all expectation, and she put up with a great deal of sulking and posing on the part of her darling earl for the sake of his contagious smile and winning looks. But when in February of 1601 he sought to touch her sceptre and tried to raise the City of London in an abortive revolt against her, she quickly "taught him better manners."

Essex united the most irresponsible attributes of the feudal baron with the even more pernicious conceit of the sublime egotist, and he voiced the one question that Gloriana could not allow to go unpunished. When he had been denied a favor by the queen, he wrote to Sir Thomas Egerton in a raging fury: "What! Cannot princes err? Cannot subjects receive wrong? Is an earthly power or authority infinite? Pardon me, pardon me, my good Lord, I can never subscribe to these principles." The words were ominous, for they meant that the magic of Elizabeth's rule was finally being called in doubt. Spoken by an unstable and churlish Essex they meant little, and most Englishmen gave a sigh of relief when he was executed in 1601, but Tudor society, especially parliament, had heard and recorded his question, though as yet it did not care to give an answer.

The Elizabethan House of Commons

A dangerously unstable political situation was rapidly developing during the final decade of the reign, and not even Gloriana's feminine guile and royal tact could entirely conceal the mounting tension within the body politic. The fat years of economic expansion and plenty were past. In their place came the depressed nineties when the kingdom was beset with bad harvests, soaring food prices, peasant revolts, declining trade, high taxes, and criticism of the crown's economic policies and political leadership. Nowhere was the restlessness so pronounced as in parliament, where only the charm of a Virgin Queen, long accustomed to the vagaries of parliamentary life, prevented a rupture between crown and Commons.[4] Elizabeth acknowledged that parliament was the sole instrument through which the sound of authority was heard in its most weighty guise, but the voice that spoke was her own. Slowly and hesitantly, however, another voice was making itself heard: the direct will of the landed classes speaking through the House of Commons. In Tudor political theory this was a cancerous usurpation and distortion of the function of one element of the commonweal by another. The proper role of parliament, especially that of the lower house, was to beseech and petition, not to command or initiate. Unfortunately, it was difficult for the queen to chastize her Commons or curb its growing independence because of the crown's financial embarrassment. Elizabeth sensed that it was essential never to go to parliament hat in hand to beg for money, and for years she avoided frequent sessions and requests for subsidies, and she forfeited the Stuart future by selling her capital in order to avoid excessive taxation. But war made her insolvent, and potential bankruptcy made her solicitous of the good will of Commons and the taxpayers which it represented. In the end the weight of financial responsibility proved overpowering: Henry VII had averaged £11,500 annually from parliamentary subsidies; his son's rate rose to £30,000; and Elizabeth's stood at £50,000.

Of all the signs of change and of growing self-consciousness on the part of parliament, the most obvious was the phenomenal increase in the size of the House of Commons. The Tudors may have been stingy in their presentation of noble titles but they were lavish in their creation of MPs. While the House of Lords actually decreased in number throughout the century as a consequence of the removal of the monastic spiritual lords, the House of Commons almost doubled in size. In Henry VIII's first parliament 74 knights sat for the thirty-seven shires, and 224 burgesses represented the chartered and franchised boroughs of the realm. As the century progressed, two interrelated movements developed: landed country gentlemen of the shires violated the historic residence laws and sat for borough seats, and the number of towns holding the right to send delegates to the House of Commons increased. Henry added 14 borough seats,[5] Edward 34, Mary 25, and Elizabeth was most prodigal of all and created 62. One element of king in parliament was obviously growing at an alarming pace and was being monopolized by the gentry, who now stood for both shire and borough seats. Socially and economically the Commons was becoming a vocal, self-conscious, and opinionated group; politically it was replacing

---

[4] What has in recent years become the "standard" view of Elizabeth's parliaments was first worked out by W. Notestein, *The Winning of the Initiative by the House of Commons* (1924); and by J. E. Neale, *The Elizabethan House of Commons* (1949), and *Elizabeth and Her Parliaments*, 2 vols. (1957).

[5] Henry also gave representation to the border shires of Monmouth and Chester (two knights each) and to the six new Welsh shires (12 knights and 11 burgesses).

the Lords in importance and was potentially capable of seizing the initiative from the crown if royal leadership and control faltered.

By 1580 Commons was a very different body from that hesitant and reluctant assembly which had been bullied by Henry VIII into discussing and enacting laws sanctioning the spiritual power of the king and establishing the faith of Englishmen. As the custodians of the national purse strings, as the possessors of land and the arbiters of etiquette, and as the jealous guardians of law and order in the shires, the gentry indulged in the presumption that their opinion should not only be listened to with respect but should be solicited. As yet privy councillors and kings were not viewed as servants of a realm where the highest authority resided in parliament; but even under Elizabeth, Commons had the audacity to suggest that it could decide on matters of state just as well as the queen herself. Here, obviously, was what traditionalists most feared: "the foot taketh upon him the part of the head, and Commons is become a king."

Though Elizabeth desperately endeavored to avoid an open conflict with her Commons, a head-on clash materialized in 1601 when parliament began to criticize the crown's right to grant monopolies regulating and licensing the economic life of the country. At stake was the queen's prerogative which stood above earthly criticism, and the theory of paternalistic government by which the crown interfered in the actions of individuals in order to insure economic justice for all. During the controversy, the Privy Council tried to explain to a Commons filled with landed country gentlemen and wealthy city merchants the government's authority to curb free enterprise and impose economic controls without statutory sanction. Elizabeth's dutiful subjects listened in angry silence to a philosophy totally at variance with their own thoughts, and, when the queen at the end of the first parliamentary session, passed through their chamber, the customary greeting—"God bless your majesty"—was halfhearted. Gloriana was deeply alarmed, and she had cause: the essence of her political magic, her personal popularity, was beginning to give way before the growing demands of Commons to initiate and even to control royal policy. As usual Elizabeth knew when to retreat. She saved her prerogative from becoming a topic for debate in Commons by promising a complete inquiry into the abuse of monopolies. Nevertheless, a constitutional issue had been raised, one which would find fervent supporters the moment an irritating and pedantic Stuart sovereign came to the throne: the question whether crown or parliament possessed ultimate responsibility for determining state policy.

The growing self-confidence of parliament was a symptom of a more basic social and psychological change within Tudor society itself, for a bumptious and pushing Commons was the institutional reflection of a vocal and articulate gentry. The growth in the size of the lower house was in itself an indication of the increasing activity of the landed and commercial classes within the kingdom. The gentry flocked to parliament to combine business, pleasure, and politics. The city of London was the swollen and teeming hub

ELIZABETH AND THE PARLIAMENT OF 1584
"The controlling mind within that mystical union of crown and
parliament belonged to the Queen." *British Museum.*

of the commonwealth, the delight of the eye, the disgust of the nose and the center of entertainment both legal and illicit. In an age of ferocious litigation, when scarcely a landowner in England did not occasionally have to travel to town to pursue a suit, the member of parliament was in a favored position by his association with privy councillors and courtiers close to the sovereign. Parliament and London were the crossroads of the realm, windows to the world, and avenues to promotion. London and the royal court were the center of influence for all who coveted an office, urged a suit, had a son to push, or wished a quick return on some investment. Finally, Commons was the most exclusive family club of the realm, and a gentleman from the shires might expect to find a host of close friends and near relatives. In 1576 Sir Francis Knollys sat with his brother and five sons; in 1597 Robert Cecil, his half-brother, a nephew, seven first cousins, and endless relatives formed a family coterie.

Puritans and Puritanism

Elizabeth's parliamentary troubles were made doubly difficult by the presence in the Commons of a stiff and opinionated gentleman, the Puritan.[6] In a way, Puritans were "another people," for Puritanism was an attitude of mind alien to most of Protestant England. Elizabeth's subjects were comfortably content to believe the dictates of established authority; they desired no windows into men's souls. Conformity in faith and obedience in religion were essential to the concept of a divinely ordained body politic in which the queen and the vast majority of her subjects subscribed. Yet the fact remained that Puritanism was on the increase. With each passing decade there seemed to be an ever greater number of men who were willing to risk their bodies' fiery destruction to avoid the flames of their souls' damnation. Had the Smithfield fires burned two decades later, the blaze would have been no candle but a mighty beacon. Only six upper-class leaders of the Protestant movement died under Bloody Mary; the rest fled to Geneva or conformed, while the fuel of martyrdom was supplied by the "common sort." By 1580 ideological truth had engulfed a significant portion of the gentry and mercantile classes, giving to the Puritans a strength and position in society out of all proportion to their numbers. Why more Englishmen were increasingly fervent in their faith and more militant in their religious opinion in 1580 than in 1554 is a profound mystery. All that can be said with safety is that the Puritan stood in the same relationship to Protestantism as the Jesuit did to Catholicism. Both were militant soldiers of their faith; both were driven on by the voice of passionate conviction; both were utterly uncompromising;

---

[6] Anyone interested in the elusive subject of Puritanism might try his hand at W. Haller, *The Rise of Puritanism, 1570–1643* (1938); P. Collinson, *The Elizabethan Puritan Movement* (1969); C. Hill, *Society and Puritanism* (1964); C. H. and K. George, *The Protestant Mind of the English Reformation, 1570–1640* (1961); and above all else R. H. Tawney, *Religion and the Rise of Capitalism* (originally published in 1926).

both placed spiritual values above human prudence; and both viewed religion as the key to life. In this sense James I was accurate if didactic in his *bon mot:* "One puritan presbyter equals one popish priest."

The Puritan was first and foremost a Protestant, holding the Bible as the sole source of religious authority and believing in the sanctity of individual interpretations. He held to the doctrine of predestination, in which an omnipotent God ordains every aspect of the universe and not a leaf can drop from a tree without His foreknowledge. He believed in election, by which God selects certain of His creatures for everlasting salvation. The church was viewed as the body of the faithful, and ministers were regarded as teachers and expounders of scripture, not as priests imbued with miraculous authority. For both Puritan and Protestant the miracle of salvation came solely through God's grace and through the individual's willingness to open his soul, cast out the sins of humanity and pray for a deliverance which he in no way merits, but which God of His mercy may or may not allow.

What distinguished a Puritan from his Protestant brothers was the literalness with which he subscribed to the Protestant creed, the rigorous logic of his approach which led him to advocate the most extreme conclusions, the discipline with which he watched his soul's health, the militant nature of his conviction, and above all the sense of rebirth and conversion which set him above and apart from the rest of humanity. The Puritan was, almost without exception, the man who had experienced a sense of conversion. He was a member of a spiritual elite endowed with rights and privileges denied to lesser men. He was the soldier of the living Christ, the elect of God who alone in a depraved and degenerate world had experienced a rebirth and regeneration.

The Bible was viewed as the literal mirror of life, and church and state were held up to scriptural inspection and generally found to be woefully lacking in piety and godliness. The trouble with the Puritan in the eyes of the established church was his determination to thunder against the evils of society. In the righteous view of Christ's evangels there was much to criticize and purify, for the world was a wicked place and the devil whistled seductively at unwary souls in every corner—in the alehouse, the theater, the country house, the court, and the bedroom. The Puritan was a deeply medieval man in that he believed that life was a spiritual drama, and that the material affairs of today must be judged by the spiritul concerns of tomorrow. It was not that everything cheerful, gay and bright was sinful, for Puritans danced, wined and laughed so long as gaiety was the fruit of godliness and not a sign of man's preoccupation with himself.

Militant, disciplined, elite, and elected, Puritans felt themselves to be separate from the corruption of the world, and it was natural that they should have organized as an exclusive society of God's saints on earth. Everywhere during the 1570s and '80s cells were founded to spread the word of God, to defend the faithful and to transform the realm of England into the kingdom of heaven. These exponents of sanctimoniousness flocked into the House of Commons, and early in the reign an embryonic Puritan parliamentary party clashed with the queen over two basic issues—the purification of that putrefied old oak, the Church of England, and the stamping out of Catholicism, root and branch. What made the presence of Puritanism in parliament doubly dangerous was the union between Commons' desire for freedom of speech, discussion, and legislation, and the Puritan's urge to speak out against a corrupt world. The constitutional issue of free speech and parliamentary initiative was fervently and vocally supported by Puritans, who were especially anxious to reform the church of which Elizabeth was the Supreme Governor.

The established church, so infamous in the eyes of God's elect, was a comfortable and confused organization catering to the muddled desires of mild Protestants and apathetic Catholics who placed loyalty above faith and prudence above conviction. It was largely Catholic in structure, substituting a sovereign lady for a pope but retaining bishops, archdeacons, ecclesiastical courts, and tithes. It was weighed down with sinecures and ignorance, and it was deliberately vague on crucial points of doctrine. Elizabeth, the Supreme Governor, was God's lieutenant on earth, and the Anglican episcopate never renounced the idea that it was a divinely inspired organization deriving authority from God and the queen. The Bible was viewed as the Word of God, but the Church of England argued that it was not for simple folk to inquire too deeply into such mysteries as predestination or the nature of sin. It was far better and infinitely safer to leave Scripture to official interpretation, which tended to be more allegorical than literal. Elizabeth was at great pains to warn her parliament that it was "over-bold with God Almighty" when subjects scanned "His blessed will as lawyers do with human testaments." The presumption, she concluded, "is so great as I may not suffer it . . . nor tolerate newfangledness." The threat of newfangledness was the core of the controversy, for Puritans were dangerously radical in their insistence that the sole purpose of life was a spiritual one and that the duty of the church was to serve God, not the crown.

Puritans had been frustrated in their effort to dominate the Elizabethan settlement of 1559–60, but within a decade they launched another campaign to seize the church from within and to legislate the new Jerusalem into existence through parliamentary statute. The campaign commenced in 1570, when both press and pulpit were utilized to re-educate the queen and her people. In the following year the fight was carried to parliament, and the Puritan party soon learned that in parliamentary freedom of speech they had a popular cause, and a weapon that might induce the queen to ease her opposition to religious reform. It was the Wentworth brothers of biblical name—Paul and Peter—who led the war for free speech and a purified church. Peter publicized the root of the controversy when he told Archbishop Parker that "we will pass nothing before we understand what it is; for that were but to make you popes." In 1576 he again spoke out against the queen's refusal to allow parliament to discuss matters of religion, saying that, during the last session of parliament, God had been "shut out of doors." Next, Paul persuaded Commons in 1581 to hear a godly sermon at the commencement of each daily meeting, but the queen, sensing the righteous Puritan hand of the Wentworths, forbade it.

The crisis came in the parliament of 1586, when the Puritan party introduced Cope's Bill and Book, two statutes which called for the abolition of the state episcopacy and the Anglican Prayer Book, and their replacement by a Presbyterian church and a Puritan creed. The Bill and Book had short shrift with the Supreme Governor, who ordered both withdrawn from Commons. In answer Peter Wentworth submitted ten articles to the House in which he defended the constitutional privilege of free speech, and suggested that anyone who violated the liberties of parliament was an enemy of God. Inasmuch as it was Elizabeth herself who had infringed these doubtful rights, Wentworth's words were both blasphemous and seditious, and he found himself in the Tower of London for his audacity.

The intransigent opposition of the queen was not the only danger faced by the Puritan party. Equally serious was its inability to present a united front on the exact organizational structure of God's church. Puritans were split by two fundamental issues: whether the true church should be Presbyterian or Congregational in form, and whether God's elect should remain in the state-church and purify it from within or break away and set up an independent ecclesia. Wealthy and conservative elements tended to favor a state-church modeled on the Kirk of Scotland whereby the queen's episcopate would be replaced by a Presbyterian synod with authority to purify the faith, determine doctrine and appoint parish ministers. A more radical, less wealthy, and socially less respectable minority led by Robert Browne and Henry Barrow believed that the godly should covenant together, not on a national scale as the Presbyterians argued, but on a local level, and that each congregation should be free to determine its own doctrine and elect its own minister. The Congregationalists or Brownists tended to be anarchistic in spirit and democratic in organization, but under the Tudors they were voices crying in the wilderness of an authoritarian age which accepted the principle of religious and political uniformity and was anxious to root out any sign of such dangerous dissent. A deeper rift in the Puritan ranks began to appear as frustration and dissent from within and persecution from without grew apace. Those who sought to take over the existing ecclesiastical order and purify it clashed with the more extreme elements who wished to separate church from state, so that the one would not pollute the other. Though Presbyterians and Congregationalists were not always easy to differentiate, Congregationalism, almost by definition, bred men of a more radical ilk, and most separatists tended to be Congregationalist in their view of the true church.

As the special vessel of God's will and the saintly soldier of His Kingdom, the Puritan was "a poor security risk." There is no doubt that God's people were loyal to the queen, but when Peter Wentworth proudly told the House of Commons: "I will never confess it to be a fault to love the Queen's Majesty," he significantly added "neither will I be sorry for giving Her Majesty warning to avoid her dangers." The dilemma was inherent in the Puritan faith. What if the queen rebuked godly council, ignored the truth, and endangered the spiritual welfare of the realm? Worse, what if the crown turned upon the soldiers of Christ, harried them out of the land, suppressed the Word of God, and openly allied with the devil? From 1590 this was exactly the problem that all Puritans faced.

Elizabeth perceived that a community of religious idealists deriving spiritual authority from on high was contrary not only to the political theory of the organic Tudor state but also to the very existence of a monarchy which claimed divinity from God. As early as 1573 the Anglican church had recognized the threat, and the dean of York Cathedral summed up the dialectic of Puritanism when he wrote: "At the beginning it was but a cap, a surplice, and a tippet [over which these Puritans complained]; now, it is grown to bishops, archbishops, and cathedral churches, to the overthrow of the established order, and to the Queen's authority in causes ecclesiastical." Elizabeth's reaction was to find an archbishop who would exterminate an organization which so obviously smacked of treason. Throughout the 1590s her new archbishop, John Whitgift, worked with a will, uncovering secret Puritan presses, crushing their cells, imprisoning Presbyterian leaders, and enforcing legislation that threatened exile and execution upon all who refused to attend Anglican services. Once the Spanish menace was past, Elizabeth rightly suspected that her crown, her supremacy, and the entire theory of Tudor government had far more to fear from Puritans than from Catholics. How correct she was in her estimation, the Stuart sovereigns would later discover to their sorrow.

A world of Puritans, parliamentarians, and profiteers was passing the old queen by, and the end came on a cold day in March of 1603. She died not so much of old age (she was sixty-nine) as of want of anything for which to live. Death was hastened by melancholy caused by the loss of her last close friend, the countess of Nottingham. Gloriana retired to bed, and turned her head to the wall. Ere she died, however, her chief councillor, Robert Cecil, the son of her old and valued adviser, Lord Burghley, faced the question which Elizabeth had left unanswered throughout her life. For over a year before the queen's death, he had been in secret contact with James VI of Scotland; and when Elizabeth's council asked her to name her successor, it was carefully arranged that she should gasp: "Who should that be but my nearest kinsman, the King of Scots."

Gloriana was gone. In life she had been, as the Spanish ambassador once reported, "much attached to the people and is very confident that they are all on her side." Not everyone had favored her politics, but as the ambassador admitted, they were all, Catholic and Protestant, peasant and nobleman, on her side. Elizabeth had possessed marvelous magic—the affection of her people. Her subjects may have heaved a quiet sigh of relief that their beloved but difficult lady was dead, but the love that they had given her was not easily transferred to the Scottish son of Mary Stuart. As the queen's godson, Sir John Harington said, since "my good mistress is gone, I shall not hastily put forth for a new master."

OLIVER CROMWELL, THE LORD PROTECTOR, 1553–1558.

IV

THE DEMISE OF
THE TUDOR STATE
1603 to 1660

Straining the System:
The Reign of James I

11 The news of Elizabeth's death and the proclamation of the Scottish king's succession "sounded so sweetly" in James' ear "that he could alter no note in so agreeable an harmony," and his entry into his new possessions was a triumphal march, one thousand strong. He had come, he said, into "the promised land, where religion was purely professed, where he sat among grave, learned, and revered men"; no longer was he "a king without state, without honour, without order, where beardless boys would brave him to his face." Unfortunately for James, he was not through with beardless boys, and his son Charles was again to know the meaning of "a king without state, without honour, without order." Within thirty-eight years of Elizabeth's death, the promised land exploded into civil war and seven years later God's anointed ruler would stand trial for treason against an even higher authority, the people of England. Though the crown of the Tudors was eventually placed upon the third generation of the Stuart line, the luster of its divinity was gone forever.[1]

The failings of the new dynasty were legion but the flaw that proved most fatal was Stuart blindness to the political and religious realities of English life. James and Charles were rigidly Tudor in a generation that greeted Elizabeth's death with relief. They were dazzled and misled by the glitter of Gloriana's throne, and they failed to perceive the tensions and divisions that had been building up long before the old queen died. In 1603

---

[1] G. M. Trevelyan, *England Under the Stuarts* (1st edit. 1904) is still the best single-volume survey of the seventeenth century. Quite different in emphasis and organization is C. Hill's *The Century of Revolution* (1961), which emphasizes the economic and social aspects of the age.

there was nothing inevitable about the course that Stuart England was to take. The political, religious, and economic burdens inherited by James were far outbalanced by the goodwill that accompanied him on his journey to London; and none of his difficulties were so pressing that they could not have been eased, or even healed, by political urbanity and royal tact. Unfortunately as the Elizabethan age waned and Stuart England dawned, principles loomed larger than politics, the disciples of dogma replaced men of caution, and on the throne sat a Scottish Solomon, a pedant who was pithy of speech but short of temper, a master of the ingenious but unflattering epigram guaranteed to antagonize even the most ardent Stuart well-wisher.

James VI and I

Of all the kings of England, James I is the most vulnerable to caricature. He was lumpish and lazy, foul-mouthed and not overly clean. Yet James Stuart was neither a bad man nor, by continental standards, an unsuccessful sovereign. Only in contrast to his Tudor predecessors was he unkingly and ridiculous. Elizabeth had driven her councillors to distraction by her disregard for security measures, but James was almost pathological in his abhorrence of violence, and he wore an ungainly, quilted, dagger-proof doublet for fear of assassination. The Tudor Queen had dazzled England by innate dignity and consummate showmanship, but the first Stuart was comical in "his breeches in great pleats and full stuffed." Gloriana had willingly sacrificed privacy to court her people, but James hated publicity; when he was told that he ought to show himself more often to his eager subjects he inelegantly asked whether as a king he was also expected to "pull down my breeches and they shall also see my arse?" Good Queen Bess had rarely talked about her royal rights but had spoken of her love for Englishmen, while James earned the reputation of being "God's silly vassal" for his scholarly insistence upon legal prerogative and the divinity of kings.

In 1603, James was no stranger to kingship, and in his own estimation he was an old hand in the art of monarchy. He had been a king at thirteen months, a ruler at nineteen years, and on his succession to the English throne at thirty-seven he was a sovereign wise in the ways of political survival. James was doubtless the most successful of the ill-starred Stuart line. His great-grandfather had been killed at Flodden Field in 1513 at the age of forty; his grandfather, James V, had died of "shame" in 1542 after the battle of Solway Moss where a Scottish army, 18,000 strong, had floundered in a bog and surrendered to 3,000 English soldiers; his father, Lord Darnley, had been blown to pieces by gunpowder ignited by his wife's lover; and his mother, Mary Queen of Scots, had died upon an English execution block. Survival was no mean accomplishment in Scotland, and under the circumstances it cannot be said that James was a royal failure.

Sixteenth-century Scotland was a kingdom where feudal loyalty flour-

JAMES I. FROM A PORTRAIT ATTRIBUTED TO GHEERAERTS THE YOUNGER.
"His breeches in great pleats and full stuffed." *Governors of Dulwich
College.*

ished, religious differences were as much a matter of clan as of creed, and respect for royalty was largely a question of "liberating" the king from some rival faction. The realm was backward and impoverished, the king's revenues were only one-sixth of the normal resources of the English crown, and Calvinist minister and highland laird were quite ready to take up arms in defense of kirk and clan. It is small wonder that James VI grew up dreading violence and that he detested the association of armed men and Presbyterian preachers. Considering the life expectancy of his family and the stultifying education reserved for monarchs who ascend their thrones in infancy, James came through surprisingly unscathed, and during the 1590s he proved himself to be the political match of any feudal lord. He successfully frustrated Catholic murder plots and Protestant kidnappings, Presbyterian intrigues and baronial deceits. The influence of the kirk was curbed, a modified episcopacy introduced to govern the church, and the independence of the clans checked. In fact, by 1603 the Scottish monarchy was stronger than it had been at any time during the sixteenth century, and James had justification for propounding exalted notions of the divine right of kings in his scholarly if impracticable tome, *The Trew Law of Free Monarchies.*[2]

James' political training should have been his greatest asset, but it turned out to be his most serious weakness. He persistently viewed the problems of his English realm in terms of Scottish experience. His education in monarchical survival was magnificent, but he was unskilled in the craft of running a centralized, semi-institutionalized, and efficient bureaucracy. He saw crown offices primarily as means of rewarding good friends and only secondarily as positions of administrative responsibility. His knowledge of English kingship and Tudor government was bookish and archaic, and although he knew in theory what was expected of him, James was never able in real life to carry out his own precepts. "The evidence of a king," he once wrote, "is chiefly seen in his selection of officers," who should be chosen on the basis of fitness for their jobs—yet he surrounded himself with Scottish cronies, charming young men, and worthless Englishmen. James was not so much extravagant as unaware of the crucial importance of economy. He was anxious never to appear mean, and he turned the English court into a treasure trove from which to reward and maintain his favorites. Elizabeth's eighteen gentlemen of the privy chamber grew to forty-eight, each with an annual fee of £50, and two hundred gentlemen extraordinary, with no observable duties to perform, were added to the royal entourage. James knew full well the truth of the sixteenth-century axiom—"bounty is an essential virtue of the king"—but, typically, he misapplied the principle. Largesse became not the cement of political loyalty, nor the means of multiplying and confirming the "affection and duty" of his subjects, but a method of advertising his own generosity. The king loved nothing better than to

---

[2] Over the centuries James has had a bad press. The fairest account is D. H. Willson, *King James VI and I* (1956).

raise men of humble origin to high estate so long as they frequently and fervently announced "their indebtedness to their only begetter."

The effect of James Stuart's character and education upon the structure and function of Tudor administration was not immediately apparent, but by the end of his reign in 1625 the Elizabethan organic and balanced commonwealth was very near collapse. The fault did not rest solely with James. But the fact remains that during most of the seventeenth century the wishes, ambitions, and above all, the failings of the sovereign were crucial to the operation of government. James' habit of rarely washing, his hopeless extravagance and susceptibility to favorites, and his unpopularity with the ladies, who tore "him to pieces with their tongues," were important matters of state. That he turned Elizabeth's "council into a grammar school" and transformed her throne into a "doctor's chair," from which he pontificated on topics ranging from history and theology to sorcery and hawking, produced grave constitutional and political consequences. In fact, the history of the early Stuarts is a lesson in the failure of leadership: James and Charles misjudged and misunderstood the issues of their reigns and, by the nature of their personalities, destroyed the reserve of public favor existing in 1603.

Kings versus Parliament

James' very first problem was exacerbated by his inability to economize and by his doctrinaire propounding of the royal prerogative. He inherited a serious financial crisis. Elizabeth had bequeathed him land revenues depleted by one-fourth, and a debt of £473,000, yet he was expected to maintain a court appropriate to the dignity of a married man with two sons and a daughter. War had wrecked the fiscal independence of the crown. The struggle with Spain and the queen's Irish wars had cost her over five million pounds, and during her reign, Gloriana had had to sell land valued at £800,000 to stave off her creditors. The government's financial position relative to the wealth of the kingdom had deteriorated markedly from the days of Henry VIII, and also in comparison with the French monarchy. Henry VIII during 1545, his most affluent year, had been able to scrape together, by legal and illegal means, revenues somewhat in excess of £900,000. His royal cousin across the channel had enjoyed about the same income, extracted from a population four times the size of England's. By 1603 the situation had materially altered: the king of France could boast of revenues worth three million pounds while James had to manage with less than a million. To make matters worse, inflation had doubled the cost of government, while neither rents from crown lands nor monies from parliamentary subsidies had kept abreast of rising prices. James I was a poorer monarch then Henry VIII or even Elizabeth, and the fiscal facts of Stuart life were discouragingly simple: the king could not live on his own in the accepted feudal fashion unless he economized unsparingly or succeeded in siphoning a larger proportion of the national wealth into the

Exchequer. The first solution was uncongenial to James' sense of royal dignity; the second produced a prolonged constitutional struggle when the king arbitrarily raised the customs on certain commodities. The hue and cry were prodigious, and James became involved in a debate over the nature and scope of the royal prerogative, which strained to the breaking point the historic union of king in parliament.

By and large Elizabeth had listened to the voice of her Commons; she constantly scolded them, but on occasion she actually gave in to them, and she always took pains to control the legislative process. In contrast, James lectured and preached to his parliaments as if they were an assembly of obstreperous schoolboys, and he dismissed the art of parliamentary politics as beneath his dignity. In his opinion, the proper function of parliament was to enact only those laws presented to it by the sovereign, for, he said, "the King, he is the maker of them and ye are the advisers, councillors and confirmers of them." Such a position was not only somewhat archaic but dangerously tactless, and grated upon the ears of MPs who had come to regard themselves as a partner in government and the guardian of liberty. There is no doubt that Gloriana's later parliaments had been dutiful largely out of respect for their aging sovereign, and that any ruler following Elizabeth would have had to move cautiously and artfully; but it is equally apparent that James' inability to comprehend the changed position of parliament and his failure to emulate Elizabeth's studied handling of her Commons antagonized a body which in 1603 had still been willing to accept monarchical leadership and to finance royal policy.

Relations were further aggravated by James' tendency to view the London scene as if he were still in Edinburgh surrounded by feudal henchmen. The Tudor bureaucracy became a lush pasture for jobbery and corruption, and though the consequences were pleasing to the king, they were disastrous to administrative efficiency and the crown's relations with parliament. The Privy Council was doubled in size and filled with men congenial to the sovereign but neither eligible to sit in Commons nor trained in parliamentary procedure. During Elizabeth's final years six privy councillors out of a body of thirteen had regularly sat in Commons; under James the number fell to three in a council of twenty-three. The result was that the Privy Council began to falter in its most crucial role—it failed to give direction to the kingdom. There was no one who could present the government's view in debates, let alone control parliamentary machinery. The situation became so serious that one good friend of the crown wrote: "I think the state scorneth to have any privy councillors of any understanding in that House." James never understood that the secret of Tudor paternalism rested not so much on the divinity of kings as upon the hard work of devoted servants and the knowledge of men experienced in the ways of parliament. Speakers of the House of Commons were shouted down by rebellious and bumptious members, privy councillors were hissed when they entered the House, and the ultimate insult was administered in 1626 when the chancellor of the Exchequer had to wait two hours for leave to speak. Members of parliament no longer looked to the crown nor asked what the Privy Council thought. Instead they turned to their own leaders and preferred their own opinions to that of the sovereign.

The growing independence of Commons was reflected in the revolutionary parliamentary technique, introduced in 1607, of the "committee of the whole" whereby the Speaker, who was customarily a royal appointee, was deprived of his control over the subject and length of debate. Moreover, the lower house demanded, and eventually extracted, from James official recognition of its claim to decide disputed elections and to judge the legal qualifications of its own members. Early in the reign Commons made its attitude perfectly clear when it politely but firmly informed the king that "the voice of the people, in the things of their knowledge, is said to be as the voice of God." Since James was also claiming to speak for the deity, it was evident that the two elements of that indivisible union of king in parliament were no longer working in unison. Commons was becoming the organ of public opinion in the shires. "If," said one MP in 1610, "we should now return into our country with nothing for the good of the commonwealth, they will say we have been all this while like children in catching butterflies." Parliament no longer regarded itself as a child; it had grown up and assumed, together with the monarch, responsibility "for the good of the commonwealth."

Corruption at Court

One of the complaints most often sounded in Commons was of James' extravagance and dependence upon court favorites. It was useless, so the argument went, to supply the king with funds unless he practiced economy, rooted out corruption, and freed himself from the expense of Scottish parasites. "For his part," said one high-minded MP, "he would never give his consent to take money from a poor frize jerkyn to trappe a courtier's horse with all," and he called for the appointment of a parliamentary committee to investigate waste and dishonesty at court.

How much peculation and mismanagement there actually were in the king's government is difficult to assess, but certainly the moral vigor and efficiency of the Tudor administrative machine began to deteriorate under the Stuarts. The decay derived in part from James' personality—particularly his weakness for pretty young men and his total inability to judge character. Parliament complained that the king was prodigal with titles and pensions for "hungry Scots"; but more damaging to James' reputation was his promotion of Robert Carr, a handsome if not overly intelligent page boy, who caught the king's eye when the young man was thrown from his horse and broke his leg during a court joust. From such an unlikely beginning, Carr rose to be Viscount Rochester and to covet the fascinating, but totally unprincipled, Frances Howard, wife of the earl of Essex. With royal connivance and a great deal of faked evidence the judges were persuaded to grant the countess a divorce, and she married Carr in 1613. As a wedding present James advanced his handsome sycophant to the earldom of Somerset, but congratulations were scarcely over when it was revealed that connubial bliss had been made possible not only by political pressure but also by murder. During the divorce proceedings, Somerset and Lady Frances had first arranged the imprisonment and then the poisoning of Sir Thomas Overbury, onetime confidant and close friend of Carr and a bitter opponent of his marriage. Though James did not attempt to save his favorite (another even more attractive gentleman had already put in his appearance at court) and allowed both Carr and Frances Howard to stand trial for murder, the crown was nevertheless besmirched by association with a scandal which shocked the kingdom. The reputation of the government was further shaken by the revelation that the earl of Suffolk, father of Frances Howard, had been misappropriating funds and accepting bribes as lord treasurer of England.

James' relations with parliament were not helped by the dismissal from court of the earl of Somerset, for the king had already turned to George Villiers, the threadbare second son of a genteel county family. Villiers was introduced to James in 1616 to counter the influence of Somerset and the Howard clan. He was tall, athletic, beautifully proportioned, and seductive. "No one," wrote one caustic observer of court life, "dances better, no man runs or jumps better"; indeed he jumped in seven years "from a private gentleman to a dukedom," with an annual income of £80,000 at a time when the government was running a yearly deficit of £90,000.

It is unjust to blame James for the turpitude of his officials. Most men accepted bribes under Elizabeth, and a certain amount of controlled corruption had always been present in a century when government salaries lagged far behind the cost of living. Nevertheless, a sovereign is customarily judged by the company he keeps, and if England was, as the Spanish ambassador claimed, a land where everyone had his price, the king was largely responsible. He fostered the most rapacious and unprincipled elements in society, he allowed favorites and flatterers to sponge on his generosity, and he engendered in those around him the belief that success in government depended not on hard, dedicated work but upon saccharine words, charming manners, a well-turned calf, an open purse, and knowing the right people at court. Certainly by the time James died, the reputation of the monarchy had been badly shaken and respect for royal government was on the decline.

"No Bishop, No King"

It is more difficult to hold the king responsible for the worsening of the crown's relations with the Puritans, for James did nothing that Elizabeth would not have applauded. The only difficulty was that he irritated where Gloriana had soothed, and preached with barbed epigrams where his predecessor had won her audience with wonderfully sonorous platitudes. On James' succession the Puritans were hopeful that a Scottish king, bought up in a Presbyterian kirk, would be their Moses, leading his people into the promised land. James, however, quickly disabused them of such ideas; he found the Church of England exactly to his taste. Its episcopal organization he felt was peculiarly suited to his idea of kingship, and its ritual was in harmony with the dignity and mystery which he believed surrounded the divinity of kings. When the Puritans petitioned their new sovereign in 1604 to reform the Church of England, James met them at Hampton Court, listened to their impassioned words and coldly told them: "I will have one doctrine, one discipline, one religion, both in substance and in ceremony." So long as the one religion was inspired by the Word of God, the Puritans were all in favor of it, but James dashed any hope of a future kingdom of heaven upon earth by adding "a Scottish Presbytery . . . agreeth as well with a monarchy as God with the devil." Then, in a formula for which he is justly famous, the king stated the issue in the most succinct terms: "No bishop, no king." James did not, as he threatened, harry the Puritans "out

GEORGE VILLIERS, FIRST DUKE OF BUCKINGHAM
"He was tall, athletic, beautifully proportioned, and seductive."
National Portrait Gallery.

of the land or else do worse." This he left to his son Charles. But his opposition drove the more moderate Puritans, who merely wanted to rid the Church of England of papal trappings and Catholic ritual, into the hands of the extremists, who did advocate Presbyterian government and who might, if pushed far enough, fulfill the logic implicit in the syllogism "no bishop, no king."

"Regnum Cecilianum"—The Cecil Kingdom

The first ten years of James' reign tended to be more Tudor than Stuart in flavor because the new sovereign inherited Elizabeth's principal minister, Sir Robert Cecil. Cecil became James' "little beagle" who stayed close to his master's heels and earned his reward in the form of the earldom of Salisbury. Deformed of body but keen of mind, Sir Robert was exactly to the king's taste, a servant who relieved his sovereign of the donkey work of monarchy. Unlike that other relic of the Elizabethan past, the unpredictable but flamboyant Sir Walter Raleigh, Cecil preferred to remain in the shadows. Moreover, master and servant were in accord on foreign and domestic affairs—a policy of peace with Spain, neutrality in Europe, and financial reform at home. Peace with Spain was a matter of principle with James and of fiscal necessity for Cecil. Much to Raleigh's disgust, Stuart England turned its back upon the glorious tradition of Drake and Hawkins and the dream of empire, and in 1604 concluded a peace treaty with the ancient enemy.

The end of a conflict that had lasted almost twenty years, and the ceaseless efforts of Salisbury in his office of lord treasurer, eventually began to have a salubrious effect on the king's finances. James' debts had doubled during the first five years of the reign, partly as a consequence of war, partly from extravagances, but mostly as a result of rising prices and inadequate revenues. But in 1606 the crown won an important legal decision: the judges of the Exchequer decided in Bate's case that James' rather hesitant raising of the customs duties the previous year by royal decree was perfectly legal: foreign trade was part of foreign policy, and control of foreign affairs traditionally came under the royal prerogative. On the strength of this decision, a new book of import and export rates was issued from which the government expected to realize an additional £70,000. Cecil, however, was a cautious and conservative gentleman; he knew Commons constituted the deepest financial well, and he was reluctant to alienate such an important source of income by exaggerating the crown's prerogative rights. Moreover, he was opposed to James' quick and ready solution to his monetary troubles —the sale of crown lands. In all, the first Stuart king divested the monarchy of lands worth £775,000, or about one fourth of his patrimony. Most of his responsible financial advisers were opposed to such measures, for the selling of property was the equivalent of consuming capital wealth and merely postponed the day of reckoning. It also accentuated a trend that was ultimately to prove fatal to the Tudor-Stuart crown: land, with all the political and economic power associated with it, was passing out of the hands of the monarchy and into those of the gentry and nobility. Later, when Charles I had sold acreage worth £650,000 to pay for his early wars against France and Spain, and the Civil War had stripped the sovereign of his remaining estates, the king was no longer the greatest landowner in the realm. By 1660 a situation had again developed similar to that of the fifteenth century: the crown no longer had a private and landed income twice that of its greatest subject—the balance set by Sir John Fortescue as essential to the independence and vitality of the monarchy. Lord Treasurer Lionel Cranfield spoke the truth when he told James that "in selling land he did not only sell his rent, as other men did, but he sold his sovereignty, for it was a greater tie of obedience to be a tenant to the king than to be his subject."

Cecil knew the worth of this advice as well as Cranfield, and in 1610 he sought to ease his sovereign's insolvency and end the dangerous constitutional bickering between king and parliament by offering a compromise: the crown would relinquish its income from such feudal sources as wardship and limit its rights to tamper with the customs, in return for a parliamentary promise to pay off the king's debts and guarantee him a fixed annual income of £200,000 from a new tax on land. The negotiations collapsed because Commons was reluctant to grant a regular tax lest it lose control over the royal purse strings, and the king's favorites and court extremists reminded James that in giving up his historic and feudal revenues he was endangering his control over the landed classes and was sanctioning "a ready passage to a democracy which is the deadliest enemy of a monarchy."

James on His Own

The failure of the "Great Contract," as Cecil's proposal was called not only left intact a source of endless irritation but also destroyed Salisbury's reputation with the king. From 1610 to his death in 1612 Cecil's influence declined, as that of Robert Carr and the Howards rose. When the last of the great Elizabethan ministers died, his death was unmourned and his absence unnoticed by a monarch who had determined to embark upon his own fiscal and foreign policies. Cecil's key position as lord treasurer was left vacant, and James decided that he was sufficiently skilled in the craft to be his own financial expert—at least until he wearied of the post. The king's fiscal policy was to exploit the royal prerogative to the full, to sell off crown lands, and to convert titles of nobility into marketable commodities. The rank of baronet had purposely been created in 1611 to be sold to the highest bidders, and the competition was so keen that a baronetcy went for as much as £10,000, and the sales netted the government the enormous sum of £100,000. James and his son viewed knighthood and the peerage in the same light. Twenty-six hundred Knight Bachelors and 126 Knights of the Bath were created, and membership in the House of Lords rose from 59 in 1603 to 121 by 1625, and to 186 under Charles I. Fiscal, not social, pressure lay behind most of these creations, and though it was said that such transactions defiled the flower of nobility, it seemed to be a small price to pay for such a painless source of income.

James also tried his hand at politics, and in his second parliament of 1614 he took considerable pains to assemble a Commons susceptible to discipline and agreeable to his views. He was instantly criticized for trying to pack parliament, and many members, who might otherwise have been favorably inclined, were irritated by the king's obtuse efforts to exert pressure in the elections. Actually there were probably no more than 160 members in a body of 463 who were beholden to the monarch; but by 1614 James' relations with his Commons had reached a point where he could do no right, and his second parliament was dissolved within two months, having passed no bills and granted no money.

More and more, as James grew older, he turned for advice and comfort to his new favorite, George Villiers, shortly to become duke of Buckingham. Unlike Robert Carr, Villiers fancied himself to be a diplomat—he sought renown for himself and honor for England in the European holocaust of religious and national war which broke out in 1618. In Germany during the latter half of the sixteenth century, an uneasy political stalemate had been established in which Catholics and Protestants learned to tolerate one another, not out of principle, but because neither side was strong enough to exterminate the other. What upset the balance and aroused latent religious bigotry were the actions of Ferdinand of Styria, a crusading Catholic and ardent believer in a centralized and German-oriented Habsburg Empire. The Austrian branch of the Habsburg dynasty was to the seventeenth century what the Spanish had been to the sixteenth—champions of a unified, imperial Europe and God's instrument to purge the continent of heresy. The princes of the German Empire, however, suspected with considerable cause that when Ferdinand became emperor the ancient and cherished liberties of Germany, as well as heresy, would be exterminated. War broke out when the Protestant nobility of Bohemia rebelled against their Habsburg and Catholic overlord and elected in Ferdinand's stead Frederick V, Elector of the Palatinate, the son-in-law of James of England. James might have prevented a general European war had he been willing to order Frederick not to accept such a risky crown, but the king badly underestimated Habsburg family solidarity and mounting religious frenzy, and hopelessly overestimated English influence in the continental balance of power, believing he could prevent Philip III of Spain from aiding his Austrian cousins. Habsburg vengeance in Bohemia was swift and overwhelming; Frederick became known as the Winter King, so short was his reign; his own Palatinate was overrun by Spanish troops; and the Protestant-Catholic balance in Germany was so badly upset that both Denmark and the Netherlands were drawn into the conflict in order to check Habsburg-Catholic domination. By 1620 the situation had deteriorated to the point where it looked as if German Protestantism might finally be destroyed and central Europe overrun by Habsburg armies.

In England there was rising religious hysteria, cries of "no popery," a growing demand that James intervene to save Frederick, and mounting pressure to recommence the glorious crusade against Spain. The king was not opposed to unofficial military aid to his son-in-law, but financially and emotionally he hesitated at the idea of war against Spain. Buckingham was passionately pro-Spanish; the cost of any really effective aid to Frederick was prohibitive since it was estimated at £900,000; and James had no wish to risk his financial well-being on a wild commitment in Germany or to expose himself to further fiscal blackmail by his none-too-loyal Commons. On one point only king and Commons were agreed: armies sent to recover the Palatinate were expensive. Parliament, however, urged the antiquated and unrealistic strategy of a cheap, profitable, and glorious naval war against Spain and her treasure fleets. As one rather inaccurate MP put it, "England never throve so well as when at war with Spain."

James now faced controversy with his Commons on two counts— money matters and foreign and military policy. Throughout the early 1620s he roundly lectured parliament on the true nature of the royal prerogative —peace and war were matters which belonged exclusively to the crown and were no concern of Commons. Despite opposition, he persisted in a pro-Spanish position. Raleigh was sacrificed to appease Spain and executed in 1619; and in 1623 young Prince Charles and the incurably romantic Buckingham started off for Spain to cement Anglo-Spanish relations. Sporting false beards and riding posthaste for Madrid, they appeared unannounced at the residence of the Spanish Infanta, whom they planned to woo with whirlwind speed and carry off to England in the proper tradition of swashbuckling romance. Things did not turn out quite as anticipated. Buckingham was snubbed by the Spanish court, the Infanta was unamused by such juvenile antics and shuddered at the prospect of marriage to a heretic, and the Spanish government refused to budge in its determination to support Habsburg power in Germany and punish Frederick of the Palatinate.

Buckingham and Charles returned home humiliated and hotly anti-Spanish, and they promptly stampeded the reluctant and prematurely senile James into war with Spain. For once the king found a "parliament of love," for in 1624 a majority favored the conflict. James allowed a full debate on foreign policy, and Commons granted him a handsome subsidy. England allied herself with the Netherlands in June of 1624; 8,000 men were promised for the recovery of the Palatinate; and a small naval expedition was organized to plunder the Spanish Main. As a final step, negotiations were begun to bring France into the war against the Habsburgs, and arrangements were made for Prince Charles to marry Henrietta Maria.

In the midst of all these military preparations, James' peaceful reign came to an end on March 27, 1625, in a more favorable atmosphere than at any time since he entered his promised land and "the people of all sorts rid and ran, nay rather flew to meet him." England was again united as it had been during the great days of '88 in the national effort to vindicate the Protestant faith and tweak the king of Spain's nose. Under the first Stuart sovereign the bonds of loyalty and tradition had been strained but not broken; the sinews of the body politic still held; respect for paternalism and guidance, though shaken, survived; and above all else, enough of the habit of obedience endured so that it was difficult to say even as late as 1625 whether the political and constitutional situation was irredeemable. The only jarring note in the perfect harmony which king in parliament was once again enjoying was that Spain in 1625 was no longer the unwary and unprepared colossus of the days of Philip II, and that the new King Charles and the ebullient duke of Buckingham had never proved their competence in war.

Charles I and
the Royal Road to War

12 In the dreary annals of mankind, dullness, obtuseness, well-meaningness, and mental rigidity on the part of kings have been the absolute prerequisites to revolution and rebellion. Had Charles I been more tactful, more ruthless, even more humorous, he might not have ended his days a sovereign "without state, without honour, without order." [1] Unfortunately, the second Stuart was designed by God to die upon the scaffold, for he made a far better martyr than ruler, and his bones were venerated more sincerely in death than his body had been in life.

Charles I (1625–1649): A Difficult King

Archbishop Laud had no illusions about his master; he delivered a gentle but devastating indictment when he said that Charles was "a mild and gracious prince who knew not how to be or be made great." Taciturn, secretive, and reserved, Charles never achieved the dignity of inscrutable silence; instead his quietness concealed a stammer in speech, a slowness in mind, and a lack of confidence in himself. In his first address to parliament he pompously informed his Commons that he "thanked God that the business of this time is of such a nature that it needs no eloquence to set it forth, for I am neither able to do it, nor doth it stand with my nature to spend

---

[1] Strangely enough there is no first-class single-volume biography of Charles I; instead there is a great pile of polemical writing. The most judicious treatment of the monarch is C. V. Wedgwood, *The King's Peace* (1955), *The King's War* (1958), and *The Trial of Charles I* (1964). The royalist point of view can be found in E. Wingfield-Stratford, *Charles, King of England* (1949) and *King Charles and King Pym* (1949). Charles is best studied and understood in terms of other people and the problems of his reign.

CHARLES I
"Dullness, obtuseness, well-meaning and mental rigidity on the part of kings have been the absolute prerequisites to revolution and rebellion." *National Maritime Museum.*

much time on words." The contrast to his father's garrulous pedantry and academic wit must have been refreshing, but Commons could hardly have missed the implication that it was not worth the effort to learn eloquence.

For all Charles' good intentions and the deadly seriousness with which he approached his office, he was coldly impersonal in human contacts and rigidly narrow in his moral and intellectual approach to life. He made a virtue of inflexibility and proudly announced that he could not "defend a bad or yield in a good cause." He constantly confused technicality with principle; if he could convince himself of the justice of the technical merits of his position, he was adamant. As the Venetian ambassador pointed out, he sought "to open the entrance to absolute power" with a lawyer's casebook and "the key to the laws." Charles knew the law and every privilege which it conferred upon him, but he had no understanding of the true meaning of power. In the face of the inevitable he would yield, but he generally did so with bad grace, contriving to give the impression that his actions were merely a temporary and strategic retreat. On one subject he was unbending; he would "suffer all extremities than ever to abandon my religion," and in the end he staked and lost his kingdom in defense of the episcopal structure of his church.

In moments of great crisis Charles could and did win the love and self-sacrifice of many men, but he was never the man to earn the confidence of a parliamentary group which was determined to transform the Tudor-Stuart throne into a constitutional monarchy limited, and at times directed, by parliament. The root of the matter was confidence. Charles could not be trusted, for he was neither competent as a king nor honest as a man. He was "so constituted by nature," said one observer, "that he never obliges anyone, either by word or deed." The one area in which he showed considerable originality was a moral casuistry which permitted him to live in the high-minded conviction that right and justice were always on his side. His father's legacy might well have destroyed a better king and a stronger man, but even an impoverished and somewhat shoddy crown, the mounting reservoir of ill will between king and Commons, and the presence of his mentor and "Grand Vizier," the duke of Buckingham, were not sufficient to produce in so brief a time the mistrust and misunderstanding from whence the Civil War sprang. Charles himself was the major cause of the coming ordeal and the destruction of the Stuart-Tudor throne.

The Spiral of Suspicion

There is a strong sense of inevitability about the actions that led to civil war and revolution, and it is difficult to perceive in the seemingly preordained course of events the realities of history—indecision, freedom of choice, and accident. If there is any certainty in the unfolding drama, it is the fact that neither king nor parliament desired, expected, or had much to gain from war, and that the behavior of individuals was so varied, contradictory, and obscure that it is impossible to discern any precise pattern based on economic, political, and religious motivation. The seventeen years following the death of James I are a study in confusion in which the only clear fact is that a spiral of suspicion between king and Commons began the moment Charles and Buckingham assumed the burdens of government.

The new reign got off to a bad start. Commons continued to be annoyed by the crown's claim to increase import and export duties at will, and it committed the unprecedented act of curtailing the customary royal grant of "Tunnage and Poundage"—the historic right to tax the import of wines and certain other commodities. Traditionally this right had been voted for life at the commencement of each reign; but now it was limited to a single year, and Charles, who was always touchy about his prerogative powers, took the action as a personal insult. The king was oversensitive but not far off the mark, for the lower house was thoroughly angered by his haughty demand for money to fight the war with Spain and his calm refusal to discuss foreign and military policy. Moreover, the House was alarmed by what appeared to be the rising tide of Catholicism at court. English prejudices and Protestant bias were disgusted by the arrival, two months after Charles' succession, of his new queen, Henrietta Maria, the Catholic princess of France. Here was a papal cell at the heart of the body politic, a source of infection that might poison the entire kingdom. And the king's high-church sympathies, his appointment of William Laud to the see of London, and his failure to enforce the Elizabethan edicts against popery were all viewed as evidence of the queen's pernicious influence.

Commons still held to the traditional argument that a king could do no wrong; consequently its annoyance and suspicions were directed at the duke of Buckingham, who was blamed for the French marriage and the court's toleration of Catholicism. Peeved by the criticism of his favorite and frustrated by Commons' niggardly wartime appropriations, Charles dissolved his parliament in August of 1625, and in the hope of a quick victory and ready plunder he determined to invest his wife's dowry in an amphibious expedition against Cádiz. The results were not what he expected; his troops got drunk on Spanish wine, the royal navy proved totally unseaworthy, and the king was faced with the prospect of begging Commons for funds to stave off bankruptcy. Charles did his best to purge his new parliament of critics, but the removal of old enemies only placed the leadership of the lower house in the hands of Sir John Eliot. The fiery Cornishman from St. Germans fiercely informed Commons that "our honour is ruined, our ships are sunk, our men perished, not by the sword, not by the enemy, not by chance" but by the criminal negligence of "those we trust." Eliot held Buckingham, as lord admiral, responsible for the Cádiz humiliation, and he commenced action to impeach the duke. An ominous change had taken place in parliament. Throughout much of James' reign, Commons had stood alone in its opposition to the king, but by 1625 the monarchy had succeeded in antagonizing the House of Lords by the mercenary sale of titles and by Buckingham's zealous efforts to advance his many friends and greedy relations. Both houses were now ready to make common cause against the duke; and in order to save his friend and chief adviser from impeachment, Charles had to dissolve his second parliament without even having persuaded Commons to grant him Tunnage and Poundage for a second year.

The king congratulated himself that strong action had saved the day: Eliot was learning better parliamentary manners in the Tower; Commons was packed off home; Buckingham was safe; and Charles had had the pleasure of informing the lower house that he would not tolerate the interrogation of one of his servants, least of all "one that is so near to me." The crown, however, could not survive on constitutional principles alone. It had to have money, and Charles proceeded to collect Tunnage and Poundage as a prerogative right and to levy the largest forced loan in history. The revenues so raised were gratifying, but the cost in terms of the goodwill of the propertied and mercantile classes was prodigious. Seventy gentlemen, of whom twenty-seven were members of parliament, had to be imprisoned for refusing to contribute to the loan. Five of the prisoners brought action against the crown for arbitrary arrest and sued to be charged or released on grounds of habeas corpus. The "Five Knights' Case" was judged in favor of the government, for it was argued that the "special command of the King" was sufficient cause for arrest and imprisonment. Strict legality doubtless lay with the king, but men of property throughout the realm began to wonder whether the decision of royal judges could make executive action just, as well as legal.

Had Charles been able to prove the vigor of his government by victory in war, he might have been able to muzzle his opponents and exercise his prerogative powers without too much criticism. Unfortunately, in 1627 Buckingham committed the sublime folly of entangling the kingdom in a conflict with France while still at war with Spain. There were substantial reasons for animosity between France and England—historic antagonism, English claims to search and seize French shipping in the channel, and unofficial English aid to French Huguenot rebels. The duke assumed full responsibility for the conduct of the war, and personally led a fleet of ninety ships and ten thousand men to strengthen the French Huguenot port of La Rochelle. The expedition was bungled from ill-conceived start to ignoble finish, and Buckingham returned home to face Charles' third and thoroughly provoked parliament.

Sir John Eliot was again in evidence; so was that aging defender of historic law and onetime chief justice of the Court of the King's Bench, Sir Edward Coke. Even more portentous was the presence of another parliamentarian, Mr. John Pym, an aggressive Somerset businessman and ex-clerk of the Exchequer, who shortly became a master of parliamentary techniques and eventually the uncrowned king of Commons. Together they directed the attack against Buckingham and the royal prerogative. Backed by the Lords, they drew up the Petition of Right, a declaration of what both Houses felt to be fundamental law which even a sovereign was expected to observe. The petition was clearly no bid for parliamentary supremacy, but it was just as certainly an indictment of the Stuart monarchy, for it listed the four areas in which James and Charles had endeavored to exercise unlimited prerogative authority. The petition stated that (1) no man should be "compelled to make or yield any gift, loan, benevolence, tax or such like charge, without common consent by act of parliament" (i.e. forced loans, tampering with the customs, and the illegal collecting of Tunnage and Poundage); (2) that no man should be imprisoned without published cause (i.e. the Five Knights' Case); (3) that soldiers and sailors should not be billeted upon subjects without their consent; and (4) that martial law should never again be used against civilians.

Confronted with a unified and aroused parliament, Charles had no recourse but to yield in the hope that he could salvage a partial financial victory out of constitutional defeat, and he signed the Petition of Right in 1628. The king did persuade Commons to grant him a subsidy, but the amount was disappointing, and the dismissal of Buckingham from all his offices was made a condition for a new Tunnage and Poundage Act. This was too much for even a chastened monarch, and in June of 1628 he prorogued parliament until the next January. Six months of inactivity improved nobody's temper. In August Buckingham was murdered with a tenpenny dagger by a disgruntled naval officer who had learned much of his politics from Eliot. Charles was incensed and held Eliot personally responsible. For its part Commons was outraged by the king's tactless imprisonment of several of its merchant-members for having refused to pay Tunnage and Poundage charges and by his deliberate provoking Puritan opinion by the promotion of crypto-Catholics at court.

When parliament met in January, both Charles and Eliot sensed that the session would be short and stormy. Commons complained about the arrest of its members, popery in high office, and illegal fiscal practices. The king in turn lectured the House on his prerogative rights and its failure to grant him Tunnage and Poundage. The crisis came in March of 1629 when Eliot proposed three resolutions: high churchmen and anyone suspected of popery should be branded as "capital enemies" of the commonwealth; the king's advisers who had urged him to collect taxes without parliamentary consent would be similarly judged; and anyone who paid customs charges would be a betrayer "of the liberties of England." This was not merely defiance, it was very nearly an invitation to revolution, and Charles had no choice but to order the Speaker to rise and dissolve the House. Commons then proceeded to express the new temper of the times: a willingness to use violence. While Eliot's resolutions were being read and voted by the House, the Speaker was forcibly held down in his chair by two members who curtly informed him, "You shall sit till we [the Commons] please to rise." The statement was tantamount to mutiny, for it presumed the right of parliament to prorogue and dissolve itself.

By 1629 it was manifest that the legal bonds uniting king and parliament into a single and indivisible body had snapped, and that all effective government was slowly being paralyzed. The constitutional clash between the executive and legislative branches of government assured the failure of all policy, both domestic and foreign; parliament would not finance actions over which it had no control, and the crown was incapable of conducting a vigorous policy without the necessary cash. As one seventeenth-century commentator summed up the situation: "I see little hope of any good unless the King and parliament shall agree, for without that no money shall be forthcoming, and without money nothing can be done." A stalemate had been reached in which the crown could not live on its own but at the same time it denied a voice in the control of policy to the one really adequate source of income.

The "Eleven Year Tyranny" (1629–1640)

The dilemma was resolved by cutting the Gordian knot; in 1629 Charles decided to go it alone and to rule without the benefit of his faithless Commons. The decision was not without precedent nor without expectation of success. The dissolution of parliament left the king's political enemies without organization or leadership. Of the major parliamentary leaders, the vocal Sir John Eliot was again clapped in the Tower, where he died unrepentant in 1632; Thomas Wentworth recanted his political heresy and entered the king's service; Edward Coke went to his grave, aged eighty-two, still garrulously expounding that "brooding omnipresence," the English Common Law; and John Pym returned to Somerset to become the treasurer of the Providence Island Company, a Puritan-cum-merchant commercial venture to colonize the New World and to carry on illegal trade in Spanish Caribbean waters. Local Puritan cells and centers of political dissent could always be scrutinized by the Privy Council and, if necessary, chastised by the prerogative Courts of Star Chamber and High Commission. It was just possible that the king might be able to live on his own if strict and scrupulous economy were observed at court and in the government. The country was prosperous and merchants, no matter what their religious ideology, could be expected to pay nonparliamentary duties on imports and exports in preference to not trading at all. There were new sources of royal income to be cultivated from the rich confusions surrounding the crown's historic and feudal rights. And most important of all, the custom of paying taxes and of obeying the king were such ingrained social instincts that, as long as Charles could administer a reasonably efficient and popular policy, the success of government without legislative blessing or subsidy was assured.

What Charles needed most in 1629 was an effective program, honest men to operate it, and money to finance it. Accordingly he turned to William Laud and Thomas Wentworth to give leadership and direction to eleven years of what royalists call paternalistic monarchy, and parliamentary critics describe as tyranny. William Laud was promoted in 1633 from the see of London to the archbishopric of Canterbury, and he became the king's chief adviser, using his positions on the Privy Council, the Star Chamber, and the Court of High Commission to enforce a policy of "Thorough" on both church and state. His close friend and colleague was Thomas Wentworth, the Grand Apostate of the parliamentary party, who became lord president of the Council in the North, lord deputy of Ireland in 1632, and finally earl of Strafford in 1640. Both men stood for the new and invigorated form of monarchical government that seemed to be thriving in Europe. Their policy of "Thorough" was largely a theoretical creed—existing more on paper than in fact—and Charles never gave it his consistent support. It was a high-minded, if not always effective, attempt by Laud, Wentworth, and a few other royal officials to introduce honesty and efficiency into government, to develop new sources of income which would free the crown from all future dependence on parliament, to maintain uniformity of faith and politics throughout the kingdom, and to construct a rational and tidy structure of government based on the Elizabethan concept of a balanced, organic, happy, and directed commonwealth.

No policy, no matter how well meaning or well administered, could endure without funds, and in 1629 a campaign was started to increase the crown's nonparliamentary revenues and decrease its expenses. This meant economy in administration, pacifism in diplomacy and, most important of all, fiscal feudalism in taxation. Retrenchment at court was relatively easy to introduce, for Charles' personal tastes were simple, even if his ability to curb his wife's extravagances and his courtiers' pleas for pensions, sinecures, and favors were negligible. A monarch with economical habits, however, was but a trifling advantage; if the government were going to survive, it would have to arrange peace with Spain and extricate itself from the Protestant-Catholic wars of the continent. Peace was concluded in 1630, and Charles embarked on a tortuous and fragile policy which lacked force, since all the major powers of Europe were well aware that he could not make good his threats or go to war without summoning parliament into session.

Cutting down expenses was not popular with anyone, except possibly Charles. The government preferred to devise new systems of taxation and squeeze dry old sources of income: customs rates were raised; new duties were imposed; and the rent paid by tax farmers who collected much of the customs revenues was increased. The most profitable source of income and the one most susceptible to manipulation was fiscal feudalism—the drastic extension of the old Tudor policy of rummaging through long disused medieval charters and feudal obligations with an eye to monetary profit. In the remote past the monarch, as the capstone of the feudal pyramid, had claimed a variety of historic privileges, many of which had long since ceased to operate but all of which were capable of being translated into pecuniary advantage. Under Charles I, purveyance—the right to commandeer food, lodging, and transportation for the king's military forces—was used as an instrument of blackmail to extract money from wealthy subjects and corporations. Encroachments upon the king's forests, the original boundaries of which had been lost to memory, were now suddenly punished, as legal experts chased down the ancient holdings of the crown, and the earl of Salisbury was confronted with a fine of £20,000, while Rockingham Forest grew from six to sixty square miles. Likewise, knighthood was transformed into a tidy source of profit. At one time any gentleman who possessed freehold land worth £40 a year had been expected to assume the military burdens of knighthood. For centuries men of property had avoided such a costly privilege, and feudal kings had allowed the obligation to lapse. Suddenly in the early 1630s the gentry was fined for its failure to come forward to be knighted at the time of Charles' coronation in 1626; the proceeds were handsome even if the hostility engendered was dangerous.

Of all the feudal and historic sources of income, wardship was the most profitable and also the most burdensome to the propertied classes.[2] Under the Tudors the crown had begun the systematic investigation of the nature of all land tenure, and no one was safe from the eager eyes of government legal experts, anxious to prove that a subject's land was held by feudal

---

[2] For wardship see pp. 86–87.

knight's fee. Not only were the earls of Oxford and Essex royal wards, but so might be the son of a Middlesex yeoman with his ten acres. By 1540 wardship had become so important to the government that the Court of Wards was established to administer lands so held and to direct the education and protect the interests of the ward. The government, however, often sold its rights to favored courtiers and royal officials, who then controlled the ward's marriage, managed his estates, and as often as not left him in beggary. Under Elizabeth the profits of the Court of Wards averaged £15,000 a year; by 1640 that figure had jumped to £71,000. The growth of wardship was feared and detested by both peers and commoners, for it meant the imposition of a heavy and unpredictable inheritance tax on property or, as the earl of Nottingham said in 1603, "the ruin of every man's house once in three descents." As a consequence, by 1630 it was being said that "all the rich families of noble men and gentlemen were exceedingly incensed and even undevoted to the crown."

Equally irritating and even more politically explosive was the extension of ship money throughout the realm. Traditionally certain coastal cities had been responsible for naval defense and the maintenance of English sea power. By 1630 the obligation remained, but it was expected that the crown would impose ship money, as the tax was called, only at moments of great national emergency. In 1634 Charles not only declared such an emergency but two years later extended the tax to inland cities and counties as well. Ship money was within the letter of the law, since neither the law nor the royal prerogative had been defined; but it certainly violated the spirit of the past, and it raised a touchy constitutional issue—whether or not the king was the sole judge of what constituted a state of emergency. Yet it placed in the hands of the monarch a source of income that might permanently release him from dependence upon parliamentary taxation, and by 1636 ship money alone was worth £196,000. Fiscal feudalism and ship money between them allowed Charles to increase his revenues by almost 50 percent and to balance his budget at close to £900,000 without recourse to parliament.

Makeshift Absolutism

Had financial extortion and fiscal expediency been accompanied by honesty in administration, the cry against extra-parliamentary taxation might not have been so loud. Unfortunately, however, Stuart absolutism was a shabby, makeshift affair, and it lacked the two essentials of European despotism—sufficient money and a trained and salaried bureaucracy. With the exception of Thomas Wentworth and William Laud, the king's servants were neither particularly honest nor particularly competent. Richard Weston, Earl of Portland, was in charge of the Treasury, and though he staved off governmental bankruptcy, he was personally corrupt, filled his office with friends and favorites, and was a secret Roman Catholic, all of which exposed Charles to the charge of harboring papal spies and venial officials. Moreover, as the years of personal rule lengthened, the influence of the queen advanced. To the public she represented the most detestable aspects of foreign rule. She was a Catholic who presided over a priestly coterie at court and maintained her own emissary at the Vatican; and she constantly urged Charles to model himself and his government on the French pattern.

Even had Laud and Wentworth received the full support of the king, or had government by Privy Council, Star Chamber, and Court of High Commission been more efficient and effective, the king's government would still have remained at the mercy of unpaid justices of the peace, sheriffs, and local officials—the very men who had been silenced by the dissolution of Commons and who were complaining of ship money and wardship. The case of John Hampden was an example of the government's potential helplessness if the natural leaders of society ever decided that Charles' "tyranny" had gone too far. Hampden was a prosperous Buckinghamshire gentleman who was closely allied by family and politics to the parliamentary opposition, and who decided not to pay ship money. He was promptly arrested and in 1637 brought to trial for tax evasion. His legal counsel did not deny the crown's right to raise ship money during a moment of crisis; it merely pointed out that the emergency had been going on for three years and that there had been sufficient time for the king to call a parliament to raise the necessary money, and that therefore Hampden had been right in resisting what by 1637 had become an improper exercise of royal authority. John Hampden lost his case, but the seven to five decision revealed that even the king's own judges were far from unanimous in their interpretation of historic law or in their approval of ship money. More and more taxpayers in the future would follow Hampden's lead by refusing to pay ship money; and as England approached the end of eleven years of personal rule, the chief condition for rebellion was beginning to materialize—a growing willingness on the part of the gentry to disobey the king's law.

Money was at the root of the government's troubles; without the wherewithal to pay salaries, to play a positive role in the European family of nations, or even to enforce a policy of paternalism designed to protect less fortunate Englishmen against their more predatory brethren, Charles' eleven year "tyranny" deteriorated into a sordid and petty scramble for money wherever it could be gleaned. Fiscal feudalism was squeezed dry, monopolies were sold or used as blackmail to extract cash from existing companies, the crown jewels were sold, and the government indulged in financial practices that would have brought any other organization into the criminal's dock. As a final desperate measure of arbitrary financing, the government confiscated £130,000 of gold bullion kept in trust for the merchants of London, and at the same time Charles sanctioned the purchase, on credit, of £65,000 worth of pepper, which was then immediately sold for £50,000 in cash—a form of deficit financing designed to destroy what little confidence remained in the king's honesty.

In foreign policy the same frantic search for money prevailed. Not only could England be bought, but she could be bought by the highest bidder. The moment peace was signed with Spain, England became a Spanish errand boy, conveying Catholic gold to the Netherlands and allowing Spanish troops to land at Plymouth and march overland to Dover in order to escape Dutch naval vessels. Finally in 1640, Charles tried to borrow four million ducats from Spain in return for thirty-five English naval ships to convoy Spanish vessels in the Channel.

Even when Charles did enforce policy and Laud and Wentworth had their way in administering a program of "Thorough," the results further antagonized the very men on whom the monarchy ultimately rested for support—the landed country gentlemen. In the north, Wentworth labored diligently to maintain the Elizabethan edicts to protect the poor from the rich and mighty. Tudor poor laws and anti-enclosure statutes were enforced, and justice became somewhat less susceptible to influence and corruption. Tudor paternalism, however, was no longer popular in an area which was growing increasingly prosperous and had long since ceased to be a military buffer between Scotland and the civilized south. When Wentworth went to Ireland to become the king's lord deputy, he left behind a wave of thankfulness that his policy of "Thorough" would no longer be applied to Yorkshire gentlemen but only to Irish barbarians. In Ireland he was certainly more thorough and possibly more successful than in the north of England.

Ireland by 1633 had not only been tamed by Elizabeth but also colonized by James, who had exported great numbers of Scottish landowners and settlers to Ulster. An Irish-Catholic and landless peasantry was ruled by English-Scottish Protestant overlords. Some of the landowners were Jacobean and Presbyterian newcomers; others were old English settlers who dated back to the days of the Tudors or before, and who were half Irish in mentality and half Catholic in faith. A strong hand was required to govern such a kingdom, and Wentworth did his best. He assiduously promoted colonization, purged the crown's administration of laxity and dishonesty, made the government financially self-supporting for the first time in a century, raised and trained a small standing army, tried to end the poverty of the church by reclaiming ecclesiastical lands, and sought to introduce the high-church doctrines and ritual so favored by his friend, Archbishop Laud. The results produced laudable efficiency in government and a secret yearning in the hearts of almost everybody of importance to get rid of the lord deputy as soon as possible. Wentworth became the personification of the most ruthless and irritating aspects of royal policy, a kind of living warning of what Charles might do in England if he ever got the chance and the financial means to do it.

It was not, however, Wentworth's efficiency but Archbishop Laud's religious fervor that ultimately proved fatal to Charles' rule. An anachronistic and uncompromising disciple of Tudor paternalism, Laud was a high-church, doctrinaire idealist who was convinced that due proportion and order within the state must begin with uniformity of thought and ceremony in the church. Above all else, the archbishop wanted a better paid, better trained, better disciplined, and more obedient clergy, and he sought to achieve his purpose by urging the return of church lands and revenues. He fought a long and losing battle with the city fathers of London to have church tithes increased so as to represent a genuine tenth of Londoners' incomes, and to regain control over the spending of such sums. He used the ecclesiastical Court of High Commission to impose orthodoxy and discipline on the ecclesia, to enforce episcopal decrees and visitations, and to root out Puritan bodies and propaganda within the established church. Under Laud the Puritans received blow after blow. Not only did they find themselves persecuted and rigorously forced to conform to the Anglican creed, but the Church of England itself seemed to be headed for a reunion with Rome. Stress was placed on ritual and the sensuous beauty of holiness, and the doctrine of predestination was de-emphasized. An almost Catholic position, called Arminianism, was adopted, whereby free will and man's ability to earn salvation and God's grace were again in part accepted. The result was the emigration of God's chosen people. In 1617 a tiny band of the elect left for a new spiritual homeland in the Netherlands, and from thence in 1620 they set sail for the New World and Plymouth Rock. By 1640, 20,000 Englishmen had fled the devil's hand and Archbishop Laud's Court of High Commission for Ecclesiastical Affairs.

The tiny minority that migrated did so not only to escape the wrath of an authoritarian regime but also to avoid the dilemma of conflicting loyalties to God or king. Their less fortunate but far more numerous brethren who remained in England had to struggle with their consciences, and in the end they harkened to the call of the spirit in preference to the voice of obedience. A community of saints had to be founded; if treason and civil war, revolution, and bloodshed were necessary, Puritans by 1640 were willing to pay that price. Mr. William Prynne, an ardent pamphleteer, sounded the Puritan cry to battle in 1639. As his cheek was being branded for seditious libel and his ears clipped for having written against Archbishop Laud, he cried out: "The more I am beat down, the more am I lift up." Whether there would have been civil war without this small but persistent voice of conscience is not even a matter of opinion; it is simply guesswork. But this can be said: Puritanism by definition was disruptive to the Tudor-Stuart system. It imposed strains which, when aggravated by profound economic, political, and social tensions, exploded first into constitutional revolution and then into civil war. Puritanism certainly supplied political rebels with the uncompromising righteousness which induced them to risk their necks in war, and it allied Jehovah on the side of parliamentary supremacy, making victory divine, moral, and predestined.

Religious frustration may not have caused the civil war, but Laud's tampering with God's Word certainly caused the end of Charles' eleven years of personal rule. To both Charles and his archbishop the existence of a Presbyterian kirk in Scotland seemed a hopeless anomaly within a divinely inspired monarchy, and a vicious distortion of the perfect and tidy hierarchy of an episcopal church headed by a royal Defender of the Faith. James I had carried the battle of uniformity as far as he dared, but had wisely decided to be content with an episcopal organization grafted onto a solidly Presbyterian base. In 1630, however, Laud and Charles set about anglicizing the Church of Scotland by increasing the authority of the episcopate and by soft-pedaling Calvinistic doctrine, and they then pushed through the Scottish Assembly the Act of Revocation, which decreed the return of all ecclesiastical property that had fallen illegally into lay hands. The first action angered Presbyterian church leaders; the second antagonized Scottish lairds who were aghast at any suggestion that their deeds to monastic and ecclesiastic estates might not be valid. How far out of touch the creed of religious "Thorough" was with the realities of Scottish life was revealed in 1637 when Laud tried to thrust a new prayer book, modeled on the English Book of Common Prayer, down the Calvinistic throats of Presbyterian Scotland. The result was a riot in the Cathedral of Edinburgh, where chairs were hurled at the dean in defiance of the English. A year later Charles was bluntly told he must make a choice: either give up his Prayer Book or send 40,000 armed soldiers to enforce Anglicanism upon the dour Scots. The king could never forgive rebellion, and he determined to safeguard Scotland for episcopacy and the English Prayer Book.

War and the Collapse of Personal Rule

War was fatal to Charles' system of government; it revealed the dry rot that had set in and the isolation in which the king had been living for the past decade. The treasury was empty and the king's call for a patriotic loan from the City of London went unheeded in a metropolis heavily populated with secret admirers of Scottish resistance and Presbyterianism. Charles traveled north to inspire his troops, which were largely unpaid, untrained, and badly led. It was soon obvious even to an obtuse monarch that he could not defeat in open battle an army of enraged Scotsmen ready to die for kirk and Scripture. In June of 1639 he reluctantly began negotiations with his rebellious subjects and withdrew the offending prayer book. The king was patently insincere in his peace overtures, and on Wentworth's over-optimistic advice, he sent out writs for a new parliament in April of 1640. Charles expected that English patriotism would be aroused by the presence of an invading army on the border, and he hopefully called upon Commons for £800,000 to discipline his Scottish subjects. What he got was a two-hour speech from John Pym, listing the sins of his government and demanding reform in church and state before a penny was voted to rescue the crown. In anger, Charles dissolved his Short Parliament. A "short" parliament, however, was merely a prelude to a "long" one, which lasted twelve years and six months, passed from reform into revolution, usurped the authority of the throne, and in the end sanctioned the execution of the king.

Charles was anything but chastened by the turn of events, and he again set out, without a parliamentary subsidy, to teach Scottish Calvinists a lesson in obedience. By July he had scraped together a second force, but in August his troops fled in panic without a fight, and the "general dissatisfaction" with the king's service was dramatically revealed. It was perfectly apparent that the landed country gentlemen who raised the king's armies and enforced his edicts were the only elements capable of giving strength and backbone to the sovereign's fainthearted troops, and by 1639 Charles had lost the confidence and the respect of this ruling class. The fiscal antics of a bankrupt and irresponsible government had produced apprehension among men of property and commerce. The government's foreign policy had caused Anglicans as well as Puritans to wonder whether Charles was soft on Catholicism; and Laud's tactlessness and doctrinaire notions about uniformity earned the hatred even of those who approved his aims.

The Long Parliament

When a victorious Presbyterian army had invaded England and routed Charles' troops in August of 1640, it had demanded that Charles pay the Scottish army £850 a day until a final settlement could be reached. The king had no other way to finance these obligations than to summon the Long Parliament. Within the year a constitutional revolution had been enacted. John Pym had claimed that "a parliament is that to the commonwealth, which the soul is to the body," and legislation was quickly passed translating that proposition into legal reality. The Triennial Act of May 1641 guaranteed the calling of parliament every three years even without the consent of the king, while yet another act prevented parliament from being dissolved without its own permission. Tunnage and Poundage were forbidden unless sanctioned by parliament; fiscal feudalism was abolished by legislation which declared all non-parliamentary taxation to be illegal. Those pillars of Tudor paternalism, the prerogative Courts of Star Chamber and High Commission, were abolished; and the king's evil councillors, Thomas Wentworth and Archbishop Laud, were attainted and sentenced to death: the layman decapitated amidst great fanfare in April of 1641, the ecclesiastic executed almost as an afterthought four years later. Their technical crime was treason; their real fault was their loyalty to a king in whom the majority in Commons had no trust, and their support of a concept of royalty which parliament was determined to destroy.

Charles bowed to the inevitable: he sacrificed his servants to the wrath of parliament, and he signed statutes that made a mockery of the divinity that doth hedge a king. By August of 1641 parliament had achieved a legal and overwhelming victory without a shot being fired; yet within the year civil war exploded. Once started, the juggernaut of political and religious change was difficult to halt; unalterably it pushed on, leaving behind the timid of heart and moderate of politics, and giving the advantage to that small minority which wanted to introduce a Puritan revolution and was ready to risk war to achieve this purpose.

Mistrust, misunderstanding, and the willingness to resort to arms are matters of habit and mind. Parliament had been suspicious of the king for so long that it continued to suspect the worst out of force of habit. Each side persisted in misunderstanding the aims of the other. Pym and his followers were doubtful of Charles' sincerity in acknowledging restraints upon his prerogative and of his outward devotion to the Protestant cause. They were at pains to point out that his queen was Catholic; that he had allowed Spanish troops and gold, destined to wage war against Protestants in Europe, to be shipped in English vessels; that his Archbishop Laud had been so high-church that he might as well have been a papist; and that the king himself had sent soldiers to Scotland to destroy the Presbyterian kirk. It certainly looked as if the king of England were in league with the forces of Satan, Rome, and the Counter Reformation. Then in October, religious hysteria and constitutional crisis merged: reports arrived of bloodthirsty Irish peasants who had risen in the night against their overlords and murdered 30,000 Protestants in their beds. The figures were the product of overwrought imaginations, but the rebellion was real enough, and it confronted parliament with an impossible choice: Catholics and Irish insurgents could not be allowed to go unpunished, but historically the responsibility for military action belonged to the king, but parliamentary leaders did not trust Charles. They feared that instead of commanding an army against papist treason in Ireland he might turn the military against God-fearing Protestants in England.

Sir Edward Hyde, chronicler of the Civil War, adviser to King Charles and lord chancellor to his son, was probably correct in his warning that religion was often "a cloak to cover the most impious designs" of men. There is considerable evidence that John Pym may have consciously inflamed credulous London apprentices with the specter of a Catholic bloodbath and rumors of a popish plot to murder the captains of parliament. Moreover, he may have deliberately goaded the king into violent and illegal action by suggesting that parliament should impeach his Catholic queen. Certainly religious consciences were tender on both sides. Men tended to think in spiritual terms, and it was easy enough to confuse religious and political issues. The appeal to arms was a ready solution in an atmosphere of passionate and mutual distrust; and the controversy over the control of the military went to the core of the constitutional struggle, forcing moderate men to take sides, and driving a permanent wedge between the king and his parliament.

Throughout the fall and early winter of 1641, Lords and Commons were swept along by the revolutionary spirit. In September, the lower house voted favorably on a "Root and Branch Bill" abolishing the episcopacy; and it began a highly critical debate on the nature of the Anglican Book of Common Prayer. Two months later came the Grand Remonstrance, cataloguing the king's sins since the first day of his succession, describing the deplorable state of the realm, and listing the many reforms still required. Finally, in February of 1642, parliament delivered the ultimate insult to the king's sovereignty and stripped Charles of the last vestiges of his ancient rights by enacting the Militia Bill, which placed all naval and military appointments under parliamentary inspection. Then in March both houses declared that the statute had the force of law even if the king withheld his signature.

"King Pym" was not without his critics both in and out of parliament. Slowly an isolated, but nevertheless legitimate, monarch in Whitehall found himself once again at the head of a political party; the unanimity that had marked the early months of the Long Parliament began to dissolve. After a long and bitter debate, the Grand Remonstrance passed Commons in November by only eleven votes and the Militia Bill by just twenty-three votes. During the winter of 1641–42 it was clear that a royalist party was forming. The demand to abolish the episcopacy, the insistence that Commons control the king's advisers as well as his armies, the threat to impeach the queen, the execution of Wentworth in May of 1641, and the growing frenzy of the London mobs—all these made men of substance and caution wonder where the process of revolution would end. Lord Paget voiced the alarm of Englishmen who welcomed limitations imposed upon royal government, but who could never sanction parliament's blatant seizure of the crown's sovereignty. It was a thoroughly aroused peer who said that when he saw Englishmen taking up arms against their king, he resolved to throw himself down at the king's feet "and die a loyal subject." More and more parliamentarians and royalists were accusing each other of planning bloodshed and war; during December of 1641 for the first time the offensive epithets Roundhead and Cavalier were heard in the streets of the city—the one a phrase of denigration for the shorn heads of the London apprentices and the other synonymous to "Cavaliero," the brutal Spanish and Catholic butchers of godly Protestants in Europe.

It was all too easy to counsel violence in an emotional atmosphere which induced a practiced parliamentarian like John Pym to describe Wentworth as a sink of "foulness and unjustness [that] will never be wiped off neither from his heart, nor from his actions." Where reform ended and revolution began is difficult to say. Possibly the atmosphere of vengeance that had surrounded Wentworth's death poisoned men's minds. More probably the massacre of Protestants in the Irish rebellion of October swept away reason and restraint. Or again it may have been growing easier to act than to argue and compromise. Whatever the cause, the sides began to polarize, to indulge in mutual recriminations and to sanction the appeal to arms.

Deliberately incited by John Pym and his colleagues, and urged on by his wife who told him "Go, you coward, and pull these rogues out by the ears," Charles was the first to resort to a show of force. On the 4th of January, 1642, at the head of 400 armed guardsmen, he strode into the chamber where Commons sat, and demanded the arrest of Mr. Pym and four others. The five members had stayed just long enough to bait the trap and fled minutes before the king arrived, and Charles, as planned, was made to look both ridiculous and despotic. All his birds had flown; they could no longer be caught by a pinch of salt and must henceforth be shot down. In February the queen left for Holland in search of money and friends, and Charles moved north to gather support. By June the drift toward war had gone so far that parliament sent Charles Nineteen Propositions, ostensibly a basis for settlement, actually a declaration of war. The propositions placed the supreme authority of government squarely in parliament; they required that all privy councillors and royal advisers be subject to legislative approval and that judicial, military, and ecclesiastical appointments be open to parliamentary inspection. Then followed the creation of the Committee of Safety as a rival governing agency to the crown, the formation of a parliamentary army, and finally the declaration in the summer of 1642 branding Charles as the aggressor.

The king knew his duty. He was determined that if he could not "live as a King," he would "die as a gentleman." War was the only solution, for Charles had announced that he could forgive "no subject of mine who comes deliberately to shed my blood." Parliament had shown its wicked design and its intention to destroy the king, the episcopacy, and the ancient constitution; and in defense of all three on August 22, 1642, Charles raised his standard at Nottingham to the shouts of "God save King Charles and hang up the Roundheads." Civil war had begun.

Profiteers and Pioneers

 "Who ever he be," wrote Archbishop Laud, "he must live in the body of the commonwealth and in the body of the church." Long before these words were written they had become archaic. The impulses that were ripping asunder the organic unity of the Tudor state and stampeding the kingdom into war included not only the voices of conscience-stricken Puritans and the irate rumblings of JPs and MPs, but also the growing resentment of two new gentlemen—the profiteer and the pioneer—against a government which imposed heavy restraints upon the right of the individual to "make of his own the best he can." [1]

The Theory of Paternalistic Government

Tudor-Stuart paternalism was grounded upon the theory of government regulation to maintain harmony, balance, and accord within the realm. The usurer, the profiteer, and the capitalist were as destructive to society as the irresponsible baronial magnate; economic individualism was as great an evil as the political individualism of a willful Essex who placed pride above obedience. The Tudors and Stuarts were essentially medieval in their economic outlook, decrying cutthroat competition and expounding strict government regulation of all aspects of economic life so as to achieve an ordered, fixed, and stable society and a fair living for all. Their motives were not so much economic as political; the healthy body politic was that

---

[1] Works on capitalism and Stuart society are legion. The following is a sampling: L. Stone, *Social Change and Revolution in England, 1540–1640* (1965); and B. E. Supple, *Commercial Crisis and Change in England, 1600–1642* (1959). W. K. Jordan, *Philanthropy in England, 1480–1660* (1959) is very suggestive, and the "Storm over the Gentry" can best be read in J. H. Hexter, *Reappraisals in History* (1962).

commonwealth in which all elements prospered according to their station, and wise councillors knew that obedience and respect on the part of the common sort were in large measure contingent upon full bellies and fat children. The evicted tenants of "progressive" landlords, the starving and homeless victims of land enclosures, and the jobless textile workers and miners were potential dangers to a kingdom devoid of police force or standing army. William Cecil voiced the haunting fear of all men of substance, and acknowledged the hard pragmatic foundation upon which Tudor economic policy rested when he wrote that trade, both foreign and domestic, was the salvation of the realm; for once trade was curtailed subjects "must either perish for want or fall into violence to feed their lewd appetites with open spoil of others, which is the fruit of rebellion."

Medieval social theory had advocated the twofold doctrine of economic and moral justice for all and competition for none, so that the kingdom might not suffer from outrageous prices and shoddy goods and individuals might escape the sins of avarice and usury. By the sixteenth century the same creed, divested of much of its religious trappings, still held true. The fair price was no longer a moral issue, but regulation was still the order of the day. Tudor economic control was not yet synonymous with the mercantilism of the second half of the seventeenth century, for no Tudor or early Stuart sovereign ever consciously associated state regulation with economic power. Instead the ideal remained the medieval one of achieving an ordered and static class structure by guaranteeing a fixed labor supply, discouraging social mobility, and curtailing economic freedom. Such a code was anticapitalistic to its core. It was opposed to economic individualism, industrial growth, free enterprise, unrestrained competition, and the absolute freedom of employer and employee to contract on the basis of the worker's skill and the demand for what he could produce.

In the words of James I, the crown regulated for "the general good of this our state and kingdom." The Privy Council, which had once spent its time scrutinizing the liveried servants of great peers, now directed its labors at relieving the consequences of unemployment in the cloth industry, helping wounded war veterans, issuing zoning proclamations, enforcing health and sanitation regulations, and protecting lesser merchants and artisans from their more predatory colleagues. The council branded the ribbon-making machine as a "devilish device," and an engine for manufacturing needles was suppressed as being dangerous to the king's interests, "spoiling and maiming his subjects." Wages and working conditions were inspected and controlled; justices of the peace were ordered to buy wheat in periods of scarcity and to sell it below cost in order to prevent famine; and they were told to prevent employers from firing their workmen during times of economic distress.

The Statute of Apprentices enacted in 1563 enshrined the Elizabethan concept of an ordered society and reflected the basic social premises of the century. It postulated the obligation of all men to toil as a social and moral duty. It assumed the existence of priority and degree and arrayed the occupations of the realm in terms of utility, imposing on all crafts including agriculture a system of apprenticeship and a strict code of labor conditions. The statute also tacitly presupposed that town and country, court and shire were separate but interdependent parts of the total commmonwealth, and it sought to prevent unbalance and change by legislating that every man should stay in the parish and occupation of his birth. The government endeavored not only to insure the regulated employment of the many-headed multitude but also to assure a minimum standard of living, and, when this was impossible, at least to prevent starvation. Poverty was traditionally viewed as the wages of laziness and the manifestation of divine wrath, and the mitigation of suffering was left to the church and the individual. When Elizabeth's government reluctantly assumed responsibility for the alleviation of poverty, a giant stride was taken in the development of the secular, bureaucratic, modern state. After 1590 England experienced a generation of economic recession during which the peasantry came close to starvation. The need for charity on a national scale was manifest; but the church, divested of its riches during the Reformation, was helpless in the face of unemployment, progressive malnutrition, famine, and rioting. Only the state had the means to handle poverty on such a scale, and with the Elizabethan Poor Law of 1601 the crown, for the first time, seriously entered the field of social welfare. The ancient ecclesiastical unit of the parish was utilized as the basic administrative division for poor relief, and overseers of the poor were appointed to administer charitable funds raised by local taxes on all property holders.

Far more important than the actual dispensing of charity by state officials was the fact that a government contrived by man had accepted not only the philosophy that all Christians had a duty to labor but also the corollary that all men had a right to work. The parishes were ordered to provide work for the unemployed, aid for the sick, protection for the aged, and punishment for those who preferred begging to an honest day's work. The doctrine behind state control of wages and prices and the relief of human suffering was not the theory of the modern welfare state. Instead it was the logic that if God ordained each man to live without envy or malice in that station into which he had been born, then society could not risk revolution by allowing the victims of economic dislocation, human avarice, and natural calamity to die miserably in their peasant hovels. Some help, if only reluctant and minimal, had to be offered, and even a parliament monopolized by property owners, taxpayers, and employers realized that poverty was too great a social danger to be ignored. The natural leaders of the body politic by necessity had to accept the political and economic responsibilities of their birth and fortune and give their time to government and their money to the relief of the poor.

Monopolies and Chartered Companies

If the common sort were the subject of endless economic and social regulation, so also were men of property and enterprise, but with far less success. Government-licensed monopolies[2] and chartered trading companies were the keystones of Tudor-Stuart economic control. In theory the granting or selling of monopolies protected essential military industries, assured fat revenues to the crown, and safeguarded both the producer and consumer from cutthroat competition and shoddy standards of production. All items except the staples of life such as meat and bread were organized and licensed as monopolies, which ran the alphabetical gamut from belts, buttons, and butter to timber, tobacco, and tar, and from beer sold in monopoly barrels and distributed in licensed alehouses to soap manufactured in government factories. By 1630 the licensing of monopolies, which brought in annually some £100,000, had become essential to the financial existence of the crown.

The same was true of chartered trading companies, of which there were basically two types—regulated and joint-stock. The oldest of the regulated companies was the Merchant Adventurers, first organized in the early fifteenth century, chartered in 1505 by Henry VII and rechartered in 1564. A governor and twenty-four assistants controlled the company, which had its home office in London and self-governing branches in such provincial cities as Newcastle, Hull, York, and Exeter. By 1600 perhaps two to three thousand merchants, each paying an entrance fee of £200, composed the membership. It was, as one member exclaimed, "the most famous company of merchants in Christendom." Its control was primarily regulatory, and each member was free to sell or buy cloth within the rules prescribed by the company. In contrast, the joint-stock companies were enterprises in which each merchant bought shares and left the buying and selling to officials of the corporation. The Muscovy Company belonged to this type of enterprise and was chartered in 1553 to deal directly with the government of the czars. Each subscriber paid £25 and the company was able to operate, pay its officials, hire sea captains, and purchase Russian furs and grain with a capitalization of £6,000.

The greatest of all joint-stock companies was the East India Company, founded in 1599 and consisting of twenty-four directors and 218 original

[2] Generally there were three kinds of monopolies: (1) a grant by the government to some favored individual to break the existing mercantile laws of the realm—for instance, a patent to export or import some restricted commodity; (2) trade monopolies granted to privileged companies such as the Staplers, the Merchant Adventurers, or the East India Company; (3) grants to individuals to monopolize the selling of articles which otherwise would have been exposed to unrestricted competition. A variant of this last type were monopolies to exploit such things as mineral resources or the riches of the New World.

subscribers who paid an entrance fee of £50. The company was established on the grandiose notion that England was "the mistress of the ocean, her navies putting a girdle round about the world." In this belief London financiers and merchants were sadly mistaken. The initial impetus had been the monopolistic actions of the Dutch, who in 1599 boosted the price of pepper from three to eight shillings a pound. Elizabethans were dependent upon heavily seasoned foods to conceal the stench of putrefaction, and on spiced drinks to warm their stomachs. Spice was more precious than gold, and the first company ships set sail to the Spice Islands of Sumatra and Java. There they met the Dutch and were promptly evicted; only as second best did the company turn to India, where it established a foothold north of Madras at Masulipatam and then in 1612 a station on the west coast at Surat.

The profits for those favored few who invested in trading companies or could procure a license for a monopoly at home were fantastic. The Russia Company paid a 90 percent dividend in 1611. The East India Company earned 500 percent on its investment in 1607, and the value of the company's assets, originally something over £60,000, rose to £370,000 by 1660. Even greater riches flowed into the silken pockets of aristocratic monopolists and favorites at court. The second earl of Salisbury netted £7,000 a year by 1622 from his monopoly on silk, and the earl of Suffolk managed to extract £5,000 from soap. The profits for courtiers and financiers were immense, but the effect of monopolies upon the economy was serious. By 1600 licensed companies could no longer be justified as a means of protecting the consumer, since they increased the cost of living without achieving a corresponding rise in the standard of production. Worse, the system was not even an effective governmental sales tax since the crown realized only about one-and-a-half pence on every shilling that monopolies added to the cost of production and distribution. The lion's share went to the private owners.

Economic and Intellectual Change

As the century progressed, an economic theory based on monopolies, chartered trading companies, and a regulated society became more and more at variance with economic reality. Two fundamental changes were slowly taking place. First, between 1540 and 1640 England was experiencing economic change of a magnitude which has sometimes been dignified with the name of the first industrial revolution; second, there was growing emotional and intellectual resentment against government control and interference, both of which were becoming increasingly irresponsible, venial and arbitrary. Trade and industry remained the social inferiors to land and title, and the countenance of the city man was described as "a dull plodding face, still looking in a direct line forward." The mercantile expression may have been that of the clod, but the direction was one of immense expansion. Iron production during the century following 1540 increased fivefold; coal mining rose from 200,000 tons a year to 1.5 million. By 1640 English coal production was three times that of Europe and the truth of John Cleveland's lines—"Correct your maps: Newcastle is Peru"—was manifest. Spain might possess the wealth of the New World, but England found far greater riches in her own backyard, where the coal mines of Yorkshire kept London hearthfires burning, supplied the white heat needed in cannon foundries, converted ore into iron and cane into sugar, and made fortunes for the mineowners.

On the high seas English shipping doubled between 1570 and 1650, and the largest merchantman afloat during the first half of the seventeenth century was a thousand-ton East Indiaman, symbolically christened *The Trades Increase*. Though Englishmen complained that the Stuart crown failed to protect mercantile interests against Dutch competition in the Baltic and the Orient and against French encroachment in the Mediterranean, trade and the earnings of commerce continued to grow. In fact, peace with Spain in 1604 was concluded as much for reasons of trade and commercial profit as out of fiscal necessity.

In all the new enterprises as well as in the manufacture and export of English broadcloth (which remained the golden fleece of British economy) fat profits were being stored away, but greater quantities were being reinvested in industry. Coal mining, draining, and digging required vast sums of money as shafts went deeper and deeper into the earth. The manufacture of soap, bricks, and glass, the refining of salt and the brewing of beer, all demanded capital. One iron smelter employed 4,000 men. At the mouth of the Tyne, where coal was cheap and available, salt was produced by heating iron pans twenty feet square and five feet deep. Four men were needed to operate a single pan and by 1589 one producer employed 300 men and had a capital investment of £4,000. Under James I, one London brewer bragged that he was worth £10,000. Despite the sums spent buying noble sons for merchant daughters, greasing the palms of corrupt Stuart ministers, purchasing estates and pedigrees and "ladifying" aldermen's wives, greater amounts were poured back into commerce and industry. As a consequence, England by the end of the seventeenth century was per capita the wealthiest kingdom in Europe with the financial strength to play the costly game of continental power politics, to invest in long-term colonial adventures, to pay for its mania for architectural extravagance, and to supply the endless capital needed for the factories, the canals, and later the railroads of the Industrial Revolution.

Merchants may have felt themselves to be inferior to country gentlemen, but the governors of high finance and the directors of economic expansion were wealthy enough to insure themselves a place in heaven by heeding the advice of Bishop Curteys of Chichester, who asked them to "consider wherefore did God give you such great store of riches and large possessions in this life, above your brethren; was it not to do good with them and to help them that have need?" Their answer was overwhelming: the merchants of the city of London in the years between 1485 and 1640 supplied £1,889,211 for charity, or one-fourth of the total contributed by men of substance throughout the realm.

Possibly mercantile generosity was a reflection of another economic fact of seventeenth-century life: the spectacular growth of London. Elizabethan authorities deplored this grotesque development, which seemed to be transforming the body politic into a distorted monster with its head out of all proportion to its body, but the city continued to grow, both in terms of size and in economic importance. Its consumption of wheat doubled between 1605 and 1661, and by 1600 seven-eighths of the cloth trade was monopolized by London merchants. At the beginning of the seventeenth century the population of England and Wales stood in the neighborhood of four and a half million, and during the century it increased by another million. Great as this rate of growth was, it was fractional compared to that of London. The city that James entered in 1603 numbered 200,000 souls; by the time the last Stuart died in 1714 the population was well over 500,000, and one Englishman in every nine lived within the boundaries of greater London. Ever since 1500 London had been sucking up great armies of men and women, for whom society felt little social and only slight Christian responsibility, and who died in droves in the plague-infested slums of Westminster and Southwark. Forty thousand persons perished in the plague of 1603, but still the stampede into the disease-ridden metropolis continued, and any pretense of government zoning collapsed. Once upon a time London had been a city of brick, mortar, and slate roofs; by Elizabeth's death it had become a vast cluster of jerry-built, thatched and plastered houses which continued to spread until everything—rats, lice, slums, and palaces—was swept away in the purging holocaust of 1666.

The inability of the Tudors and early Stuarts to regulate the growth of London was symptomatic of the force of change and the failure of government control in the face of determined opposition. Everywhere the story was the same: rich and poor alike conspired to violate and ignore the official concept of a static and paternalistic state. Suffolk justices of the peace reported in 1622 that two-thirds of the textile workers were no longer apprenticed but were merely hired laborers; a sure sign that the Statute of Apprentices was a dead letter. The growth of the city of London itself was eloquent evidence of the ineffectiveness of the laws limiting the movement of labor and the migration of peasants into the city. In 1604 parliament for the first time tried to pass a free trade bill opening foreign commerce to all; and twenty years later it succeeded in destroying much of the effect of monopolies by abolishing the crown's right to grant licenses to favored individuals.

Not only did merchants and industrialists, vagrants and apprentices ignore and circumvent government economic regulations, but also the ruling class as a whole came to detest the monarchy's clumsy and tactless efforts to impede economic growth and to enforce an archaic policy upon a people resentful of incompetent despotism. Even under Elizabeth there had been signs of trouble, especially over monopolies. The first outburst came during the depression year of 1577 when bad harvests had driven up the price of grain from 20 to 60 shillings a quarter (eight bushels). Monopolies in the midst of economic stagnation and starvation seemed to many to be immoral and the cause of high prices and depressed trade. In Commons angry censure was voiced against "salt petre men," who "dug in every man's house" for the precious soil heavy with nitrate found in cellars and outhouses, and against inspectors keen on detecting the sale of soap, glass, cards, hats, and tapestries which lacked the monopolist's stamp. In the face of such scrutiny no Englishman's home was his castle, no tradesman was safe from the avarice of a monopolist determined to extract the last penny from his license. Merchants and industrialists who were excluded from the profits of certain trades and industries, JPs who blamed the high cost of living and the equally heavy burden of poor relief on the holders of monopolies, and MPs who rebelled against search warrants and prying inspectors, united to decry the government's economic policy. The second parliamentary attack came in 1601 and was so severe that the queen was constrained to interfere, and she promised a complete investigation into the theory and practice of monopolists. Unfortunately Gloriana had less than two years to live and her Stuart successors were both less tactful and more dependent on the sale of monopolies.

Stuart Paternalism

Under James and Charles, Tudor economic philosophy was abused and economic practices perverted. More and more the government viewed mercantile regulation simply as a means of raising money and rewarding court favorites. Zoning proclamations were enforced not to curb or to direct London's growth, but as a means of raising fines from contractors who offended the law or bought licenses to violate it. The theory behind monopolistic and chartered companies was that in return for the price of a license their commercial ventures would be protected against outside competition, but the Stuarts were too often tempted to press their pecuniary rights and ignore their economic duties. They licensed competing companies and then allowed the original monopoly to buy off the potential threat. By 1612 pirates were inflicting £40,000 worth of damage upon English shipping, but little could be done because the lord admiral himself was in their pay. The situation by 1622 had grown so serious that the Venetian ambassador wrote that the great trading companies were suffering from a surfeit of "privileges," for which the sovereign extracted vast sums of money and offered little protection in return. In order to maintain themselves, he added, companies had to "disburse great sums to the favorites, the Lords of the Council and other ministers.... Thus burdened and protected, they are enabled and compelled to tyrannize over the sellers without and the buyers within the king-

LONDON, FROM AN ENGRAVING BY VISSCHER, 1616
"A vast cluster of jerry-built, thatched and plastered houses."
British Museum.

dom." It was bad enough when monopolies fell to the Cecils, Raleighs, and Essexes of Elizabeth's court, but Englishmen became incensed when the system was used by James and Charles to reward destitute Scottish favorites and worthless courtiers.

Stuart distortion of Tudor economic paternalism produced political friction and social bitterness, and the system itself and the philosophy on which it rested were attacked both in and out of parliament. In 1631 the justices of Hertfordshire denounced Charles' efforts to interfere in local affairs when they wrote that "this strict looking to markets is the reason why the markets are smaller, the corn dearer." Laissez-faire was in the air, if only because the end of government interference would assure absolute control over local government to the ruling oligarchy of landlords, employers, factory owners, and merchants. Moreover, it would open up the profits of an unrestrained and expanding economy to the most favored, the most ruth-

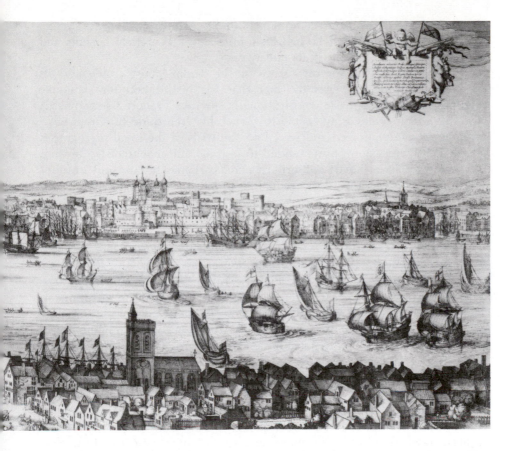

less, and the most intelligent; in other words, to the propertied classes. The earl of Clarendon in the middle years of the seventeenth century sadly acknowledged the existence of the new economic spirit when he admitted that money "was entertained as the truest wisdom," and that society accepted as lawful anything "which would contribute to being rich." It is well to remember that the hatred incurred by Archbishop Laud stemmed not only from Puritans who loathed his high-church authoritarianism, but also from enclosing landlords who detested his efforts on the Enclosure Commission of 1636–38, and from profiteers who abhorred his use of the Star Chamber to enforce old-fashioned economic paternalism. When corruption and inefficiency were joined to a mercantile policy which ran counter to the interests of the moneyed and ruling classes, one major ingredient of political revolution was present. It made no difference that both James and Charles endeavored to maintain a kind of benevolent despotism, trying to protect artisans and peasants against unscrupulous capitalists and greedy landlords in much the same way that their ancestors had once tried to protect the common sort against the extortions of overmighty barons. Stuart fiscal insolvency made a mockery of such ideas, for the rich and the favored could always bribe and purchase exemptions, and the enforcement of the system rested upon local officials who had little faith in its theoretical benefits and even less economic interest in its effectiveness.

More serious yet, for the future of the Tudor-Stuart crown and its concept of government, was the fact that the justification for economic regulation involved a basic constitutional issue. As Francis Bacon put it: "trading in companies is agreeable to monarchy; free trade to a republic." Monopolies were enforced and issued on the basis of the royal prerogative. Consequently anti-monopolists tended to become anti-monarchists. In their opposition to Tudor-Stuart authoritarianism, parliamentarians and Puritans found an influential ally in the economic profiteer.

Pioneers

If coal miners, factory owners, and enclosing landlords were cramped and frustrated by the doctrine and operation of the organic and static state, the colonial expansion of England likewise could find no comfortable place within the structure of early seventeenth-century paternalistic government. The spirit of pioneering is as characteristic of western man as the urge for profiteering, and the winds that scattered "young men through the world to seek their fortunes," were not unique to the beardless boys of Elizabeth's reign. Angles and Saxons who swept across the English Channel to conquer Roman Britain, their descendants who unified the island, the Viking "swift sea kings" who harried and plundered the land, and their blood cousins, the Normans, who conquered and made England their own and who carried Anglo-Norman culture deep into Scotland, Wales, and Cornwall, were all explorers and exploiters. The jump across 3,000 miles of ocean to a New World was merely the next step in a process that had begun when the first Saxon set foot in Britain.

In the sixteenth century English eyes and thoughts for the first time looked outward. The glitter of Spanish gold and the legend of a direct sea passage over the top of the world to China and the Orient enthralled the imagination. As early as Henry VIII's reign Englishmen were boasting that "there is no land uninhabitable, no sea innavigable" to men of courage and adventure; and one of the avowed purposes of the Muscovy Company in 1553 was to discover "how men may pass from Russia either by land or sea to Cathaia [China]." The idea of planting Englishmen beyond the seas and the lure of the fabled wealth of imaginary civilizations, where kitchen utensils were forged of gold and grotesquely-shaped people had eyes in their shoulders and mouths in their stomachs, caught men's fancy long before Captain Christopher Newport set sail for Jamestown in 1607.

From the start English expansion overseas was unique, for the course of British colonization fulfilled Sir Walter Raleigh's prophecy that he would yet live to see the New World "an English nation." Englishmen expected "to plant a nation where none before hath stood." From Maine to Georgia, from Bermuda to the Barbados, from Newfoundland to Ireland, England exported her peoples and transplanted a living social organism into the wilderness of a new world. As Francis Higginson marveled in 1629, "those that love their own chimney corner and dare not go far beyond their own towns . . . shall never have the honor to see the wonderful works of Almighty God." The hand of the deity may have been present; but hard economic facts were even more apparent, for neither Puritan nor profiteer, pilgrim nor promoter could have built his temple or trading post without the wealth of England standing behind him. The age of colonial expansion was possible because it happened to coincide with an era of capitalistic and industrial growth in which money was available to finance the pioneering energies of the seventeenth century.

The picture, treasured by generations of Americans, of God-fearing pilgrims dressed in "black plug hats—truncated cones with silver buckles—" piously turning their energies to the creation of a Puritan paradise in "the place that God will show us to possess in peace and plenty," is not strictly true. Not only did God's elect wear clothing in the height of Stuart fashion, but they also came to the New World for profits of the purse as well as those of the spirit. Colonial settlements were expensive, requiring long-term investments and confidence in the future to realize a return on the original capital outlay. Francis Bacon acknowledged this fact when he compared the founding of colonies to the planting of trees. "You must make account," he said, "to lose almost twenty years' profit, and expect your recompense in the end." The Massachusetts Bay Company spent almost £200,000 during the first decade of its existence; the settling of the Barbados between 1627 and 1629 cost £10,000; South Carolina in 1620 involved an outlay of £17,000 without a penny in return; and the Virginia Company spent £100,000 during the first fifteen years of its uncertain existence, and then went bankrupt in 1622.

Funds on such a scale were collected in the expectation of fabulous profits, and colonial investors organized themselves into joint-stock companies in the hope of a quick return on their monies. The Virginia Company, chartered in 1606, was founded by merchants from London and Plymouth who had been precise in their instructions to the 105 hardy souls who eventually landed at Jamestown on May 24, 1607. The company expected the colony to produce "all the commodities of Europe, Africa, and Asia and to supply the wants of all our decayed trades." Besides the establishment of a thriving community, the settlers were ordered to search in their spare time for gold, a northwest passage to China, and heathen souls to convert to Christianity. Unfortunately this wonderful picture of a bustling community of iron smelters and glass blowers, tar makers and wood cutters was never realized. Three thousand miles of chilly water, a death toll that reduced the Jamestown colonists by three-fourths, and the terror of the wilderness smashed the optimistic dreams of London financiers, but two years later stubborn promoters sent out another 600 settlers, determined this time to "take fast hold and root in the land." They arrived in the nick of time, for the remnants of the original settlers of Jamestown had already abandoned their site when relief arrived. London businessmen poured thousands of pounds into the Virginia adventure only to end up in bankruptcy; but the dream of profits was finally achieved when the colonists sent home to England the rolls of dried tobacco leaves smoked by the Indians. When Englishmen acquired the habit, branded by James I as "loathsome to the eye, hateful to the nose, harmful to the brain, dangerous to the lungs," the economic salvation of the colony was assured. Tobacco exports rose from 20,000 pounds in 1619 to 60,000 within five years, and the population of Virginia reached 38,000 by 1670.

The Plymouth settlement, though more godly in its design, was no less commercial in its conception. Mr. Thomas Weston, a London ironmonger, and John Pierce, a London clothmaker, received a patent from the Virginia Company in 1620 to found a neighboring colony. They induced William Bradford and his Puritan band of exiles in Holland to join them in an informal stock company. Cautious men who preferred to invest their riches but not their lives in such a problematical venture were urged to do so at the cost of £12/10s per share; more daring investors who actually sailed to the New World were rewarded with two shares for the same price; and settlers who could contribute nothing but their persons received one share apiece for their labor and the risk of their lives. The capital thus raised, as well as all future profits, were assigned to the company for seven years, at the end of which time the venture was to be dissolved and the money divided proportionately among the shareholders. Of the 101 passengers on board the *Mayflower*, only 35 were Puritans from Holland; the remaining 66 came from Southhampton and London. Many of these were the elect of God, but many more were men of Mammon.

The early history of the Plymouth colony is a tale of constitutional confusion and commercial struggle as well as of theocratic achievement. Having chosen to land at Plymouth, the colonists found themselves illegal squatters with only doubtful claim to the land, and their relationship to the Virginia Company was hopelessly confused by the fact that they had failed to settle in Virginia. In 1626 the original pilgrims, strengthened by a steady stream of colonists, bought out the London financiers for £1,800 and assumed the company's debt of £600. Eight of the wealthiest settlers raised most of the money, in return for which they received a monopoly of the colony's trade and the income from a tax paid by each shareholder. The Puritan settlement at Plymouth was peculiarly successful from the start. Trading posts were established at Kennebec and Penobscot in Maine; and in 1628 the Plymouth colony sent a troop under Miles Standish to destroy a competing settlement at Quincy, where Mr. Thomas Morton outraged Puritan souls by his dissolute life and his success at trading with the Indians. Puritans, whether in the Plymouth colony or at Salem (founded by the Massachusetts Bay Company in 1629), were uniquely astute in showing an economic profit. Unlike Jamestown, where the settlement suffered from a surfeit of unruly adventurers in quest of quick and easy riches, the New England colonists were disciplined and industrious. They labored in the Lord's vineyard, secure in the knowledge that a profit shown in the ledger was pleasing to God. They took pride in the certainty that they were God's stewards, transforming the wilderness and its heathen inhabitants into a land of milk and honey, populated with God-fearing Christians.

Throughout the New World, Englishmen were on the move—some to the granite outcroppings of New England, some to the fisheries of Maine and Newfoundland, some to the red earth of Virginia, some to the Carolinas, some to the garden paradises of the West Indies rich in sugar cane. By 1700 there were twenty colonies planted in the New World. The trickle of daring souls who were willing to risk 3,000 miles of water and one to two months on the high seas became a flood. In 1630 seventeen vessels with a thousand men and women landed in the Boston region; within the year that number had doubled. By 1634, four thousand had arrived in Massachusetts, and New England boasted a population of 50,000 in 1675. The city of Boston, the largest town in the colonies, doubled in size every generation: 1,200 in 1640; 3,000 in 1660; and 7,000 in 1690. The total population of the mainland colonies rose to 100,000 by 1650, and possibly 250,000 Englishmen lived overseas by the end of the century.

Expansion and the pioneering urge had little place in the Tudor-Stuart scheme of things. Settlements located in the wilderness and populated with men of independent and rebellious spirit, hardly fitted into the official picture of a tidy, organic, and static society. Charles I and his Archbishop Laud viewed both the Plymouth and Massachusetts Bay Colonies with the deepest misgivings; Puritans may have been good colonists, but they were generally bad subjects. Very early in their history, the New World settlements evidenced a deplorable sense of independence and acquired rights which few Englishmen at home enjoyed. Only ten years after the first settlers landed at Jamestown, Virginians had been awarded the dangerous liberty of holding a general assembly once a year. The Massachusetts Bay Colony soon proved even more rebellious and disobedient, showing little regard for authority when, during the Civil War in England, it announced that "our allegiance binds us not to the laws of England any longer than while we live in England." The pioneers who sailed for America may have "resolved to be Englishmen gone to the world's end," but they shortly discovered that their country was where "the heart and blood are given." A new nation, struggling to shape its own ideals and laws, was born the moment Englishmen turned their backs on the Old World. Their hopes and aspirations, their loyalties and devotion were directed to something new: to "dear New England! dearest land to me."

If so many ventured forth into a wilderness thousands of miles from their chimney corners, still more preferred the shorter trip to Ireland. Of all the colonies, Ireland received the greatest number of immigrants throughout the seventeenth century, was economically the most important, and was the single enterprise in which the crown played a direct role. Except for the colonization of Ireland, the history of England's expansion is one of private enterprise, private funds, and private dreams. Elizabeth and James were largely interested in colonies as possible military bases, bits "in the ancient enemy's mouth." The prospect of revenue, however, always interested the state, and the charters of all the early settlements reserved for the crown one-fifth of all gold and silver discovered, and imports and exports to and from the colonies paid a heavy tariff. Except for this, the government paid slight attention to overseas development. On occasion, it actually discouraged it, as when James endeavored to curtail colonization in the interests of peace and trade with Spain.

Ireland was the one exception to the crown's laissez-faire colonial policy. The island was Roman Catholic in faith, tribal in social structure, and only a short sea voyage away. From every point of view it was ideal for colonization conducted in the name of religion, civilization, and trade. In 1600 the time seemed propitious for the completion of a conquest begun 500 years before under Henry II. James I accepted the Protestantizing and civilizing of Ireland as his special care, and between 1609 and 1625 fifty-nine Scottish "undertakers" were selected by the crown. Each settler was granted anywhere from 1,000 to 3,000 acres in the county of Ulster on the understanding that he populate his estate with good and godly Presbyterians. Ulster was filled with Englishmen and Scotsmen, and it remains today Protestant and Anglo-Saxon and part of the United Kingdom. The policy of fostering English emigration to Ireland was continued under the Cromwellian Protectorate, when thousands of English soldiers and immigrants were settled in the wake of Oliver Cromwell's military conquests. There they thrived as the elect of God, ruling over a Celtic and Catholic population which never forgot nor forgave their English overlords.

The flow of immigrants into Ireland is not difficult to understand, but what induced thousands to leave the comfort and security of their homes for the inhospitable, rockbound shores of New England and the dreadful silence of endless forests is more difficult to explain. Of all the great powers, only England exported her peoples. Spanish imagination was caught by the glitter of gold and the anguish of souls crying out for salvation; France sought trade and raw materials. Only England developed plantations, exported homes and a way of life, and established entire nations in the wilderness. Permanent colonization demanded a type of recruit different from the missionary, the conquistador, or the trapper. It required men, women, and children to build, to toil, and to pray. The Indians, in the eyes of such settlers, were not heathens in need of conversion or even potential assets as trappers of animals, but menaces to the well-being and very existence of the colonists. Long before the advent of the cowboy and the conquest of the prairie lands, the only good Indian was a dead Indian.

The lure that could succeed in the face of disease, famine, and privation must have been prodigious. At Jamestown only 32 colonists survived out of 105; at Plymouth 50 died within the year, and at one moment during the first winter only seven men were fit to work. Quiet folk were enticed from their homes "to seek new worlds for gold, for praise, for glory." As one Englishman put it, "God sends me to go. If His will be, I shall die, for I had rather die with credit than live with shame." Whether the credit which was uppermost in his mind was economic or spiritual is immaterial, since the seventeenth century tended to see no distinction between the two. Certainly the hope of a Garden of Eden rich in profits and in godliness was a potent motive, but an equally important if less positive influence was at work: escape from that ugly trinity, religious persecution, economic exploitation, and social discrimination. England in the first years of the seventeenth century saw herself as overpopulated, and many men argued that "we must starve or eat up one another" unless the surplus was sent out to the colonies. In point of fact, the realm was not overpopulated, merely underemployed. The plague, the jails, and the gallows took their grisly toll, but thousands more remained, unwanted burdens upon an already inadequate relief system. The New World quickly became a haven for all who could find neither religious nor economic comfort in the organic state of the Tudor-Stuart commonwealth, and a place to unload the undesirable and unwanted. In 1618 a hundred homeless and starving young boys and girls from the slums of London were shipped to Virginia. Jail sentences and capital punishments were regularly commuted to deportation, for brawn and muscle, though they might be morally depraved, could yet "yield a profitable service" in the New World where labor was at a premium.

If the common sort were often shipped off against their will, men of substance went forth of their own accord. The hazards of the New World seemed slight compared to the harsh realities of life at home. The dream of a future world, where men could live freely "without sergeants or courtiers or lawyers or intelligencers," attracted all who suffered from economic, political, or religious privation. The desire for change, the urge to avoid conditions imposed by the accident of birth, and the demand for free land were motives strange and foreign to the Tudor system, which in the hands of the Stuarts was growing increasingly rigid, corrupt, and archaic. Yet in point of numbers, few men escaped the bondage of the Old World through emigration. Discontent at home found but an inadequate safety valve in colonization, and it is well to recall by way of introduction to the Civil War that for every Puritan who fled, a hundred stayed behind; for every embittered gentleman who risked his patrimony on a gamble in the New World, a thousand clung to the old way of life at home; and for every adventurer who sailed westward, many more remained in England awaiting the grand adventure of civil war and rebellion.

The Anatomy of Rebellion

Slowly, reluctantly, a divided realm prepared for war.[1] The moment of decision had arrived; debate must give way to action, and throughout the land men were called upon to choose sides.

The War Between the Historians

The controversy over who fought whom, and why, commenced the moment men made their choice and picked up weapons with which to fight. Analysts from Hyde, Harrington, and Hobbes to Marx, Tawney, and Trevor-Roper have sought to find the explanation "in society, not in individuals."[2] That ponderous social and economic forces were at work is undeniable, and the specter of class war is certainly discernible. Geographically the divisions were suggestive. All the cathedral cities save Oxford and Chester sided with parliament; so did the industrial centers, the ports, and the economically advanced regions of the south and east. Conversely, the strongholds of royalty were the countryside, the shires, and the backward areas of the north and west. The words "populous, rich, and rebellious" seemed to go

---

[1] The classic and multivolume account of the early Stuart period and the civil war years is S. R. Gardiner, *History of England, 1603–1656* (18 Vols., 1894–1904) and Sir Charles Firth's continuation, *The Last Years of the Protectorate* (1909). At the other end of the spectrum is Crane Brinton, *An Anatomy of Revolution* (rev. ed. 1953), a provocative analysis of the English Civil War, the American Revolution, and the French Revolution; and L. Stone, *The Causes of the English Revolution 1529–1642* (1972).

[2] Edward Hyde, Earl of Clarendon, *The History of the Great Rebellion*, ed. W. D. Macray (1888); Thomas Hobbes, *Behemoth: The History of the Causes of the Civil Wars in England*, ed. W. Molesworth (1840); R. H. Tawney, *Harrington's Interpretation of His Age* (1941); H. Trevor-Roper, "Social Causes of the Great Rebellion," in *Historical Essays* (1957); C. Hill, *Puritanism and Revolution* (1958); and P. Zagorin, "The Social Interpretation of the English Revolution," *Journal of Economic History*, Vol. XIX (1959).

hand in hand. Social alignments reflected the geographic, and contemporaries were not unaware of the economic and social interests which were beginning to emerge on either side. "Freeholders and tradesmen are the strength of religion and civility in the land," concluded Richard Baxter, and "gentlemen and beggars and servile tenants are the strength of inequity." It was not accidental that eighty peers chose the king, twenty others preferred neutrality, and only thirty remained in London, loyal to the "liberties" of parliament. Men of new wealth, of economic enterprise and capitalistic sentiment, who were busily building industrial and commercial empires, enclosing land, and buying out their less prosperous landed rivals, seemed to be arrayed against "gentlemen of ancient families and estates." As Professor Tawney succinctly put it: an aggressive creditor and capitalistic class "discovered, not for the first time, that as a method of foreclosure war was cheaper than litigation." [3]

Not only did the patterns of economic determination appear, and a feudal and anachronistic past give way to a progressive and vital capitalistic future, but England's Civil War harbored yet another element of revolution: the revolt of the poor and downtrodden against the rich and mighty. In 1642 the "heady multitude," quiet since the days of the Peasant Revolt, was once again growing restive and resentful, and dangerous political notions were in the air. "The gentry have been our masters a long time," it was said, "and now we may chance to master them." Men of property directed worried glances at the "commonality" who sought "not only to abuse but plunder any gentleman." As war and violence progressed, novelty in politics, radicalism in social theory, and extremism in religion were on the increase, and Levellers and Diggers and other "strange voices" grew bold and spoke out against their ancient masters.

In spite of all this, Edward Hyde's term "the Great Rebellion" has not prevailed, and England's ordeal is still called the Civil War. In the final analysis the choice of sides was personal, not economic, political, or social, and it was made by men of the same class, not between classes. Englishmen may have been aware of the growing rigidity of Tudor-Stuart paternalism; they may have unconsciously sensed the truth of economic determinism and realized that economic change must necessitate political reformation; they may have felt, sometimes fervently, that God allowed them no choice but to defend the right as they knew it; yet men's decisions were intensely personal. Sir Edmund Verney made such a choice when he decided that his loyalty to Charles outweighed his devotion to parliamentary liberties and spiritual purity. "I have eaten the King's bread and served him near thirty years, and will not do so base a thing as to forsake him." The Civil War was fought between men like Edmund Verney, who for reasons of their own elected different sides.

---

[3] R. H. Tawney, "The Rise of the Gentry," *Economic History Review*, Vol. XI (1941), p. 12.

Cromwell, Charles I, Fairfax, Essex, and Hyde all had one thing in common: no matter what their politics or religion they were the "natural leaders" of society. They were men of varying degrees of property, and though they often disagreed violently over whom should exercise discipline and who should be obeyed, they were in accord in their belief that both discipline and obedience were necessary to a well-ordered society. The ancient law, the historic constitution, was not being called in doubt; no one questioned that it should safeguard property and "the liberty of all those that have a permanent interest" within the realm. They fought, as William Bradshaw stated at King Charles' trial, not over the law but over "who shall be the expositors of this law." No man of estate had any wish that anyone except men of property should be "the expositors." The royalist Cavalier agreed with the parliamentary colonel who warned that if the master and the servant were equal in law and in vote, then "there may be a law enacted that shall be an equality of goods and estates" as well.

The community and solidarity of interests among the ruling elements momentarily dissolved, producing civil, not revolutionary, war. Yet ties of friendship, breeding, and class remained so strong that Sir William Waller could write Sir Ralph Hopton on the evening of battle that "my affections to you are so unchangeable that hostility itself can not violate my friendship. We are both upon the stage, and we must act the parts assigned us in this tragedy. Let us do it in a way of honour and without personal animosities." The old school tie constantly acted as a check to bitterness and passion, curbed the horrors of war, and made possible the restoration of the Stuarts in 1660. In the end, after a generation of godliness and violence, the gentry, regardless of whether they were represented by the 236 members of Commons who decided for the king or by the 270 odd who chose for parliament, reunited in their determination to preserve order, obedience, and respect for property. The moment that happened, the restoration of the Stuart monarchy was assured.

The Civil War

At first the war went badly for parliament. The crux of the matter was expressed by the earl of Manchester in November 1644, when he complained that "if we beat the King ninety-nine times yet he is King still . . . but if the King beats us we shall be hanged and our posterity be made slaves." Roundheads were rebels; and despite their control of the navy and their ability to raise money from the prosperous and heavily populated south, rebels carried the stigma of treason. The habit of loyalty to God and king remained strong, and parliament had the difficult task of building the machinery of war upon unconstitutional foundations and of convincing a doubtful nation that God and justice were on its side. The old organs of government could not be used since most of the lord lieutenants of the counties had remained loyal to the sovereign, and the top personnel of the

Exchequer, the Chancery, and the law courts had fled north when Charles left London. Devoid of executive and administrative machinery, parliament turned to committees to rule those regions under its control. County committees were organized to administer the shires and muster the local militia, and eventually the Committee of Both Kingdoms became the supreme executive agency responsible to parliament.

Parliament's difficulties lay in the twofold fact that its leaders were determined to be as unrevolutionary as possible, and that many of them were of two minds whether they actually wanted to beat the king. Certainly conservative opinion in both houses had no intention of destroying the monarchy and was aghast at the thought of the dangers of continued violence. The more cautious elements of the gentry still retained control. They staffed the county committees, and they raised their own tenants and drilled them into military units. In London, parliament was loath to tax men of wealth too heavily and preferred to finance the war through loans from the city fathers and wealthy merchants. Such a policy was simply an effort to beat the king at his own game, and it was doomed to failure. The tide of royal victories continued until parliament learned to capitalize upon its greater financial potential, and leadership was taken over by men who were determined to win the war no matter what the cost in terms of money, men, or time-honored customs.

It quickly became apparent that parliamentary victory would require outside aid, and in September of 1643, Commons reluctantly entered into a Solemn League and Covenant with the Scots, promising to reform religion in England "according to the word of God," who presumably spoke the language of Scottish Presbyterianism. Scottish arms helped win the battle of Marston Moor in July of 1644, but the results were embarrassingly disappointing. There was no follow-up to the victory; there seemed to be no will to win; and two weeks later the earl of Essex received a resounding licking at Lostwithiel by Charles' devoted Cornishmen.

If the king were to be defeated in battle, more than Scottish allies were needed; a clean sweep from within was required. The first step was to rid the army of its aristocratic leadership under the earl of Essex, and to purge the military of incompetence by enacting a Self-Denying Ordinance whereby members of parliament resigned their military positions. The ordinance passed through Commons in December of 1644 but was blocked by the old guard in the Lords until April of the following year. In the meantime, parliament had created a unique military organization known to posterity as the New Model Army, commanded by Lord Thomas Fairfax, a highly proficient professional trooper, and his lieutenant general, Oliver Cromwell, the most inspired of the new amateur soldiers. Promotion was based on merit, not blood, and the army was staffed with men who "made some conscience of what they did." Parliament had forged a weapon of righteousness and discipline, dedicated to victory. Cromwell had once said that he would rather "have a plain russet-coated captain that knows what

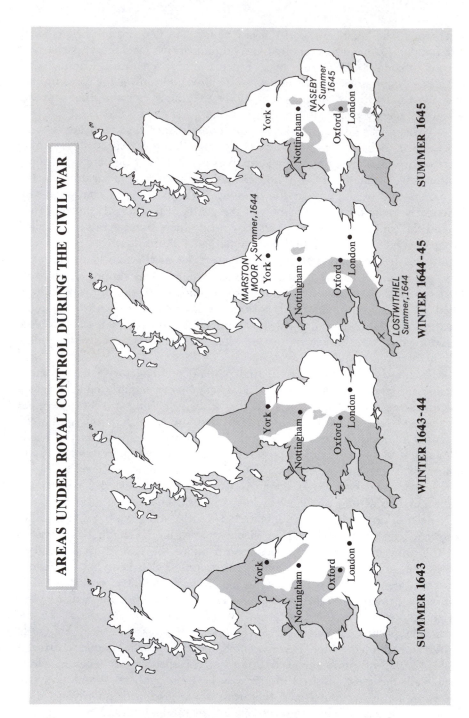

AREAS UNDER ROYAL CONTROL DURING THE CIVIL WAR

SUMMER 1643

York ●
Nottingham ●
Oxford ●
London ●

WINTER 1643-44

York ●
Nottingham ●
Oxford ●
London ●

WINTER 1644-45

MARSTON
MOOR ✕ Summer, 1644
York ●
Nottingham ●
Oxford ●
London ●
LOSTWITHIEL
Summer, 1644 ✕

SUMMER 1645

York ●
Nottingham ●
NASEBY
✕ Summer
1645
Oxford ●
London ●

he fights for and loves what he knows than that which you call a 'gentleman' and is nothing else." By March of 1645 he had obtained his wish, and four months later at the battle of Naseby his raw recruits held firm, and God gave victory to His militant saints.

The New Model Army was not only well disciplined, it was well and regularly paid, for parliament after 1644 began to utilize its immense fiscal reserves. It collected the rents on crown lands seized during the war; it raised vast sums of money through the customs; it imposed first voluntary and then forced loans upon wealthy merchants; it levied subsidies based on a new and more realistic assessment; and it collected what was called the "weekly pay" from all owners of land and chattels. Victory, however, was not merely purchased with money; it was won by the inspired leadership of such men as generals Harrison, Fairfax, and Ireton. Above all it was achieved by Oliver Cromwell, who started life as a simple country gentleman, justice of the peace and member of parliament, and who emerged at the age of forty-three as the one parliamentary leader who could win battles. He proved to be a man of action who could shout back at verbose parliamentarians: "Haste what you can. . . . The enemy in all probability will be in our bowels in ten days." It was his haste and vitality that

> First put arms into religion's hand
> And timorous conscience unto courage manned.

The moment parliament fully mobilized for war, Charles' defeat was merely a matter of time. The battle of Naseby was the ruin of the royalist cause, and within the year, on May 5, 1646, a fugitive king elected to surrender his person to his old enemies, the Scots, in the hope that they might remember that he too had been born in Scotland.

The Drift Toward Revolution

There was nothing extraordinary about civil war in England. Rebellion, rioting, and treason were time-honored practices, and in the fifteenth century the crown had become a political football to be kicked and pummeled by the great magnates. Civil disturbances in the past, however, had been of a distinct type; they were waged within the structure of government and framework of a society that sanctioned a wide degree of violence. They were fought within a class to which the king himself, as the greatest baron of the realm, belonged; and they were waged not to destroy the crown but to use and control it. Though the Civil War began in this tradition, the tempo of violence and change increased, moving steadily from reform to revolution, from limited monarchy to no monarchy. In the end the customs and restraints of centuries were torn aside, the ancient constitution violated and finally discarded.

The drift toward revolution commenced the moment war broke out; in a sense the Self-Denying Ordinance of 1645 was the first of a series of purgations in which conservatism and caution gave way to radicalism and extremism. Though self-administered, the ordinance constituted a decisive defeat for the grandees of parliament, especially for the aristocratic leadership of what remained of the House of Lords. As control of the military was taken over by men of a lesser social position but a greater desire to win the war, the composition of the county committees passed to revolutionists of energy, if not of breeding. Inherent within parliament and the parliamentary party was a basic social, and in part religious, split between timid constitutional monarchists such as the earls of Essex, Bedford, and Manchester, together with their conservative brethren in the House of Commons who were inclined to Presbyterianism in religious conviction, and the religious radicals who ranged in politics from the advocates of parliamentary supremacy and limited monarchy to the republicans and devotees of social as well as political revolution.

Though the political radicals tended to be Congregationalists or Independents, the royalist propagandists who tried to equate Presbyterianism with aristocracy and Congregationalism with democracy were considerably off the mark. Some of the most revolutionary leaders in politics were Presbyterians in religion. Conversely many Independents were politically conservative. Oliver Cromwell may have been no monarchist, but he was certainly no democrat. What distinguished an Independent or Congregationalist from a Presbyterian, and divided a radical from a conservative, was his willingness to experiment, his desire to act, and his readiness to use strong medicine in both state and church. Few Independents started off as republicans by conviction but many, like Cromwell, ended up voting to execute the king by necessity.

The moment the pressure of the Civil War ended in 1646, the radicals, who had taken over the control of the army, had to face the consequences of victory; they were in danger of having won themselves out of a job. In 1647 the conservatives struck at the wartime political leadership of such radicals as Sir Henry Vane and Oliver St. John, and tried to dissolve the New Model Army. In retaliation the military occupied London, and in August the House of Commons was purged at bayonet point of eleven of its most conservative Presbyterian members. Government by coup d'etat had commenced, but the final defeat of the conservatives was delayed until the summer of 1648. In the face of mounting radical pressure from the army and the extremists in parliament, the conservative Presbyterian members made their last bid to stem the tide of revolution and to turn the clock back to the days of 1641. They made common cause with Charles, who promised to reform the Church of England along Presbyterian lines; and they found the military means to defy the New Model Army by alliance with the Scots, who suddenly remembered that after all Charles was a Stuart and a Scotsman. The unholy league of conservative parliamentarians, Scottish Presbyterians, and Anglican Charles Stuart was no match for the soldiers of righteousness, and the Scottish forces were badly defeated in August of 1648 at the battle of Preston Pans. In December Cromwell and his victorious army returned to London, surrounded the ancient palace of Westminster, and purified parliament of the fearful of heart, the sinful of soul, and the uncertain of politics. Colonel Pride excluded 143 members from Commons, and the Long Parliament of 1641 became very short of members, only 78 remaining, of whom 20 refused to take their seats.

The End of the Old Constitution

The more Commons was "liberated" of its conservative elements, the greater became its claim to absolute supremacy over all other organs of government. The episcopacy had been abolished as early as 1646, but after Pride's purge the tempo of constitutional change attained revolutionary proportions. In January of 1649 Commons declared itself to "have the supreme power in this nation," and whatsoever it enacted "hath the force of law . . . although the consent of the King or the House of Peers be not had thereunto." Within days both king and Lords went the way of episcopacy. Kingship was declared "unnecessary, burdensome and dangerous"; Charles I was executed on Sunday, January 30, 1649; and a week later the House of Lords was abolished.

The decision to try and execute the king was momentous. In the past monarchs had been defeated in war, killed in battle, or quietly murdered in their beds, but never before had a sovereign been executed "as a tyrant, traitor, murderer and public enemy to the good people of this nation." The final decision was Cromwell's who, for better or for worse, was a man incapable of allowing a decision to go by default. Charles had proved his incompetence in defeat, his untrustworthiness in his alliance with the Scots and Presbyterians, and his sinfulness in the deceit with which he approached any negotiation with the army or parliament. Cromwell and the leaders of the army faced the dilemma which ultimately confronts all convinced minorities who have acquired the power to impose their will; the question whether the better part must give way to the more part. God had given His saints victory in war. It was unthinkable to a man who believed that he alone could save England from "a bleeding dying condition" that an ungodly majority should snatch the fruits of victory from God's elect. Charles had to be destroyed because it was clear that he felt in no way bound by sworn promises, and that he would undo God's work just as soon as he could find the means to do so. So determined was Oliver Cromwell that the king must die that he informed the 135 commissioners who tried Charles that, if necessary, he would "cut off the King's head with the crown on it."

In death Charles proved infinitely more dangerous than in life. He died as became a man and a sovereign, and he associated his death with the one principle that could wipe clean a lifetime of criminal folly: the rights of all Englishmen under law as they had been enshrined in the ancient and historic constitution. He died, as he claimed, "the Martyr of the People," a victim of naked force which denied not only his rights as king but the rights of all subjects, "for if power without law may make laws, may alter the fundamental laws of the kingdom, I do not know what subject he is in England that can be sure of his life or anything that he calls his own."

The Rump Against the Army

After seven years of war nothing remained of the ancient constitution except a Rump parliament which now stood face to face with a military monster of its own creation. England had become a commonwealth ruled by a Council of State of forty-one and a Rump of fewer than seventy-eight members. The council was still relatively conservative in composition, and continued to reflect the will of parliament, not of the army, for it was composed of three judges, three army officers, five peers, and thirty MPs. Any serious showdown, however, between the military and the tattered remnants of the Long Parliament was postponed until April of 1653 since the army was busy crushing mutiny within its own ranks and rebellion at home and in Ireland.

If Oliver Cromwell faced a historic decision in ordering the execution of a king, three months later he made an equally grave choice: the supression of the left wing of the revolutionary movement. The moment the crust of custom had been broken and the forces of innovation allowed, the scent

THE EXECUTION OF CHARLES I, SUNDAY, JANUARY 30, 1649
"He died . . . a victim of naked force which denied not only his rights as king but the rights of all subjects."

of social revolution from below became stronger and stronger. The numbers of Levellers, egalitarians, and religious communists were small throughout the realm, but their arguments sounded dangerous to conservative ears, and their heavy representation in the enlisted ranks of the army lent strength to their demand for radical reform. Levellers defied the most hallowed and cherished right of property—that a stake in society was an absolute prerequisite to a voice in government. The Leveller argument that "the poorest that lives hath as true a right to give a vote as well as the richest and greatest" was anathema to all men of substance. Cromwell and most of the grandees of the army were gentlemen of considerable property, and Cromwell informed the Council of State in March of 1649 that "you have no other way to deal with these men but to break them in pieces. . . . If you do not break them they will break you." Both army officers and Rump politicians could make common cause against enlisted men and Levellers, who impudently asked: "We were ruled before by King, Lords and Commons, now by a general, court martial and Commons, and we pray you what is the difference?" In May of 1649 three regiments mutinied, and General Cromwell followed his own advice: he destroyed the Leveller-inspired mutinies at Burford. Victory over rebellious Levellers was as crucial as Charles' execution in restoring the monarchy, for the battle of Burford marked the end of the revolutionary drift toward the left. Both military and political leaders came down hard on the side of social conservatism, which in the end inevitably led to conservatism in politics and the restoration of the ancient constitution in 1660.

Once Cromwell had chastened his mutinous troops, the army was called upon to crush rebellion in Ireland and Scotland. Across the Irish Sea the fire of the uprising of 1641 continued to smolder. Ireland was Catholic, royalist, and seditious—three good reasons to warrant God's vengeance—and in August His instrument, in the shape of Oliver Cromwell, arrived to punish the ungodly and disloyal Celts. At Drogheda the disciplined army of the saints put the hateful heretics to the sword. Within the year Ireland was prostrate and bleeding, and by the Act of Settlement of 1652 two-thirds of the land was expropriated, the bulk of the Irish population forcibly transplanted to County Connaught, and the island populated by London land speculators and Cromwellian soldiers. The terms of the settlement were never carried out in full, but enough was accomplished to embitter English-Irish relations for the next 300 years, and to convince most Irishmen that Oliver Cromwell had come from the land where a man could light his pipe with his finger.

With Ireland safe for the English, Cromwell turned on Scotland. There the Stuart dynasty still exercised its ancient magic, and rigid Scottish Presbyterians had risen again in defense of a Stuart king, this time in the person of young Charles II. At the battle of Worcester, in September of 1651, God again gave victory to His Roundheads, and Scotland like Ireland found itself garrisoned with English troops and joined with England into a united commonwealth. With all its enemies utterly routed, the Rump had no choice but to call upon its virtuous army for "aid and comfort"; and in April of 1653 the military were of a mind to give advice aplenty, for the grandees of the army were anything but pleased with the course of events in London and Whitehall. With each passing year the Rump seemed more and more unbending, self-perpetuating, and oligarchical. Its energy for reform had died, and it lacked the respect of the nation. The officers of the army were disgusted by the spectacle of parliamentary lawyers arguing over legal quibbles and never getting around to such important matters as reforming the church and the legal system or paying the arrears of the military.

Both Rump and army were aware that the revolutionary government was becoming less and less representative of opinion in the boroughs and the shires, and that it was slipping into incompetence and apathy. Parliament's solution was to enlarge itself with "persons of the same spirit and temper," and to allow existing members to exercise a veto over new recruits. The army's answer was to abolish the Rump entirely and to call into existence an assembly of saints. "We are not a mere mercenary army," they said, "here to serve an arbitrary power of the state." Instead they had taken up arms "in judgment and in conscience." Technically the military was the servant of parliament, but when the master did not "have a heart to do anything for the public good," then it was clear, as Cromwell told the Commons, the Lord was "done with them" and must choose "other instruments for carrying out of His work." In almost hysterical tones Cromwell informed the Rump that "you are no parliament; I say you are no parliament; I will put an end to your sitting!" And he did; the House was cleared at sword's point, and the next day, on April 21, a note was pinned to the door which read: "This house to Lett now Unfurnished."

The Search for Legality

When Cromwell justified his coup d'etat by arguing that the Rump itself had forced such violence upon him, he spoke only part of the truth. The course of novelty had moved from reform to revolution, sweeping away parliament as well as the crown. When Commons was purged out of existence by a military force of its own creation, a profound, if bitter, lesson was learned: parliament could no more exist without the crown than the crown without parliament. The ancient constitution had never been king *and* parliament but king *in* parliament; when one element of that mystical union was destroyed, the other ultimately perished.

The legal authority that had called the New Model Army into existence had vanished, but the army remained. From April of 1653 on, the military made a series of sincere if abortive efforts to find a legal justification for its authority, and a godly structure of government in which it could participate. Unfortunately the leaders of the army discovered that the clothing of naked power with the garments of legality was a job to tax the ingenuity of even the most accomplished political stylist. In July godliness and goodwill were tried, and a parliament of 144 saints, selected by the army and local church congregations, was called. Ever since, it has been known by the name of one of its members—Praise God Barebones. Never were reformation and reform approached with greater zeal, piety, and confidence of success; never were hopes more bitterly disappointed. Saintliness proved no substitute for political acumen or parliamentary experience, and sorrowfully Cromwell had to confess his error in imagining that "men of our judgement, who had fought in the wars and were all of a piece upon that account," would be able to work in accord and achieve God's will. In the end the general discovered that he was plagued more by pious fools than devilish knaves, and by December the Barebones Parliament had been sent home bag and baggage.

Faced with the problem of creating some kind of legal government other than martial law, the military unconsciously took the first hesitant steps which eventually led to the restoration of the monarchy. Imperceptibly men's minds turned back to the idea of monarchy as the single structure of government that offered legality, security, and permanence. The Instrument of Government, drawn up in December of 1653, inaugurated the drift that ended in restoration. By the terms of instrument, Cromwell exchanged the title of lord general of the army for lord protector of the commonwealth; executive power was placed in a Council of State composed of civilians and army officers who acted as a check on the protector's control; and legislative authority was vested in a single house elected from men of "known integrity, fearing God and of good conversation." Godfearing men were equated with those who had proved themselves to be careful stewards of the Lord, and the franchise was limited to persons worth £200 in real or personal property. The army was too cautious to place its future solely in the hands of the godly, and therefore Cromwell was given the right to exclude doubtful individuals from parliament (100 were in fact barred), and a standing army of 30,000 was written into the constitution.

The Instrument of Government lasted less than two years, for saints proved as unwilling to pay taxes as country squires, especially when the lion's share of the money was going to maintain a military force over which they had no control and which was rapidly deteriorating into a self-perpetuating armed caste. By January 1655, relations between the protector and his parliament were so bad that Cromwell, like Charles, chose to rule alone.

Charles had succeeded in making his "tyranny" endure for eleven years; Cromwell's rule of the major generals lasted barely twenty-two months. The difference between eleven years of Stuart absolutism and twenty-two months of Cromwellian dictatorship revealed the underlying weakness of the protector's position: it was easier to rule by legal and historic means than by military force. "If nothing should be done but what is according to law," Cromwell once said, "the throat of the nation might be cut while we sent for someone to make the law." Men who hate, who seek revenge, or who feel close upon them the fire of damnation or the hope of salvation, have no time to wait. A decade and a half of indecent haste produced the final irony—there was no law left, and the throat of the nation was cut upon the sword that had been forged to protect it. Charles had endured because law, habit, and custom were on the side of monarchy. He collected ship money and wardship and benevolent loans, because subjects were used to paying taxes to a king whom most people continued to accept as divine and who could discover endless precedents for his actions. Sheriffs and justices, constables and lord lieutenants enforced his law and raised money in his name out of a sense of historic duty, despite the fact that some of them dragged their feet and opposed royal policy. But a king was still a king and had to be obeyed. Only total bankruptcy, produced by the Scottish war, had forced Charles to call his parliament.

In contrast, Cromwell was neither divine nor legal. His authority did not stem from his title of lord protector, since there was neither precedent nor legality inherent in such a rank. Instead his power was vested in his command of troops, and in the end he and his military colleagues had to use the army, first to prop up the crumbling habits of lawfulness and obedience, and then to take over and operate the administration of government. Under the major generals the realm was divided into twelve parts, each governed by a military regime determined "to discourage and discountenance all profaneness and ungodliness" and to collect a Decimation Tax of 10 percent upon the estates of former Cavaliers. The results discredited the military and forged a bond among all men of substance regardless of their politics or religion. Rule by the major generals revealed that only the restoration of the ancient constitution could safeguard property and assure to "the natural rulers" of society their control of local and national government.

As with Charles in 1640, lack of money and the cost of war forced Oliver Cromwell's hand: he would have to try again to prop up his rule with some semblance of legality and parliamentary sanction. For the first five years of the commonwealth's life (1649–53) the Rump had been living in a fiscal paradise maintained by the sale of confiscated crown, church, and Cavalier lands. Some 7 million pounds had been raised from these sources which, when supplemented by occasional subsidies and income from the customs, had carried the government through the first years of its existence and had given it the financial means to suppress rebellion in Ireland and Scotland. In 1653, however, the pinch began on a level unimaginable in the days of the Stuarts. Under the commonwealth Englishmen learned for the first time that "an army is a beast that has a great belly and must be fed." Throughout most of the 1650s the budget stood at 2.7 million pounds, or three times what had been considered feasible under Charles I. The army alone was costing anywhere from 1.5 million to 3 million pounds annually, depending upon the nature of the government's military involvements. By 1655 the situation was desperate, for the Decimation Tax was proving to be unprofitable as well as illegal, and money from the sale of Cavalier estates and fines imposed upon royalists was beginning to run out. Moreover, the protector faced the added strain of a victorious but extremely costly war against Spain.

A New Foreign Policy

A revolutionary government in 1649 required a new foreign policy, and the moment that parliament took over first the initiative and then the crown itself, new ideas and interests in foreign affairs began to make themselves heard. With dynastic interests dead, the voice of trade rang unchallenged in the halls of Commons. The argument was clearly articulated that the state, by means of war and legislation, should actively seek to expand trade, protect the interests of Englishmen in foreign parts, and formulate a policy of economic aggression. A conscious policy of mercantilism in which the power of the state was marshaled in defense of chartered trading companies was accepted by the commonwealth government, which no longer had to heed the interests of the royal family, courtiers, and favorites. The only debate was the direction of commercial expansion and whether the influence of the Merchant Adventurers or the East India Company should prevail.

Economic aggression and a commercial policy in which English colonies were viewed as "subordinate to and dependent" on the mother country led to war with Holland in May of 1652. Anglo-Dutch relations had been deteriorating ever since England had made peace with Spain in 1604. Throughout the first forty years of the century, the Dutch tricolors had dominated the high seas "from China to Peru." The harbors of the world had been explored and monopolized by Dutch commercial interests, and the Netherlands East India Company had successfully closed the East Indies to English ships. England continued to resent the so-called massacre of Amboyna in 1623 when the Dutch seized and tried twelve English East India Company merchants for treason; and relations between the two countries were further strained by the execution of Charles I, which shocked public opinion in Holland. Moreover, the Netherlands saw in the enactment of the English Navigation Acts of 1650 and 1651 a direct challenge to their commercial empire. The Dutch claimed the right to "trade to all countries and plantations in America and elsewhere, without difference of people." The Navigation Acts required that English trade be carried in English ships, and that all foreign powers be excluded from the profits of the empire. Equally serious was England's claim to sovereignty over the channel, and her demand that foreign vessels strike their flags on meeting English men-of-war. Though the Dutch had no intention of admitting the freedom of the seas in the East Indies which they controlled, elsewhere they claimed it as the right of all maritime nations.

The First Dutch War of 1652 was disastrous to the Netherlands: her navies were defeated, her commerce disrupted, and her ports blockaded. By February of 1654 Oliver Cromwell was in a position to dictate the peace. The Stuart pretender, Charles II, was declared *persona non grata* by the Dutch States-General; Holland recognized English supremacy in the channel, and agreed to pay a tribute for fishing in British waters. "The judgement of heaven" had been appealed to, and though good Dutch Calvinistic merchants had their doubts and would make another appeal eleven years later during the Second Dutch War, the Lord had obviously declared for the English.

War with the Netherlands had never been popular with those economic interests in England which viewed Spain as the national enemy and advocated expansion into the West Indies. Moreover, English Calvinistic republicans were unhappy with a conflict that they regarded as a form of religious fratricide. Cromwell and many a country gentleman thought nostalgically of the days of Good Queen Bess, when glory, profit, and righteousness had united to singe the Spanish beard, loot Catholic treasure ships, and strike a blow for God and country. Militant Protestantism, lured on by the ancient shibboleth of cheap and profitable naval war, could not resist the temptation of war against Spain. Cromwell's "design" for English expansion into the West Indies and his grandiose dream of a crusade of all Protestant countries throughout Europe against Catholicism got under way in 1655. In the hope of emulating past glories, English ships again blockaded Cádiz and sought out the treasure fleets carrying the wealth of the New World. Unfortunately the profits proved meager, and for once England was more victorious on land than upon the high seas. She was joined by France in the capture of the Spanish port of Dunkirk in Flanders, a victory which allowed Cromwell to carry "the keys of the continent at his girdle." Had he lived, the protector might have been tempted to reenact the design of Henry V and carve for England a new European empire. As it was, only the capture of Jamaica from Spain was of enduring consequence, since it became the center for English domination of the West Indies. Of more immediate concern was the cost of the war, which forced renewed efforts to find a parliamentary government that could ensure a sufficient flow of funds and would cooperate with the military.

Restoring the Monarchy

The army's final solution to the constitutional impasse was called the Humble Petition and Advice by which the military decided to restore the monarchy in all but name. Cromwell was offered the crown but preferred the less conspicuous title of "His Highness"; however, he accepted the right to name his own successor. The ghost of the House of Lords was resurrected in the form of a second chamber nominated by the lord protector and approved by Commons. Even the historic franchise based on forty

OLIVER CROMWELL
"A good constable to keep the peace
of the parish." *Bibliothèque Nationale.*

shilling freehold land and borough representation was reestablished. The
moment, however, that the "natural leaders" of society again sat in the lower
house, they proved as difficult as any Stuart Commons. The upper house,
which possessed the right of veto, was filled with generals and Cromwellian
friends and therefore could be trusted; but unfortunately, the lower chamber,
with many of its members promoted to the new House of Peers, proved
more rebellious than ever. As with his other parliaments, Cromwell had to
resort to force; and in February of 1658 he disbanded this final legislative
experiment, announcing that he dissolved "this parliament and let God judge
between you and me." The Commons impudently answered back: "Amen."

If Oliver Cromwell was a failure, it was not for lack of courage or
endeavor. He has been called a "puzzled Atlas"; he might better be compared to the tortured Laocoön, destroyed by serpents called forth by his
own actions. Cromwell's failure was the tragedy of all men of goodwill who
recognize evil but find it difficult to describe the right. He and his army
colleagues were masterful men of war; they fought with conviction, but they
were innocent in the ways of statecraft. The lord general had had greatness
thrust upon him, and he looked to God as his guide. As one of the natural
rulers of society, he viewed himself as "a good constable to keep the peace
of the parish," and he accepted the post of lord protector "not so much out of
the hope of doing any good, as out of a desire to prevent mischief and evil."
Cromwell, however, was considerably more than a landed country gentleman; he was a saint. When East Indian merchants, sly lawyers, and ambitious politicians proved that at heart they despised "the cause of the people
of God," then the soldier-saint had no choice but to accept the responsibility
for forging a New Jerusalem. No matter how often parliament was resurrected or purged, it always showed itself to be "a worldly constitution, a

body fitted for a king . . . and every whit as Babylonish as kingship itself." Cromwell could not escape the conclusion that only the military, the hard core of God's elect, contained the life, the spirit, and the virtue of really good people.

The more the lord protector labored in the Lord's vineyard, the more evident it became that either men would have to be forced on to the path of righteousness or the old way of life and the ancient habits of thought would have to be restored. In the end history proved more powerful than the sword, and had Cromwell lived he would probably have endeavored to restore the monarchy in his own person. As it was, the Stuart court was copied by the protector with one essential exception: Charles I had had only a token military force, but Cromwell dined with every door guarded by armed sentries. Not only was the lord protector styled "His Highness" but his children became princes and princesses, and his country wife had to learn that a queen does not haggle over the price of oranges. Though the new court abounded with the regalia of royalty, Cromwellian monarchy was kingship without conviction or tradition. What held the Protectorate together was the force of the protector's own personality: he never achieved the New Jerusalem, but few men doubted his sincerity. His strength rested in his conviction that he was the Lord's instrument and not merely a common manipulator of men and parties. When he died, exhausted but not embittered, the revolution collapsed from within; it had in truth been dead for over a decade. Even in failure, the lord protector remained magnificent. How God ultimately judged between his chosen vessel and the impudent men in parliament, who forced the protector into greater and greater acts of violence, is not for man to record. History has long since given up writing about *Cromwell's Bloody Slauter House* or *The English Devil: Hell's Higher Court of Justice.* Today the verdict is simply that of a "puzzled Atlas" who was eventually destroyed by the means forced upon him to attain his ends. The Kingdom of God belongs to heaven, the city of man to earth, and not even a Cromwell could unite the two.[4]

The lord protector died on the third of September, 1658, and within eighteen months Charles II reclaimed his throne "without one drop of blood and by that very army which rebelled against him." The Bishop of Winchester is not to be laughed at for believing that "never was there so miraculous a change as this, nor so great things done in so short a time. But this is the Lord's doing; no human wisdom can claim a share in it." A peaceful restoration was indeed an extraordinary achievement, for the legacy of Cromwellian dictatorship was hatred, and the future in 1658 boded nothing

---

[4] An extraordinary number of people, including President Theodore Roosevelt, have had something to say about Oliver Cromwell. See the biographies by Ashley, Firth, Hill, and Wedgwood listed in the Bibliography; also W. C. Abbott, *Bibliography of Oliver Cromwell* (1929).

but anarchy and further civil war. What the good bishop, however, did not perceive was that Cavaliers and republicans had had their fill of civil war and military rule, and that no one, not even the major generals, could think of any political solution other than the restoration of the monarchy.

The utter failure of nonroyal monarchy was revealed when Oliver Cromwell's son, Richard, tried to inherit the protector's authority. What the father could do, his civilian son could not, and in April of 1659 the military forced Richard to dissolve the Protectorate and to reinstate the Rump. Incredible as it seems the Rump proved as unforgiving and as ungodly as ever, and promptly defied the grandees of the army by refusing to vote the arrears of pay and to abolish clerical tithes. With the military and the Rump again at sword's point, the realm began the long slide into anarchy. Associations sprang up urging people not to pay their taxes; the law courts ceased to function because the judges had no legal commission by which to act; and the lunatic fringes of the religious sects were again distributing their pamphlets and inflaming hungry apprentices and petty tradesmen in the city of London. The Levellers had been curbed but not silenced by Cromwell in 1649, and their strength had been manifest during the trial of their leader, John Lilburne—colonel, financial speculator, soap manufacturer, and demigod. At his trial thousands of spectators had chanted:

> And what? Shall then honest John Lilburne die?
> Three score thousand will know the reason why.

Levellers did not believe in complete political equality, but they did advocate the extension of the vote to all "freeborn Englishmen." Economic well-being in the seventeenth century was still the measure of liberty, and laborers, apprentices, and paupers were not included in the Leveller's definition of freedom. To the left of the Levellers stood the Diggers, whose views on freedom had nothing to do with property or prosperity. The liberty that they promoted lay "where a man receives his nourishment and preservation, and that is the use of the earth"; they advocated the abolition of wage labor and private property and the introduction of a Christian communism devoid of avarice and ambition.

Political radicalism tended to amalgamate with religious extremism. The fruits of contention and diversion, as Laud had warned, were harvested in the form of religious anarchy. Freedom of faith led inevitably to the disintegration of the state-supported church. Presbyterians, particularly of a conservative hue, had no faith in everyman's fancy to decide the truth for himself, and they never gave up their plea for uniformity and centralization of religion along Presbyterian lines. Independents also believed in a state church, if only because the truth was self-evident and good men must unite in its defense. While they urged a looser organization in which each congregation would have freedom to select its own minister, they never imagined either anarchy of thought or action. Toleration, however, was forced upon the lord protector and his Congregationalist followers as an answer to Presbyterianism, and as a means of winning the support of the religious splinter groups, which were legion.

Seekers and Ranters, Quakers and Baptists abounded, flourishing in the warm air of Cromwellian toleration and finding their greatest support among the enlisted ranks of the army. Religious radicals might be tolerated, but when they propounded not only that Christ had died for all mankind but also that men were equal on earth as well as in the eyes of God, they were branded as dangerous lunatics and political rebels. When such sects as the Fifth Monarchists argued the use of military action to prove their faith, both church and state had good cause for alarm. The Fifth Monarchists were millenarians who believed in the imminent second coming of Christ. Though many of them quietly awaited his arrival, others preferred to celebrate with riots and rebellions in defiance of established authority which they believed would shortly be cast down and destroyed. In the face of the "giddy, hot-headed, bloody multitude" which was beginning to harken to the voice of religious ranters, the ruling classes came to the conclusion that a state church and a historic king were absolutely essential to the maintenance of social discipline and obedience. As one gentleman complained: "I love old England very well, but as things are carried here, the gentry can not enjoy much to be in it." When these words were spoken, the swan song of revolution was sung.

In an atmosphere of anarchy, and with men of substance putting aside their religious and political disputes to unite in defense of order and degree, the army and the Rump continued to harangue each other to death. In May of 1659 the Rump cashiered General Lambert and ordered the army to disband. In answer the military for a second time closed the doors of parliament. But the army itself was beginning to disintegrate, since it was uncertain whether the rank and file would follow their officers against the Rump, and the generals were unable to unite upon a single policy. Some remained loyal to the idea of a protectorate, others sought yet another try at government by God's elect, and still others, such as George Monck, declared for the Rump. In the end it was General Monck who made the crucial decision—he ordered his soldiers out of Scotland and began the long march toward London. Hopelessly split, the military gave in to public pressure and the threat of Monck's approaching troops. "The Lord hath blasted them and spit in their faces, and witnessed against their perfidiousness," and as an act of repentance the Rump was restored for a third time on December 27th.

What would a thrice restored remnant of a dead revolution do in the face of the rising clamor for a new and free parliament? Would it allow elections or permit the inclusion of excluded members? In the streets of London apprentices spitted every steak they could find to signify the "roasting of the Rump." Even so that body hesitated, since either course of action meant the restoration of the monarchy. In the end the decision rested with General Monck, whose advance on London became a victory march. He entered the city on the 3rd of February 1660, and immediately commenced the process of unpurging parliament. On April 21 his soldiers quietly opened the doors to eighty of the one hundred and forty-three members who had been barred from their seats ten years before by Colonel Pride. The new additions were enough to outvote the diehards, and Commons set up a monarchistic Council of State with authority to invite Charles II back to his native land, and to order new elections on the basis of the historic franchise. Having done what General Monck ordered, parliament then proceeded to dissolve itself. The Long Parliament was finally over and so also was the Civil War.

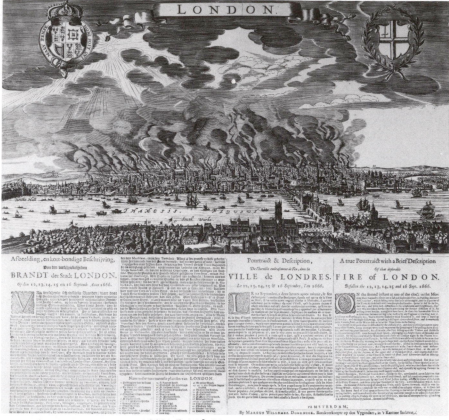

THE GREAT FIRE OF LONDON, 1666. *British Museum.*

V

SOCIETY RESTYLED
1660 to 1688

Charles II and
the Fruits of Revolution

15 On Friday afternoon, the 25th of May, 1660, Charles II's exile came to an end. Four days later, on his thirtieth birthday, the Merry Monarch made his triumphal entry into the city of London. "The shouting and joy" were "past imagination." His way was strewn with flowers, bells rang out a noisy welcome, the streets were hung with tapestries, fountains ran with wine, balconies were crowded with gaily-decked ladies, and the procession took seven hours to reach the royal palace of Whitehall. There, in the same room where his father had waited eleven years before to walk out upon the scaffold, Charles II was acclaimed by his loyal Commons. King, Lords, and Commons were united in their determination to turn back the clock to the days of 1641. The skeletons of war, rebellion, and regicide were firmly and securely shut into the closet of forgetfulness. The pretense was observed, at law and in the statute books, that twenty years of treason had never existed. Two decades of Civil War and Cromwellian Protectorship became an Interregnum, a limbo between periods of legality. The experience of saints and idealists and the advice of Mr. Thomas Hobbes were carefully set aside. The Restoration rested on neither godliness nor reason but on history.[1]

Fashions in Political Theory

The Civil War had produced two great political thinkers: the Puritan poet John Milton (1608–74) and the rationalist Thomas Hobbes (1588–

---

[1] The best surveys of the last half of the seventeenth century are G. N. Clark, *The Later Stuarts* (1934); D. Ogg, *England in the Reign of Charles II* (1955); J. H. Plumb, *The Growth of Political Stability in England 1675–1725* (1967); and A. Bryant, *The England of Charles II* (1935) and *Samuel Pepys* (3 vols., 1934–38).

1679). Each differed from the other as night from day, each reflected divergent facets of the Cromwellian revolution, and each was equally unacceptable to the restored monarchy of 1660. Milton had preached tyrannicide and republicanism on the grounds that man was born free, and that "the power of kings and magistrates is nothing else, but what is only derivative" and "committed to them in trust." When monarchs betrayed that trust, the free and godly had a moral duty to revolt. In his last political tract, *The Ready and Easy Way to Establish a Free Commonwealth,* Milton expounded the ultimate justification of the Cromwellian dictatorship. "Nature," he said, "appoints that wise men should govern fools." Wisdom was equated in Milton's mind not so much with godliness as with goodwill, and his most enduring treatise was the *Areopagitica* (1644), in which he defended freedom of speech on the grounds that the truth will always prevail over error when both are tested "in a free and open encounter" by men of wisdom and moderation. The truth needed "no policies, nor stratagems, nor licensings to make her victorious." Unfortunately neither the truth, as Milton conceived it, nor men of goodwill had been able to prevent the Cromwellian regime from deteriorating into despotism. Milton's "ready and easy way" proved to be inadequate, for it presumed the existence of men devoid of prejudice and filled with Christian charity. Charles II could scarcely have been expected to favor a political faith that sanctioned tyrannicide; and he and his advisers knew enough about human nature to realize that the Restoration, if it were to endure, could not be built on a Christian dream; it had to be firmly rooted in self-interest and a "vile and sordid love of money."

If Milton was too much the idealist, Thomas Hobbes was too much the realist. Hobbes wrote of the godless Leviathan, the secular state that was the product of social need and naked power. Law and order rested neither on divine precepts nor on the inalienable and historic rights of man, but upon the will of the sovereign which had the physical force to secure order and enforce law. Human nature, according to the Hobbesian creed, destined man to lust for power and to live in perpetual fear of destruction at the hands of the strong, the intelligent, and the greedy. Self-preservation compelled each individual to convey all his rights to a sovereign body which as a consequence became the source of all coercive authority within society and created and executed its own laws. Rebellion against such a sovereign power was the ultimate act of social folly since its destruction meant the end of society and a reversion to a state of nasty brutishness and anarchy.

The Leviathan was written between 1641 and 1651 as a defense of the crown and a warning against rebellion, but ironically it cost Hobbes his welcome at the exiled court of Charles II. The first Charles had died a martyr to something akin to Hobbes' sovereign—the military might of Oliver Cromwell's New Model Army. Eleven years later his son claimed the throne of England upon the same principles for which his father had died: the law of God and history as enshrined in the ancient constitution. Charles II was no Hobbesian sovereign; instead he was a legitimate ruler who accepted limitations upon his own authority because he recognized the historic rights of his subjects. A godless sovereign, created by man for reasons of social necessity and claiming absolute authority, was totally unacceptable to the Stuarts and to the seventeenth century as a whole. Charles, as an exiled sovereign returning to his throne at the sufferance of General Monck and public opinion, could hardly have condoned the Hobbesian doctrine that might makes its own right. It was because England had been exposed to the tyrannical consequences of unrestrained political power that the traditional sovereign was being restored. Men of substance saw in the ancient kingship a safeguard to their property, and they applauded a king who could write that "without the safety and dignity of the monarchy neither religion nor property can be preserved."

The Restoration: What Was Restored

In theory the Restoration was unconditional and limited only by Charles' promises, granted at Breda in April of 1660 just before setting sail for England. The Declaration of Breda pledged "liberty to tender consciences," a general pardon for all except for those whom parliament specified, the safeguarding of all land transfers made during the Interregnum until parliament had decided upon a just settlement, and the disbanding of the army. In actual fact, of course, the restored monarchy was unconsciously conditioned by the precedent of twenty years of rebellion and regicide. Not only did Charles make promises at Breda, but it was clear to all in 1660 that the divinity of kings was fast fading. The Stuart throne had been restored as an act of political necessity, not as the result of divine judgment. If any institution could claim to be the voice of heaven it was parliament, not the king. Even as Charles set foot in England the new position of the monarchy was recorded by Samuel Pepys. When the king was being rowed to the wharf at Dover, one of his favorite dogs fouled the boat. This mishap, Pepys noted, "made us all laugh and methink that a King and all that belong to him are but just as others are. . . ." If any idea of divine right existed in Charles' mind, it was probably similar to that of the happy pontiff who, on his election to the papal throne, is recorded to have said: "God has given us the papacy, now let us enjoy it." If nothing else, the new monarch was determined to enjoy what God and General Monck had given him.

England was fortunate in this ugly, big-nosed, "tall man, above two yards high," who stepped ashore at Dover. Like his grandfather, the second Charles was almost a foreigner; and having lived fifteen years in France, he was more French than English in taste and politics. Yet Charles understood England and his English subjects better than any Stuart sovereign before or after him: he instinctively sensed that the rock upon which the monarchy stood was popularity. Puritans were revolted by his scandalous self-indulgence, parliamentarians suspected that at heart he was an absolutist, and Protestants were scandalized by his free thinking and shocked by his Catholic proclivities. Yet few Englishmen felt sufficient animosity to act upon their hatred, and many thousands saw in Charles the affectionate symbol of "a very merry, dancing, drinking, quaffing and unthinking time." Though the righteous minority had serious doubts, the multitude loved a monarch who could announce that "God will not damn a man for taking a little unregular pleasure by the way."

Charles endeared himself to his subjects because he had a sense of humor and an appreciation for timing, joined with an absolute determination never again to go upon his travels. He had the sensitivity, intelligence, and tact not to drive himself or his enemies to extremes. In victory he was moderate, in defeat he was understanding, and his epitaph, spoken by the marquis of Halifax, has about it the ring of truth. "Let his royal ashes then lie soft upon him, and cover him from harsh and unkind censures; which, though they should not be unjust, can never clear themselves from being indecent." For all his faults, Charles Stuart was never indecent in his sex life, his faith, or his politics, and this was all that most men demanded of him. England in 1660 had had its fill of indecent godliness and military rule, and it was satisfied with a sovereign who could learn from the past, yet forget and forgive the bitterness of his experiences.

If fervent royalists thought that the Restoration would bring sweet

CHARLES II, 1659
"The multitude loved a monarch who could announce that 'God will not damn a man for taking a little unregular pleasure by the way.'" *National Portrait Gallery.*

revenge and that henceforth the sun would shine on their "side of the hedge," they were sadly mistaken. Charles had promised at Breda pardon to all except those named by parliament, and he kept his royal word. In the end only 57 names were omitted from the Act of Indemnity. Of these, 30 were condemned to die but only 13 were finally sacrificed to the demand for vengeance. Though the people greeted the spectacle of hanging and disemboweling with "great shouts of joy," and Mrs. Pepys left her wifely duties to view the hanging of the exhumed corpses of Cromwell and his brother-in-law General Henry Ireton, the monarchy was not restored in a bath of blood. The men who had committed treason against the sovereign and had cast down the crown were themselves members of the ruling class, and it had been their disaffection with the revolution that was largely responsible for Charles' return. They were as useful and necessary to him as his faithful royalists.

The king had scarcely reached London before it became apparent that rebels as well as steadfast friends would have to be rewarded. Those old Cromwellian military men George Monck and Edward Montagu each earned a peerage. Monck received the coveted Order of the Garter and a dukedom, and Montagu was appointed general of the fleet and created earl of Sandwich. The men who triumphed in 1660 were politic individuals in both camps, who were able to make the best of all possible worlds. Charles' council of thirty in 1661 contained twelve men who had committed treason against his father. In part, forgiveness was deliberate policy; in part it was dictated by necessity, for the king had to have advisers of experience and only the parliamentary party could supply him with what he needed. In all honesty, the new monarch had to agree with Samuel Pepys' conclusion that the Cavalier party was unable to supply "nine commissioners or one secretary fit for the business." Twenty years of exile had been no training in the art of government. Merchants and Presbyterians, rebellious landlords and Cromwellian generals had been ruling the realm for two decades through parliamentary committees; and after the Restoration many of them continued in the service of the crown.

The man who typified the Restoration and its policies was the king's chief minister and lord chancellor, Edward Hyde, the newly created earl of Clarendon. Hyde had been an opponent of ship money and an ally of Pym when the Long Parliament first met. His purpose in 1660 was to restore to England "its old good manners, its old good humour and its old good nature." This did not mean bloodshed, revenge, or the restoration of Tudor-Stuart paternalism. During the years of exile the earl's greatest accomplishment had been to keep his king free from the religious passions and furious vengeance of the queen mother and hotheaded Cavaliers. He sought the return of king in parliament which would not be a blind and slavish imitation of the days of Elizabeth but instead a constitutional balance reflecting the changes legally introduced during the first years of the Long Parliament. Though royalists might weep for their martyred king, a ruling monarch had been dethroned and executed by parliament, and the restored crown had to recognize this unpleasant fact.

The sceptre and sword of state returned untarnished, but the crown that rested upon Charles' brow was sadly lacking in its ancient luster. The prerogative courts of Star Chamber and High Commission, the two pillars of Tudor-Stuart paternalism, had been legally abolished in 1641 and were not restored. Without the machinery to enforce royal will in church and state or to discipline "the natural leaders" of society in the shires, any pretense of an organic and ordered society vanished, and the direction of government fell into the hands of men of property. The greatest accomplishment of the earl of Clarendon was his success in associating "the rule of the restored House of Stuart with the sense of universal security for persons and goods." It was exactly here that the royalists' cup of bitterness ran over; for they learned that the Restoration did not mean the redemption of lost estates and rewards for past sacrifices, but instead "Indemnity for the king's enemies and Oblivion for his friends."

The Act of Indemnity and Oblivion of 1660, establishing the land settlement, acknowledged the sanctity of private property even when held by rebels, and proved the wisdom of William Prynne's words that "if Charles Stuart is to come in, it were better for those that waged war against his father that he should come in by their votes." Crown lands worth 3.5 million pounds, church property valued at 2.4 million pounds, and the estates of 700 royalists which had been confiscated during the Interregnum were returned to their original owners. Although many a parvenu Cromwellian officer was stripped of his lands and hard-won social dignity, Cavalier estates, sold to support the king's armies or to pay the fines and crushing taxes levied by the Rump and the military government under Cromwell, were never restored. Between 1644 and 1652, £1,300,000 in fines had been extracted from 3,000 royalists; and possibly an even larger sum was later raised by the Decimation Tax. How many Cavalier gentlemen went under, destroyed by debts and loyalty to their king, is beyond reckoning. One study indicates that in Staffordshire half the land changed hands between 1609 and 1669, the presumption being that the highest rate of change occurred during the Interregnum years. Certainly the royalists in 1660 felt that they had been cheated of the fruits of Restoration. The wealthy, the influential, the astute, but not necessarily the just, triumphed. It seemed to many supporters of the king that they had "endured the heat of the day and become poor," only to be "put off with inconsiderable nothings." Charles himself escaped their hatred, but Cavaliers never forgave Clarendon for what they considered to be rank betrayal.

Though the earl of Clarendon was branded a Judas, he was no traitor to his class, only to an unlucky minority within it. The king's party, he argued, consisted not solely of royalists but of all persons of "considerable fortunes and families in the kingdom." In 1660 England stood upon the threshold of 170 years of government of, by, and for the well-bred, the well-connected, and the well-established, in which freedom was equated with property and liberty with privilege. With a single voice the oligarchy acclaimed Hyde's words that "whatsoever is of civility and good manners, all that is of art and beauty," is the "child of beloved property." Even that excellent Presbyterian Richard Baxter agreed that "want of riches" keeps "men out of freedom."

It was crucial to the defense and security of men of substance that a parliament dominated by gentlemen be financially and politically supreme; that local government be firmly in the hands of the squirearchy; and that the Church of England be converted into a form of outdoor relief for the oligarchy. All three were in part achieved by the Restoration. The rule of property in government had in large measure been achieved when parliament established its right to be the sole taxing instrument within the realm. The crown's feudal and historic sources of revenue were never revived. In the place of ship money, wardship, and purveyances, Charles II was promised an annual income of £1,200,000 for life, only half of what Cromwell had gone bankrupt on, but a third more than his father had managed with during his eleven years of personal rule. The first Restoration parliament, known as the Cavalier Parliament, was loud in its devotion to monarchy; but it was equally determined not to create a financially independent crown, nor to reintroduce the system of direct land and property taxes that had existed in the days of Elizabeth and James I. In the sixteenth century a parliamentary subsidy had generally been levied at a rate of four shillings to the pound on the assessed value of land, and at the rate of two shillings, eight pence, on personal property. By 1628 property assessment had become so outdated that the upper classes had been able to escape the full weight of taxation, and even during the Civil War years parliament had been hesitant to burden its members too heavily. Though subsidies based on a new rate of assessment were passed, the Rump and the military preferred to live off the custom duties, excise taxes, and fines imposed upon royalists. The Cavalier Parliament of 1661 showed the same reluctance to depend upon direct taxation. The last of the ancient subsidies was passed in 1663; thereafter an excise tax on beer, ale, tea, coffee, and soap, a hearth tax, and the customs carried the cost of government.

The fiscal supremacy of parliament undoubtedly meant a tax policy favorable to landlords and merchants. Before judging the class nature of the tax structure, however, it is well to recall that nearly a million pounds was voted in 1660 to pay off the arrears of the army, and that throughout Charles' reign men of property were contributing on the parish level nearly £700,000 a year for poor relief. This was the price oligarchy was willing to pay for the control of local government. The country gentleman had always exercised immense influence in the shires, but after 1660 within his own estate he was "prince." The demise of the Star Chamber and the failure of the Privy Council to discipline and control justices of the peace removed royal influence from the countryside, leaving supreme the sheriff, the high constable, the lord lieutenant, the justice of the peace, and the local squire. At the same time, the abolition of feudal military tenure in 1660 further increased the power of the local gentry by transforming feudal landholding, which had been in the past subject to fiscal and military obligations to the crown, into private property. Copyholds were left largely unprotected, and tended to deteriorate into leaseholds held at the sufferance of the local land-owner.

As a further safeguard against a monarchy balanced, and in local affairs heavily outweighed, by oligarchy, parliament made good its claim to freedom of speech and debate. It demanded that statute take precedence over royal proclamation and that the crown's prerogative be translated into law. The Book of Customs Rates of 1660, for example, was based on statute, not royal decree. Finally, it insisted on the right of habeas corpus, first enacted into law in 1641 and restated in 1679, whereby the critics of the crown were protected and limits were placed upon the actions of arbitrary government. England, as the French ambassador noted, had a monarchical appearance because there was a king, "but at bottom it is very far from being a monarchy." Members of parliament, he said, not only spoke their minds freely but even called "the highest people to the Bar."

The crown was inseparable from religion, and the restoration in the state of the ancient constitution required the resurrection in the church of the episcopacy. Unfortunately Anglicans and Presbyterians refused to be reconciled. Twelve bishops and twelve Presbyterian elders, like Lewis Carroll's maids, could not sweep away the sand of discord. The only thing they could settle upon was that "the Church's welfare, unity and peace, and His Majesty's satisfaction were ends on which they were all agreed." With the failure of churchmen to find a solution, the Cavalier Parliament of 1661–62 took a hand and re-established Anglican uniformity, episcopacy, and discipline. The Act of Uniformity of 1662 ordered the clergy to give "unfeigned assent and consent" to the Anglican Prayer Book, and 250 Puritan pastors were removed from their posts. Those expelled became known as Dissenters or Nonconformists since they refused to revert back to Anglicanism. Having purged the clergy, parliament struck at the non-conforming ranks of the laity. The Corporation Act of 1661 required all town officials to take an oath of allegiance to the crown and to accept communion according to the rites of the Church of England. The Conventicle Act of 1664 made all meetings of five or more persons for non-conformist worship seditious; and the Five Mile Act passed a year later ordered that no dissenting minister might live within five miles of a town, nor teach unless he had taken the oath of allegiance. Taken together the religious settlement became known as the Clarendon Code, though in fact it represented the failure, not the triumph, of the earl's policy. Although Clarendon had been responsible for Charles' promise at Breda to grant "liberty to tender consciences," and both he and Charles sought a more moderate and broader religious settlement, the Cavaliers, who had been denied their wish in land and politics, had their say in religion.

In defeat Puritanism found its grandest voice in the blind Milton. Evicted from his position as Latin secretary to the Council of State under Cromwell, silenced as a political pamphleteer, and cut off by law from the comfort of his faith, the poet posed the question hidden in every Puritan heart:

> Now blind, disheartened, shamed, dishonoured, quelled,
> To what can I be useful, wherein serve
> My nation and the work from Heaven imposed?

Satan's triumph in *Paradise Lost* is the cry of blind, disheartened Puritanism; *Paradise Regained* is the hope of inward victory and heaven. Dissent after 1660 turned to pietism, toleration, and finally to democracy. Those who could not be persuaded to conform for the sake of political privilege began to close their ranks. Congregationalists and Presbyterians, Quakers and Unitarians after 1660 stood united in quiet but determined opposition to Anglican episcopacy and the state-enforced uniformity on which it rested.

If militant Puritanism died with the Restoration, so also did Laudian Anglicanism. The restored church became the instrument of oligarchy, not of monarchy; and the alliance of the altar and the throne gave way to the union of the miter and the ermine. Under Archbishop Laud, the church of Henry VIII and Elizabeth had retained one essential feature of its Catholic heritage: ministers were "ambassadors of God" ordained "to supply the room of Christ." The old Anglican Church had been the dictator of morals, the censor of opinions, and had constituted a separate caste, and Laud had encouraged the simple parson "to hold up his head in the presence of the country families." Once upon a time ministers had been "as good as any Jack Gentleman in England," but after 1660 the church became the preserve of the squirearchy.

The king continued to be the governor of the ecclesia and the defender of the faith, but his powers of discipline had died with the Court of High Commission. Parliament now accepted the burden of ordaining and enforcing religious uniformity, and it removed from the church's hands the right to tax itself. Henceforth the ecclesia lost its position as a divinely sanctioned caste and became a profession, to be taxed and disciplined like any other occupation. The church was worth saving, not for the sake of religion, but because it was one of the pillars of respectability and an essential prop to oligarchical rule. The sons of gentlemen were sent to college to "learn the art or trade of preaching." Five hundred years earlier the church had thundered with the mighty voice of God. By the sixteenth century it sang an obedient treble to the crown's bass. After 1660 it became the silent and humble partner in that scheme of things so confidently described by the marquis of Newcastle, who "loved monarchy as it was the foundation and support of his own greatness; and the church as it was well constituted for the splendor and security of the crown; and religion as it cherished and maintained that order and obedience that was necessary to both."

Restoration Politics

The Restoration was a brilliant accomplishment, achieved without bloodshed and with a minimum of bitterness, but the resurrection of the ancient constitution created almost as many questions as it solved. It remained to be seen whether the treasured Tudor doctrine of uniformity of faith could survive in a society where religious dissent was extensive, or whether spiritual orthodoxy was possible in a universe run by the mechanical laws of Sir Isaac Newton's world machine. Equally problematical was the restoration of the ancient but muddled political formula of king in parliament at a moment when Englishmen were demanding a more precise definition of the powers of monarchy. The Restoration left the exact relationship between king and parliament in dangerous obscurity; and by 1666 both crown and Commons were beginning to articulate their own definition of that formula.

The restored crown may have been stripped of much of its divinity, but it still retained many of its ancient prerogatives. The king could prorogue and dissolve parliament at will, could veto acts of legislation, and was not obliged to account for how much or how well he spent his revenues. He was responsible for the conduct of foreign policy, was head of the military forces of the realm, and could choose his own advisers and listen only to those he preferred. Most important of all, the king still retained the right to suspend and dispense with any law of parliament. As James I had put it, "general laws made publicly in parliament may by [royal] authority be mitigated and suspended upon causes only known to him." The right to pardon is inherent in any executive authority, but the power to suspend the operation of law could in its most extreme form have destroyed the fruits of war and revolution for which parliament had fought.

In order to counterbalance the weighty authority of the monarch, parliament possessed the right of impeachment of royal advisers, and it tenaciously maintained its grasp over the purse strings of government. The crux of the constitutional issue was that parliament had asserted its supremacy but as yet lacked the institutional machinery and the precedents to make good its demand. The right to tax was undisputed, and the crown recognized that its revenues stemmed from parliament, but the power of appropriation remained in controversy. It was clear that the legislature would never be able to harness the executive unless it possessed the right to allocate money for specific purposes and to require an account of the sums spent. Charles in 1660 had been granted an annual revenue of £1,200,000. In theory he was expected, in good feudal tradition, to live within his income, and how he spent his revenues and the amounts he assigned to the court and the various branches of government were not matters for parliament to decide. Theory collapsed when the king failed to receive the full sum promised him and when Commons refused to vote additional revenues until it felt confident that the money spent reflected its policies and not the whims of royal mistresses and favorites. Without statistical knowledge it was also difficult to correlate anticipated income with actual taxes. When Charles commenced his reign in 1661, receipts were short by £250,000, and the king had to operate on a shoestring. In the face of bankruptcy, Charles, like his father, slowly gave way; and in 1665 the principle of appropriation of monies was reluctantly conceded in theory, if not always in fact. Two years later parliament created the crucial piece of machinery necessary to enforce its financial will—a Committee of Public Accounts.

Underlying the controversy between a restored monarchy and a Cavalier Parliament was the recurrent question of advice. The power to impeach royal ministers was a blunt weapon unless Commons knew who was giving "bad" advice to the sovereign. As yet the concept of total cabinet or council responsibility had not evolved, and if the king could do no wrong, it was essential that parliament know the names and the policies of his most intimate advisers, who might be giving evil advice. Sir Henry Neville urged that the sovereign rely only on councillors approved by parliament and that "there shall be a register kept of all the votes of these several councils . . . with the names as well of those who consent, as of such who dissented." Charles had no intention of allowing Commons to intrude upon the sacred precincts of his council chamber, if only because both he and his cabinet were increasingly in disagreement with the wishes of parliament. The crisis came when the architect of the Restoration, the earl of Clarendon, was impeached in November of 1667 and fled to France in order to escape imprisonment and possible decapitation. Clarendon's fall involved three interrelated events: the misappropriation of funds during an ineptly fought Dutch war; Charles' clash with parliament over the crown's right to suspend the law; and the disasters of fire and plague in the city of London.

War with the Netherlands in 1665 was a continuation of commonwealth policy. The Cavalier Parliament was as anxious as its republican predecessors to enact legislation protecting English maritime and imperial interests. The Navigation Act of 1660 aimed at establishing a self-sufficient empire and extending the principle of "English ships with English crews" to the colonies. The statute was specifically directed at excluding foreign competition from the empire and assuring English commercial dominion throughout the seven seas. With such a goal in mind, war with the Dutch was caused by the simple fact, as stated by Samuel Pepys, that "the trade of the world is too little for us two, therefore one must down." Moreover, dynastic pique as well as commercial rivalry entered the picture, for Charles had never forgiven Dutch animosity toward the Stuart cause during the Interregnum.

The war only highlighted the incompetence of English arms in contrast to the days of Cromwell and Admiral Blake. Admiral DeRyter sailed up the Thames in June of 1667, set fire to naval installations, and towed away the flagship, *The Royal Charles,* right under English noses. War against Holland also suffered from lack of money and energy. Clarendon failed to give the needed leadership, and parliament failed to supply the necessary funds; but, as Pepys complained, the major fault lay with the royal brothers, Charles and James, "who mind their pleasures and nothing else." Parliament had no intention of granting supplies that might be wasted on favorites, dogs, and mistresses. Consequently English military honor fell victim to the constitutional conflict over appropriations.

Dutch victory at sea was not solely the result of English naval incompetence and constitutional squabbling between king and Commons. The enemy also profited from the plague that raged through London during the summer of 1666 and from the catastrophic, if purging, fire which destroyed three-fourths of the old city. During the plague year of 1665–66, 68,495 Londoners perished from the bubonic bacillus carried by fleas that lived on the hordes of rats that infested the slums of the city. Twenty-two more people died during the night of Sunday, September 2, 1666, when London went up in flames: four died by fire, five by drowning, six from fright, and seven by accident. St. Paul's Cathedral, the Royal Exchange, the Guild Hall, the Custom House, the halls of 44 trading companies, 87 parish churches, and 13,200 houses were destroyed. The total loss was estimated at over £11,000,000, ten times the royal income. The fire started in the home of the king's baker in Pudding Lane. Timber houses with plaster walls, pitch-boarding, and thatched roofs went up like torches, spreading their sparks throughout the city. For once the king moved swiftly and decisively, saving what he could of his capital. The parishes of the city were divided among members of the Privy Council under the command of the king's brother, the duke of York. Justices of the peace and the local nobility were marshaled; each division received three justices of the peace, thirty soldiers, and a hundred constables, all intent on demolition, the only possible method of containing the conflagration. From 5 A.M. to 11 P.M. Charles himself moved from parish to parish, passing buckets, swinging pickaxes, paying workmen, and offering encouragement. The next day 100,000 Londoners were homeless, but the fire was out and rebuilding commenced within the hour.

Singed at home and beaten on the high seas, England sued for peace at Breda in July of 1667. She regained the city of New York but gave up trying to break the Dutch monopoly over the spice islands of the East Indies, and momentarily withdrew her claim that the Channel was a *Mare Anglia.* The earl of Clarendon was held responsible for all the evils of the day. He was blamed by parliament for having urged Charles to issue a stillborn Declaration of Indulgence in 1662, softening the harshness of the religious code that bore his name. He was held accountable for the king's

THE GREAT PLAGUE OF LONDON, 1665–66
"68,495 Londoners perished." *Clarendon Press, Oxford.*

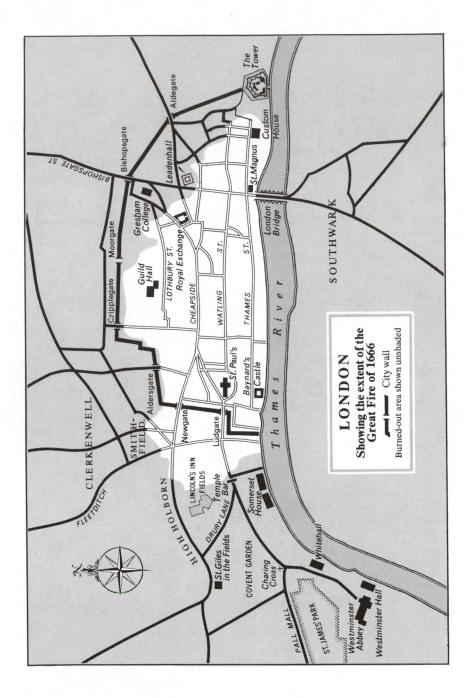

LONDON

Showing the extent of the Great Fire of 1666

━━━ City wall

Burned-out area shown unshaded

The Tower
Aldgate
Bishopsgate
BISHOPSGATE ST.
Leadenhall
Custom House
St. Magnus
London Bridge
Moorgate
Gresham College
Royal Exchange
LOTHBURY ST.
Cripplegate
Guild Hall
CHEAPSIDE
WATLING ST.
THAMES ST.
SOUTHWARK
Thames River
Aldersgate
St. Paul's
Baynard's Castle
SMITHFIELD
CLERKENWELL
Newgate
Ludgate
FLEETDITCH
Lincoln's Inn Fields
Temple
Drury Lane Bar
HIGH HOLBORN
Somerset House
Whitehall
St. Giles in the Fields
COVENT GARDEN
Charing Cross
PALL MALL
ST. JAMES' PARK
Westminster Abbey
Westminster Hall

Portuguese marriage to Catherine of Braganza, which brought with it Tangier in the Mediterranean and Bombay in India but no children born in wedlock in Whitehall. He was blamed for the sale of Dunkirk to the French in 1662 for £400,000, which was regarded as a deliberate betrayal of the victory won by English arms in the days of Oliver Cromwell. Finally, both parliament and the king made him the scapegoat for the ignominious defeat of England at the hands of the Dutch.

With Clarendon's fall in 1667, England was ruled by a Cabal, or inner council. The age of government by alphabets had begun, for the Cabal took its name from the first letters of the ruling clique—Clifford, Arlington, Buckingham, Ashley, and Lauderdale. Ashley was a free thinker and parliamentarian, Arlington a psuedo-Catholic, Clifford a papist, Buckingham an Independent gone libertine, and Lauderdale a Scottish Presbyterian. Government with five heads almost instantly floundered. The Cabal could agree on nothing except religious toleration, not because it believed in the principle but because each member sought to profit from it. The Cabal, in Charles' view, had but a single advantage; it left him free to develop his own foreign policy and in 1672 to introduce for a second time a Declaration of Indulgence suspending the operation of the Clarendon Code.

By 1670 Charles had determined on a pro-French policy. He was himself French by taste and breeding, and his mother was Louis XIV's aunt. He admired the ease, freedom, and brilliance of Louis XIV's absolutism, and he sincerely desired to free English Catholics from the Draconian laws of Elizabeth's reign which still, in theory at least, existed. The ultimate purpose of Charles' policy remains in doubt. If he aimed, as some historians have argued, at a second Stuart tyranny based on "Catholicism, toleration, a standing army and the French alliance," he never informed those around him. The king was both too lazy and too humorous to be a successful despot or fanatic. Moreover, he was too intelligent to believe seriously that he would be able to get away with it. In all three—his laziness, his humor, and his intelligence—he differed from his brother and successor, James II, who was hardworking, humorless, and stupid, qualities which in 1688–89 again sent the Stuarts into exile.

In 1670 Charles signed the secret Treaty of Dover with France, whereby Louis XIV promised to relieve his cousin of dependence upon parliament by an annual pension and to send troops to enforce Catholicism in England. In return Charles offered to make a public declaration of his adherence to the Catholic faith as soon as it was "convenient" to do so. "Convenient" was the saving word, since there is considerable doubt whether Charles seriously imagined that there would ever be such a "convenient" occasion, except possibly on his deathbed. Whatever the ultimate purpose of the treaty, its immediate effect was to put into the hands of an impecunious king a considerable sum of money and a French promise to help England revenge herself upon the Dutch. Anglo-French designs upon the Netherlands were the only aspects of the treaty publicized, and they led to the Third Dutch

War in 1672, which inaugurated England's entrance into the European system of alliances and realliances to maintain the balance of power.

France dominated the last half of the seventeenth century as Spain had overshadowed the final years of the sixteenth. If any country can be said to have profited from thirty years of European war in which outrage, atrocity, and aggrandizement on the part of men and states were cloaked in the pious platitudes of religious idealism, that country was France. Almost the moment that the Treaty of Westphalia was signed terminating the Thirty Years War in 1648, France emerged as the colossus of Europe and sought to extend her dominion to her "natural boundaries" of the Rhine, the Alps, and the Pyrenees. The avowed policy of the French crown was to realize at home and abroad the maxim: "The king first in France, and France first in Europe." Under Louis XIV (1638–1715) that policy seemed on the verge of completion. France was the wealthiest and most stable kingdom in Europe. Paris and the new royal court at Versailles were regarded as the cultural centers of the continent. French became the language of diplomacy and polite society, and every petty dynasty throughout Germany and Italy slavishly modeled itself upon the court of the *Grand Monarque*. French hegemony did not limit itself to the arts and letters. The wealth, security, and economic prosperity of France upset the military balance of power, and permitted Louis to train and finance a standing army of 100,000 men. Fear of French arms and, at the same time, a willingness to accept French gold became the pivots of European diplomacy. In 1672 French expansion was directed at destroying the Dutch Republic and claiming the Spanish Netherlands in the name of Louis' Spanish wife. It was essential to French plans that the two maritime and commercial powers—England and Holland—should not be allied to one another. The offer of gold to finance the Stuart government, the desire for revenge upon the Dutch, and Charles' Francophilia were sufficient to bring England into the European alliance system on the side of France.

If Louis planned on active and successful English support in the Third War against Holland, he was sadly mistaken. Despite the trade rivalry between England and the Netherlands, the war was not popular. English navies were again shamefully defeated; there was mounting xenophobia against France; and parliament had strong objections to Charles' pro-Catholic policy. In accordance with his promise to Louis in the secret Treaty of Dover, Charles issued the second Declaration of Indulgence, in which he suspended the Clarendon Code against Dissenters and the Elizabethan penal laws against Catholics. As a consequence, king in parliament once again became king versus parliament, for the Cavalier Commons of 1672, though a trifle elderly, was just as fiercely anti-Catholic and anti-Dissenter as ever. In the end the king was faced with a choice: either a parliamentary grant of £1,200,000 with which to fight the Dutch war and a Test Act (1673) barring all Catholics and Dissenters from civil and military offices, or his Declaration of Indulgence and a bankrupt state. Charles was always one to accept cash in hand in preference to religious scruples in the bush. He withdrew his declaration and signed the Test Act. The statute was in part aimed at the king's Catholic brother, James, Duke of York, who was forced to resign his position as lord high admiral; and it was the first skirmish in the long battle to prevent the Catholic duke from succeeding to his brother's throne.

Parliament proved its control over those aspects of foreign policy that involved large sums of money by forcing Charles to conclude peace with Holland in 1674 and to give up the French alliance. Thereafter Charles lived on his secret French pension of over £100,000 a year and the receipts from the customs; his revenues for the first time reached the 1.2-million-pound level originally authorized by parliament in 1660. The crown by 1674 had finally achieved a degree of fiscal independence and had successfully weathered the financial crisis of the early years of the reign; but the Stuart monarchy was almost wrecked a second time by the efforts of parliament to exclude the duke of York from the succession and by the religious and constitutional conflict that culminated in the extraordinary activities of Mr. Titus Oates and the Popish Plots of 1678–81.

My Lord of Shaftesbury and the Popish Plot

Government by Cabal had been replaced in 1674 by the more personal rule of the sovereign and his new chief minister, Thomas Osborne, Earl of Danby, who helped solve the king's monetary embarrassments and sought to construct in Commons a court party loyal to church and king. The English domestic scene during the 70s was a picture of befuddlement and confusion. Behind his ministers' backs, Charles, with the aid of his mistresses, was indulging in petticoat diplomacy, continuing to assure Louis that England was ripe for a Catholic triumph. At the same time Danby was striving to rally support for the monarchy by bribing and influencing members of parliament. In 1679 it was alleged that 214 MPs were beholden to the earl either for pensions or for offices. It is closer to the truth to say that Danby had at his disposal £84,000 annually from the Secret Service Fund to spend as he saw fit in organizing the king's friends. Besides the judicious use of money, Danby espoused a pro-Dutch, anti-French, and anti-Catholic policy to weld his party together. As a final measure of confusion, French gold could be found everywhere, for Louis was generous to the king's enemies as well as his friends. Out of this quagmire of moral delinquency, political opportunism, and diplomatic chaos, three factors are discernible: (1) the growing resentment against the heir apparent, James, Duke of York, and his Catholic faith; (2) the wave of religious hysteria which led even Englishmen of reason and moderation to believe that papists were hidden behind every bush, plotting to murder the king and overthrow the Protestant church; and (3) the formation of a country party under the leadership of that spiritual father of ward-healing, lobbying, and bossism, Anthony Cooper, Earl of Shaftesbury.

The earl of Shaftesbury was either "the father of liars" and "the favorite of the devil," or the hero of parliamentary supremacy, the father of Whiggery, and the defender of English liberties. The earl was all things to all people and a master at abandoning the ship at the crucial moment. He had been a Cavalier soldier until the royalist defeat at Naseby; he then became a zealous Presbyterian and supporter of the Protectorate, until he happened to perceive the drift of events and worked for the return of Charles II. He was rewarded first with the title of Baron Ashley and then in 1672 with the earldom of Shaftesbury. He became a member of the Cabal and lord chancellor of England, but fled the king's government to found the Green Ribbon Club, which became the organizational nucleus for the Whig party and the center of opposition to Charles. What Anthony Cooper believed remains a mystery. What he claimed to stand for was parliamentary supremacy, constitutional and Protestant monarchy, the exclusion of Catholic James from the succession, and anti-French and anti-Catholic foreign policy. The fact that the earl, like everybody else in Restoration England, was in the pay of the king of France merely befuddles the picture further. Whatever his purpose, his achievement was monumental. He forged a political machine, known to this day as the "Whigs," or Scottish horse thieves—a name bestowed upon it by his enemies. Determined to overthrow Danby, defeat the court or "Tory" party, force a Whig cabinet upon the king, and pass the Exclusion Bill barring the duke of York from the succession, Shaftesbury deliberately used his party machine to spread religious hysteria and fabricate plots purporting to overthrow the "Establishment." Whether he manufactured the Popish Plot remains one of the great mysteries of the century. Certainly Shaftesbury became the ardent supporter of Mr. Titus Oates, whose fertile and unscrupulous mind invented the whole thing.[2]

Danby fell in December of 1678 when, at the height of the hysteria, Charles' negotiations for a French pension were suddenly revealed. The earl had in fact not approved of these secret dealings and had acted only upon orders from Charles himself. The king could do no wrong, but his unfortunate minister could, and in December Danby's impeachment was voted by a Whig-dominated parliament. A month earlier, Titus Oates had stood before the bar of the House of Commons and had sworn that the queen and her private physician, Sir George Wakeman, had plans to poison the king and lead a Catholic insurrection. To save Danby and his queen, Charles dissolved parliament in January of 1679, but he could not save the

---

[2] Anyone interested in one of the great mysteries of English history and in an exciting account of the Popish Plot by one of the masters of detective fiction should read John Dickson Carr, *The Murder of Sir Edmund Godfrey* (1936), which should be balanced by a more recent account by J. P. Kenyon, *The Popish Plot* (1972).

TESTIS OVAT

innocent victims of religious panic, false oaths, and deliberate malice. In all, ten men were tried and executed, largely on evidence supplied by Titus Oates, whose face appeared on lady's snuff boxes, fans, and handkerchiefs, who received a generous pension of £1,200 a year from a thankful House of Commons, and on whose testimony alone five peers were imprisoned and the queen herself proclaimed a traitor. Imagination knew no bounds. Intolerance and incredulity, unreason and superstition had been banished from the center of court and social life; but they lurked still in the minds of worthy and upright men who were fearful of their souls' salvation and in the hearts of tradesmen and apprentices ready to believe the worst, especially when the news was accompanied by free beer supplied by the Green Ribbon Club.

Desperate for money even to feed his immediate family, Charles risked a new parliament, and elections were called for February of 1679. Everywhere Whigs were triumphant and Shaftesbury introduced the Exclusion Bill in the full expectation that it would pass both houses. Charles would never fight for his faith, but he was willing to risk all to defend his queen and his brother's rightful inheritance; and in May, although he had received no money, the king prorogued parliament and in July dissolved it. Then at the height of the crisis Charles was struck down with fever, and by August it appeared that he was dying. The news shocked the leaders of the nation into sanity and drove home to the Whig party the realization that, should Charles die, the country would again be thrown into civil war, between factions supporting Charles' illegitimate Protestant son, the duke of Monmouth, and his legitimate Catholic brother, the duke of York. The memory of civil war and its social consequences prevailed, and the country slowly began to rally to the king.

Time was on Charles' side. Throughout 1680 and '81 the heat of hysteria receded and men could jokingly remark: "I can not tell you what today's plot is. 'Tis something to do with yesterday's plot, but I have not heard about yesterday's plot yet." A sure sign of a return to sanity was the reduction of Titus Oates' pension to two pounds a week. By 1681 the king was strong enough to order Shaftesbury's arrest on the charge of high treason and to rule without parliament. The nation's economic prosperity assured him a handsome income from the customs and excise taxes, and Louis of France decided that French gold would have to restore what it had so nearly destroyed—the Stuart throne. Charles became a French pensioner to the amount of approximately £500,000 a year.

Even in victory Charles was not indecent. He had saved the doctrine of the inviolability of the hereditary monarchy and the right of his brother to the crown, but he introduced no standing army paid with French silver, no Catholic altars built upon swords. Instead, during his final years of personal rule he out-politicked the Whigs and beat them at their own game. The king achieved control by giving in to the Tory party and becoming the greatest Tory of them all. French money continued to help sustain his throne, but Charles never tampered with the basic tenet of Tory faith: the union of the honorable and the reverent. While the Merry Monarch reigned, England remained safe for Anglicanism; episcopacy was protected from Catholicism on one side and Dissent on the other. In return Tories were staunch supporters of the Stuart dynasty.

Charles died in his fifty-sixth year on February 6, 1685, and at the last moment he professed his Catholicism and received the sacraments. He also apologized for taking such an "unconscionable long time" in dying. Though there had been moments of passion and violence, his reign, like his personality, had been restful. On only one subject had Charles been willing to go to extremes—the preservation of the throne for the Stuart line. Nevertheless, he had his doubts about a brother who, he predicted, "would never be able to hold it out for four years to an end." The prophecy was accurate, almost to the day.

The Triumph of the Oligarchs

The Civil War, which swept Charles I from his throne, had smelled of the sewer and the fury of religious fanaticism, but the Glorious Revolution, which unseated James II, was sanely rational and safely aristocratic.[1] It had been called "glorious" and "bloodless" and "sensible"; it savored somewhat of comic opera, but the events of November 1, 1688 through February 6, 1689 justly deserve the name of glorious, if only because they signify that men can on occasion learn from experience. The memory of the revolutionary consequences which followed in the wake of political excess, regicide, and republicanism haunted Whigs and Tories when they again faced the embarrassing problem of ridding themselves of a monarch whose actions threatened their leadership of society.

James II (1685–1689)

If Whig and Tory had ascertained a lesson in the past, the same cannot be said for James II, who learned nothing from his father's martyrdom and his own lean and hungry years in exile. It is difficult to be fair to James either as a king or as a man. If ever a revolution was the result of blundering and misguided good intentions on the part of a single individual, the second and final fall of the house of Stuart is the perfect example. The burden of responsibility rests with James. He was not urged on by hotheaded supporters or goaded into action by radical opponents, for the heat of revolu-

---

[1] Any serious student of the reign of James II will eventually have to turn to T. B. Macaulay's brilliant description in his *History of England* (6 vols., 1849–61). More modern but not necessarily better are F. C. Turner, *James II* (1948); D. Ogg, *England in the Reigns of James II and William III* (1955); G. M. Trevelyan, *The English Revolution, 1688–1689* (1938); H. and B. Van der Zee, *William and Mary* (1973); and S. Prall, *The Bloodless Revolution* (1972).

tionary fire was spent. Whigs in parliament were cautious oligarchs, not militant Puritans or rebels by principle as in the days of King Pym. By 1688 they bore little resemblance to the hot and furious party forged by the earl of Shaftesbury. The Green Ribbon Club boys were dead or exiled. Whigs now listened to the unenthusiastic voices of the earls of Devonshire and Shrewsbury and the reasoned advice of the marquis of Halifax, who preferred the designation "Trimmer" to that of either Whig or Tory. Tories, for their part, were no longer dashing Cavaliers or Laudian ecclesiastics, but well-fed, well-bred defenders of a church which looked to parliament to enforce its spiritual monopoly and of a restored and legitimate crown which was bound by law to protect property and religion. Tory squires and their cousins, the parish rectors, loudly acclaimed their faith in the divine right of kings and the doctrine of nonresistance to the actions of God's anointed lieutenant on earth; but hidden in the back of their minds was the reservation that the king and his office were not inseparable. The precedent of 1649 remained, and not even a Tory could escape the enigma: "If the King can do no wrong, somebody did the late King a great deal of wrong." When James II turned on the Church of England and, in the name of a divinely ordained prerogative, violated the sanctity of private property, Tories came to the conclusion that a Catholic sovereign could not be protected by the Anglican divinity of kings.

The reservoir of goodwill that lifted James onto his brother's throne appeared bottomless. The Stuart monarchy seemed more secure and respected than since the days of the first James. The grandeur of the Tudor throne had vanished, but Charles II had succeeded in restoring some of the luster of royalty by mastering the machinery of parliamentary politics. Taking a leaf from the earl of Shaftesbury's book, Charles had learned a basic lesson of Restoration existence: he could not presume upon the faithfulness of his Commons, but he could manufacture it. Neither tradition nor the divinity of kings could guarantee parliamentary obedience unless the monarch controlled the machinery which sent loyal members to the House of Commons. Triumphant over religious frenzy and Whig schemes to limit the king's authority in 1681, Charles had decided to "reform" the source of most of his political difficulties—the boroughs which sent disloyal members to parliament and placed local government in the hands of those opposed to the Stuart dynasty. Throughout the last years of his reign, borough charters were scrutinized and, if found lacking, were revoked and reissued, giving the crown the authority to nominate town officials, veto their election, and restrict the franchise to holders of municipal office. The result was to place local and parliamentary government firmly in the hands of the Tories. When parliament met at the commencement of the new reign, James II had to admit that his brother had done his work so well that "there were not above forty members but such as he himself wished for." Yet within three years a majority party, predisposed to tolerate the monarch's Catholicism and maintain the prerogative and divine nature of his royal office, joined the Whigs

The House of Stuart

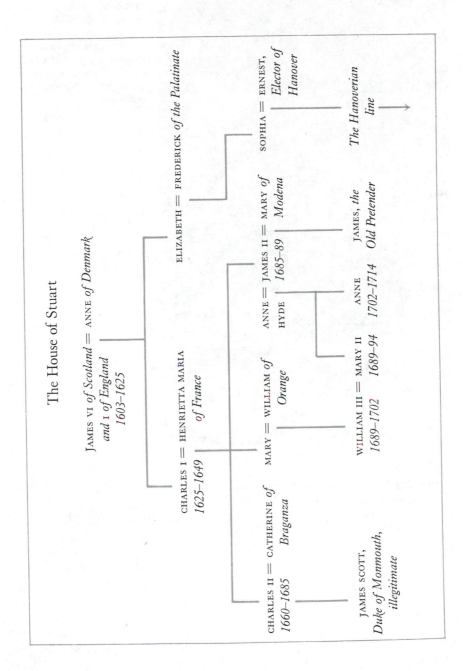

JAMES II
"Stodginess, stubbornness and stupidity were the prevailing qualities of a man whom Bishop Burnet analyzed as having 'no true judgment.'" *National Portrait Gallery.*

in inviting the king's Protestant daughter and her husband, Prince William of Orange, to replace him on the throne.

It is fashionable for historians to be polite about James; to applaud his aim of toleration but to deplore his means; to bewail his intelligence but to presume his righteousness. Before the accolades are bestowed it might be well to ponder whether James' high regard for toleration was based on principle or was merely a weapon with which to establish an even greater intolerance; whether he spoke for the welfare of all subjects or only for a militant and anachronistic minority who clung to notions unacceptable to the century of enlightenment into which England was moving. Whatever the final judgment, the record of his reign indicates that stodginess, stubborness, and stupidity were the prevailing qualities of a man whom Bishop Burnet analyzed as having "no true judgment." In the bishop's view, James lacked his brother's tact and humor; he held to "high notions of kingly authority; and laid it down for a maxim that all who opposed the King were rebels in their hearts." Even his secret dalliance achieved a stuffiness that had once led his brother to remark that one might thing his mistresses were "given him by his priests for penance." He took himself, his office, and his duty to God with a seriousness that ultimately destroyed his dynasty. Lord Chesterfield's stilleto-sharp characterization must stand: "though we have now a prince whose study is his country's glory, whose courage will give him luster without a throne, whose assiduity in business makes him his own chief minister, yet heaven, it seems, has found a way to make this all more terrible than lovely."

In February of 1685 there was no whisper of the thunder to come. Well-wishers of a moral bent noted that "the change upon the face of the English court is very remarkable; in the last King's time mirth, plays, buffoonery, etc., domineered, and were encouraged; now there is little to be seen but seriousness and business." Unfortunately, the new reign did not bring the anticipated "happiness to the nation," for James' Tory supporters made two assumptions, neither of which materialized: that the king would keep his religion private, and that the heir to the throne would be Protestant. James II had been born and bred an Anglican. His first wife was the Protestant Anne Hyde, daughter of the earl of Clarendon, and by her he had two daughters, Mary and Anne. It was not until 1672 that he publicly declared himself a Catholic. The following year he married the Italian and Catholic Maria of Modena, but at his succession he was fifty-three, childless by his second wife, and the dynasty seemed secure in the Protestant line of Mary and her Stuart husband, the champion of European Protestantism, Prince William of Orange, the Statholder of Holland.

Parliament met in May. The king received for life the same revenues granted his brother, and members of the lower house held it to be in bad taste to embarrass James by asking him to enforce the penal legislation against Catholics. Though Lords and Commons were willing to ignore the Test Act, they were adamantly against repealing it. In the name of obedience, parliament was willing to accept a Catholic interlude, close its eyes to the deliberate violation of the law and wait patiently for James' Protestant daughters to inherit the throne. Unfortunately the king was not content with religious sufferance. He yearned for a Catholic triumph, the first step of which would be the repeal of the Test Act barring Catholics from civil and military office. Before James could urge parliament to reconsider its attitude toward Catholics, the realm was shocked by the news of a double invasion— the Presbyterian earl of Argyll's descent upon Scotland and the Anglican duke of Monmouth's landing at Lyme Regis on the border between Dorset and Devonshire.

Putting Back the Clock

Argyll's escapade led promptly to the executioner's block. The Monmouth invasion had no better conclusion, but it did involve the last battle ever fought on English soil. The duke was the illegitimate son of Charles II, and he expected to raise the countryside in the name of nationalism and

Protestantism. It is significant that peasants and artisans flocked to his standard but yeomen and gentlemen remained coldly aloof. They preferred a sovereign from the right side of the bed and were anxious to do nothing that might restore the hateful days of the Civil War and the Interregnum. Devoid of upper-class support and led by a frivolous fop, the invasion had little hope of success. Parliament granted James £400,000 to finance an army with which to defend his throne, and at Sedgemoor in July of 1685, Monmouth's troops were routed. The duke's forces consisted of some 3,000 foot soldiers armed with barbarous but ineffective sickles and scythes, 500 horse troops mounted on plough horses, and four Dutch cannons. The royal army was well trained and professional and the results were inevitable: the slaughter of 1,384 of Monmouth's men and the duke's capture, two days later, in a bean field in Hampshire where he had been cowering, filthy and hungry. Within the week he was executed, and James commenced a policy of grim retribution that shocked his Tory supporters out of their unquestioning loyalty to his Stuart person. In September Judge George Jeffreys' Bloody Assizes sat in brutal judgment upon peasants, 400 of whom paid with their lives for their folly, and 1,200 of whom were deported to the Barbados.

The wages of sin when directed against the Lord's anointed were death; but generally such bloody spectacles were reserved for the natural leaders of society, not the humble toilers who were relatively secure in their obscurity. The law was on Judge Jeffreys' side, but precedent and public opinion were not. The nation was aghast at the sight of common folk dancing their grizzly jig three feet off the ground. James' revenge smacked not of deliberate political calculation but of religious hysteria; it appeared to many Englishmen that the simple sons of Devon were in fact dying for their Protestant faith, not for their treasons. Whether Jeffrey's judicial decisions were motivated by religious hatred is beside the point. The effect was to conjure up the memory of the Smithfield Fires and the fate of Protestants under Bloody Mary.

Victorious over his Protestant nephew, James looked to further laurels in parliament, and he demanded of his Lords and Commons that the Test Act be repealed. But even a parliament packed with royal nominees had been shocked by the fury of the Bloody Assizes; and it was still more alarmed by the presence of James' standing army, fresh from Sedgemoor and now encamped 13,000 strong just outside London. A standing army, illegally officered with Catholics and loyal to the Stuart dynasty, was feared as the prelude to French-style despotism in England. Throughout Europe all the signs pointed to a Catholic resurgence. Only a month before, Louis XIV of France had revoked the Edict of Nantes which protected the political and religious rights of French Protestants. At the same time James was becoming more and more outspoken in his Catholicism and admiration of his French cousin. In an atmosphere of rising religious tension, parliament was uncompromising in its determination not to repeal the penal laws against Catholics. For its impudent lack of cooperation, James prorogued parliament on November 20, and set forth on a policy which led within two years to the ruin of his house and the loss of his throne.

Unable to Catholicize the realm with Tory aid and parliamentary consent, James turned to the suspending powers of the crown to subvert the law and unite Catholics and Dissenters in support of the monarchy. In April of 1687 he issued the first of his Declarations of Indulgence, giving freedom of worship to Catholics and Nonconformists and permitting both denominations to hold public and military office. The king hoped that the two persecuted minorities would stand together against Tory and high-church bigotry and become the prop and stay of the Stuart monarchy. Suspending the law was not enough; the government had to be Catholicized, the Church of England purged and disciplined, and the Tories who controlled the boroughs and shires replaced with Dissenters and Catholics. Military commissions were given to papists; the lord lieutenant of Ireland and the lord admiral of the fleet were Catholics; the papal nuncio was accorded a public welcome in 1687; the king's Jesuit confessor was admitted to the Privy Council, which became a Roman Catholic Cabal; and, if the realm needed further evidence of his zeal, James appointed as his lord chancellor Judge Jeffreys, who not only possessed a bloody reputation but had been regarded by Charles II as a man of "no learning, no sense, no manners and more impudence than ten carted streetwalkers."

The Court of High Commission for Ecclesiastical Affairs was resurrected in defiance of parliamentary statute and used to suspend bishops who allowed anti-Roman preaching in their dioceses. As bishoprics fell vacant, James filled his episcopal bench with high-church Anglicans favorable to Rome, in the hope that the Church of England might be brought back into the papal fold. The ecclesia did not take kindly to such pressure; it renounced its doctrine of nonresistance and showed surprising vigor in defending the Prayer Book, the Anglican communion, and independence from Rome. In retaliation James struck at the root of the opposition, that seminary of Anglicanism, Oxford University. Christ Church, University and Magdalen Colleges were placed under Catholic control and the fellows of Magdalen were evicted for refusing to elect a popish president. When Dr. Hough, the president of Magdalen, was expelled from his office, he complained that the government was illegally depriving him of what was tantamount to private property. Whigs and Tories agreed with him; if Dr. Hough lost his presidency then no inalienable right was safe, and resistance to royal tyranny was therefore a sacred duty.

Not content with tampering with private property, James committed an even worse sin in the eyes of the leaders of society: he tried to wrest local government from the hands of the gentry. His brother had revoked borough charters so that the crown could control the nomination of solid Tory supporters of church and monarchy. Now James used the same means to bully the towns into electing Catholics and Nonconformists and men of no property. Royal commissioners were dispatched into the countryside to inquire whether the local squirearchy, if elected to parliament, would favor the repeal of the Test Act and support the Declaration of Indulgence. The evasive and negative nature of the answers convinced James to purge county administration of its substantial citizens. Whigs and Tories were dropped from the lists of justices of the peace and other shire officials, and Catholics and Dissenters were appointed in their stead. It was bad enough that some of the new appointees could neither read nor write; it was far worse that others had not "one foot of freehold land in England." In London "all the jolly, genteel citizens" were "turned out and all the sneaking fanatics put into their places." James' actions removed the most weighty deterrent to revolution: fear of social upheaval from below. It was becoming obvious to the ruling classes that this time rebellion might be necessary for the defense of property and order.

The climax was reached in 1688. In January James ordered home six English and Scottish regiments stationed in the Netherlands, a sure sign to many that the king was preparing to ally England with France against the Dutch. In May he issued a second Declaration of Indulgence and ordered that it be read from every pulpit within the realm. When Archbishop Sancroft and six other bishops refused, on the grounds that the king could not suspend the operation of religious law, he clapped them in the Tower and accused them of seditious libel. Then in June a son was born to his Catholic wife; the king rejoiced, but Protestant England was suddenly deprived of the single most powerful argument for obedience to the king: the expectation that the succession would pass to Mary and William of Orange. In England and in Holland men were reaching the decision that revolution had to be risked, and on June 30, 1688, Whig and Tory magnates sent an urgent appeal to William of Orange to save their land from Catholic domination. If any doubt remained about the overwhelming sentiments of the country, lower as well as upper class, it was dispelled when a London jury acquitted the seven bishops. The king, however, continued to take no notice of the approaching storm, and even Judge Jeffreys admitted that James was guided solely by the Virgin Mary.

The European Scene

In Europe events were synchronizing with those in England with fatal results. Louis XIV broke the peace of Europe in September and sent his armies against the German Empire. Throughout the summer Prince William had been hesitating to accept the invitation to claim the throne of England for fear that Louis might strike first at Holland. When the French finally settled down to a war of siege against Philippsburg, the stadtholder decided to risk the invasion of England. He set sail on November 1 with a carefully organized fleet of 225 vessels and an army of 15,000 men replete with a portable bridge, a mobile smithy, a printing press with which to flood England with Protestant propaganda, a mold for striking new coinage once the invasion succeeded, four tons of tobacco, 1,600 hogsheads of beer, 10,000 pairs of boots, and Prince William's personal coach and horses.

Once again an English monarch faced the consequences of having acted as landlord of England, not king; once again an invader arrived under the banner of liberation. What Henry IV had done in 1399, William of Orange, the future William III, did in 1689; he endeavored to transform treason into a crusade against tyranny by championing the liberties of Englishmen and defending property against a despotic government. James II, like Richard II, discovered that legitimacy was no defense for a monarchy devoid of popular support, and like the last legitimate male Plantagenet, the last male Stuart found himself forsaken and alone. William and his professional troops were not to be compared to the duke of Monmouth and his farm boys, and this time the English gentry came forward to welcome the invader. Even the men in the king's confidence quietly slipped away to join the Dutchman. The standing army, for which James had sacrificed parliamentary subsidies and upper-class popularity, faded away; and the loyalty of the navy was never tested, for a "Protestant wind" kept it harborbound. James himself proved his mettle by attempting precipitous flight, a venture so fraught with ill luck that it took two weeks and the connivance of Prince William to achieve. The queen and her infant son slipped away to France on December 10; early next morning James followed them, dropping the Great Seal of England into the Thames as he headed for the channel. Unfortunately he was recognized and returned to London where it had to be carefully arranged that the king could once again manage to escape.

English supporters of William assumed that the stadtholder came "only to maintain the Protestant religion; he will do England no harm." Actually the Prince of Orange had little love for English domestic affairs. His single interest was the defense of Holland and the defeat of France. At worst, England had to be kept neutral, at best transformed into a weapon with which to destroy Louis XIV. William's concerns were England's wealth and her naval and military potential, not Dr. Hough's presidency at Magdalen. In a cold and tight-lipped fashion William was a fanatic, a soldier who cared nothing for politics and who had little interest in his fellow men except as diplomatic and political instruments or as infantry for his armies. Short, asthmatic, and stooped, with bad teeth and beaked nose, the prince gave himself and those around him unsparingly to his single obsession—the destruction of France.

The final irony of William's bloodless victory and England's Glorious Revolution is that neither would have been possible without the cooperation of Louis XIV and James II. The Most Christian King of France badly miscalculated; for he sent no aid to his Stuart cousin, and he failed to redirect his troops against Holland. Instead, he welcomed the Dutch invasion in the mistaken belief that Whigs and Tories would plunge England into civil war, involving Holland in a hopeless military venture and leaving Europe to French conquest. What Louis failed to discern was the crucial fact that Whigs and Tories, for all their political differences, had one thing in common: they were property owners and therefore the ruling elite of the kingdom. As such, they were united in their opposition to James.

The Glorious Revolution

As for James, he guaranteed the bloodless nature of the revolution [2] by fleeing with his baby son to the security of Louis XIV's court. William of Orange, despite his invitation signed by six solid English peers and an Anglican bishop, was still a foreigner, and plenty of Englishmen remained loyal to the Stuart name. There were many Stuart well-wishers who could not understand "what could make our master desert his kingdom and his friends?" Presumably James lost his nerve, and in doing so he lost his kingdom. The king's flight not only assured a peaceful change of monarchs but it also solved the constitutional dilemma confronting William and his Whig and Tory supporters—how to legalize the violent overthrow of a legitimate sovereign. The same issue had faced Henry IV, and the same solution was now invoked. James' decision to flee (which received all the help William could decently give) and his casting of the Great Seal into the Thames were accepted as acts of abdication. Had he remained, the prince of Orange would have been confronted, as Henry IV had been, with the embarrassing presence of a live and legitimate king who possessed an indisputable male heir.

James' "abdication" solved the crucial problem of how to remove a sovereign; it did not, however, answer the related question of how to replace him with someone else. Without a sovereign nothing was legal, not even parliament. Under the circumstances, men did the best they could. William was invited to issue writs for a Convention Parliament which met on January 22, 1689. At one end of the political spectrum stood certain of the Whig magnates who wanted the throne declared vacant on the grounds that James II had subverted the "constitution of the kingdom by breaking the original contract between king and people"; and they demanded the appointment of a successor by act of parliament. This was too much for the Tories, who still clung to the doctrine of hereditary monarchy and opposed any notion of a sovereign who possessed his authority by the grace of parliamentary election. Moreover, William had his own views on the subject. He dismissed as unacceptable the idea that the crown should pass to his wife as next in line of succession while he became "his wife's gentleman

---

[2] Besides Turner, Macaulay and Trevelyan, see D. W. R. Bahlman, *The Moral Revolution of 1688* (1957); G. M. Straka, *The Revolution of 1688—Whig Triumph or Palace Revolution?* (1962); S. B. Baxter, *William III* (1966); L. Pinkham, *William III and the Respectable Revolution* (1954); and M. Ashley, *The Glorious Revolution* (1968).

usher." He insisted upon equal status with Mary on the basis of military conquest and his own blood claim as the grandson of Charles I. In the end the Whig magnates and the Dutch prince both got their way. In February of 1689 William and Mary were recognized as joint monarchs and were forced to accept parliamentary limitations upon their sovereignty.

The fiction of royal inheritance and even the myth of the divine right of kings were preserved in 1689, but in reality it was transparently clear that the sovereignty of parliament had triumphed. Though William III didn't like it, he had to listen to "Honest Tom" Wharton, who tactlessly reminded him: "We have made you King." The crown in theory may have remained unrestrained, but the man and woman who wore it did so on the sufferance of men of property, and statutes were enacted prescribing the use to which royal authority might be put. The Declaration of Rights, later translated into law as the Bill of Rights of 1689, propounded no doctrine of limited monarchy or parliamentary supremacy. It merely forbade the use of royal and prerogative rights as they had been exercised in the past by Charles and James. The power to dispense with law was not abolished, it was simply outlawed "as it hath been assumed and exercised of late." The royal claim to maintain a standing army was not denied; only armies raised without parliamentary consent were prohibited. What parliament enacted was not a statement of rights, but a bill of limitations. To safeguard those limitations it reverted to the time-honored method of asserting its authority through the

THE DOUBLE CORONATION OF WILLIAM AND MARY, APRIL 1689
"He insisted upon equal status with Mary on the basis of military conquest and his own blood claim as the grandson of Charles I." *Rijksmuseum, Amsterdam.*

purse. William and Mary were offered an annual income of only £600,000, which was hopelessly insufficient by itself; the rest had to be appropriated yearly by parliament for specific purposes. In the end William extracted from Commons sums that no Stuart king had imagined possible; but such monies were granted annually, and they were offered only for the purpose of implementing policies agreeable to a majority in parliament. As a further safeguard a Mutiny Act was passed, limiting to a single year the crown's right to enforce martial law in the army, thus making it impossible to maintain a military force for more than twelve months at a time without recourse to parliament.

The final step of the revolution was the Act of Toleration, passed in 1689 for reasons more of political necessity than of principle. William was a Calvinist while his wife was an Anglican. He insisted that the Church of England abide by the promise of toleration which had been made to Nonconformists in order to lure them from Catholic James and his Declaration of Indulgence. The tide of religious bigotry was receding, and even Catholics were left in peace, although they and the Unitarians were carefully excluded from the Act. On all fronts men were weary of emotion. In religion as well as politics, Whigs and Tories were ready to accept the marquis of Halifax's policy of never rocking the political boat. In William and Mary, England found sovereigns uniquely fitted to the temper of the times. Mary was ignorant of history, politics, science, and mathematics; her spelling was quaint, her grammar faulty, and her "mind as sluggish as an island river." William confessed himself to be "a Trimmer and would continue so," if only because he had come to England in order to trim Louis XIV down to size and redress the European balance of power.

Two bloodless revolutions, 300 years apart, are worth a moment's thought, for one was the prelude to a hundred years of civil war and anarchy, the other to the dawn of England's Augustan Age. The kings involved may have had much in common—Richard II and James II were incompetent, Henry IV and William III unscrupulous—but the men who stood behind royalty, who in fact made the two rebellions, were worlds apart. It is true that both the fourteenth-century feudal baron and the late seventeenth-century aristocrat attempted to control monarchy, but while the one found his defense in private law and the absence of government, the other sought protection in the rule of law common to all Englishmen. The glory of the Glorious Revolution resided not so much in its bloodlessness as in the security it offered all men of property, both Whig and Tory. The real victors of '89 and the architects of eighteenth-century England were the great estate owners, the lesser gentry, the merchant-princes, and those three vocal apologists of oligarchical respectability—the lawyer, the parson, and the educator. The revolution was their doing, and to understand it, it is necessary to turn away from acts of parliament and the peculiarities of kings to the education of a country gentleman and the commonplaces of county life.

It has been said with the usual conceit of historical generalizations that all history is intellectual history, for actions in war, commerce, and government presume at least a modicum of activity on the part of the human brain. Presumably then, a political upheaval that could sweep away the ordained and organic Tudor state, and replace it with a social mechanism contrived by men of good breeding for "the preservation of their property" involved a profound revolution of the mind.[3] Whatever the truth about the causal relationships between thought and deed, this much is beyond dispute—earth and sky, man and God were judged very differently in 1399 and 1689, and reality in state, church, and nature was viewed and described in new and diverse ways.

No better symbol of the revolution in mind and spirit exists than the contrast between the two St. Paul's Cathedrals: the old, dilapidated structure with its broken spire, vaulted ceilings and towering Gothic windows through which the light of God's grace entered, giving visual meaning and comfort to the humble Christians within; and the new, Classical-Renaissance St. Paul's, built by Sir Christopher Wren, the mathematician, astronomer, city planner, and architect who intended his house of God as a harmonious and lucid monument dedicated to the "philosophic" world-view.

Three centuries of history had wrought a revolution in mind and spirit; and the ideals and preconceptions most dear to the medieval knight, priest, and craftsman had become as outmoded as feudal kings, guilds, and monasteries. By 1689 Squire Jones and Parson Brown looked out upon a new and wonderful kingdom, secure, prosperous, and self-confident; and in their thankfulness they beheld the hand of God. Even the deity they worshiped had divested Himself of much of His medieval trappings, and though He continued to reveal His purpose through Scripture, there were now three new sources of divine light that completely upset the traditional picture of the universe: Nicholas Copernicus' *On the Revolution of the Heavenly Orb* (1540); Robert Boyle's *The Sceptical Chemist* (1661); and Isaac Newton's monumental *Philosophiae Naturalis Principia Mathematica* (1687). Only a generation before, Henry Peacham in *The Compleat Gentleman* [4] was still assuring his young readers that the structure of the heavens consisted of a series of crystal spheres, revolving in majestic serenity around a fixed and stationary earth located, like the yolk of an egg, in the center of the universe. For Peacham's students the millennium of faith was not yet over; although doubt had entered in, man in his own estimation remained

---

[3] Something of the intellectual ferment of the century can be gleaned from B. Willey, *The Seventeenth Century Background* (1934); H. Butterfield, *The Origins of Modern Science, 1300–1800* (1949); R. S. Westfall, *Science and Religion in Seventeenth Century England* (1958); and G. P. Gooch, *Political Thought in England from Bacon to Halifax* (1915).

[4] *The Compleat Gentleman* was originally published in 1622 but it remained standard reading down to the time of its last edition in 1661. For a modern reprint see the Folger Shakespeare Library edition, ed. V. B. Heltzel (1962).

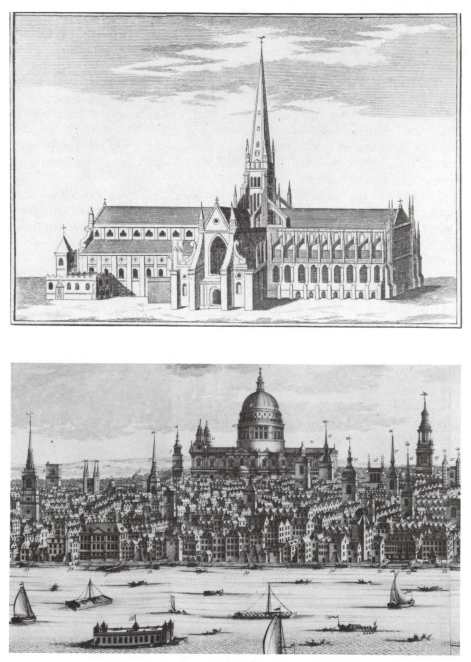

OLD AND NEW ST. PAUL'S CATHEDRAL
"The old . . . giving visual meaning and comfort to the humble Christians within; and the new Classical-Renaissance St. Paul's . . . dedicated to the 'philosophic' world view." *National Monuments Record and the Ashomolean Museum.*

God's unique and special creation. The firmaments and all that they contained were presumed to have been established so that humanity could enact the drama of salvation and damnation. Aristotelian physics, which propounded one set of physical principles for man's constantly changing world of earth, water, fire, and air, and another for God's immutable domain of moon, planets, stars, and firmaments, remained supreme. The titans of the new astronomy, Copernicus and Galileo, were suspect, the expounders of a foolish and absurd heresy which, in the words of John Donne, called "all in doubt." For most of Peacham's gentle readers the old language of pre-Copernican physics and astronomy accorded with reality: the sun rose and set (the earth certainly did not spin on its axis giving the illusion of moving sun and stars); the pump sucked water up from the well (it was not pushed up by the pressure of the atmosphere); the arrow still fell to the ground of its own accord (it was not pulled down and deflected by the force of gravity). Most men of the early seventeenth century agreed with the royal scholar, James I, who dismissed Francis Bacon's brilliant efforts to invest scientific thought with the cardinal principles of exact observation and reasoned conclusion with the quip: "like the peace of God, it passeth all understanding."

By 1689, however, Parson Brown and Squire Jones had discarded Aristotelian physics and dismissed the medieval heavens as mere folklore. Bacon's labors were being understood even by untutored dilettantes, and Copernicus and Galileo had become commonplaces of the dining-room table. The Royal Society, founded in 1660, had fostered a new generation of gentlemen scientists, who accepted with equanimity the idea of a limitless universe in which earth, sun, and stars hurtled in orderly but soulless eternity, and who understood the scientific principle of the water pump, which was no longer said to operate on the Aristotelian dictum of nature abhorring a vacuum, but on Boyle's law $pv = C$. The men who made the Glorious Revolution regarded as preposterous the Shakespearean view of the atmosphere as an "excellent canopy" and a "majestical roof fretted with golden fire." Instead they accepted it as a sea of air which lay heavy upon the earth and exerted an immense pressure on man and beast.

Men's minds were slowly beginning to embrace the idea of change in all areas of human interest and speculation. The interests of the Royal Society were as eclectic as its members were brilliant. Originally an "invisible college" meeting in London coffee-houses and taverns, the society included almost every Englishman of intellectual distinction during the second half of the seventeenth century. There were John Evelyn, the botanist, coin collector and political diarist; Mr. Samuel Pepys, bureaucrat, commentator, and naval expert; Sir William Petty, the "political arithmetician" and father of modern demography; Sir Christopher Wren; the poet John Dryden; Robert Hooke, the universal scientist and near equal to Newton; Dr. Edmund Halley; John Locke; John Aubrey, the first of the group biographers; and, of course, Sir Isaac Newton. The existence of such versatility, however, did not mean that conservative country gentlemen or wealthy city merchants had either the intelligence or the economic means to follow in the footsteps of that perfect seventeenth-century aristocratic scientist, the honorable Robert Boyle, promoter of the gospel, government inspector of the mines, director of the East India Company, theologian, inventor, and fourteenth child of one of the greediest English estate owners in Ireland, the earl of Cork. Even the most optimistic reader was discouraged by the titles of Boyle's books: his famous "law" on the elasticity of gases was first outlined in *New Experiments Physico-Mechanical Touching the Spring of the Air and Its Effects, Made, for the Most Part, in a New Pneumatical Engine*. Nor did enthusiastic gentlemen have the training to comprehend the mathematical propositions of Sir Isaac Newton and René Descartes. Instead their imaginations were excited by science fiction and polite popularizations of Newtonian and Cartesian science. They devoured Cyrano de Bergerac's *Voyage to the Moon* (1657) and Bishop Francis Godwin's *The Man in the Moon* (1638), in which they read about a spacecraft powered by forty swans. They learned their Descartes from Fontenelle's *The Plurality of Worlds* (translated in 1688), and came to rely on John Harris for their Newtonian theory. Fontenelle's countess with an astronomical turn of mind discoursed upon the philosophy of a mechanical universe that was likened to a watch "which is very regular and depends only upon the just disposing of the several parts of the movement." In Harris' *Astronomical Dialogues Between a Gentleman and a Lady* the Newtonian universe was presented in the elegant language of the day:

> O! pray! move on, Sir, said she, this is amazingly fine: I fancy myself travelling along with that little Earth in its course round the gilded Sun.

English property owners remained confident in the conviction that they, and to a lesser extent all mankind, were God's special gift to creation, but in the books they read and absorbed it was perfectly clear that the deity Himself no longer had a secure place in the Newtonian World Machine. He had become little more than a first cause, a divine and marvelous clockmaker, who started but thereafter did not tamper with his own universal and eternal laws of motion, inertia, and gravity. Throughout the seventeenth century the hand of God had been pushed back by the mind of man; and authors who had been branded in their own day as dangerous atheists became respectable philosophers. Sir Walter Raleigh partially removed God from the historical scene, leaving *The History of the World* (1614) as a record of human events and motives. Lord Herbert of Cherbury wrote of *Henry VIII* (1649) as a man, not as God's or the devil's instrument on earth. Francis Bacon offered the new scientific methodology as man's hope in his struggle to liberate himself from the consequences of Adam's fall; man's power over nature, not God's grace, would henceforth be his salvation. In politics, men talked about man-made societies and the inalienable rights of life, liberty, and property, not of governments instituted by God or the divinity of kings.

Slowly the secular, analytical, and categorical mind began to predominate: the habit of thought that conceives of statistical data and accuracy as being a positive good, that classifies and breaks down scientific knowledge into its smallest component part, and that delimits and defines every phase of government and society. The seventeenth-century revolution which tore asunder the unity of the Tudor state was in part the result of this tendency to view political reality in increasingly exact terms. The age of constitution writing was beginning, and men required that the relationship between the executive and the legislature be determined and recorded. Had king and parliament, royal judges and common lawyers, antiquarians and historians never sought to define and analyze such formless medieval political equations as "king in parliament," "the sovereign is over man but under God and law," and "to the king belongs authority over all men, but to subjects belong property," there would have been no controversy over political theory and possibly no appeal to arms.

By 1689 the statistical and analytical mind had triumphed. Gregory King in his *Natural and Political Observations and Conclusions upon the State and Conditions of England* (1696) began to count heads and to present population statistics. Consequently historians have for the first time a fairly reliable notion of demographic growth and breakdown: five-and-a-half million men inhabited England, of whom 2.7 million ate meat daily and one million were on poor relief. Two million lived in Ireland, one million in Scotland, 250,000 in the colonies, and a half million in London. King estimated that for the year 1688 the average family income of a peer was £2,800, of a gentleman £450, of a tradesman £45, of a laboring man £15, and of a soldier £14. The average income in England was £7/18s per head, in contrast to Holland where it was £8/1s/4d, and to France where the average was only £6. Mr. Thomas Mun wrote during the 1630s an important treatise on *England's Treasure by Forraign Trade*, concluding that "to sell more to strangers yearly than we consume of theirs in value" was the secret of English prosperity. In country manor and town house, table conversation began to take on a modern ring—free trade, censorship of the press, the rights of man, the purpose of government, the rebuilding of London, the control of colonies, and the ebb and flow of finance. No one spoke of usury any longer; instead they referred to a decent rate of interest and chatted about trade figures that were duly recorded for posterity: foreign trade in 1662 was valued at £7,750,000, but by 1688 it had jumped to £11,500,000. In industry and finance, the same attitude of mind prevailed, and the Restoration merchant or country gentleman poured his pounds into a host of new schemes, each the result of careful analysis of man's world—water companies, postal enterprises, paper and glass manufacturing, banking schemes, fire insurance, life insurance, and 236 new patents taken out be-

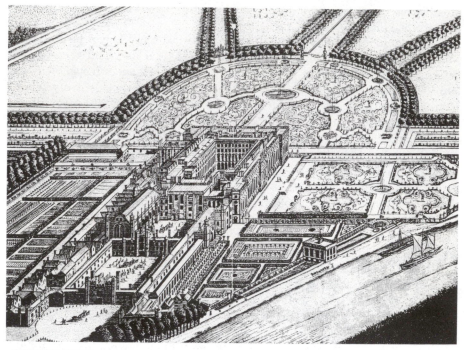

HAMPTON COURT, 1724
"Parks, lawns, and garden beds were laid out with geometrical perfection—
every curve of every flower bed was as perfectly elliptical as any planetary
orbit, every shrub was in schematic balance with its neighbor, and every
maze contrived with mathematical exactitude." *After an engraving by
L. Kniff.*

tween 1660 and 1700. Even the gentleman's parkland was subjected to the
categorical mind. Tudor gardens, once untamed and almost parvenu in the
indecency of their color schemes and designs such as Tudor roses and
heraldic beasts, gave way to a more restrained and mathematical approach.
Parks, lawns, and garden beds were laid out with geometrical perfection—
every curve of the flower bed was as perfectly elliptical as any planetary
orbit, every shrub was in schematic balance with its neighbor, and every
maze was contrived with mathematical exactitude.

   The seventeenth-century Englishman was becoming not so much an
"economic animal" as a statistical being, and the ultimate intellectual conceit
was recorded and distilled into its simplest form by Descartes, who declared
the reality of human existence to be *cogito ergo sum,* "I think therefore I
am." Doubtless many Englishmen still hungered for an older and passing
way of life which persisted in viewing existence as a spiritual phenomenon,
and required that governments should strive to achieve a society fit for
Christians in need of salvation. But a certain amount of godlessness in the

affairs of man and nature seemed a small price to pay for the material, constitutional, and intellectual strides of the century.

For the unwashed multitude, England in 1689 may have been almost as nasty, brutish, and unhealthy as it had been three centuries earlier. But for the oligarchs, the privileged few, she stood upon the threshold of an age in which physical discomfort was masked with massive elegance, religious enthusiasm carefully restrained by the reasoned conclusions of deism, wealth properly dressed in good breeding, and politics predicated upon the marquis of Halifax's dictum that "to know when to leave things alone is a high pitch of good sense." England had become a paradise for men of property. Juries, after 1670, could safely hand down verdicts which even went against the interests of the crown. The Habeas Corpus Act of 1679 protected the critics of government from arbitrary arrest. The press, though still answerable to sweeping libel laws, was virtually free to criticize men, policies, and institutions. In religion, it was found necessary to suppress the words of that dangerous iconoclast, Thomas Hobbes, for the oligarchs were not yet willing to accept his argument that salvation was open to all who held to the virtues, "Faith in Christ, and Obedience to Laws." They preferred the more lofty sentiments of Milton—"Give me the liberty to know, to utter, and to argue freely according to conscience, above all liberties." Religious nonconformity still suffered certain political disabilities even after the Toleration Act of 1689, but if Catholics, Dissenters, and even Unitarians kept their thoughts to themselves, they were allowed a certain degree of liberty of conscience. Gentlemen of wealth and leisure, however, could and did converse on any subject they chose; they had the time and security, and they were beginning to have the education. The age of Lord Chesterfield, Doctor Samuel Johnson, and Horace Walpole could not be far in the future, when the Restoration courtier and patron of letters, Charles Sackville, sixth Earl of Dorset (1676–1705), could match wits with Mr. John Dryden. Dorset once proposed at dinner that his guests each jot down an "impromptu" and that Mr. Dryden should be judge of the literary merit. The dramatist, having perused each contribution, proclaimed the earl to be the victor, and he read the winning entry:

> I promise to pay Mr. John Dryden five hundred pounds on demand.
> Signed, Dorset.

Not only was the world of letters their oyster, to be opened and savored, but so was all of England. Gentlemen could walk safely through the countryside, stick in hand, no longer obliged to go armed with a sword, for their lives were relatively safe and their properties absolutely secure. Two generations of civil war and revolution had transformed England into a kingdom where birth, breeding, and estate had become the pillars of society. The Glorious Revolution guaranteed that government, irrespective of party control, would protect the sanctity of private property, reflect its views, and insure its future.

In achieving such a blessed state of affairs, the leaders of society were fortunate in having a gentleman philosopher who united reason, religion and good breeding into a philosophical justification for rebellion, and who marshaled God and history in the defense of property. Thomas Hobbes had been too secular and shocking, the Levellers and Diggers too dangerous, Milton too spiritual, but John Locke, like the porridge in *Goldilocks and the Three Bears,* was found to be exactly right. He presumed the existence of men of birth and self-restraint who joined together to preserve and to defend their inalienable rights of life, liberty, and estate. He advanced the political doctrine that the purpose of government was to achieve a society fit for the dignity of man (preferably gentlemen). States instituted by men of common sense and property never deteriorated into tryanny, because government was assumed to be a social convenience created to protect every kind of estate—property, wealth, title, and historic position. Society consisted of men who possessed rights bestowed by a benevolent deity; and government, be it crown or parliament, was regarded as nothing more than the trustee of those rights. When the guardian abused the authority conferred upon him (as James II had done) rebellion was not only justified, it became a sacred duty. John Locke in his *Two Treatises of Government* (written 1681 and published 1689) had made society respectable, to accompany a respectable revolution. The revolution had found a philosophical "Trimmer" as well as a royal one. Together John Locke and William III guided England into a century of economic prosperity, military triumph, and political self-satisfaction.

Security on such a massive and enduring scale produced confidence in royal government, in the future, in England, and in oligarchy. "The world," said the marquis of Halifax, has "grown saucy, and expecteth reasons, and good ones too, before they give up their own opinions to other men's dictates." And why shouldn't they expect good reasons? Locke assured them that "we are born free and we are born rational." With a Glorious Revolution behind them and 143 years of rule ahead of them, the oligarchs in 1689 were ready to maintain a government which reflected their wishes, to invest in an economic future which inspired confidence, and to concede the truth of Milton's words about "God's Englishmen."

> Consider what nation it is whereof ye are, and whereof ye are the governors; a nation not slow and dull, but of a quick, ingenious, and piercing spirit; acute to invent, subtle and sinewy to discourse, not beneath the reach of any point the highest that human capacity can soar to.
>
> —*Areopagitica*

Bibliography

Bibliographies

Abbott, W. C. *Bibliography of Oliver Cromwell.* 1929.
Davies, G. *Bibliography of British History—Stuart Period.* 2nd ed., 1970.
Furber, Elizabeth C. *Changing Views on British History; Essays on Historical Writing Since 1939.* 1966.
Grose, C. L. *A Select Bibliography of British History, 1660–1760.* 1939.
Levine, M. *Tudor England, 1485–1603.* 1968.
Read, C. *Bibliography of British History—Tudor Period.* 2nd ed., 1959.
Sachse, William L. *Restoration England, 1660–1689.* 1971.

General Works

FIFTEENTH CENTURY

Chrimes, S. B. *Lancastrians, Yorkists and Henry VII.* 1964.
Costain, T. *The Last Plantagenets.* 1962.
Coulton, G. G. *Chaucer and his England.* 1946.
———. *Medieval Panorama.* 1938.
Du Boulay, F. R. H. *The Age of Ambition: England in the Late Middle Ages.* 1970.
Jacob, E. F. *Henry V and the Invasion of France.* 1947.
———. *The Fifteenth Century.* 1961.
Kendall, P. M. *The Yorkist Age.* 1962.
Myers, A. R. *England in the Later Middle Ages.* 1952.
Scofield, C. L. *The Life and Reign of Edward IV.* 1923.
Storey, R. L. *The End of the House of Lancaster.* 1966.
Trevelyan, G. M. *England in the Age of Wycliffe.* 1920.

Sixteenth Century

Bindoff, S. T. *Tudor England.* 1950.
Black, J. B. *The Reign of Elizabeth, 1558–1603.* 2nd ed., 1959.
Elton, G. R. *England Under the Tudors.* 1955.
Froude, A. *History of England, 1529–1588.* 12 vols. 1877–1878.
Hurstfield, J. *Elizabeth I and the Unity of England.* 1960.
Mackie, J. D. *The Earlier Tudors.* 1957.
Morris, C. *The Tudors.* 1957.
Pollard, A. F. *England Under Protector Somerset.* 1900.
Rowse, A. L. *The England of Elizabeth.* 1951.
Smith, L. B. *The Elizabethan World.* 1967.
Storey, R. L. *The Reign of Henry VII.* 1968.

Seventeenth Century

Ashley, M. *England in the Seventeenth Century.* 1952.
Aylmer, G. F. *A Short History of Seventeenth Century England.* 1963.
Brinton, C. *The Anatomy of Revolution.* Rev. ed., 1953.
Bryant, A. *The England of Charles II.* 1935.
Clark, G. N. *The Later Stuarts.* 1934.
———. *The Seventeenth Century.* 1961.
Davies, G. *The Early Stuarts, 1603–1660.* 1959.
Firth, C. *The Last Years of the Protectorate.* 1909.
Gardiner, S. R. *History of England, 1603–1656.* 18 vols. 1894–1904.
Hill, C. "Recent Interpretations of the Civil War." *History* 41 (1956).
———. *The Century of Revolution.* 1961.
Jones, I. D. *The English Revolution, 1603–1714.* 1931.
Kenyon, J. P. *The Stuarts.* 1959.
Laslett, P. *The World We Have Lost.* 1965.
Macaulay, T. B. *History of England.* 6 vols. 1849–1861 (esp. vol. one).
Mathew, D. *The England of Charles I.* 1951.
———. *The Jacobean Age.* 1938.
———. *The Social Structure in Caroline England.* 1948.
Ogg, D. *England in the Reign of Charles II.* 1955.
———. *England in the Reigns of James II and William III.* 1955.
Taylor, P. *The Origins of the English Civil War: Conspiracy, Crusade or Class Conflict.* 1960.
Trevelyan, G. M. *England Under the Stuarts.* 1904.

European Background

Aston, T. *Crisis in Europe, 1560–1660.* 1965.
Cheyette, F. L. *Lordship and Community in Medieval Europe.* 1967.
Cheyney, E. *The Dawn of a New Era.* 1936.
Elliot, J. H. *Europe Divided, 1559–1598.* 1968.
Elton, G. R. *Reformation Europe, 1517–1559.* 1963.
Fowler, K. *The Age of Plantagenet and Valois.* Esp. intro., chaps. III, IV. 1967.
Friedrich, C. J. *The Age of Baroque, 1610–1660.* 1952.

Gilmore, M. *The World of Humanism.* 1952.

Huizinga, J. *The Waning of the Middle Ages.* 1st ed., 1924.

Jones, J. R. *Britain and Europe in the Seventeenth Century.* 1966.

Koenigsberger, H. G., and G. L. Mosse. *Europe in the Sixteenth Century.* 1968.

Major, J. R. "The Crown and the Aristocracy in Renaissance France." *American Historical Review* 69 (1963–64).

Nussbaum, F. L. *The Triumph of Science and Reason, 1660–1685.* 1953.

Perroy, E. *The Hundred Years' War.* Tr. by W. B. Wells. 1951.

Trevor-Roper, H. R. "The General Crisis of the Seventeenth Century." *Past and Present* 16 (1959).

Wedgwood, C. V. *The Thirty Years War.* 1949.

Wolf, J. B. *The Emergence of the Great Powers, 1685–1715.* 1951.

SPECIAL SURVEYS

Allen, J. W. *A History of Political Thought in the Sixteenth Century.* Rev. ed., 1957.

Byrne, M. S. C. *English Life in Town and Country.* 1954.

Chambers, J. D. *Population, Economy, and Society in Pre-Industrial England.* 1972.

Clapham, J. *A Concise Economic History of Britain.* 1949.

Clarkson, L. A. *The Pre-Industrial Economy in England, 1500–1750.* 1971.

Darby, H. C. *A New Historical Geography of England.* 1973.

Davis, Ralph. *English Overseas Trade, 1500–1700.* 1973.

Ernle, Lord (R. W. Prothero). *English Farming, Past and Present.* 1936.

Hexter, J. H. *Reappraisals in History.* A collection of key articles. 1962.

Holdsworth, W. *The History of English Law.* Vol. 4. 3rd ed., 1945.

Lipson, E. *The Economic History of England.* 1931.

Ogilvie, C. *The King's Government and the Common Law, 1471–1641.* 1958.

Pinchbeck, J. and M. Hewitt. *Children in English Society.* 2 vols. 1969.

Postan, M. M. *The Medieval Economy and Society, 1100–1500.* 1972.

Schubert, H. R. *A History of the British Iron and Steel Industry to 1775.* 1957.

Stone, L. "Social Mobility in England, 1500–1700." *Past and Present* 33 (1966).

Thirsk, Joan, ed. *The Agrarian History of England and Wales.* Vol. 4. 1967.

Thompson, F. *A Short History of Parliament, 1295–1642.* 1953.

Wrigley, E. A. *An Introduction to English Historical Demography: From the Sixteenth to the Nineteenth Century.* 1966.

Legal, Constitutional and Governmental History

FIFTEENTH CENTURY

Bean, J. M. W. *The Decline of English Feudalism, 1215–1540.* 1968.

Cam, H. H. "The Decline and Fall of English Feudalism." *History* 25 (1940).

Chrimes, S. B. *English Constitutional Ideas in the Fifteenth Century.* 1936.

Hay, D. "Late Medieval–Early Modern." *Bulletin of the Institute of Historical Research* 25 (1952).

Lander, J. R. *Conflict and Stability in Fifteenth Century England.* 1969.

_____. "Edward IV: The Modern Legend and a Revision." *History* 41 (1956).

_____. *The Wars of the Roses.* 1965.

McFarlane, K. B. "Bastard Feudalism." *Bulletin of the Institute of Historical Research* 20 (1943–45).

_____. "England and the Hundred Years War." *Past and Present* 22 (1962).

_____. *Lancastrian Kings and Lollard Knights.* 1972.

_____. "The Wars of the Roses." *Proceedings of the British Academy* (1965).

_____. "War and Society 1300–1600." *Past and Present* 22 (1962).

Myers, A. R. "The Character of Richard III." *History Today* 4 (1954).

_____. *The Household of Edward IV.* 1959.

Tey, J. *The Daughter of Time.* 1953.

Wilkinson, B. *Constitutional History of England in the Fifteenth Century, 1399–1485.* 1964.

Wolfe, B. P. "The Management of English Royal Estates Under the Yorkist Kings." *English History Review* 71 (1956).

_____. "Yorkist and Early Tudor Government, 1461–1509." *Historical Association Pamphlet* (1966).

SIXTEENTH CENTURY

Atkinson, T. *Elizabethan Winchester.* 1963.

Van Baumer, F. L. *The Early Tudor Theory of Kingship.* 1940.

Brooks, F. W. *The Council of the North.* 1953.

Cooper, J. P. "Henry VII's Last Years Reconsidered." *Historical Journal* 2 (1959).

Davies, C. S. L. "The Pilgrimage of Grace Reconsidered." *Past and Present* 41 (1968).

Dunham, W. H. "Regal Power and the Rule of Law: A Tudor Paradox." *Journal of British Studies* 3 (1964).

Elton, G. R. "Henry VII: A Restatement." *Historical Journal* 4 (1961)

_____. "Henry VII: Rapacity and Remorse." *Historical Journal* 1 (1958).

_____. *Henry VIII, An Essay in Revision.* Historical Association. 1962.

_____. "King or Minister?: The Man Behind the Reformation." *History* 39 (1954).

_____. *Policy and Police: The Enforcement of the Reformation in the Age of Cromwell.* 1972.

_____. *Reform and Renewal: Thomas Cromwell and the Common Weal.* 1973.

_____. *Star Chamber Stories.* 1958.

_____. *The Tudor Revolution in Government.* 1953.

Figgis, J. N. *The Divine Right of Kings.* 1914.

Gleason, H. *The Justices of the Peace in England, 1558–1640.* 1969.

Harbison, E. H. *Rival Ambassadors at the Court of Queen Mary.* 1940.

Harriss, G. L. and P. Williams. "A Revolution in Tudor History: Dr. Elton's Interpretation of the Age." *Past and Present* 25 (1963).

Hurstfield, J. "Was There a Tudor Despotism After All?" *Transactions of the Royal Historical Society.* 5th ser., 17 (1967).

_____. "Political Corruption in Modern England." *History* 47 (1962).

_____. "The Revival of Feudalism in Early Tudor England." *History* 37 (1952).

James, M. E. "Obedience and Dissent in Henrician England: The Lincolnshire Rebellion, 1536." *Past and Present* 48 (1970).

Jones, W. R. D. *The Tudor Commonwealth, 1529–1559.* 1970.

Lehmberg, S. E. *The Reformation Parliament.* 1969.

Levine, M. *Tudor Dynastic Problems, 1460–1571.* 1973.

Loades, D. M. *Two Tudor Conspiracies.* 1965.

MacCaffrey, W. T. "England, the Crown and the New Aristocracy." *Past and Present* 30 (1965).

———. *Exeter, 1540–1640: The Growth of an English Country Town.* 1958.

———. "Place and Patronage in Elizabethan Politics." In Bindoff, S. T., J. Hurstfield, and C. H. Williams, eds. *Elizabethan Government and Society.* 1961.

———. *The Shaping of the Elizabethan Regime.* 1968.

Morris, C. *Political Thought in England, Tyndale to Hooker.* 1953.

Neale, J. E. *Elizabeth I and Her Parliaments.* 2 vols. 1957.

———. *The Elizabethan House of Commons.* 1949.

Notestein, W. *The Winning of the Initiative by the House of Commons.* 1924.

Pickthorn, K. *Early Tudor Government: Henry VII, Henry VIII.* 2 vols. 1934.

Pulman, M. B. *The Elizabethan Privy Council in the 1570s.* 1971.

Richardson, W. C. *The History of the Court of Augmentations, 1536–1554.* 1961.

———. *Tudor Chamber Government.* 1952.

Samaha, J. B. *Law and Order in Historical Perspective: The Case of Elizabethan Essex.* 1974.

Smith, A. G. R. *The Government of Elizabethan England.* 1967.

Whitney-Jones, R. D. *The Tudor Commonwealth Men.* 1969.

Wolffe, B. P. "Henry VII's Land Revenues and Chamber Finance." *English Historical Review* 79 (1964).

SEVENTEENTH CENTURY

Ashley, M. *Oliver Cromwell and the Puritan Revolution.* 1958.

———. *The Glorious Revolution of 1688.* 1968.

Aylmer, G. E. "Attempts at Administrative Reform, 1625–1640." *English Historical Review* 72 (1957).

———. "Office Holding as a Factor in English History, 1625–1642." *History* 4 (1959).

———. *The King's Servants.* 1961.

Bahlman, D. *The Moral Revolution of 1688.* 1957.

Bosher, R. S. *The Making of the Restoration Settlement, 1649–1662.* 1951.

Brailsford, H. N. *The Levellers and the English Revolution.* 1961.

Brunton, D., and D. H. Pennington. *Members of the Long Parliament.* 1954.

Burne, A. H., and P. Young. *The Great Civil War.* 1959.

Davies, G. *The Restoration of Charles II.* 1955.

Feiling, K. *A History of the Tory Party.* 1924.

Gooch, G. P. *English Democratic Ideas in the Seventeenth Century.* 1959.

———. *Political Thought in England from Bacon to Halifax.* 1915.

Gough, J. *John Locke's Political Philosophy.* 1950.

Hexter, J. H. *The Reign of King Pym.* 1941.

Hobbes, T. *Behemoth: The History of the Causes of the Civil Wars in England.* Ed. by W. Molesworth. 1840.

Hyde, Edward (Earl of Clarendon). *The History of the Great Rebellion.* Ed. by W. D. Macray. 1888.

Jones, J. R. *The First Whigs: The Politics of the Exclusion Crisis, 1673–83.* 1961.

Judson, M. A. *The Crisis of the Constitution.* 1949.

Kearney, H. F. *The Eleven Years Tyranny of Charles I.* 1962.

Keeler, M. F. *The Long Parliament, 1640–41.* 1954.

Kemp, Betty. *King and Commons, 1660–1832.* 1957.

Kenyon, J. P. *The Popish Plot.* 1972.

———. *The Stuart Constitution, 1603–1688.* 1966.

Lee, M. *The Cabal.* 1965.

MacCormack, J. *Revolutionary Politics in the Long Parliament.* 1974.

Mitchell, W. M. *The Rise of the Revolutionary Party in the English House of Commons, 1603–1629.* 1957.

Mosse, G. L. *The Struggle for Sovereignty in England from the Reign of Elizabeth to the Petition of Right.* 1950.

Pennington, D. H. *Members of the Long Parliament.* 1954.

Pinkham, Lucile. *William III and the Respectable Revolution.* 1954.

Plumb, J. H. *The Growth of Political Stability in England, 1675–1725.* 1967.

Prall, S. *The Bloodless Revolution, England, 1688.* 1972.

Roberts, C. *The Growth of Responsible Government in England.* 1966.

Roots, I. *The Great Rebellion, 1642–1660.* 1966.

Solt, L. F. *Saints in Arms.* 1959.

Straka, G. M. *The Revolution of 1688—Whig Triumph or Palace Revolution?* 1962.

Tanner, J. R. *English Constitutional Conflicts of the Seventeenth Century.* 1928.

Trevelyan, G. M. *The English Revolution, 1688–1689.* 1938.

Underdown, D. *Pride's Purge: Politics in the Puritan Revolution.* 1971.

Walzer, M. *The Revolution of the Saints.* 1965.

Wedgwood, C. V. *The King's Peace.* 1955.

———. *The King's War.* 1958.

———. *The Trial of Charles I.* 1964.

Western, J. R. *Monarchy and Revolution: The English State in the 1680's.* 1972.

Worden, B. *The Rump Parliament, 1648–1653.* 1974.

Zagorin, P. *A History of Political Thought in the English Revolution.* 1954.

———. *The Court and the Country: The Beginning of the English Revolution.* 1969.

Zaller, R. *The Parliament of 1621.* 1971.

Economic and Social History

Fifteenth Century

Bean, J. M. W. "Plague, Population and Economic Decline in the Later Middle Ages." *European History Review* 2nd ser., 15 (1962–63).

———. *The Estates of the Percy Family, 1416–1537.* 1958.

Bennett, H. S. *The Pastons and Their England.* 1922.

Beresford, M. W. *The Lost Villages of England.* 1954.

Bridbury, A. R. *Economic Growth: England in the Later Middle Ages.* 1962.

Dobson, R. B. *The Peasants' Revolt of 1381.* 1970.

DuBoulay, F. R. H. *The Lordship of Canterbury: An Essay on Medieval Society.* 1966.

Dunham, W. H. *Lord Hastings' Indentured Retainers, 1461–83.* 1955.

Gairdner, J., ed. *Paston Letters.* 6 vols. 1904.

Holmes, G. A. *The Estates of the Higher Nobility in Fourteenth Century England.* 1957.

Kingsford, C. L., ed. *Stonor Letters.* 2 vols. 1919.

Postan, M. "Some Social Consequences of the Hundred Years' War." *Economic History Review* 12 (1942).

———. "The Cost of the Hundred Years' War." *Past and Present* 27 (1964).

Power, E., and M. Postan. *Studies in English Trade in the Fifteenth Century.* 1933.

Russell, J. C. *British Medieval Population.* 1948.

Thompson, J. W. *Economic and Social History of the Later Middle Ages.* 1931.

Thrupp, S. *The Merchant Class of Medieval London, 1300–1500.* 1948.

Ziegler, Philip. *The Black Death.* 1969.

SIXTEENTH CENTURY

Ames, R. *Citizen Thomas More and His Utopia.* 1949.

Aydelotte, F. *Elizabethan Rogues and Vagabonds.* 1967.

Bowden, P. J. *The Wool Trade in Tudor and Stuart England.* 1962.

Brenner, Y. S. "The Inflation of Prices in Early Sixteenth Century England." *Economic History Review* 2nd ser., 14, no. 2 (1961).

———. "The Inflation of Prices in England, 1551–1650." *Economic History Review* 2nd ser., 15, no. 2 (1962).

———. "The Price Revolution Reconsidered: A Reply." *Economic History Review* 2nd ser., 17 (1964).

Campbell, Mildred. *The English Yeoman under Elizabeth and the Early Stuarts.* 1942.

Caspari, F. *Humanism and the Social Order in Tudor England.* 1954.

Charlton, K. *Education in Renaissance England.* 1965.

Copeman, W. S. C. *Doctors and Disease in Tudor Times.* 1960.

Cornwall, J. "English Population in the Early Sixteenth Century." *Economic History Review* 2nd ser., 23, no. 1 (1970).

———. "The Early Tudor Gentry." *Economic History Review* 2nd ser., 17 (1965).

Dietz, F. C. *English Government Finance.* Rev. ed. 1964.

Dyer, A. D. *The City of Worcester in the Sixteenth Century.* 1973.

Esler, A. *The Aspiring Mind of the Elizabethan Younger Generation.* 1966.

Ferguson, A. B. *The Articulate Citizen and the English Renaissance.* 1965.

———. *The Indian Summer of English Chivalry.* 1960.

Hexter, J. H. "The English Aristocracy, Its Crises, and the English Revolution, 1558–1660." *The Journal of British Studies* 8 (1968).

Hurstfield, J. *The Queen's Wards.* 1958.

Jordan, W. K. *Philanthropy in England, 1480–1660.* 1959.

Kerridge, K. *Agrarian Problems in the Sixteenth Century.* 1969.

Miller, H. "The Early Tudor Peerage 1485–1547." *Bul. Inst. of Historical Research* 24 (1951).

Onions, C. T. *Shakespeare's England.* 2 vols. 1917.

Outhwaite, R. B. *Inflation in Tudor and Early Stuart England.* 1969.

Ramsay, G. D. *English Overseas Trade During the Centuries of Emergence.* 1957.

Ramsey, P. *Tudor Economic Problems.* 1963.

Rowse, A. L. *Tudor Cornwall.* 1941.

Simpson, A. *The Wealth of the Gentry, 1540–1660.* 1961.

Stone, L. *Social Change and Revolution in England, 1540–1640.* 1965.

———. *The Crisis of the Aristocracy, 1558–1641.* 1965.

Tawney, R. H. *Religion and the Rise of Capitalism.* 1926.

———. *The Agrarian Problem of the Sixteenth Century.* 1912.

Thirsk, J. *Tudor Enclosures.* Historical Association. 1958.

Wilson, F. P. *The Plague in Shakespeare's London.* 1927.

Wright, L. B. *Middle Class Culture in Elizabethan England.* 1935.

Zeeveld, W. G. *Foundations of Tudor Policy.* 1948.

SEVENTEENTH CENTURY

Ashley, M. *The Stuarts in Love.* 1963.

Baxter, S. B. *The Development of the Treasury, 1660–1702.* 1957.

Coleman, D. C. "Labour in the British Economy of the Seventeenth Century." *Economic History Review* 2nd ser., 8 (1956).

Fischoff, E. "The Protestant Ethic and the Spirit of Capitalism: The History of a Controversy." *Social Research* 11 (1944).

Hinton, R. W. K. "The Mercantile System in the Time of Thomas Mun." *Economic History Review* 7 (1954–55).

MacPherson, C. B. *The Political Theory of Possessive Individualism.* 1962.

Notestein, W. *The English People on the Eve of Colonization.* 1954.

Pease, T. C. *The Leveller Movement.* 1916.

Pepys, Samuel. *The Diary.* 7 vols. Ed. by Robert Latham and William Mathews. 1970–72.

Rabb, T. K. *Enterprise and Empire: Merchant and Gentry Investment in the Expansion of England, 1575–1630.* 1967.

Speck, W. A. "Social Status in Late Stuart England." *Past and Present* 34 (1966).

Supple, B. E. *Commercial Crisis and Change in England, 1600–1642.* 1959.

Tawney, R. H. *Business and Politics Under James I.* 1958.

Trevor-Roper, H. R. "Religion, the Reformation and Social Change" and "The General Crisis." In *Religion, the Reformation and Social Change.* 1967.

———. "Social Causes of the Great Rebellion." In *Historical Essays.* 1957.

———. *The Gentry, 1540–1640. Economic History Review,* Supplement I (1953).

Weber, Max. *The Protestant Ethic and the Spirit of Capitalism.* 1930.

Wilson, C. *Mercantilism.* Historical Association. 1958.

Zagorin, P. "The Social Interpretation of the English Revolution." *Journal of Economic History* 19 (1959).

Religious History

Abernathy, G. R. *The English Presbyterians and the Stuart Restoration. American Philosophical Society Transactions.* New series, 55 (1965).

Baskerville, G. *English Monks and the Suppression of the Monasteries.* 1937.

Blench, J. W. *Preaching in England in the Late Fifteenth and Sixteenth Centuries: A Study of English Sermons, 1450–1600.* 1964.

Bosher, R. S. *The Making of the Restoration Settlement: The Influence of the Laudians.* 1951.

Clebsch, W. A. *England's Earliest Protestants, 1520–1535.* 1964.

Collinson, P. *The Elizabethan Puritan Movement.* 1967.

Cragg, G. R. *Puritanism in the Period of the Great Prosecution, 1660–1688.* 1957.

Cross, C. *The Royal Supremacy in the Elizabethan Church.* 1969.

Dickens, A. G. *Lollards and Protestants in the Diocese of York, 1509–1558.* 1959.

——. *The English Reformation.* 1964.

——. *Thomas Cromwell and the English Reformation.* 1959.

Dickinson, J. C. *Monastic Life in Medieval England.* 1961.

Donaldson, G. *The Scottish Reformation.* 1960.

Foxe, John. *Acts and Monuments of the English Martyrs.* Ed. by S. R. Cattley and G. Townsend. 1837–1841.

Gasquet, F. A. *The Eve of the Reformation.* 1923.

George, C. H., and K. *The Protestant Mind of the English Reformation, 1570–1640.* 1961.

Haller, W. *Foxe's "Book of Martyrs" and the Elect Nation.* 1963.

——. *Liberty and Reformation in the Puritan Revolution.* 1955.

——. *The Rise of Puritanism, 1570–1643.* 1938.

Havran, M. J. *Catholics in Caroline England.* 1962.

Heath, P. *The English Parish Clergy on the Eve of the Reformation.* 1969.

Hill, C. *Intellectual Origins of the English Revolution.* 1965.

——. *Puritanism and Revolution.* 1958.

——. *Society and Puritanism in Pre-Revolutionary England.* 1964.

——. *The Economic Problems of the Church, from Whitgift to the Long Parliament.* 1956.

Hughes, P. *The Reformation in England.* 3 vols. 1954.

Jordan, W. K. *The Development of Religious Toleration in England.* 4 vols. 1932–1940.

Knappen, M. M. *Tudor Puritanism.* 1939.

Knowles, David. *The Religious Orders in England.* Vols. 2, 3. 1955–1959.

MacFarlane, A. *Witchcraft in Tudor and Stuart England: A Regional and Comparative Study.* 1970.

Maclure, M. *The Paul's Cross Sermons, 1534–1642.* 1958.

Manning, R. *Religion and Society in Elizabethan Sussex.* 1969.

McFarlane, K. B. *John Wycliffe and the Beginnings of English Nonconformity.* 1952.

McGrath, P. *Papists and Puritans Under Elizabeth I.* 1967.

Meyer, A. O. *England and the Catholic Church Under Elizabeth.* Trans. by J. R. McKee. 1967.

Miller, P. *The New England Mind.* 1939.

New, J. F. *Anglican and Puritan: The Basis of Their Opposition.* 1964.

Ogle, A. *The Tragedy of the Lollards' Tower.* 1949.

Owst, G. R. *Preaching in Medieval England: An Introduction to Sermon Manuscripts of the Period, c. 1350–1450.* 1965.

Pollard, A. F. *Thomas Cranmer and the English Reformation.* 1904.

Porter, H. C. *Reformation and Reaction in Tudor Cambridge.* 1958.

Powicke, F. M. *The Reformation in England.* 1941.
Robson, J. A. *Wyclif and the Oxford Schools.* 1961.
Rupp, G. *Studies in the Making of the English Protestant Tradition.* 1947.
Smith, H. M. *Pre-Reformation England.* 1938.
Smith, L. B. "A Matter of Conscience." In T. Rabb & J. Seigel, *Action and Conviction, Essays in Memory of E. H. Harbison.* 1969.
———— "The Reformation and the Decay of Medieval Ideals." *Church History* 24 (1955).
————. *Tudor Prelates and Politics.* 1953.
Thomas, K. *Religion and the Decline of Magic: Studies in Popular Beliefs in Sixteenth and Seventeenth Century England.* 1971.
Thompson, A. H. *The English Clergy and their Organization in the Later Middle Ages.* 1947.
Thomson, J. A. F. *The Later Lollards, 1414–1520.* 1965.
Trimble, W. R. *The Catholic Laity in Elizabethan England, 1558–1603.* 1964.
Walzer, M. *The Revolution of the Saints.* 1965.
Yule, G. *The Independents in the English Civil War.* 1958.

Intellectual and Cultural History

Auerbach, Erna. *Tudor Artists.* 1954.
Barker, A. *Milton and the Puritan Dilemma, 1641–1660.* 1942.
Boas, Marie. *Robert Boyle and Seventeenth Century Chemistry.* 1958.
Brandt, W. *Shaping of Medieval History: Studies in Modes of Perception.* 1966.
Burtt, E. A. *The Metaphysical Foundations of Modern Science.* 1924.
Bush, D. *English Literature in the Earlier Seventeenth Century.* 1945.
Butterfield, H. *The Origins of Modern Science, 1300–1800.* 1949.
Butterworth, C. *English Primers, 1529–1545.* 1953.
Chambers, E. K. *English Literature at the Close of the Middle Ages.* 1945.
Cruttwell, P. *The Shakespearean Moment and Its Place in the Seventeenth Century.* 1954.
Curtis, M. H. *Oxford and Cambridge in Transition, 1558–1642.* 1959.
Einstein, L. *Tudor Ideals.* 1921.
Evans, J. *English Art, 1307–1461.* 1949.
Fink, Z. *The Classical Republicans.* 1962.
Fussner, F. S. *The Historical Revolution: English Historical Scholarship in the Sixteenth and Seventeenth Centuries.* 1956.
Hall, A. R. *The Scientific Revolution.* 1954.
Harvey, I. *Gothic England.* 1947.
Hexter, J. H. *More's Utopia: The Biography of an Idea.* 1952.
Kearney, H. F. *Origins of the Scientific Revolution.* 1964.
———— "Puritanism, Capitalism and the Scientific Revolution." *Past and Present* 28 (1964).
Laslett, P. *John Locke's Two Treatises of Government: A Critical Edition with an Introduction and Apparatus Criticus.* Rev. ed. 1965.
Lewis, C. S. *English Literature in the Sixteenth Century, Excluding Drama.* 1954.
Lovejoy, A. C. *The Great Chain of Being: A Study of the History of an Idea.* 1936.

McConica, J. K. *English Humanists and Reformation Politics Under Henry VIII and Edward VI.* 1965.

Millar, O. *English Art, 1625–1714.* 1957.

Pocock, A. *The Ancient Constitution and the Feudal Law.* 1957.

Prior, M. E. *The Drama of Power: Studies in Shakespeare's History Plays.* 1973.

Seebohm, F. *The Oxford Reformers.* 1938.

Simon, J. *Education and Society in Tudor England.* 1966.

Smith, L. B. "English Treason Trials and Confessions in the Sixteenth Century." *Journal of the History of Ideas* 15 (1954).

Stone, L. "The Educational Revolution in England." *Past and Present* 28 (1964).

Strong, R. *The English Icon: Elizabethan and Jacobean Portraiture.* 1969.

Summerson, J. *Architecture in Britain, 1530–1830.* 2nd ed. 1955.

Sutherland, J. *English Literature of the Late Seventeenth Century.* 1969.

Tillyard, E. M. W. *The Elizabethan World Picture.* 1934.

Waterhouse, E. *Painting in Britain, 1530–1790.* 1953.

Watson, C. B. *Shakespeare and the Renaissance Concept of Honor.* 1960.

Webb, G. *Architecture in England: The Middle Ages.* 1956.

Wedgwood, C. V. *Poetry and Politics Under the Stuarts.* 1950.

Westfall, R. S. *Science and Religion in Seventeenth Century England.* 1958.

Willey, B. *The Seventeenth Century Background.* 1934.

Wolfe, D. M. *Milton in the Puritan Revolution.* 1941.

Military and Colonial History

Bagwell, R. *Ireland Under the Stuarts.* 1936.

Beckett, J. C. *A Short History of Ireland.* 1958.

Beer, G. L. *The Origins of the British Colonial System.* 1908.

Boynton, L. *The Elizabethan Militia, 1558–1638.* 1967.

Brown, P. N. *History of Scotland.* 3 vols. 1908–09.

Clark, G. N. *War and Society in the Seventeenth Century.* 1958.

Craven, W. F. *The Southern Colonies in the Seventeenth Century, 1607–1689.* 1964.

Crowson, P. S. *Tudor Foreign Policy.* 1973.

Cruickshank, C. G. *Elizabeth's Army.* 2nd ed. 1966.

Dickinson, W. C. *Scotland from the Earliest Times to 1603.* 2nd ed. 1965.

Donaldson, G. *Scotland: James V to James VII.* 1965.

Dunn, R. S. *Sugar and Slaves: The Rise of the Planter Class in the English West Indies, 1624–1713.* 1972.

Falls, C. *Elizabeth's Irish Wars.* 1950.

Grant, I. F. *The Social and Economic Development of Scotland Before 1603.* 1930.

Hale, J. R. "Sixteenth Century Explanations of War and Violence." *Past and Present* 51 (1971).

Lee, M. *James I and Henry IV: An Essay in English Foreign Policy, 1603–1610.* 1970.

Mattingly, G. *Renaissance Diplomacy.* 1955.

——. *The Armada.* 1962.

Oman, C. W. C. *The History of the Art of War in the Middle Ages.* 1953.

Parry, J. H. *The Age of Reconaissance.* 1963.

Rowse, A. L. *The Expansion of England.* 1955.

Wernham, R. B. *Before the Armada.* 1966.

Williamson, J. A. *A Short History of British Expansion.* 1931.

_____. *The Age of Drake.* 1938.

Wilson, C. H. *Profit and Power: A Study of England and the Dutch Wars.* 1957.

_____. *Queen Elizabeth and the Revolt of the Netherlands.* 1970.

Woodroffe, T. *Vantage at Sea, England's Emergence as an Oceanic Power.* 1958.

Woolrych, A. *Battles of the English Civil War.* 1961.

Biography

Adamson, J. H., and H. F. Folland. *Sir Henry Vane, 1613–1662.* 1973.

Airy, O. *Charles II.* 1904.

Allmand, C. T. *Henry V.* Historical Association. 1968.

Anderson, F. H. *Francis Bacon, His Career and His Thought.* 1962.

Armitage-Smith, S. *John of Gaunt.* 1904.

Ashley, M. *The Greatness of Oliver Cromwell.* 1958.

Bald, R. C. *John Donne, A Life.* 1970.

Baxter, S. B. *William III.* 1966.

Beer, B. L. *Northumberland; the Political Career of John Dudley, Earl of Warwick and Duke of Northumberland.* 1974.

Bowen, C. D. *The Lion and the Throne, the Life and Times of Sir Edward Coke.* 1956.

Brook, V. J. K. *A Life of Archbishop Parker.* 1962.

Bryant, A. *Samuel Pepys.* 3 vols. 1934–38.

Chamber, E. *A Short Life of William Shakespeare.* 1935.

Chambers, R. W. *Thomas More.* 1948.

Chrimes, S. B. *Henry VII.* 1972.

Cranston, M. *John Locke.* 1957.

Elton, G. R. "The Good Duke." *Historical Journal* 12 (1969).

_____. "Thomas Cromwell." *History Today* 6 (1956).

Emmison, F. G. *Tudor Secretary: Sir William Petre at Court and Home.* 1961.

Ferguson, C. W. *Naked to Mine Enemies* (Wolsey). 1958.

Firth, C. *Oliver Cromwell.* 1900.

Fraser, Lady Antonia. *Mary Queen of Scots.* 1969.

Gairdner, J. *The Life and Reign of Richard III.* 1898.

Gammon, S. R. *Statesman and Schemer: William, First Lord Paget, Tudor Minister.* 1974.

Gibb, M. A. *Buckingham.* 1935.

Gregg, P. *Free Born John: A Biography of John Lilburne.* 1961.

Greenblatt, S. J. *Sir Walter Raleigh, The Renaissance Man and His Roles.* 1973.

Haley, K. H. *First Earl of Shaftesbury.* 1968.

Handover, P. M. *The Second Cecil.* 1959.

Havran, M. J. *Caroline Courtier: The Life of Lord Cottington.* 1973.

Henderson, T. F. *Mary Queen of Scots.* 1905.

Hill, C. *Oliver Cromwell.* Historical Association. 1958.

Hulme, H. *The Life of Sir John Eliot.* 1957.

Hutchinson, H. F. *The Hollow Crown: A Life of Richard II.* 1961.

Jenkins, E. *Elizabeth the Great.* 1958.

Jordan, W. K. *Edward VI: The Young King.* 1968.

———. *Edward VI: The Threshold of Power.* 1970.

Kendall, P. M. *Richard III.* 1955.

———. *Warwick the Kingmaker.* 1957.

Kenyon, J. P. *Robert Spencer, Earl of Sunderland, 1641–1702.* 1958.

Lacey, R. *Robert Devereux, the Earl of Essex.* 1971.

———. *Sir Walter Ralegh.* 1974.

Lander, J. R. "Edward IV: The Legend and a Revision." *History* 41 (1956).

Lang, A. *The Mystery of Mary Stuart.* 1901.

Manuel, F. E. *A Portrait of Isaac Newton.* 1968.

Mason, A. E. W. *The Life of Francis Drake.* 1941.

Mattingly, G. *Catherine of Aragon.* 1941.

Merriman, R. B. *The Life and Letters of Thomas Cromwell.* 2 vols. 1902.

Muller, J. A. *Stephen Gardiner and the Tudor Reaction.* 1926.

Neale, J. E. *Queen Elizabeth.* 1934.

Paul, J. *Catherine of Aragon and Her Friends.* 1966.

Pollard, A. F. *Henry VIII.* 1902.

———. *Wolsey.* 1929.

Prescott, H. F. M. *Mary Tudor.* 1953.

Read, C. *Lord Burghley and Queen Elizabeth.* 1960.

———. *Mr. Secretary Cecil and Queen Elizabeth.* 1955.

Ridley, J. *Thomas Cranmer.* 1962.

Rowse, A. L. *Sir Richard Grenville of the Revenge.* 1937.

Scarisbrick, J. J. *Henry VIII.* 1968.

Schenk, W. *Reginald Pole.* 1950.

Simons, E. N. *Henry VII.* 1968.

Slavin, A. J. *Politics and Profit: A Study of Sir Ralph Sadler, 1507–1547.* 1966.

Smith, L. B. *A Tudor Tragedy, the Life and Times of Catherine Howard.* 1961.

———. *Henry VIII, The Mask of Royalty.* 1971.

Steel, A. *Richard II.* 1941.

Stone, L. *An Elizabethan: Sir Horatio Palavicino.* 1956.

Trevor-Roper, H. R. *Archbishop Land.* 2nd ed. 1962.

Turner, F. C. *James II.* 1948.

Van der Zee, H. and B. *William and Mary.* 1973.

Wallace, W. M. *Sir Walter Raleigh.* 1959.

Waugh, E. *Edmund Campion.* 1935.

Wedgwood, C. V. *Oliver Cromwell.* 1939.

———. *Thomas Wentworth, First Earl of Strafford.* 1961.

Williams, N. *Thomas Howard, Fourth Duke of Norfolk.* 1964.

Williamson, J. A. *Sir John Hawkins.* 1927.

Willson, D. H. *King James VI and I.* 1956.

Wingfield-Stratford, E. *Charles, King of England.* 1949.

Index

Act of Succession, 110, 114, 125
Act of Supremacy, 111, 114, 148, 150
Agincourt, Battle of, 18
Agriculture. *See also* Enclosures, Gentry
    Peasantry
  feudal, 27–28, 34
  fifteenth-century recession, 34–35
  labor shortage, 35–36, 71
  plague, effect of, 33
  revival of, in sixteenth century, 68
Amboyna, Massacre of, 257
Anglican Church *See* Church of England
Ann, Queen of England (1702–1714),
    291
Anne of Cleves, 130–32
Apprentices, Statue of, 229–30, 234
Argyll, Archibald Campbell, Ninth
    Earl of, 291
Armada, 178, 181–82
Arthur, Prince, 86, 87–88
Ascham, Roger, 76

Bacon Francis, 171, 172, 174, 238,
    239, 301, 302
Barnet, Battle of, 55
Bate's case, 206
Baxter, Richard, 245
Beaufort family
  Bishops of Winchester, 22, 118
  control by, 52
  Edmund, Duke of Somerset, 22, 52
  Joan, 39
  Margaret, 22
Bedford, Duke of, 19, 21

Bill of Rights, 297
Bilney, Thomas, 123–24
Black Death, 18, 29–33
  effects of, 30–33, 68
  origins of, 29–30
Blois, Treaty of, 161
Bloody Assizes, 292
Bodin, Jean, 71
Boleyn, Anne, 76, 103, 107, 108, 109,
    129
  execution of, 129
Bolingbroke, Henry, Earl of Derby.
    See Henry IV
Bonner, Edmund, Bishop of London,
    78, 111, 126, 146, 153
Bosworth Field, Battle of, 59, 62
Boyle, Robert, 299, 301, 302
Bradford, William, 240
Bradshaw, William, 246
Brandon, Charles, Duke of Suffolk,
    84, 137
Breda, Declaration of, 269, 271, 274
Buckingham, Dukes of
  Edward Stafford, 82, 84
  family wealth, 39, 68
  George. *See* Villiers
Burford, Battle of, 253
Burgundy, Duchy of, diplomatic
    relations with, 54–55
Burgundy, Margaret, Duchess of, 55,
    77, 84

Cabal, 281, 283
Cade, Jack, rebellion of, 24

Cádiz
  under Elizabeth I, 179
  under Charles I, 214
  under Cromwell, 258
Calais, 18, 35
  loss of, 154, 159, 161
Cambrai, Treaty of, 104
Campion, Edmund, 181
Carr, Robert, Earl of Somerset,
  203–04
Cateau Cambrésis, Treaty of, 159
Catherine of Aragon
  death of, 129
  divorce, 104–09, 150
  marriage to Arthur, 87–88
  marriage to Henry, 88, 100, 104
Catherine of Braganza, 281, 284
Catherine de Medici, 155, 159,
  161, 182
Cavalier, use of term, 226
Cavalier Parliament. *See* Parliament
Caxton, William, 77–78
Cecil, Robert, Earl of Salisbury,
  188, 192, 206–07
Cecil, William, Lord Burghley, 166–67,
  168, 176, 177, 182, 192, 229
Chantries, 146
Charles I (1625–1649), 201, 209–10,
  211–27, 235–38, 241
  character as cause of Civil War, 211–
  12
  and Civil War, 246–51
  compared to Cromwell, 255–56
  "Eleven Year Tyranny," 216–23
  execution, 251–52
  financial policy, 217–19, 220
  foreign policy, 215, 221
  parliament, conflict with, 213–14,
  215–16, 223, 224–27
  religious policy, 214, 220, 221–22,
  225
  Scotland, policy with, 223, 224
  "Thorough," policy of, 217, 221–22
  trial, 246
Charles II (1660–1685), 253, 258,
  267–86
  and the Cabal, 281
  character of, 269–70, 281, 286
  death of, 286
  and Exclusion Bill, 285–86
  financial policy, 273–74, 276–77,
  282–83

foreign policy, 277–78, 281–83
French pension, 281, 283, 286
and parliament, 282–83, 284–86, 288
and the Popish Plot, 284–86
religious views, 270, 274–75, 282
and the Restoration, 267–77
return from exile, 263
and Tory Party, 286
Charles V, Duke of Burgundy, King of
  Spain, Emperor of the Holy
  Roman Empire, 101, 103, 152
  relations with Henry VIII, 103–05,
  130
  relations with Mary I, 150, 154
Charles V, King of France, 14
Charles VI, King of France, 14–15,
  17, 19
Charles VII, King of France, 19
Charles IX, King of France, 161
Chaucer, Geoffrey, 78
Chesterfield, Lord, 291
Church
  medieval: commercial attitude,
  29, 70; effect of plague, 30–31;
  failure of, 40–41; legal position
  of, 119–20
  pre-Reformation: apathy in, 120;
  corruption and failure of, 118–23;
  Hunne's case, 119
  See also Counter-Reformation,
  Protestantism, Reformation
Church of England
  Court of High Commission, 217,
  220, 222–23, 224, 272, 275, 293
  under Henry VIII, 114, 126–27, 132–
  33: *King's Book* (1543), 132–
  33; Ten Articles, 127
  under Edward VI: Acts of Uniformity, 143, 147; Ordinal of 1550,
  147; *Prayer Book* (1549), 142–43;
  Prayer Book (1552), 147, 158
  under Elizabeth I: the Puritans,
  190–92; religious settlement,
  157–59, 190; Thirty-Nine
  Articles, 158
  under Charles I: Root and Branch
  Bill, 225–26
  under the Restoration, 274–76: Act
  of Uniformity, 274; Conventicle
  Act, 274; Corporation Act, 274;
  Five Mile Act, 274; Test Act, 282–
  83, 291, 292, 293–94

Church of England (*continued*)
 under James II, 288, 292–94
 under William III: Act of Tolera-
  tion, 298, 305
Civil War
 causes of, 211–13, 223–24, 225–
  27, 243, 244–46
 First Civil War, 246–49
 revolutionary nature of, 249, 250
 role of religion in, 250
 Second Civil War, 250–51
Clarence, George, Duke of, 55, 56, 82
Clarendon Code, 274
Clarendon, Earl of. *See* Hyde, Edward
Clement VII. *See* Papacy
Coke, Edward, 215, 217
Colet, Dean John, 122
College of Arms, 74
Colonies, 238–43
 and Charles I, 241
 immigration to, 222, 238–41
 and Puritans, 239, 240–41
Comines, Philippe, 62
Commissions of Array, 89
Commonwealth, the (1649–1660),
  255–63
Commonwealth Party, 144
Congregationalism. *See* Protestantism
Convocation, 107–08
Cooper, Anthony, Earl of Shaftsbury,
  284–85, 288
Copernicus, Nicholas, 299, 301
Council
 for the Northern Parts, 127, 170
 Privy: under Henry VII and VIII,
  93–94; under Elizabeth I, 166,
  169–70, 202; under James I,
  200, 202–03, 229; under Charles II,
  271, 273–74, 277, 278, 281; under
  James II, 293
 of regency under Edward VI, 138
 of Wales, 91, 170
Counter-Reformation
 on continent, 149, 160
 in England, 152–54, 180–81
Court of High Commission. *See* Church
 of England
Cranfield, Lionel, 207
Cranmer, Thomas, Archbishop of
 Canterbury, 78, 108, 143
 character, 108
 death, 152, 153

role in Henry VIII's divorce, 109
Cromwell, Oliver, 250–51
 character, 249, 259
 and Charles' execution, 250
 death, 260
 efforts to find legal basis for government, 254–56, 258–59
 finances under, 256–57, 272
 foreign policy, 257–58
 and the Humble Petition and
  Advice, 258
 and Ireland, 242, 253
 as Lord Protector, 255–58
 and New Model Army, 247–49
 and parliament, 251, 254–55
Cromwell, Richard, 261
Cromwell, Thomas, 112–13
 administrative reforms, 112
 death, 130–32
Crown
 Glorious Revolution, effects of,
  297–98
 "New Monarchy," 80–82
 and parliament, 7, 50, 168
 political unity, 77, 91
 restoration of, 269
 royal prerogative: under Elizabeth I, 186; under James I,
  202–03; under Charles I, 213–16;
  under Charles II, 273–74, 276–77,
  283–86; under James II, 293–94
 termination of, by Cromwell, 251
 under the Lancastrians, 43, 46–47
 under Edward V, 56
 under Richard III, 57
 under Henry VIII, 114–16
 under Edward VI, 138–40
 under Elizabeth I, 167–69
 under James I, 197
Culture. *See also* Science
 cosmology, 97–98, 299–301
 Elizabeth, 171–74
 late–seventeenth-century, 302–04

Dacre, Thomas, Lord, 91–92
Declarations of Indulgence
 under Charles II, 278, 282
 under James II, 294, 298
Descartes, René, 302, 304
Devereux, Robert, Earl of Essex,
  172, 184

Diggers, 245, 261, 306
Donne, John, 172, 301
Dover, Treaty of, 281, 282
Drake, Francis, 171–72, 179, 182
Drogheda, Battle of, 253
Dryden, John, 301, 305
Dudley, Edmund, 93, 94
Dudley, John, Earl of Warwick,
    Duke of Northumberland, 145–48
  his son, 151
Dudley, Robert, Earl of Leicester,
    165, 176, 179, 182
Dunkirk, sale of, 281

East India Company, 231–32, 257
Economic theory
  Elizabethan Poor Law, 221, 230
  free trade, 234
  laissez-faire, 236–37
  medieval, 11, 27–29, 70–71, 229
  mercantilism, 257
  monopolies, 231–32, 235–36
  and the oligarchs, 303
  paternalism, opposition to, 232–38
  Statute of Apprentices, 229–30, 234
  Tudor-Stuart, 228–32
Edward III (1327–1377), 4, 7, 83
Edward IV (1461–1483), Earl of
    March, Duke of York, 52–56, 82
Edward V (1483), 56–57, 83
  his brother, 83
Edward VI (1547–1553), 133,
    137–48
  birth, 129
  character, 147
  death, 148
  and Northumberland, 145–47
  the Protectorate, 138–45
  religious policy, 142, 147
Edward, Prince of Wales, 22–24, 52, 54
Eliot, John, 214, 215, 216, 217
Elizabeth I (1558–1603), 155–93
  birth, 109
  and the Catholics, 159, 179–81
  character, 140, 156–57
  coronation, 157
  death, 192
  and Essex, 184
  and marriage, 165
  and Mary of Scots, 163–65,
    177, 179–81

and Northern Rebellion, 176–77
  paternalistic government, 168–71,
    235
  and Philip, 159, 160, 175–77
  and the Puritans, 188–92
  recessional, 182–92
  religious settlement, 157–59, 190
  and Scotland, 161–63
  under Mary I, 151–52
Elizabeth of York, 83
Elyot, Thomas, 76
Empson, Richard, 93, 94
Enclosures, 71–73, 144, 237
Erasmus, Desiderius, 76, 121, 140
  and the New Testament, 76
Erastianism, 123
Exclusion Bill, 284–86

Fairfax, Thomas, Lord, 247, 249
Feudalism
  bastard feudalism, 43–47, 50–51;
    livery and maintenance, 44, 50–51
  education, 75
  the knight, 26–27, 36–37
  landholding, 27–28, 71–73
  lordship, 37–38
  military ideal, 13–14, 27: decline
    of 26–29
  money economy, 29
  social theory, 35
  See also Agriculture, Church,
    Nobility, Peasantry, Yeoman
Fisher, John, Bishop of Rochester, 126
Five Knights' Case, 214–15
Flodden Field, Battle of, 102
Fortescue, John, 44, 45
Fox, Bishop Richard, 93
France
  and the Counter-Reformation,
    160–61
  diplomatic relations with, under:
    Edward IV, 55; Henry VIII, 101,
    102; Edward VI, 142; Elizabeth I,
    159, 161; Charles II, 281–82;
    James II, 294
  domestic situation in fifteenth
    century, 14–15
  and Glorious Revolution, 294–96
  government of, 14, 171
  power in seventeenth century, 282
  war with, under: Henry V, 14–21;

Henry VII, 88; Henry VIII
102–03, 132; Edward VI, 142;
Mary I, 154; Charles I, 215
Francis I, King of France, 101, 102,
103, 152
Francis II, King of France, 160
Frederick V, Elector of the Palatinate,
208–09
Froissart, Jean, 27

Gallileo, 301
Gardiner, Stephen, Bishop of
Winchester
under Henry VIII, 125, 127,
133
under Edward VI, 143, 146, 149
under Mary I, 149–50, 152, 153
Gentry
and charity, 234, 273
education of, 75–76
and Glorious Revolution, 298
Knights of the Shire, 13, 36–37,
41, 46
and the merchant, 74
prosperity of, 73–75
triumph of, 273–74, 298, 306
under Elizabeth I, 170, 185, 186–88
under Charles I, 214–23, 244–45
under Charles II, 272–74
under James II, 293–94
Germany, diplomatic relations with
under Henry VIII, 130–32
under James I, 208–09
Gilbert, Humphrey, 172
Glendower, Owen, 12
Glorious Revolution, 287–88, 294,
295–98, 306
Act of Toleration, 298
Declaration of Rights, 297
Mutiny Act, 298
Gloucester, Dukes of
Humphrey, 21–22
Richard. *See* Richard III
"Great Contract," 207
Green Ribbon Club, 284, 285
Grenville, Richard, 172
Gresham, Thomas, 167
Grey, Lady Jane, 147–48, 151,
156–57
Grünewald, Matthias,
31

Habeas Corpus, 214–15, 274, 305
Hales, John, 144
Halifax, George Saville, First Marquis of
("the Trimmer"), 270, 288,
298, 305, 306
Hampden, John, case of, 220
Hanseatic League, 34
Hastings, William, Lord, 39
Hawkins, John, 176, 182
Henrietta Maria, 209, 213–14, 220,
225–27
Henry II, King of France, 152–53,
159
Henry III, King of France, 161, 182
Henry IV (1399–1413), 9–13
character, 9, 62
loss of inheritance, 5
seizure of throne, 6–7
Henry V (1413–1422), 13–19, 21, 118
character, 13, 17, 62
claim to French throne, 17
dual monarchy, 19
Hundred Years War, 13–19
Henry VI (1422–1461), 19, 21–24,
46–47, 51–55
character, 22, 62
death, 55
deterioration of government under,
22–24
finances, 21, 44, 46
parliament under, 47–51
Henry VII, Earl of Richmond (1485–
1509), 80–94
at Bosworth, 59, 62
character, 62, 82, 94
children of, 84
claim to throne, 59, 82–83
commercial policy, 70
finances of, 85–88
law, administration of, 87, 88–91
liquidation of rivals, 83–84
the "New Monarchy," 80–82
Henry VIII (1509–1547), 99–133,
168
and the church: medieval, 118–23;
as Supreme Head, 107–08, 109–16,
120, 121
character, 100, 132, 133, 140
and Cromwell, 112–13
death of, 133
diplomacy, early, 101–03
divorce, 103–09

Henry VIII (*continued*)
  Last Will and Testament, 137–38
  law, enforcement of, 91–92, 95–97
  religion, attitudes toward, 108–09
  wives of, 88, 100, 104, 107–08, 110,
    129, 130–32
Herbert, Edward, Lord of Cherbury,
  302
Hobbes, Thomas, 267–69, 305, 306
Hooper, John 124, 153
Hotspur, Harry, 12
Hough, Dr., 293, 295
Howard, Catherine, 132
Howard, Charles, Lord Admiral,
  172, 182
Howard, Frances, 203–04
Howard, Thomas, Earl of Surrey,
  Second Duke of Norfolk, 89,
  102, 118–19
Howard, Thomas, Fourth Duke of
  Norfolk, 177, 181
Humanism, 75–76. *See also* Renaissance
Hundred Years War, 14–21, 31, 33–34
  Agincourt, Battle of, 18
  brutality of, 18
  causes of, 14
  English defeat, 52
  indenture system, 17
  Treaty of Troyes, 19
Hunne, Richard, 119
Hyde, Anne, 291
Hyde, Edward, Earl of Clarendon,
  225, 237, 245
  and Clarendon Code, 274
  impeachment, 277, 278–81
  as Lord Chancellor, 271, 272–73,
  278

Industrialization, 232–33, 303
  manufacture of wool, 69–70, 143–44,
  233
Inflation, 70–71, 143, 201
Instrument of Government, 255
Intercursus Magnus, 70
Interregnum, 267
Ireland
  Act of Settlement, 253
  colonization of, 221, 242
  revolts of, under: Elizabeth I, 183–84;

  Charles I, 225; Cromwell, 253
  and "Thorough," 221–22

James I (VI of Scotland) (1603–1625),
  164, 198–210, 229, 242
  birth of, 164
  character and its effect on govern-
    ment, 198–201
  compared to Elizabeth, 198, 202, 204
  corruption at court, 202, 203–04
  and divine right, 200
  financial troubles, 201–02, 204, 206,
    207–08, 209
  foreign policy, 206
  and parliament, 202–03, 208
  paternalism, failure of, 235–38
  political training and background,
    198–201
  and Puritans, 188–89, 205–06
  and science, 301
  succession, 192, 197
James II (1685–1689), 278, 283,
  285–86, 287–96
  "abdication," 296
  birth of son, 294
  and Catholicism, 281, 291, 293–94
  character, 290–91
  and divine right, 288
  and Exclusion Bill, 285–86
  succession, 291
  Tory Party, attack on, 294
  universities, attack on, 293
James IV of Scotland, 86, 102
James V of Scotland, 132, 163, 198
Jamestown, 238, 239–40, 241, 243
Jeffreys, George, 292, 293, 294
Jesuits, 160, 180–81, 188–89
Joan of Arc, 19–21
John of Gaunt, Duke of Lancaster,
  5, 7
  and Catherine Swinford, 22, 59
Jonson, Ben, 171
Justices of the Peace, 170–71, 228

King, Gregory, 303
Kingmaker. *See* Neville, Richard
Knox, John, 152, 155,
  163

Lancaster, Duchy of, 5, 9, 12, 85, 91, 170

Lancaster, House of. *See* Henry IV, V, VI, VII

Language, English, development of, 77–78

La Pole, John de, Earl of Lincoln, 83

Latimer, Hugh, Bishop of Worcester, 36, 144, 153

Laud, William, Archbishop of Canterbury, 211, 214, 217, 219–20, 237, 241, 261, 275
  death, 224
  religious policy, 221–22, 224
  "Thorough," policy of, 217, 220, 221–23

Law
  and the Civil War, 252
  common and equity, 90
  corruption of, in fifteenth century, 44–47, 50–51
  Court of Chancery, 90
  Court of King's Bench, 56
  crime rate under Elizabeth, 95
  enforcement, 95–97
  in London, 95
  Inns of Court, 78–79
  Star Chamber, 90, 217, 220, 224, 237, 272
  under Edward IV, 56
  under Henry VII and VIII, 87, 88–92
  under the oligarchs, 305

Levellers, 245, 253, 261, 306

Lilburne, John, 261

Lluyd, Humprey, 172

Locke, John, 301, 306

Lollardy, 11, 14, 41–42, 119, 124
  John Wycliffe, 41

London, 78–79, 186–88
  fire of, 278
  growth of, 234
  plague of, 278
  violence in, 95

Long Parliament, 224–27, 252–54, 261–63
  the Civil War, 227, 246–51
  House of Commons: purged, 250, 251

House of Lords: abolished, 251; restored, 258

legislation: Grand Remonstrance, 226; Militia Bill, 226; Nineteen Propositions, 227; Root and Branch Bill, 225–26; Self-denying ordinance, 247, 249–50; Triennial Act, 224
  Praise God Barebones Parliament, 255
  the Rump Parliament, 252–54, 261–63

Lords Appellant, 4

Louis XI, King of France, 55, 59

Louis XIV, King of France, 281–82, 283, 286
  and Edict of Nantes, 292
  and Glorious Revolution, 294–96

Loyola, Ignatius, 160

Luther, Martin, 123–24

Machiavelli, 82–83

Malory, Thomas, 27, 78

Margaret of Anjou, 22, 52–54
  alliance with the Kingmaker, 55

Margaret Tudor, Queen of Scots, 84, 86, 137

Maria of Moderna, 291

Marlowe, Christopher, 171, 172, 174, 182

Marston Moor, Battle of, 247

Mary I (1553–1558), 133, 148–54
  birth, 100, 104
  character, 148, 151, 154
  death, 154, 159
  marriage to Philip, 150, 154
  restoration of Catholicism, 150
  Smithfield Fires, 152–54
  succession of, 148

Mary II (1689–1694), 291
  character, 298
  See also William III

Mary of Guise, 155, 161–63

Mary Stuart, Queen of Scots, 132, 155, 163–65
  character, 164
  in England, 176–77, 179–80
  execution, 180
  marriages, 142, 164
  and David Riccio and James Hepburn, 164

Mary Tudor, Queen of France,
Duchess of Suffolk, 84, 102,
137
Massachusetts Bay Company, 239,
240, 241
Mercantilism, 257
Merchant adventurers, 35, 70,
231, 257
Merchant class, 74–75
charity of, 234
paternalism, opposition to, 232–38
and the Protectorate, 256–57
See also Gentry, Industrialization,
Trade
Milton, John 267–68, 275, 305, 306
Monasteries
and charity, 122
dissolution of, 111
sale of lands under: Henry VIII,
111–12, 132; Mary I, 150
See also Chantries
Monck, George, Duke of Albemarle,
262–63, 269, 271
Monmouth, James Fitzroy, Duke of,
286
invasion by, 291–92
Monopolies, 186, 220, 231–32,
235–38
Montague, Edward, Earl of Sandwich, 271
More, Thomas
social attitudes of, 70
trial and martyrdom, 122, 125–26
Utopia, 93
Mortimer, Edmund, Earl of March, 7
his uncle, Mortimer, Sir Edmund, 12
Mowbray, Thomas, Duke of Norfolk, 5
Mun, Thomas, 303
Muscovy Company, 231, 238

Naseby, Battle of, 249
Navigation Acts (1650, 1651),
257, 277
Netherlands
competition with, 232
diplomatic relations with, under:
Elizabeth I, 160, 176;
James I, 209
and Philip, 178–79

war with, under: Oliver Cromwell,
258; Second Dutch War, 277–78;
Third Dutch War, 281–83
Neville, Ralph, Earl of Westmorland,
6, 39
Neville, Richard, Earl of Warwick
death of, 55, 85
family of, 39, 48
as Kingmaker, 54–55
and Wars of the Roses, 52–55
wealth, 39–40
New Learning, 75–76
New Model Army, 247–49, 250–51,
252–55
against the Rump, 252–55, 258–59,
261–63
"New Monarchy," 80–82
Newton, Issac, 299, 301, 302
Nobility
barons in the fifteenth century,
4, 9, 38–40, 43
incomes of, 36–37, 38–39, 44, 170
lawlessness of, 44
patronage, 44–45
under the Tudors, 89, 91, 127
under Elizabeth I, 170
under Charles I, 244–45
Norfolk, Dukes of. *See* Howard,
Thomas; Mowbray, Thomas
Northern Rebellion, 176–77
Northumberland, Duke of. *See* Dudley,
John

Oates, Titus, 283, 284–86
Oldcastle, John, 14
O'Neill, Hugh, Earl of Tyrone, 183–84
Osborne, Thomas, Earl of Danby, 283,
284
Overbury, Thomas, murder of, 204

Papacy
anti-papal feeling in England, 118–19
Clement VII and Henry VIII's divorce,
103, 104–07
the Great Schism, 25
Paul IV, 149, 154, 160
Parker, Matthew, Archbishop of
Canterbury, 167, 190

Parliament
Cavalier Parliament, 271, 272–86
Convention Parliament, 296–98
and Danby, 283, 284
failure of, in fifteenth century,
43, 47–51
feudal parliaments, 7–9, 47–51
Habeas Corpus, 214–15, 274,
305
House of Commons: independence
under James I, 202–03, 207;
membership in fifteenth century,
48; role in fifteenth century,
48–49; size under Tudors, 185–86
House of Lords, 44, 47–48; increase
in size under Stuarts, 207–08;
under Elizabeth I, 185
organization of, 48
and Shaftsbury, 284–86
Short Parliament, 223
triumph of, 297–98
under Henry IV, 7–9
under Henry VII, 89
under Mary I, 150
under Elizabeth I, 166–71,
185–88
under James I, 202–03,
207, 208–10
under Charles I, 211–12,
213–16
under Charles II, 269, 272–86,
288
under James II, 292–93
See also Long Parliament,
Reformation Parliament
Parma, Duke of, 179, 182
Parr, Catherine, 132
Parsons, Robert, 181
Paston family, 26–27, 45, 47
Peacham, Henry, 299
Peasantry, 35–36
and enclosures, 71–73
Ket's Revolt, 145
Revolt of 1381, 42
under James II, 292
Pepys, Samuel, 269, 271, 277,
278, 301
Percy, Henry, Earl of Northumberland, 6, 12
family wealth, 39

Petition of Right, 215
Philip II, King of Spain. *See*
also Armada
character of, 178
and Counter-Reformation, 160
death of, 182
and Elizabeth I, 159, 160, 175–77
and Great Enterprise, 177–82
and Mary I, 150, 154
and Netherlands, 176, 178–79
Pilgrimage of Grace, 127–28
Pinkie, Battle of, 141
Plague. *See* Black Death
Plantagenet, House of. *See* Richard
II
Plymouth settlement, 240–41, 243
Pole, Reginald, Cardinal, 150–51,
153, 154
Political theory
of Charles II, 269, 276–77
colonies, Tudor-Stuart attitude
toward, 241
of the Commonwealth, 251,
254–56
divine right of kings, 138, 200,
202, 248, 288
Glorious Revolution, 297–98
Hobbes, Thomas, 268–69
Locke, John, 306
medieval, 4–5, 7, 11, 13
Milton, John, 268
paternalistic government, 168–69,
202, 217, 228–32
the secular mind, 301–04
under the Tudors, 76–77, 78, 88–
93, 114–116, 138–40; Elizabeth
and the Tudor organic state,
167–71, 185
Poor Law of 1601, 230
Popish Plot, 283–86
Population
of colonies, 240, 241, 303
of England, 30, 68, 234, 303
of London, 79, 234
of towns during plague, 34
Praemunire, Statute of, 107
Presbyterianism. *See* Protestantism
Preston Pans, Battle of, 250–51
Pride, Colonel, 251, 263
Printing, first press, 77–78

Protestantism
  Arminianism, 222
  Congregationalism, 191, 250,
    261–62, 275
  Dissenters and Nonconformists,
    274, 293–94, 298, 305
  Erastianism, 123
  Fifth Monarchists, 262
  Independents, 250, 262
  the nature of the mass, 142–43
  origins of, 123–24
  persecution of, 152–53, 161
  Presbyterianism, 191, 205–06,
    223, 250–51, 261–62, 275
  Toleration, Act of, 298
  See also Church, Counter-Reforma-
    tion, Luther, Puritanism, Reforma-
    tion
Prynne, William, 222, 272
Puritanism
  meaning of, 188–89
  migration, 222, 239, 240–41
  under Elizabeth I, 159, 183,
    188–92
  under James I, 204–06
  under Charles I, 217, 222
  under Charles II, 275
Pym, John ("King Pym"), 215,
  217, 223, 224–27

Raleigh, Walter, 171–72, 174,
  206, 209, 238, 302
Reformation
  break with Rome, 107–13
  and Edward VI, 142–43
  and Luther, 123–24
  Royal Supremacy, 110–16
  in Scotland, 163
  spiritual origins of, 117–25
  See also Counter-Reformation,
    Reformation Parliament
Reformation Parliament, 107–112
  legislation: Abolishing Diversity
    of Opinion, Act for, 129–30;
    Annates, Statute of (1532),
    108; Annates, Statute of
    (second), 110; anti-clerical
    legislation, 107–08; Restraint
    of Appeal, Acts in, 109, 116;
    Succession, Act of, 110, 125;

Supremacy, Act of, 111, 114,
  148, 150, 158; Treason, Act of,
  125, 126
Renaissance
  effect on: education, 75–76;
    government, 92–94
  and Italy, 101–02
  spirit of, 75, 171–74, 184
Restoration, 263, 267–77
  Act of Indemnity, 271, 272
  Steps leading to, 246, 253, 255–56,
    261–63
Revenues
  Committee of Public Accounts, 277
  Cromwellian reforms, 112
  crown lands, sale of: under
    Elizabeth I, 183; under James
    I, 206; under Charles I, 207
  debasement of currency under
    Henry VIII, 143
  decimation tax, 256–57, 272
  decline of, in fifteenth century, 34
  fiscal feudalism (wardship and
    relief), 86–87, 207, 218–19,
    220, 224
  forced loans, 214
  incomes: average in 1688, 303;
    parliamentary under Tudors,
    185; ship money, 219, 220;
    taxation, 273
  titles, sale of, 207–208, 214
  under Richard II, 11
  under Henry IV, 11
  under Henry VI, 21, 34, 46
  under Edward IV, 56, 85
  under Henry VII, 85–88
  under Henry VIII, 111–12, 143,
    201
  under Elizabeth I, 167, 183–84,
    201
  under James I, 201, 204, 206–07
  under Charles I, 214, 218–19,
    220–21, 224
  under the Commonwealth, 249,
    256–57, 272–73
  under Charles II, 273, 276–77,
    282–83
  under James II, 292
  under William III, 298
  See also Tunnage and Poundage
Richard II (1377–1399), 3–9, 93

Richard II (*continued*)
  abdication of, 7
  attitude towards peasants, 35
  collapse of good government, 5
Richard III (1483–1485), 57–59,
  83
  at Bosworth Field, 59
  character, 56–57
  as Lord Protector, 57
  as Lord Lieutenant of the North,
  56
  murder of princes, 57
Riche, Richard, 122–23
Richmond, Henry Fitzroy,
  Duke of, 104, 107, 154
Ridley, Nicholas, Bishop of
  London, 146, 153
Ridolfi, Robert, 181
Roses, Wars of the, 43, 45–46,
  51–62
Roundhead, use of term, 226
Royal Society, 301

Science, 299–304
Scotland
  and the Civil War, 247, 249,
  250–51
  effects of "Thorough," 222–23
  reformation in, 163
  relations with, under Elizabeth,
  161–63, 165
  in sixteenth century, 198–200
  Solemn League and Covenant, 247
  treaties with: of Berwick, 165;
  of Edinburgh, 164
  war with Scotland under:
  Henry VIII, 102, 132; Edward
  VI, 141–42; Charles I, 223–24,
  225
Sedgemoor, Battle of, 292
Seymour, Edward, Earl of Hertford,
  Duke of Somerset
  character, 140, 141–42
  economic policy, 143–44
  fall of, 145
  as Lord Protector, 138–45
  religious policy, 142–43
Seymour, Jane, 129
Seymour, Thomas, 156
Shaftesbury, Earl of.

See Cooper, Anthony
Shakespeare, William, 3–4, 5, 6,
  13n, 17, 56–57, 94, 104, 168,
  171, 173, 301
Ship money, 219, 220
Shrewsbury, Battle of, 12
Sidonia, Medina, 178
Simnel, Lambert, 83–84
Smith, Thomas, 50, 86
Smithfield Fires, 152–54
Solway Moss, Battle of, 132, 198
Somerset, Dukes of
  Edmund, 22
  Edward. *See* Seymour
Spain. *See also* Philip
  cold war with, 175–76, 177,
  179
  diplomatic relations with: under
  Henry VII, 88, 151; under
  Henry VIII, 101, 103; under
  Edward VI, 142; under Mary I,
  154; under Elizabeth I, 160,
  175–77; under James I, 206,
  208–09; under Charles I, 221
  government of, 171
  war with Spain: the Armada,
  177–79, 181–82; under James I,
  209–210; under Charles I,
  214–15, 218; under Cromwell,
  258
Spenser, Edmund, 171
Spurs, Battle of the, 102
St. Aibans, Battle of, 52, 54
St. John, Oliver, 250
Stanley, William, 59, 89
Staplers, 35
Star Chamber. *See* Law
Statutes. *See* Parliament
Stoke, Battle of, 83–84
Stuart, Henry, Lord Darnley, 164

Test Act, 282–83, 291, 292, 294
Tewkesbury, Battle of, 55
Thirty Years War, 208–09, 281
Tory Party, 284
  and Charles II, 286
  and the Glorious Revolution, 288,
  296
  and James II, 287, 288, 293
Towton, Battle of, 54

Trade
  collapse of in the fifteenth
    century, 34–35
  growth under Tudor-Stuarts,
    233
  Navigation Acts, 257, 277
  with Netherlands: collapse
    of trade, 151; wars, 257,
    277–78, 281–83
  with New World, 71, 176
  revival of, in fifteenth century,
    68–70, 71
  in seventeenth century, 303
  wool trade, 29, 35, 68–70,
    143–44, 151
  See also Economic theory,
    East India Company, Merchants,
    Merchant adventurers, Muscovy
    Company, Staplers
Trent, Council of, 160
Tunnage and Poundage, 11,
    213, 214, 215–16, 224

Vane, Henry, 250
Verney, Edmund, 245
Villiers, George, Duke of Buckingham,
    204, 208, 209–10, 214–16
  attack on, 215
  murder of, 216
Virginia Company, 239–40

Wakefield, Battle of, 52
Warbeck, Perkin, 84
Wardship. *See* Revenues, fiscal
    feudalism
Warham, William, Archbishop
    of Canterbury, 108, 122
Warwick, Earls of
  Edward, 83, 84
  John. *See* Dudley
  Richard. *See* Neville
Wentworth brothers, Peter
    and Paul, 190–91

Wentworth, Thomas, Earl of
    Strafford
  death, 224, 226
  in Ireland, 221
  and policy of "Thorough," 217,
    219–20
Weston, Richard, Earl of Portland,
    219
Whig Party
  and Glorious Revolution, 295–
    96
  the Green Ribbon Club, 284
  under Charles II, 285–86
  under James II, 287–88
Whitgift, John, Archbishop of
    Canterbury, 192
William III (1689–1702), 291,
    294–95, 295–306
  character, 295, 298
  and Glorious Revolution, 295–97
  invitation to invade England,
    288–90, 294
  religious policy, 298
  succession, 291, 294
Wolsey, Thomas, Cardinal, 99–100,
    102–03, 113
  abuse of power, 121
  ambitions, 102
  the divorce, 104
  fall of, 104–107
Woodville, Elizabeth (her family),
    54, 56, 57
Worcester, Battle of, 253
Wren, Christopher,
    299, 301
Wyatt, Thomas, revolt of,
    151, 153
Wycliffe, John, 41

Yeoman class, 28, 36
Yonge, Thomas, 51
York, Dukes of
  Edward. *See* Edward IV
  Richard, 22, 24, 39, 52
York, House of. *See* Edward IV
    and V, Richard III